**UNKNOWN
CALIFORNIA**

UNKNOWN CALIFORNIA

EDITED BY *Jonathan Eisen and David Fine*
with Kim Eisen

COLLIER BOOKS

Macmillan Publishing Company

NEW YORK

Macmillan Publishing Company
866 Third Avenue, New York, N.Y. 10022
Collier Macmillan Canada, Inc.

Library of Congress Cataloging in Publication Data
Main entry under title:
Unknown California.
   Bibliography: p.
   1. California—History—Addresses, essays, lectures.
2. California—Fiction. I. Eisen, Jonathan. II. Fine,
David M., 1934–   III. Eisen, Kim.
F861.5.U55   1985b   979.4   84-23020
ISBN 0-02-048070-9 (pbk.)

Macmillan books are available at special discounts for bulk purchases
for sales promotions, premiums, fund-raising, or educational use.
Special editions or book excerpts can also be created to specification.
For details, contact:

Special Sales Director
Macmillan Publishing Company
866 Third Avenue
New York, New York 10022

First Collier Books Edition 1985

10 9 8 7 6 5 4 3 2 1

Unknown California is also available in a hardcover edition from
Macmillan Publishing Company.

Designed by Jack Meserole

Printed in the United States of America

ACKNOWLEDGMENTS

We would like to acknowledge the following people, without whose help this book would have had fewer pages, or if it had the same number of pages, they wouldn't be as good. First, we want to thank John Ahouse, Curator of the Special Collections Library at California State University, Long Beach, for his personal interest in the project, his guidance and intimate knowledge of the subject matter, which he was eager to share with us far beyond what we had a right to expect. Surely this book would be less comprehensive and a lot less fun without him, or without his colleague, Robert Brasher.

It is commonplace to thank one's editor, but we have an especially good one in Alexia Dorszynski. We are grateful to her, and to her assistant at Macmillan, Jill Herbers, for their ongoing involvement, support, and enthusiasm.

This book is dedicated to the memory of CAREY McWILLIAMS.

Permission to use the following copyright material is gratefully acknowledged:
"Notes Toward an Understanding of California" by Herbert Gold, copyright by Herbert Gold from *Los Angeles Times*, January 9, 1983. "California Rising" by Wallace Stegner, copyright 1981 by *New West* magazine, from *New West*, October 1981. "Eureka! A Celebration of California" by John Gregory Dunne, reprinted by permission of International Creative Management, copyright 1979 by John Gregory Dunne. This article first appeared in *New West*, January 1979. "Lost Horizon" by Lewis Lapham, copyright 1978 by *Harper's Magazine*. All rights reserved. Reprinted from the February 1979 issue by special permission. "First Glimpse of the Sierra" from *The Yosemite* by John Muir, copyright 1912 by The Century Company, renewed by Wanda Muir Hanna. Reprinted by permission of E. P. Dutton, Inc. "The Society Upon the Stanislaus" by Nigey Lennon, copyright 1982, from *Mark Twain in California*. "The Shirley Letters, 1851–1852" by Dame Shirley, Alfred A. Knopf, Inc. "Sojourner" by Gerald Haslam, copyright 1983, from *Hawk Flights: Visions of the West*. Reprinted by permission of Seven Buffaloes Press (Box 249, Big Timber, Montana 59011). "A Social History of the Hippies" by Warren Hinckle, copyright 1967, by Ramparts Magazine, Inc. Reprinted by permission of Bruce W. Stilson. From *Ramparts* magazine, March 1967. "Hippies Without a Home" by Frank Robertson from *California* magazine, March 1982. "Country Women, The Feminists of Albian Ridge" reprinted by permission of Kate Coleman. This selection originally appeared in *Mother*

CONTENTS

III   Southern California Country

IV   Voices of Dissent

V Paving Paradise

A WORD BEFORE

As a place on the mind and on the map, California offers itself as a metaphor for the contradictions of the American—and Western—dream. In myth and reality, California has represented the ultimate frontier, the last stop on the continent, the final destination. The region has attracted, as all frontiers do, the enterprising and the dissatisfied, the optimistic seekers of the dream and those who in Nathanael West's words "have come to California to die." California has carried into the twentieth century the paradoxical meanings of the nineteenth-century frontier: the place both of new beginnings and of violent endings.

The quest has been both material and spiritual; the search has been one for the promised wealth of El Dorado (and Oil Dorado) and for the New World Eden. And it has been undertaken by young and old, healthy and infirm, Yankee and ethnic.

The encounter between promise and betrayal, fable and reality, expectation and actuality, has been played out recurrently in the California story, a story recounted in the pieces that make up this collection. Gold fever, land fever, oil fever, and Hollywood fever have left in their wake a legacy both of civilization and discontent.

Reviewing the literature on California—nonfiction and fiction—we discovered there was no one place to which the reader could turn for the best writing. There is a vast body of literature on the state, much of it by the best writers America has produced. So we became miners in the quest of California's literary gold. From thousands of pages of ore we extracted and refined, uncovering such gems as the Shirley Letters from the California gold mines, Will Irwin's 1908 study of San Francisco's Chinatown, and John Steinbeck's pre-*Grapes of Wrath* study of migrant farm workers, "Their Blood Is Strong." We found an early version of Mark Twain's "The Jumping Frog of Calaveras County" and discovered the trenchant hilarity of the early Norman Mailer in his Hollywood novel, *The Deer Park*. From the rich mine of California fiction we also extracted gold from such works as Evelyn Waugh's *The Loved One* and Cyra McFadden's *Serial*.

We included as well a number of now-classic reflections on the state, such as John Muir's evocation of Yosemite and the High Sierras, Henry George's prediction of what the railroads would bring to California, Henry Miller's celebration of the Big Sur coast, Carey McWilliams' probe of L.A.'s cults, and Thomas Pynchon's journalistic excursion into the smoke and cinder of Watts, 1965.

And we unearthed facets of contemporary California in such pieces as Richard Reeves' report on the instability of the Southern California land-scape, Randy Shilts' extract from *The Mayor of Castro Street* on the San Francisco murder of Harvey Milk and Mayor George Moscone, John McKinney's first-hand observation of the "boutiquing" of the California coast-line, Richard Stayton's comic Disneyland narrative, and James D. Houston's discovery of Silicon Valley.

And this is only part of a book-length labor of love.

The result is a meditation on the historical California and the California of the imagination. It is at once factual and contemplative, gritty and phil-osophical, depictive and reflective.

It is a book that is simultaneously recognizable and new, expanding its own boundaries, reaching into areas of meaning—personal, social, political—that address some of the larger aspects of American culture. Although our time frame is roughly 1850–1983, we have selected only works that transcend their own time. We present them as works that remain fresh and relevant because they each express in a unique way something about California that touches nearly everyone everywhere, across the boundaries of space and time.

JONATHAN AND KIM EISEN
DAVID FINE

Laguna Beach, California
December 1983

I

Doors
of Perception

HERBERT GOLD

Notes Toward an Understanding of California

E UREKA" ("I have found it") is the state motto. A few Indians were already here, wandering a universe of sea and mountain, desert, forest, humid marshlands and plains. Yesterday, when the first Spanish, English, even some Russian explorers, trappers and adventurers sailed into the bays, it was El Dorado, the land of gold, even before they found the gold; and in addition—always forgetting the Indians—it was the place where nobody came first. We are a simultaneous people with a history leapt out from rowdy imagination. What a country for laborious dreamers!

When I first visited California as a teen-age adventurer, spending my *Wanderjahr* hitchhiking around the United States—discovering that the world was not, in fact, as I had suspected, all just Cleveland, Ohio—the state was known elsewhere as a sanitarium for lungers, Okies, odd malcontents, speculators and rejects from the "real" America of winters and work. In Los Angeles I ate in a cafeteria with no posted prices; you were asked to pay whatever you considered right. The Good Lord would guide you. A pump kept a waterfall, "the Divine Chain of Water," circulating over a green stucco relief map of El Dorado. The divine pump never faltered, undeterred by deadbeats, until the cafeteria was redeveloped into a highrise complex.

Even during World War II, when I was stationed in California, waiting to be shipped to China as a Russian interpreter, this was another world. It was paradise. I found myself among a colony of White Russian exiles in San Francisco, and in their enthusiasm for a young man who had learned their language, they kept me drunk most of the time, so that I didn't see much of San Francisco, but instead gazed at ceilings, skies and the eyes of ballet dancers. The real world was far away.

And finally, in 1960, when I came to live in San Francisco, the state had entered its massive industrial, commercial and agricultural transformation into the most successful and prosperous corner of America. But the style and psychology of California was not like the rest of America. And it still isn't.

Elsewhere, there is the struggle for existence; we have heard of this in

California. Here, for the massive middle class, the struggle sometimes comes down to a courageous battle against boredom and bland, and this is why love and marriage seem to have replaced the frontier for exploration; they have become the moral equivalent of war in a state where all the marriages end in divorce, now officially called "dissolution," which doesn't take much of the pain out of it.

Another meaning of life in California is expressed by the parks, streams, mountains, waterfalls, high and low deserts, a variety and richness of land and sea which astonish the wanderer. When dailiness is too much with me, I like to flee. I hike and camp in the Las Padres National Forest, inland from Big Sur, sometimes climbing the ridges and sleeping in the wilderness among the wild boar, sometimes following the stream that leads into the Zen monastery named for the Tassajara Indians. Las Padres and the other great forests—particularly the wilderness stands of pine and redwood—utter a California which resists category. This is a place like no other; these are days and nights like no others, or rather, like those of 150 years ago.

Sometimes, hiking with a friend, I declare a Vow of Silence in the woods. I did so once with Bill Graham, the rock music promoter. He agreed with enthusiasm. The only road to peace, we decided, was in the Zen fashion—with acceptance, with breathing the air, with making our burdens light, with simplicity, calm and oneness with the universe.

Our mystic silence lasted 10 minutes. "My feet hurt from these goddamn new boots and I think I'm getting a case of goddamn poison oak," cried Bill amid the towering cathedral trees, this sudden dose of Zen peace conflicting with his turbulent spirit. "And I can't stand these goddamn raisins and nuts we're gonna eat, I want a Winchell doughnut," he added, steeped in his own high-cholesterol form of sacred harmony with the universe.

Elsewhere, between the wilderness and the coastal cities, the rural logging counties of Northern California, especially Humboldt and Mendocino, show evidence of mysterious wealth (tasteful automobiles, rustic manses, fine restaurants) despite the depression in the ranching and logging industries. How can this be? Well, many of those shy folks with the cute little kids attending cute little private schools are marijuana farmers. And since marijuana is illegal, they are unable to pay taxes on their profits; this tends to make them richer. There is an eerie parallel economy up there that does not enter the statistical world of the Department of Commerce. It's a good market for rock records, *quiche*, Brie and repeating rifles.

Occasionally the police bag a back-to-the-earth ideologue. A friend of mine was arrested for having 147 marijuana plants on his property—that's a crop worth about $150,000 a year. He was too mellow to resent the arresting officers, some of whom were volleyball-playing pals of his. When I asked how a former college English professor happened upon such troubles, he shrugged and said, "Always did want to get close to the land, growing things like in Wordsworth and Tennyson." "And now?" I asked. "What will be will be," he said. "*Shantih*"—and probably what will be will be a long set of legal plea bargains. Wordsworth and Buddha would have established a more prudent arrangement with the authorities.

A poem by Rilke about the body of Apollo ends with a charge: "You must change your life." In California, without necessarily very much effort, almost everyone changes his life. The country of the mind urges this upon us.

For example, during the glory days of the flower generation, I found myself mysteriously and thickly grown over with long hair. I'm not sure just how it happened. And my wife (I no longer have that wife, of course, like a true Californian) remarked that my face would better express its inner strength through concealment beneath a beard. Like magic, a beard began to appear, aided by a neglect of shaving. Shazam! I looked like the hippies of La Jolla, Monterey, the mountains, the deserts, the Sunset Strip, the Haight-Ashbury, the campuses, the coffeehouses, the anti-Vietnam War parades, I resembled the drug mind-expanders, the communal livers, the new-family experimenters, the Hermann Hesseans, all those who had discovered truth and beauty and a revised life and eternal salvation. It had been tested and proved. They had found it last Thursday. I was a member of the herd of independent minds.

I also know a semiretired stripteaser who proudly supplements her income from a few sex exhibitions by doing what she calls "guerrilla gardening," harvesting herbs, roots, and low-growing vegetables in the primitive fastnesses of Golden Gate Park in San Francisco. She and some Vietnamese refugees have a nice thing going there. Well, what else is open to a 58-year-old sex queen who has taken to the vegetarian life? She invited me to lunch and *nothing* comes from an over-priced health-food shop. And she is free and independent. And she doesn't look 58.

Let us now praise the fair flesh of California, because however seriously we take the gross national product, our status as an industrial power, our immense skills in factory farming (the square tomato, for machine picking, was invented at the University of California at Davis, and is perfect except for a boring taste), our rowdy history, the Gold Rush and the movies, the wild coastline and the prevalent springtime climate and the cathedral groves of redwood trees, the California girl and the throb of pleasure are part of an international fantasy. When I entertain visitors from the Soviet Union, Germany, France, England, wherever, they always marvel over the beauties of people—of haunch, hair and teeth. This Dorado of escapees from elsewhere has produced a new race—the Californian. So much athletic grace is almost unnatural. Yet life is not always easy here.

Notes Toward an Understanding of California | 5

I sat recently at a swimming pool with the 17-year-old daughter of friends. She had two schoolmates with her, and we discussed college, the future, atomic policy, President Reagan and man's fate. They smiled. When they smiled, with their perfect orthodontal teeth all even and flashing at the same wattage of amiability, it was not three separate mouths; it seemed more like one long clean bright blazing tooth with three pairs of eyes also smiling above. Suddenly, Epiphany! I had always adored those straight California teeth, so unlike my own, with the space between the upper two front molars or cuspids or whatever they are called (non-orthodontal youth). Now, with a soft sea-breeze suddenness, I was wearied of perfection! The next lady I met without perfect teeth would be the one I loved.

One of the reasons for the international mistrust of California, along with adoration, is the careless hedonism people link with it. For Scandinavians, the climate is forever June; for the inhibited, California means body aware-ness and freedom; for the poor, it is money, and for the rich, it is the place where even the poor look tanned, immorally graceful and easy with them-selves.

We come out and declare who we are by our deeds. We are free to succeed or fail according to our promises. We can lie, but then live up to our lies—this is an act of continuous dangerous creation.

Toward the end of his long life, I asked the artist Jean Varda, who lived surrounded by teen angels in his Sausalito houseboat, feeding them spa-ghetti, garlanding their hair with flowers and accepting their worship, why his paintings, collages, and sculpture suddenly began to have depth and passion in addition to the charm and energy for which Picasso and Henry Miller admired them.

"Why now, Yankel?"

We were trudging through the muck and sea-damp murk of Gate Five on a nocturnal wine-buying expedition. He had had a stroke. The next day he was taking a flight to Mexico City in pursuit of yet another angel, whose eyes, he reported contentedly, destroyed him. He chuckled at my question.

"Why now? You're nearly 80. Why profundity, and suddenly now?"

He was still laughing at the question, but he stopped in the dark and gave me a serious answer. "For 50 years I was a charlatan," he said. "I practiced charlatanry with all my heart, with all my soul, to make it perfect. Now, through charlatanry, I have become an artist! I am lucky, my friend. I took a terrible chance."

He died a few days later in Mexico City. I don't know if he died in the arms of the girl with the destroying eyes, but I know he died a winner. I own his "Avicenna the Philosopher"—a Byzantine collage which depicts the great medieval thinker with a warning finger uplifted. The warning seems to be: Remember joy! It's all we've got!

The public history of California, like that of very great nations, continually leads us to the mysterious private lives of its citizens. A person can live in Ohio and not be an Ohioan; a Californian generally knows that he comes from an elsewhere, but since he is here, he has enlisted, he is a member of the legion. Soon after my arrival in 1960 I began to notice I was often the most veteran Californian in a room where new arrivals from, say, New York had taken off their Brooks Brothers suits after two or three weeks and were already snug in the California camouflage vestments of leather, denim, or silk. A generation later I am an honorary Native Son of the Golden West, whose children all have perfect teeth.

Recently, while I was flying back to California from New York, the captain remarked over the intercom, in that laconic airline-pilot fashion, that we would soon be crossing the California border—"frontier," he said—and my heart leaped with pleasure. Desert brown, the deep gash of Yosemite, the Sierra and Mount Shasta and then the coastal verdancy, and finally the dense, cool, dramatic city of San Francisco, projecting out with its bay and its Pacific Ocean. Home at last! was the thrill that passed through me.

We have found it! It is no longer just gold, oil, money, grapes, orchards, an agribusiness that invents square tomatoes and never-spoil milk, tomatoless tomatoes and milkless milk . . . microchips, religious cults, the entertainment and aerospace industries, but also a complicated way of being human, a nationality without an army—perhaps an exaggerated mirror for the American dream, the universal dream of a sweeter elsewhere.   [1983]

WALLACE STEGNER

California Rising

O NE out of every ten Americans is a Californian. There are many more Californians in the world than there are Australians and New Zealanders combined, more Californians than all the Norwegians, Swedes, Danes, Finns, and Icelanders in Scandinavia, more than twice as many Californians as Hungarians, Portuguese, or Greeks. Nations that have shaken the world, and some that still trouble it, look puny by comparison with this single state. The California economy exceeds that of all but a handful of nations. The state has a fantastic variety of topographies, climates, products, natural beauties. It has the biggest congressional delegation, and it has produced—though not everyone brags about this—two out of the last four presidents, and become the adopted home of a third.

Ask a Hungarian, a Norwegian, or a Greek who he is, and he can tell you, probably with pride. He is bonded to his fellow countrymen by blood, language, history, folkways, evolved arts, shared triumphs and shared defeats, even by the degree of inbreeding and adaptation that produces a recognizable physical type. And he is as definable to others as to himself; outsiders have an image of him that may be wrong in detail but is broadly accurate.

But ask a Californian who he is and you may get any of two dozen answers, in two dozen languages. Native sons and daughters will identify themselves as Californians without hesitation—indeed, with the same sort of patriotic pride that a Greek or Norwegian might show. But immigrants, and we are many, may not. I tried it on the luncheon table the other day and found that the people seated at it, though they have all lived in California since at least the 1940s, still think of themselves as Iowans, Kansans, or Scotsmen. Identification with a place, they agreed, has much to do with growing up in it, and may not be fully achieved short of a couple of generations. But they agreed on something else, too: non-Californians though they were, they didn't want to live anywhere else, including the places where they grew up.

A generation ago, writing on this same subject, I concluded that California was "America only more so . . . the national culture at its most energetic end. . . . In a prosperous country we are more prosperous than most; in an urban country more urban than most; in a gadget-happy country more addicted to gadgets; in a mobile country more mobile; in a tasteless country more tasteless; in a creative country more energetically creative; in an optimistic society more optimistic; in an anxious society more anxious."

It did not seem to me then that California could be called a cultural region. It didn't have the isolation, the homogeneity, or the humility to be called a region. It didn't feel like any spur track, it felt like the main line, and it was likely to assert that if Columbus had landed on the West Coast instead of the West Indies, Manhattan Island would still belong to the Indians.

That was in 1959, at the height of the postwar boom. With the aid of hindsight I would not really change that judgment, but I would temper it. For it seems clear now that in 1959, and before it, and after it, California has not only been America only more so, it has sometimes been America in the worst sense of the word. It has plundered itself, it has permitted the wide excesses of wide-open opportunism and uncontrollable growth. Mainly over water, it has split itself politically in two.

Now things have changed and grown tighter. We are making real estate millionaires in smaller numbers. We are tearing down and selling off the schools that for a while we were completing at the rate of two or three a week. We live at a different point on the population curve than during those years when more than 50 percent of the population was under 25. We have seen the influx of millions of immigrants, many of whom will not make it to full citizenship for two or three generations, if ever. The movement of Pacific and mesoamerican peoples into the state has postponed for a long time the development of a recognizable California type—either that, or it has guaranteed the continuation and widening of the gap between haves and have-nots that has ominous economic and racial possibilities for the future.

A full generation after 1959 we are further than ever from being able to define a Californian or California culture. We are probably further from a unifying California pride, though by the evidence of our luncheon table not many of us want to move. Maturing pains turn out to be as bad as growing pains. By and large the less a Californian reads and thinks, the more satisfied he is. Even with the boat ramps overcrowded on Shasta Lake, even with far-ahead reservations necessary in most state parks and on the Muir Trail, it is still a life that few would trade for any available alternative. Children reared in California find it hard to live anywhere else. College football players used to the California climate grieve when they are drafted by Green Bay or Buffalo.

Curiously, as the boom slows and we are near the limits of available water, as we have to fight for the open space we once took for granted, as we feel the competition of the energy-rich mountain states and the Sunbelt Southwest, we show more regional stigmata than we did in 1959. We reveal a provincial self-consciousness and touchiness, we make tacit admissions of cultural inferiority. In their relations with the East, California writers, painters, musicians, and publications display the attitudes, alternately apologetic and defiant, that mark the colonial complex, as when some Bay Area writers expressed in a recent issue of the *San Francisco Examiner* their distress at being ignored by New York reviewers. Quaintly, some of the complainers had recently moved out here from the East. By becoming Californians, they complained, they had lost status.

They should not have wasted their breath. I suggest that, in matters of cultural evaluation, the colonial complex arises from first granting some other place the authority to make judgments about us, and then believing the judgments they make.

The colonial complex is nothing new. Early American writers and critics were infuriated by (because they half accepted) condescending British opinions of them. American patriots smarted under the scorn of British travelers, and tried to make up in brag what they lacked in cathedrals. Later, the regions deferred in the same way to New York opinion, and were angered for the same reasons.

American writing is done everywhere; a lot of it, and some of the best, is done in California. But American publishing is done pretty much between Broadway and Third Avenue and between 33rd and 60th streets, and American literary opinion, though its territory may extend south to take in the Village, is generated on essentially the same ground. The book reviews that every bookstore in the country accepts as the highest authorities are *The New York Times Book Review* and the *New York Review of Books*, both admirable journals that express New York superbly and either do not know or do not much care about the rest of the country. Seeing itself occasionally in those pages, California as often as not is embarrassed to find itself pictured as grotesque or trivial. But since the judgment comes from headquarters, half of us believe it.

The case of the review media is especially irritating to some Californians because those periodicals make judgments, presume to sift the important from the unimportant, and they do so from premises that often seem uninformed, biased, or condescending. But the editorial assumptions of other media are not too different. And that, it seems to me, is a change. In 1959 I think we did not feel that Gotham was against us, or indifferent to us, or affiliated with a culture that repudiated ours. Big times were afoot then, and we felt the interest in them from beyond our borders. By 1981 that interest, often amused, but interest, seems to have hardened into resistance.

Well, we have produced a lot of screwballs since 1959, and all Californians may be tainted by association. In a notably free and exuberant society, nearly anything goes, and sometimes it goes sour. But I think it is not California's failures and excesses that have bred antagonism in the East. Success has more to do with it. Emotions simple, direct, and understandable are at work. Envy and fear.

"American history is history in transition from an Atlantic to a Pacific phase," said historian Garrett Mattingly 35 years or so ago. What was apparent to a historian then is apparent to almost anybody now. The East wanes, the West waxes. It is no longer unthinkable that a distinguished scholar should leave Harvard for Berkeley or Stanford. Growth, energy, opportunity, shift westward. Our most populous and powerful state fronts the Pacific, our foremost trading partner is not Great Britain but Japan. And the garrison mentality often charged against regional patriots can affect rearguard positions as well as outposts. It cannot be entirely coincidental that the condescension and antagonism of the Atlantic states toward California grows shriller and less charitable at the precise time when population, money, and political power are bleeding out of the Atlantic states toward the South, the Southwest, and the West.

But rivalry, even when acknowledged, doesn't have to be pursued. By resenting and resisting eastern prejudice and distaste, we would only reduce ourselves to the shrillness of regional scolds. The eastern stranglehold on the publication-and-opinion industry, though it has proved hard to break, will not last indefinitely.

West Coast journals, if they are smart, will not become simply regional retorts to eastern journals. They will not be regional at all in the limiting sense. They will base themselves firmly on their own territory and shoot for an audience as wide as the English-speaking world. To do that they will need confidence. They will also need a wider view of California and the California culture than that provided by Hollywood or even by the contemporary Hollywood variety of politics. There is every sort of richness, every sort of quality, in California, to counteract a fairly pervasive vulgarity. No richness and no quality should go unreported, and the merely sensational doesn't need to be hyped.

In 1959 I said that California, if it is a region at all, is a region with a view. I meant a *wide* view. And I see no reason in 1981 to revise that description. [1981]

JOHN GREGORY DUNNE

Eureka!
A Celebration of California

When I am in California, I am not in the West, I am
west of the West. —THEODORE ROOSEVELT

I MOVED to California on the fifth day of June, 1964. I can be very specific about the date: I had to swear to it in a legal deposition, signed and witnessed and admitted into evidence in Civil Court, City of New York, in and for the County of New York, as an addendum in the case of *New York Telephone Company, plaintiff,* v. *John Gregory Dunne, Index number* 103886/ 1964. The charge against me was nonpayment of a bill from New York Telephone in the amount of $54.09. The record of the proceeding, Index number 103886/1964, noted that a subpoena had been issued ordering me to court to answer the charge, and a process server, fully cognizant, as the record shows, that his "statements are true under the penalties of perjury," swore under oath that he had served me with said subpoena on July 7, 1964, in person at my residence, 41 East 75th Street, City of New York, County of New York. The case of *New York Telephone Company, plaintiff,* v. *John Gregory Dunne* was heard on July 24, 1964, and in due course I was found guilty as charged, fined $5 plus $9 in court costs and $1.16 in interest on the unpaid bill, making the total default $69.25. A warrant was also issued for my arrest for failure to answer a court order, namely the subpoena allegedly served on July 7, 1964.

Sometime later that summer, the papers pertaining to Index number 103886/1964, Civil Court, City of New York, in and for the County of New York, were forwarded to me at my new home in Portuguese Bend, California, a peninsula protruding into the Pacific Ocean on the southwestern tip of Los Angeles County. The equilibrium of my first western summer was upset. The sealed crates containing the records of my past were drawn from storage and opened. A check of my bank statements confirmed that the bill from New York Telephone had been paid on time, the evidence being a canceled check, number 61, dated March 23, 1964, drawn in the amount of $54.09 on the Chase Manhattan Bank, Rockefeller Center Branch, and paid to the order of the plaintiff, the New York Telephone Company. Witnesses attested that I had not been out of Los Angeles County since my arrival on the fifth of June, making it difficult for the process server, whatever his affirmations that his statements were "true under the penalties of perjury," to have served me with a subpoena on the Upper East Side of Manhattan on July 7. I engaged Carmine DeSapio's attorney and on his instructions sent this information to the president of the New York Telephone Company, copy as well to Mr. John McInerney, clerk of the Civil Court, City of New York, in and for the County of New York. By return mail I received a letter from the president of New York Telephone apologizing for the unfortunate error, saying that the judgment had been vacated and that copies of the vacating order as well as his letter of apology had been put in my file. I was so warmed by this prompt recognition of corporate error that I immediately wrote back the president of New York Telephone, copies to Mr. Frederick Kappel, chairman of the board at AT&T, and to Mr. David Rockefeller at the Chase Bank, and told him to do something carnally improper to himself.

And so I was in California, on the lam, as it were, from the slam. Manifest Destiny, 1964. What was western expansion, after all, but a migration of malcontents and ne'er do-wells, have-nots with no commitment to the stable society left behind, adventurers committed only to circumventing any society in their path. For eight years on the Upper East Side of Manhattan, I had been a have-not and a malcontent. I dreamed of being an adventurer. When I was 25, I had put up $100 to buy a piece of an antimony mine in Thailand.

I was not sure what antimony was, but I saw myself in riding boots and a wide-brimmed hat in the jungles of Siam. There was a whisper of opium and there were women always called sloe-eyed, wearing *ao dais* and practiced in the Oriental permutations of fellatio. The daydream, of course, was compensation for the reality I was then living. I was a traffic clerk in an industrial advertising agency, little more than a messenger in a Brooks Brothers suit and a white buttoned-down shirt and a striped tie, taking copy and layouts for industrial toilet fixtures to the client in the Bronx. At night I tried to write a novel titled *Not the Macedonian*. The first line of the novel—the only line I ever wrote—was "They called him Alexander the Great." Not, of course, the Macedonian. My Alexander was a movie director. In Hollywood. I had never met a movie director, I had never been in Hollywood. For that matter, I had never been west of Fort Carson, Colorado, where I had spent the last three months of a two-year stint as a peacetime army draftee. Nor had I ever told anyone, least of all the girl I was then supposed to marry, that my fashionable address in New York's silk-stocking district was a rooming house, populated by men who had been beaten by the city. One roommate was a lawyer from South Carolina who had failed the New York Bar exam three times and was afraid to go home. Another was a drunk who had been out of work for eleven months. The owner-landlord of this townhouse between Madison and Park packed four people to a room, each at $56 a month, and day and night he prowled the corridors and stairwells looking for transgressions of his house rules. Once he threatened to evict me for tossing Q-tips in the toilet, another time for violating the food protocols. His kitchen was run on a nonprofit honor system; a price list was posted (2 cents for a saltine, 5 cents for a saltine with a dab of peanut butter, 7 cents for a saltine with peanut butter and jelly, etcetera) and the tenant was expected to tot up his expenses on a file card. Snitches reported to the owner-landlord that I had been negligent in the accounting of my nightly inhalation of Hydrox and milk. My only defense was rapture of the snack. I threw myself on his mercy and was sentenced to permanent loss of kitchen privileges.

Each day I scoured the Apartments to Share column in the *Times* real estate section, but it was not until a man in a green-flocked apartment on East 15th Street told me there was only one bed in his flat that I realized the meaning of the phrase in the ads, "Must be compatible." I haunted the sleazy one-room employment agencies along 42nd Street and up Broadway, looking for a better job. I felt that if I only broke through to $75 a week it would be the first step to the cover of *Time*. In the evenings I concocted résumés, listing jobs I had never held with references from people I had never met. The most elaborate fiction was the invention of a job on a daily newspaper in Colorado Springs. During my service at Fort Carson, I had noted that this paper did not give its reporters bylines and so I bought up enough back issues at the out-of-town newsstand on Times Square to create for myself an unbylined city room background. The employment agents were impressed. Except one, a man with rheumy eyes and dandruff flaking down on his shiny blue suit. Even now I sometimes awake with a start remembering that awful day when he told me he had checked out one of my soi-disant Colorado references, who reported that he had never heard of me.

I can say now what I dared not say then: I was a jerk.

In time, however, my nonexistent job on the city desk of the Colorado Springs newspaper helped me find employment with a trusting trade magazine, an opportunity that I later parlayed into a five-year sojourn on *Time*. There I learned discipline, met deadlines and became adept at dealing with the more evasive transitions, the elusive "but," the slippery "nevertheless," the chimerical "on the other hand." I also learned that the writer on a news magazine is essentially a carpenter, chipping, whittling, planing a field correspondent's ten- or twelve-page file down into a 70-line story, in effect cutting a sofa into a bar stool; in the eyes of his editors, both are places to sit.

Since days in *Time*'s New York office are counted as enhancing one's world vision, I became, after three years, the magazine's Saigon watcher, even though I had never been there. In 1962, I persuaded my editors to pay my way to Indochina, my alleged sphere of expertise, where I fornicated for five weeks and in what now seems a constant postcoital daze floated to the nascent realization that the war beginning to metastasize in Vietnam was a malignant operation. It was a difficult induction to explain to my editors back in New York. A whore in Cholon did not seem much of a source, notwithstanding the brother she claimed was in Hanoi, from whom, in her text, she received periodic messages over an RFD route I suspected was not sanctioned by President Diem or Archbishop Thuc. It was just a feeling. I had the feeling when I monitored a conversation about Swiss bank accounts over drinks at the Cercle Sportif in Saigon, an abstract discussion punctuated by long silences, the simple question, "Do you favor Lausanne?" seeming to carry an absurd consignment of symbolic freight. I had the same feeling when I flew around the countryside for a few days with a four-star U.S. Army general from MACV. The bases he dropped in on reminded me of Fort Bliss or Fort Chaffee from my own army days. The latrines were spotless, whitewashed stones lined the pathways between tents and the young volunteer American officers wore starched fatigues and spit-shined boots and their hair was clipped to the skull two inches over the ears. There were graphs and maps and overlays with grease pencil notations, and after every briefing there was coffee and optimism, but no American officer in whatever section we happened to be visiting could explain why the roads were not secure at night. Losing control of the roads at night was the nature of the war, the general said. He seemed to think this a reasonable explanation and stressed that the plans and procedures of his command were "viable"; I learned new and ambiguous meanings for the word "viable" during my short stay in Vietnam. A Turk nicknamed Cowboy had a less ambiguous expression. Cowboy was a former colonel in the Turkish air force who, after being declared redundant and forced into premature retirement, had signed on with the CIA for the Bay of Pigs. At $2,000 a month he was working off that contract in Vietnam, hedgehopping over the hills to avoid ground fire, summing up what was happening in the jungles below in two words: "All shit."

Cowboy carried no weight in the Time-Life Building. Briefed at the Pentagon, lunched at the White House, my editors saw the light at the end of the tunnel, they thought my sibylline meanderings the pornography of a malcontent. In the ensuing religious wars about Vietnam that rent *Time*, I sided with the doubters in the Saigon bureau and asked to be relieved of the Vietnam desk. My penance was reassignment to the Benelux portfolio, along with responsibility for the less doctrinaire capitals of Western Europe—a beat that encompassed by-elections in Liechtenstein, Scandinavian sexual mores and Common Market agricultural policy. "How small," I wrote, "is a small tomato?" I became sullen, a whisperer in the corridors. I did not get an expected raise, a short time later I married, a short time after that, still a malcontent, not yet a have, I quit my job. Ignorant of the impending posse from the New York Telephone Company, the adventurer routed himself to California.

Eureka, as the state motto has it: "I have found it."

I had found it.

TWO

Imagine: an Irish Catholic out of Hartford, Connecticut, two generations removed from steerage, with the political outlook of an alderman and social graces polished to a semigloss at the Hartford Golf Club. Imagine a traveler with this passport confronting that capital south of the Tehachapi called El Pueblo de Nuestra Señora la Reina de Los Angeles. My wife, Joan Didion, was a fifth-generation Californian and was in a sense returning home (although her real home was the equally impenetrable flatland of the Central Valley), but to me it was a new world: *the* new world. I watched Los Angeles television, listened to Los Angeles radio, devoured Los Angeles newspapers trying to find the visa that would provide entry. "Go gargle razor blades," advised a local talk show host pleasantly; it was a benediction that seemed to set the tone of the place. Dawn televised live on the Sunset Strip: A minister of the Lord inquired of a stringy-haired nubile what she liked doing best in the world. An unequivocal answer: "Balling." Another channel, another preacher. This one ascribed the evils of the contemporary liberal ethic to one "J. J. Russo." It was some time before I apprehended that the Italianate "J.J." was in fact Jean-Jacques Rousseau. In a newspaper I read of a man living on the rim of Death Valley who walked alone out into the desert, leaving behind a note that he wanted to "talk to God." God apparently talked back. The man was bitten by a rattlesnake and died.

Fundamentalism, the Deity, the elements—those familiar aides-mémoire that titillate the casual visitor to the western shore. I did not need a pony to find the immediate subtext of banality and vulgarity. It took a long time, however, to learn that the real lesson in each of those parables was to quite another point. Los Angeles is the least accessible and therefore the worst reported of American cities. It is not available to the walker in the city. There is no place where the natives gather. Distance obliterates unity and community. This inaccessibility means that the contemporary de Tocqueville on a layover between planes can define Los Angeles only in terms of his own culture shock. A negative moral value is attached to the taco stand, to the unnatural presence of palm trees at Christmas (although the climate of Los Angeles at Christmas exactly duplicates that of Bethlehem), even to the San Andreas fault. Whenever she thought of California, an editor at *The New York Times* once told me, she thought of Capri pants and plastic flowers. She is an intelligent woman and I do not think she meant to embrace the cliché with such absolute credulity; she would have been sincerely pained had I replied that whenever I thought of New York I thought of Halston and Bobby Zarem. (My most endearing memory of this woman is seeing her at a party in New York, as always meticulously pulled together, except that the side seam on her Pucci dress had parted. The parted seam was the sort of social detail that marked her own reportage, which had a feel for texture absent in her a priori invention of a California overrun with plastic greenery.) "I would love to see you play with the idea of California as the only true source of American culture," she wrote my wife and me, fellow conspirators, or so she thought, in her fantasy of the western experience. "I mean, what other state would have pearlized, rainbow-colored plastic shells around its public telephones?"

Notice "plastic," that perfect trigger word, the one word that invariably identifies its user as culturally superior. When I arrived in California in 1964, the catch words and phrases meant to define the place were "smog" and "freeways" and "kook religions," which then spun off alliteratively into "kooky California cults." Still the emigré, I referred to my new country as "Lotusland"; it was a while before I realized that anyone who calls Los Angeles "Lotusland" is a functioning booby. In the years since 1964, only the words have changed. California is a land of "rapacious philodendron" and "squash yellow Datsuns," Marion Knox noted on the Op-Ed page of *The New York Times*; seven months in the Los Angeles bureau of *Time* seemed to Ms. Knox an adventure in Oz. "Angel dust." "The 'in' dry cleaner." "Men in black bathing suits, glossy with Bain de Soleil." (Perhaps a tad of homophobia there, a residual nightmare of Harry's Bar in Bloomingdale's.) "The place of honor at . . . dinner parties," Ms. Knox reported, "is next to the hotshot realtor." I wonder idly whose dinner parties, wonder at what press party do you find the chic hairdresser and the hotshot realtor. I also think I have never read a more poignant illustration of Cecilia Brady's line in *The Last Tycoon*: "We don't go for strangers in Hollywood."

In *Esquire*, Richard Reeves spoke of "ideas with a California twist, or twisted California ideas—drinking vodka, est, credit cards, student revolts, political consultants, skateboards . . ." An absurd catalogue, venial sins, if sins they be at all, some not even Californian in origin. Ivy Lee had the Rockefeller ear before the term "political consultant" was invented, not to mention Edward Bernays and Benjamin Sonnenberg, who were plugged into the sockets of power when normalcy was still an idea to be cultivated. And what is est after all but a virus of psychiatry, a mutation of the search to find one's self, passed west from Vienna via Park Avenue, then carried back again, mutated, on the prevailing winds. (Stone-throwing in glass houses, this kind of exchange, a Ping-Pong game between midgets, est on one coast, Arica on the other, vodka drinking in California, Plato's Retreat in Manhattan, lacquered swimmers on the Malibu, their equally glossy brothers three time zones east in Cherry Grove.) The trigger words meant to define California become a litany, the litany a religion. The chief priests and pharisees attending the Los Angeles bureaus of eastern publications keep the faith free from heresy. A year ago a reporter from *Time* telephoned my wife and said that the magazine was preparing a new cover story on California; he wondered if she had noticed any significant changes in the state since *Time*'s last California cover.

Still they come, these amateur anthropologists, the planes disgorging them at LAX, their date books available for dinner with the hotshot realtor. They are bent under the cargo of their preconceived notions. "The only people who live in L.A. are those who can't make it in New York," I once heard a young woman remark at dinner. She was the associate producer of a rock 'n' roll television special and she was scarfing down chicken mole, chiles Jalapenos, guacamole, sour cream, cilantro and tortillas. "You cook New York," she complimented her hostess. "Mexico, actually," her hostess replied evenly, passing her a tortilla and watching her lather sour cream on it as if it were jam. Another dinner party, this for an eastern publisher in town to visit a local author. There were ten at dinner, it was late, we had all drunk too much. "Don't you miss New York?" the publisher asked. "Books. Publishing. Politics. Talk." His tone was sadly expansive. "Evenings like this."

The visitors have opinions, they cherish opinions, their opinions ricochet around the room like tracer fire. The very expression of an opinion seems to certify its worth. Socially acceptable opinion, edged with the most sentimental kind of humanism, condescension in drag. "Why can't you find the little guy doing a good job and give him a pat on the back?" the managing editor of *Life* once asked my wife. Little people, that population west of the Hudson, this butcher, that baker, the candlestick maker, each with a heart as big as all outdoors. Usually there is a scheme to enrich the life of this little person, this cultural dwarf, some effort to bring him closer to the theater or the good new galleries. Mass transit, say. I remember one evening when a writer whose subject was menopausal sexual conduct insisted that mass transit was the only means of giving Southern California that sense of community she thought it so sadly lacked. I did not say that I thought "community" was just another ersatz humanistic cryptogram. Nor did I say that I considered mass transit a punitive concept, an idea that runs counter to the fluidity that is, for better or worse, the bedrock precept of Southern California, a fluidity that is the antithesis of community. She would not have heard me if I had said it, for one purpose of such promiscuous opinionizing is to filter out the disagreeable, to confirm the humanistic consensus.

He who rejects the dictatorship of this consensus is said to lack "input." Actors out from New York tell me they miss the input, novelists with a step deal at Paramount, journalists trying to escape the eastern winter. I inquire often after input, because I am so often told that California (except for San Francisco) is deficient in it, as if it were a vitamin. Input is people, I am told. Ideas. Street life. I question more closely. Input is the pot-au-feu of urban community. I wonder how much input Faulkner had in Oxford, Mississippi, and it occurs to me that scarcity of input might be a benign deficiency. Not everyone agrees. After two weeks in California, a New York publishing figure told Dick Cavett at a party in New York, he felt "brain-damaged." Delphina Ratazzi was at that party, and Geraldo Rivera. And Truman Capote, Calvin Klein, Charlotte Ford, George Plimpton, Barbara Allen with Philip Niarchos, Kurt Vonnegut, Carrie Fisher with Desi Arnaz Jr., Joan Hackett and Arnold Schwarzenegger. I do not have much faith in any input I might have picked up at that party.

THREE

California is not so much a state of the Union as it is an imagi-nation that seceded from our reality a long time ago. In leading the world in the transition from industrial to post-industrial society, California's culture became the first to shift from coal to oil, from steel to plastic, from hardware to software, from materialism to mysticism, from reality to fantasy. California became the first to discover that it was fantasy that led reality, not the other way around. —WILLIAM IRWIN THOMPSON

Perhaps it is easiest to define Los Angeles by what it is not. Most emphatically it is not eastern. San Francisco is eastern, a creation of the gold rush, colonized by sea, Yankee architecture and Yankee attitudes boated around the Horn and grafted into the bay. Any residual ribaldry in San Francisco is the legacy of that lust for yellow riches that attracted those early settlers in the first place. Small wonder easterners feel comfortable there. They perceive an Atlantic clone; it does not threaten as does that space-age Fort Apache 500 miles to the south.

Consider then the settling of Southern California. It was—and in a real sense continues to be—the last western migration. It was a migration, however, divorced from the history not only of the West but of the rest of California as well, a migration that seemed to parody Frederick Jackson Turner and his theory on the significance of the frontier. In Turner's version, the way west was not for the judicious—overland, across a continent and its hard-scrabble history. Those who would amputate a past and hit the trail were not given to the idea of community. Dreamers or neurotics, they were individualists who shared an aversion to established values, to cohesion and stability. A hard man, Turner's western wayfarer, for a hard land.

The settlers of Southern California traveled the same route across the Big Empty—but on an excursion ticket. By the mid-1880s, the frontier, as Turner noted, was for all intents and purposes closed, the continental span traced by a hatchwork of railroad lines. Where there were railroads, there was murderous competition, and when in 1886 the Santa Fe laid its track into Southern California, it joined in battle with the Southern Pacific for the ultimate prize, the last terminal on the Pacific shore, a frontier of perpetual sunshine where the possibilities seemed as fertile as the land. The rate wars between the Santa Fe and the Southern Pacific denied sense. From the jumping-off points in the Missouri Valley, fares to Southern California dropped from $125 to $100, and then in a maniacal frenzy of price-cutting to $12, $8, $6, $4. Finally on March 6, 1887, the price bottomed out at one dollar per passenger, 100 copper pennies to racket down those trails blazed by the cattle drives and the Conestoga wagons, to cross that blank land darkened by the blood of the Indian wars.

What the railroads had essentially created in Southern California was a frontier resort, a tumor on the western ethic. Bargain-basement pioneers, every one a rebuke to Turner's hard man, flooded into Southern California, 120,000 of them trained into Los Angeles by the Southern Pacific alone in 1887, the Santa Fe keeping pace with three and four trainloads a day. In such a melee, where personal histories were erased, the Southland was an adventurer's nirvana. Land speculators preyed on the gullible, enticing them with oranges stuck into the branches of Joshua trees. But even when the land bubble burst, the newcomers stayed on, held captive by the sun, the prejudices and resentments of their abandoned life, the dreams and aspirations of their new one, cross-fertilizing in the luxuriant warmth.

And still they came, a generation on every trainload. If New York was the melting pot of Europe, Los Angeles was the melting pot of the United States. It was a bouillabaisse not to everyone's taste. "It is as if you tipped the United States up so all the commonplace people slid down there into Southern California," was the way Frank Lloyd Wright put it. In *Southern California: An Island on the Land*, Carey McWilliams replied gently to Wright: "One of the reasons for this persistent impression of commonplaceness is, of course, that the newcomers have been stripped of their natural settings—their Vermont hills, their Kansas plains, their Iowa cornfields. Here their essential commonplaceness stands out garishly in the harsh illumination of the sun. Here every wart is revealed, every wrinkle underscored, every eccentricity emphasized."

Expansion, McWilliams noted, was the major business of Southern California, the very reason for its existence. The "volume and velocity" of this migration set the tone of the place. From 1900 to 1940, the population of Los Angeles increased by nearly 1,600 percent. Everyone was an alien, the newcomer was never an exile. In an immigrant place where the majority was non-indigenous, the idea of community could not flourish, since community by definition is built on the deposits of shared experience. The fact that the spectacular growth of Los Angeles exactly coincided with the automotive age further weakened the idea of community. Where older cities, radiating out from a core, were defined and limited both by transportation and geography, Los Angeles was the first city on wheels, its landscape in three directions unbroken by natural barriers that could give it coherence and definition, its mobility limited only by a tank of gas.

The newness of Los Angeles—it is, after all, scarcely older than the century—and the idea of mobility as a cultural determinant lent the place a bumptiousness that was as appealing to some as it was aggravating to others. In a word, Southern California was different, and in the history of the land, what is different is seldom treasured. Exempt from the history of the West, the cut-rate carpetbaggers who settled in the Southland could adopt the western ethic and reinterpret it for their own uses. The result is a refinement of that ad hoc populism that has characterized California politics in this century, an ingrained suspicion of order, the bureaucracy of order and the predators of order. It is a straight line from Hiram Johnson to Howard Jarvis, and when Jerry Brown intones, "Issues are the last refuge of scoundrels," he is speaking in the authentic voice of a state where skepticism about government is endemic.

This attitude toward politics, as well as Southern California's particular and aggressive set toward the world, could be dismissed as a sunstroked curiosity as long as the region remained a provincial and distant colony, and so it did remain until World War II. Even with the steady infusion of people and ideas and capital, Southern California had almost no industrial base until the war. There was plenty of technological know-how—Los Angeles was the first city in the country to be entirely lit by electricity—and even before the turn of the century there was a sense that the city's destiny did not lie in divine guidance from the Atlantic. "The Pacific is the ocean of the future," Henry Huntington said then. "Europe can supply her own wants. We shall supply the needs of Asia."

Cowboy talk: There was no industry to supply the needs of Asia. Agriculture dominated Southern California (Los Angeles until 1920 was the nation's richest agricultural county), and the population boom had spawned an improvised ancillary economy of the most demeaning sort. It seemed a region of animal hospitals and car dealerships and roadside stands, of pool services and curbstone mediums. "Piddling occupations," James M. Cain wrote in 1933. "What electric importance can be felt in a peddler of orange peels? Or a confector of Bar-B-Q? Or the proprietor of a goldfish farm? Or a breeder of rabbit fryers?" In this service economy, Hollywood was the ultimate service industry—it required no raw materials except celluloid, which cost little to ship either as raw stock or finished film—but its payroll was enormous, and from 1920 to 1940 it gave Southern California a simulated industrial base. In 1938 the movie industry ranked fourteenth among all American businesses, in gross volume, eleventh in total assets.

And then came the war. The figures tell the story. In an eight-year period, 1940 to 1948, the federal government invested $1 billion in the construction of new industrial plants in California, and private industry kicked in $400 million more; industrial employment rose 75 percent; Los Angeles alone juggled $10 billion in war production contracts. These were just numbers, however, as ephemeral as any wartime figures. What was important was the technological scaffolding propping up the numbers. As Carey McWilliams points out in *California: The Great Exception*,* California "unlike other areas . . . did not convert to war production, for there was nothing much to 'convert'; what happened was that *new* industries and *new* plants were built overnight." "New" is a word that often takes on a suspect connotation when applied to California, but here were new plants untainted with the technological obsolescence afflicting so many older industries in the East. New processes using the new metals and new chemicals indigenous to California. New industries, such as aerospace and computers, which were mutually dependent, and in the case of aerospace particularly suited to the geography and climate of Southern California, a place where hardware could be tested on the limitless wastes of the Mojave 365 days a year.

In effect the war allowed Southern California to find a sense of itself. The self discovered was not particularly endearing. Think of Frederick Jackson Turner's hard man, glaze him with prosperity, put him in sunglasses and there you have it—a freeway Billy the Kid. There was an extravagance about the place, a lust for the new, and it was this lust that allowed Southern California to capitalize on the technologies of the future, to turn its attention away from the rest of the nation, from the bedrock of history itself. The boom years made Los Angeles an independent money mart, no longer an economic supplicant, its vision west across the Pacific to Japan and Australia, toward those frontiers envisioned by Henry Huntington; look if you need proof at the Los Angeles Yellow Pages and those corporate branch offices in Tokyo and Sydney. To some the lusts of Southern California seemed to lead only to venereal disease. "Reality . . . was whatever people said it was," J. D. Lorenz wrote in *Jerry Brown: The Man on the White Horse*. "It was the fresh start, the self-fulfilling prophecy, the victory of mind over matter. In a land without roots, reality was image, image replaced roots, and if the image could be constructed quickly, like a fabricated house, it could also be torn down quickly." It is part of the fascination of Southern California that it would enthusiastically agree with Lorenz's creed. Better the fresh start than roots choking with moral crab grass, better the fabricated house than the dry rot of cities, better mind over matter than a paralysis of will.

* It should be noted here that McWilliams's two books, *Southern California: An Island on the Land* and *California: The Great Exception*, are essential to any study of California. I think they are great books, not only because I am now and often have been in McWilliams's debt, but more importantly because they are cool and informative, history as literature in every sense.

Prosperity stroked the natural bombast of the Southern California frontier. Los Angeles, that upstart on the Pacific, looked back on the eastern littoral with a cool indifference that bordered on contempt. See what community got you, it seemed to say; what good are stability and cohesion if their legacy is the South Bronx? Economic independence, coupled with that western urge to be left alone, made Southern California in some metaphoric sense a sovereign nation, Pacifica, as it were, with Los Angeles as its capital.

And here is the other negative that defines Los Angeles: It no longer regards itself as a second city.

The history of nationhood is also largely the history of a nation's single city—that London, that Paris, that New York (with Washington as its outermost exurb) where politics, money and culture coalesce to shape a national idea. Every place else is Manchester or Marseilles. The claim of Los Angeles to be the co-equal of New York could be dismissed as the braggadocio of a provincial metropolis except for one thing. Los Angeles had Hollywood, the dream factory that is both a manufacturer of a national idea and an interpreter of it. Hollywood—the most ridiculed and the most envied cultural outpost of the century. Think of it: technology as an art form, an art form, moreover, bankrolled and nurtured by men who, in Louis Sherwin's surpassing remark, "knew only one word of two syllables and that word was 'fillum.' " At times I admit a certain impatience with Hollywood and all its orthodoxies. I hear that film is "truth at 24 frames a second" and wonder if any art has ever had a credo of such transcendental crap. Try it this way: "truth at 60 words a minute." But that is a factor of age and taste. When I was an undergraduate, the trek of the ambitious and allegedly literate bachelor of arts was to the East; to be heard, one was published, and the headquarters of print was New York. Now that trek is a trickle. The status of image has usurped the status of type. The young graduates head west, their book bags laden with manuals on lenses and cutting, more conversant with Jewison than with Joyce, almost blissfully persuaded that a knowledge of *Dallas* and *Los Angeles*, *Casablanca* and *Maracaibo* is a knowledge of the world at large.

It is this aspect of the Hollywood scene that eastern interpreters fasten upon. Zapping the vulgarity is less demanding than learning the grammar, the grammar of film, and by extension the grammar of Los Angeles, and of California itself. In the beginning, there was the vulgarity of the movie pioneers, many of whom were from Eastern Europe. No recounting of that era is complete without referring to those early movie moguls as former "furriers" or "rag merchants." It was an ethnic code, cryptological anti-Semitism. For furrier read Jew. No, not Jew: The Sulzbergers were Jews, and the Meyers; these unlettered rag-traders were nothing but ostentatious, parvenu sheenies, and there was always a good giggle in the Goldfish who changed his name to Goldwyn. I think of the Marxist critic who in the space of a few thousand words spoke about Josef von Sternberg, who "spurns as canard the rumor that he was born Joe Stern of Brooklyn"; about Mervyn Leroy, of whom "it is rumored that his real name is Lasky"; and about Lewis Milestone, "whose actual name is said to be Milstein."

It was easier to laugh than it was to examine the movie earthquake and its recurring aftershocks, easier to maintain that Los Angeles's indifference to the cultural heritage of the East was evidence of an indigenous lack of culture. But the lines had been drawn, the opinion media of the East versus the western image media of movies and television, and the spoils were the hearts and minds of America. This country had always been defined by the East. Everything was good or bad to the extent that it did or did not coincide with the eastern norm; the making of cultural rules, the fact of being the nation's social and cultural arbiter, imbued confidence. The movies were a severe shock to that confidence, all the more so because those images up there on screen did not seem to have an apparent editorial bias. "The movies did not describe or explore America," Michael Wood wrote in *America in the Movies*. "They invented it, dreamed up an America all their own, and persuaded us to share the dream. We shared it happily, because the dream was true in its fashion—true to a variety of American desires—and because there weren't all that many other dreams around."

The opinion media and the image media—each has an investment in its version of the American myth, each a stake in getting it wrong about the other. To the opinion media, Southern California is the enemy camp, and their guerrilla tactic is one of deflation. In their version, the quintessential native was born in Whittier and carries the middle name Milhous. Apostates and quislings are spokesmen: the refugee from Long Beach, now a practicing Manhattan intellectual, who reports that life in Los Angeles is the life of a turnip; the film director who curtsies to his critical constituency and says that if Solzhenitsyn lived in L.A., he would have a hot tub and be doing TM. Hatred of New York is seen as an epidemic. "What do you hate (or dislike) about New York City?" begins a letter from *New York* magazine. "We are asking a number of persons . . ." *Esquire* finds this hatred, and Woody Allen in *Annie Hall*. It is a kind of negative boosterism that I find infinitely depressing. "As a well-known New York hater, you . . ." It was a correspondent from *Time* on the telephone. (*Time* again, where the history of California is demarcated by *Time* cover stories.) I told the *Time* man that while I was gratified at being described as "well known," I did not know how I had achieved the reputation of "New York hater." He admitted it was not from anything I had ever written. Nor anything I had said; we had never met. Nor anything he had heard secondhand. I persisted: How had I achieved that dubious reputation? "You live here," he said finally.

The call troubled me for a long time. If I had not thought much about New York's financial crisis (the actual subject of the call), I certainly took no pleasure in its plight (the assumption of my caller). It just never crossed my mind. And there it was, the canker, the painful sore of reciprocity: Los Angeles was indifferent to New York. It was the same indifference that for decades New York had shown, and was no longer showing, to the rest of the country.

FOUR

The splendors and miseries of Los Angeles, the graces and grotesqueries, appear to me as unrepeatable as they are unprecedented. I share neither the optimism of those who see Los Angeles as the prototype of all future cities, nor the gloom of those who see it as the harbinger of universal urban doom. . . . It is immediately apparent that no city has ever been produced by such an extraordinary mixture of geography, climate, economics, demography, mechanics and culture; nor is it likely that an even remotely similar mixture will ever occur again.

—REYNER BANHAM
Los Angeles: The Architecture of Four Ecologies

"The freeway is forever" was the slogan of a local radio station the summer I arrived in California. Here was the perfect metaphor for that state of mind called Los Angeles, but its meaning eluded me for years. Singular not plural, *freeway* not *freeways*, the definite article implying that what was in question was more an idea than a roadway. Seen from the air at night, the freeway is like a river, alive, sinuous, a reticulated glow of headlights tracing the huge contours of a city 70 miles square. Surface streets mark off grids of economy and class, but the freeway is totally egalitarian, a populist notion that makes Los Angeles comprehensible and complete. Alhambra and Silver Lake, Beverly Hills and Bell Gardens, each an exit, each available. "The point about this huge city," observed Reyner Banham, "is that all its parts are equal and equally accessible from all other parts at once."

Driving the freeway induces a kind of narcosis. Speed is a virtue, and the speed of the place makes one obsessive, a gambler. The spirit is that of a city on the move, of people who have already moved here from somewhere else. Mobility is their common language; without it, or an appreciation of it, the visitor is an illiterate. The rearview mirror reflects an instant city, its population trebled and re-trebled in living memory. Its monuments are the artifacts of civil engineering, off-ramps and interchanges that sweep into concrete parabolas. There is no past, the city's hierarchy is jerry-built, there are few mistakes to repeat. The absence of past and structure is basic to the allure of Los Angeles. It deepens the sense of self-reliance, it fosters the idea of freedom, or at least the illusion of it. Freedom of movement most of all, freedom that liberates the dweller in this city from community chauvinism and neighborhood narcissism, allowing him to absorb the most lavish endowments his environment has to offer—sun and space.

The colonization of Los Angeles has reduced the concept of space to the level of jargon, to "my space" and "your space." Space is an idea. I do not think that anyone in the East truly understands the importance of this idea of space in the West. Fly west from the Atlantic seaboard, see the country open up below, there some lights, over there a town, on the horizon perhaps a city, in between massive, implacable emptiness. The importance of that emptiness is psychic. We have a sense out here, however specious, of being alone, of wanting, more importantly, to be left alone, of having our own space, a kingdom of self with a two-word motto: "Fuck Off." Fly east from the Pacific, conversely, and see the country as the westerner sees it, urban sprawl mounting urban sprawl, a vast geographical gang-bang of incestuous blight, incestuous problems, incestuous ideas. People who vote Frank Rizzo and Abe Beame or Ed Koch into office have nothing to tell this westerner. It is, of course, simple to say that both these views from the air are mirages, but even a mirage proceeds from some basic consciousness, some wish that seeks fulfillment. What, after all, is community? Space in the West, community in the East—these are the myths that sustain us.

When I think of Los Angeles now, after almost a decade and a half of living not only in it but with it, I sometimes feel an astonishment, an attachment that approaches joy. I am attached to the way palm trees float and recede down empty avenues, attached to the deceptive perspectives of the pale subtropical light. I am attached to the drydocks of San Pedro, near where I lived the summer I moved to California, and to the refineries of Torrance, which at night resemble an extra-terrestrial space station and which always made my wife cry that first summer on the long drive home from town. I am attached to the particular curve of coastline as one leaves the tunnel at the end of the Santa Monica Freeway to drive north on the Pacific Coast Highway. I am attached perhaps especially to the time warp of Boyle Heights and Echo Park and Silver Lake. I remember an afternoon spent in a bungalow in Silver Lake with Rasputin's daughter. Yes: Rasputin.

His daughter was a quiet and stolid woman in her middle sixties. After Lenin's arrival at the Finland Station, she had been a circus acrobat in Europe, and after that she had drifted to Los Angeles and into factory work, and then she had retired to that tiny bungalow in Silver Lake. There were faded photographs of the Czar and Czarina of All the Russias on the living room wall and there were icons and a samovar from the motherland. There was also a promoter who was trying to tie up the print, film and dramatic rights to Maria Rasputin's life. In a room that evoked one of the turning points in history, the promoter said that a boulevard in the Valley had been named after her family. I felt like Philip Marlowe and I do not think that ever again I will understand the phrase "clash of cultures" as well as I understood it that afternoon in Silver Lake.

I am attached to it all, attached equally to the glories of the place and to its flaws, its faults, its occasional revelations of psychic and physical slippage, its beauties and its betrayals.

It is the last stop.

It is the end of the line.

Eureka!

I love it.   [1979]

LEWIS H. LAPHAM

Lost Horizon

FOR the past six or seven weeks I have been answering angry questions about San Francisco. People who know that I was born in that city assume that I have access to confidential information, presumably at the highest levels of psychic consciousness. Their questions sound like accusations, as if they were demanding a statement about the poisoning of the reservoirs. Who were those people that the Reverend Jim Jones murdered in Guyana, and how did they get there? Why would anybody follow such a madman into the wilderness, and how did the Reverend Jones come by those letters from Vice-President Mondale and Mrs. Rosalynn Carter? Why did the fireman kill the mayor of San Francisco and the homosexual city official? What has gone wrong in California, and who brought evil into paradise? Fortunately I don't know the answers to these questions; if I knew them, I would be bound to proclaim myself a god and return to San Francisco in search of followers, a mandala, and a storefront shrine. Anybody who would understand the enigma of San Francisco must first know something about the dreaming narcissism of the city, and rather than try to explain this in so many words, I offer into evidence the story of my last assignment for the *San Francisco Examiner*.

I had been employed on the paper for two years when, on a Saturday morning in December of 1959, I reported for work to find the editors talking to one another in the hushed and self-important way that usually means that at least fifty people have been killed. I assumed that a ship had sunk or that a building had collapsed. The editors were not in the habit of taking me into their confidence, and I didn't expect to learn the terms of the calamity until I had a chance to read the AP wire. Much to my surprise, the city editor motioned impatiently in my direction, indicating that I should join the circle of people standing around his desk and turning slowly through the pages of the pictorial supplement that the paper was obliged to publish the next day. Aghast at what they saw, unable to stifle small cries of anguished disbelief, they were examining twelve pages of text and photographs arranged under the heading LOS ANGELES—THE ATHENS OF THE WEST. To readers unfamiliar with the ethos of San Francisco, I'm not sure that I can convey the full and terrible effect of this headline. Not only was it wrong, it was monstrous heresy. The residents of San Francisco dote on a romantic image of the city, and they imagine themselves living at a height of civilization accessible only to Erasmus or a nineteenth-century British peer. They flatter themselves on their sophistication, their exquisite sensibility, their devotion to the arts. Los Angeles represents the antithesis of these graces; it is the land of the Philistines, lying somewhere to the south in the midst of housing developments that stand as the embodiment of ugliness, vulgarity, and corruptions of the spirit.

Pity, then, the poor editors in San Francisco. In those days there was also a *Los Angeles Examiner*, and the same printing plant supplied supplements to both papers. The text and photographs intended for a Los Angeles audience had been printed in the Sunday pictorial bearing the imprimatur of the *San Francisco Examiner*. It was impossible to correct the mistake, and so the editors in San Francisco had no choice but to publish and give credence to despised anathema.

This so distressed them that they resolved to print a denial. The city editor, knowing that my grandfather had been mayor of San Francisco and that I had been raised in the city, assumed that he could count on my dedication to the parochial truth. He also knew that I had studied at Yale and Cambridge universities, and although on most days he made jokes about the future of a literary education, on this particular occasion he saw a use for it. What was the point of reading all those books if they didn't impart the skills of a sophist? He handed me the damnable pages and said that I had until five o'clock in the afternoon to refute them as false doctrine. The story was marked for page 1 and an eight-column headline. I was to spare no expense of adjectives.

The task was hopeless. Los Angeles at the time could claim the residence of Igor Stravinsky, Aldous Huxley, and Christopher Isherwood. Admittedly they had done their best work before coming west to ripen in the sun, but their names and photographs, together with those of a few well-known painters and a number of established authors temporarily engaged in the writing of screenplays, make for an impressive display in a newspaper. Even before I put through my first telephone call, to a poet in North Beach experimenting with random verse, I knew that cultural enterprise in San Francisco could not sustain the pretension of a comparison to New York or Chicago, much less to Periclean Athens.

Ernest Bloch had died, and Darius Milhaud taught at Mills College only during the odd years; Henry Miller lived 140 miles to the south at Big Sur, which placed him outside the city's penumbra of light. The Beat Generation had disbanded. Allen Ginsberg still could be seen brooding in the cellar of the City Lights Bookshop, but Kerouac had left town, and the tourists were occupying the best tables at Cassandra's, asking the waiters about psychedelic drugs and for connections to the Buddhist underground. Although I admired the work of Evan Connell and Lawrence Ferlinghetti, I doubted that they would say the kinds of things that the city editor wanted to hear. The San Francisco school of painting consisted of watercolor views of Sausalito and Fisherman's Wharf; there was no theater, and the opera was a means of setting wealth to music. The lack of art or energy in the city reflected the lassitude of a citizenry content to believe its own press notices. The circumference of the local interest extended no more than 150 miles in three directions—as far as Sonoma County and Bolinas in the north, to Woodside and Monterey in the south, and to Yosemite and Tahoe in the east. In a westerly direction the civic imagination didn't reach beyond the Golden Gate Bridge. Within this narrow arc the inhabitants of San Francisco entertained themselves with a passionate exchange of gossip.

At about three o'clock in the afternoon I gave up hope of writing a believable story. Queasy with embarrassment and apology, I informed the city editor that the thing couldn't be done, that if there was such a place as an Athens of the West—which was doubtful—then it probably was to be found on the back lot of a movie studio in Los Angeles. San Francisco might compare to a Greek colony on the coast of Asia Minor in the fourth century B.C., but that was the extent of it. The city editor heard me out, and then, after an awful and incredulous silence, he rose from behind his desk and denounced me as a fool and an apostate. I had betrayed the city of my birth and the imperatives of the first edition. Never could I hope to succeed in the newspaper business. Perhaps I might find work in a drugstore chain, preferably somewhere east of St. Louis, but even then he would find himself hard-pressed to recommend me as anything but a liar and an assassin. He assigned the story to an older and wiser reporter, who relied on the local authorities (Herb Caen, Barnaby Conrad, the presidents of department stores, the director of the film festival), and who found it easy enough to persuade them to say that San Francisco should be more appropriately compared to Mount Olympus.

I left San Francisco within a matter of weeks, depressed by the dreamlike torpor of the city. Although in the past eighteen years I often have thought of the city with feelings of sadness, as if in mourning for the beauty of the hills and the clarity of the light in September when the wind blows from the north, I have no wish to return. The atmosphere of unreality seems to me more palpable and oppressive in San Francisco than it does in New York. Apparently this has always been so. Few of the writers associated with the city stayed longer than a few seasons. Twain broke camp and moved on; so did Bierce and Bret Harte. In his novel *The Octopus*, Frank Norris describes the way in which the Southern Pacific Railroad in the 1890s forced the farmers of the San Joaquin Valley to become its serfs. The protagonist of the novel, hoping to stir the farmers to revolt and to an idea of liberty, looks for political allies among the high-minded citizens of San Francisco. He might as well have been looking for the civic conscience in a bordello. A character modeled after Colis Huntington, the most epicurean of the local robber barons, explains to him that San Francisco cannot conceive of such a thing as social justice. The conversation takes place in the bar at the Bohemian Club, and the financier gently says to Norris's hero that "San Francisco is not a city . . . it is a midway plaisance."

The same thing can be said for San Francisco almost a hundred years later, except that in the modern idiom people talk about the city as "carnival." The somnambulism of the past has been joined with the androgynous frenzy of the present, and in the ensuing confusion who knows what's true and not true, or who's doing what to whom and for what reason? The wandering bedouin of the American desert traditionally migrate to California in hope of satisfying their hearts' desire under the palm trees of the national oasis. They seek to set themselves free, to rid themselves of all restraint, to find the Eden or the fountain of eternal youth withheld or concealed from them by the authorities (nurses, teachers, parents, caliphs) in the walled towns of the East. They desire simply to be, and they think of freedom as a banquet. Thus their unhappiness and despair when their journey proves to have been in vain. The miracle fails to take place, and things remain pretty much as they were in Buffalo or Indianapolis. Perhaps this explains the high rate of divorce, alcoholism, and suicide. The *San Francisco Examiner* kept a record of the people who jumped off the Golden Gate Bridge, and the headline always specified the number of the most recent victim, as if adding up the expense of the sacrifice to the stone-faced gods of happiness.

Given their suspicion of civilization, the wandering tribes have little patience with institutional or artistic forms, which they identify with conspiracy. Who dares to speak to them of rules, of discovering form and order in the chaos of feeling? Like the detectives in the stories by Dashiell Hammett and Raymond Chandler, the California protagonist belongs to no Establishment. He comes and goes as effortlessly as the wind, remarking on the sleaziness and impermanence of things, mocking the shabby masquerades (of governments and dictionaries) by which the prominent citizens in town cheat the innocent children of their primal inheritance. No matter how grandiose the facade, every door opens into an empty room. Without rules the bedouin's art and politics are as insubstantial as tissue paper or interior decoration, and in the extremities of their sorrow they have nothing to hold onto except the magical charms and amulets sold by mendicant prophets in the bazaars. Sometimes the prophets recommend extended vacations at transcendental dude ranches.

Maybe this is why the conversation in California is both so desperate and so timid. What passes for serious talk, at the Center for the Study of Democratic Institutions as well as in the cabanas around the pool at the Beverly Hills Hotel, has the earnest texture of undergraduate confession. Everybody is in the midst of discovering the obvious. Middle-aged producers, well known for their greed and cunning, breathlessly announce that politics is corrupt, that blacks don't much like whites, and that the wrong people get killed in the wrong wars. Women in sunglasses enter from stage left saying that they have just found out about Freud; somebody's literary agent astonishes the company with a brief summary of the French Revolution. Nobody wants to ask too many questions because usually it is preferable not to know the answers. More often than not the person to whom one happens to be speaking turns out to be playing a part in his own movie. Given the high levels of disappointment in California, people retire to the screening rooms of their private fantasy. The phantasmagoria that they project on the walls seldom bears much resemblance to what an uninitiated bystander might describe as reality. Thus, if a man says that he is a writer, it is possible that he writes notes to his dog, in green ink on a certain kind of yellow paper that he buys in Paris. If a woman says she's an actress, it is possible that she once stood next to Marlon Brando in an airport, and that he looked at her in such a way that she knew he thought she was under contract to Paramount. To ask such people many further questions, or to have the bad manners to remember what they were saying last week or last year, constitutes an act of social aggression.

California is like summer or the Christmas holidays. The unhappy children think that they are supposed to be having a good time, and they imagine that everybody else is having a better time. Thus the pervasive mood of envy and the feeling, common especially among celebrities, that somehow they have been excluded from something, that their names have been left off the guest list. In New York nobody wants to be David Rockefeller. They might want his money or his house in Maine, but they don't want to change places with the fellow, to actually wear his clothes and preside over the annual meeting of the Chase Manhattan Bank. But in California, people literally want to be Warren Beatty, or Teddy Kennedy, or Cher Bono. If only they could be Teddy or Warren or Cher, even for a few hours in a car traveling at high speed on Sunset Boulevard, then they would know true happiness and learn the secret of the universe.

In California so many people are newly arrived (in almost all declensions of that phrase) that their anxieties, like those of the parvenus in Molière's plays, provide employment for a legion of dancing masters (i.e., swamis, lawn specialists, hairdressers, spiritual therapists, swimming-pool consultants, gossip columnists, tennis professionals, et cetera, et cetera) who smile and bow and hold up gilded mirrors as false and flattering as the grandiose facades with which their patrons adorn the houses built to resemble a baroque chateau or a Spanish hacienda. The athletic coaches of the human-potential movements take the place of liveried servants in the employ of the minor nobility. Every season since the Gold Rush, California has blossomed with new money—first in gold, then in land, cattle, railroads, agriculture, film images, shipbuilding, aerospace, electronics, television, and commercial religions. The ease with which the happy few become suddenly rich lends credence to the belief in magical transformation. People tell each other fabulous tales of El Dorado. They talk about scrawny girls found in drugstores and changed overnight into princesses, about second-rate actors made into statesmen, about Howard Jarvis revealed as a savior of his people. Everybody is always in the process of becoming somebody else. If the transformations can take place in the temporal spheres of influence, then why can't they also take place in the spiritual sectors?

Perhaps this is why California is so densely populated with converts of one kind of another. A young man sets out on the road to Ventura, but somewhere on the Los Angeles Freeway he has a vision. God speaks to him through the voice of a disc jockey broadcasting over Radio Free Orange County, and he understands that he has lived his life in vain. He throws away his credit cards and commits himself to Rolfing and salad. Thus, Jane Fonda discovers feminism and Tom Hayden declares his faith in "the system"; Eldridge Cleaver renounces the stony paths of radical politics and embraces the luxury of capitalism; Richard Nixon goes through as many conversions as he finds expedient; and Ronald Reagan begins as an ADA Democrat and ends as the conscience of the Republican rear guard. As with the prophets who gather the faithful in the compounds of pure truth, so the politicians conceive of politics not as a matter of practical compromise but as a dream of power and a fantasy of omnipotent wish.

Throughout the decade of the 1960s I kept reading in the newspapers about the revolutions coming out of California, about the free-speech movement at the University of California in Berkeley, about the so-called sexual revolution, about the counterculture and the "revolutionary life-styles" portrayed in the pages of *Vogue*. As recently as last year, people were talking about "the taxpayers' revolt," as if, once again, California were leading the nation forward into the future. Sometimes when reading these communiqués from the front I am reminded of Lenny Bruce and the bitter jokes with which he used to entertain the crowd at the hungry i in San Francisco. California sponsors no revolution and only one revolt. This is the revolt against time. In no matter what costumes the self-proclaimed revolutionaries dress themselves up, they shout the manifesto of Peter Pan. They demand that time be brought to a stop. They declare time to be circular, and they say that nothing ever changes in their perpetual summer, that they remain forever suspended in the enchantment of their innocent garden. History is a fairy tale, in which maybe they will consent to believe on the condition that the scripts have happy endings. The media advertise California as the image of the future, but to me the state is the mirror of the past—not the recent, historical past, but the ancient and primitive past of 90,000 years ago with the light of paleolithic fires flickering in the windows of the stores on Rodeo Drive.

Even the people who go to California to die hope to find a connection to another world. Maybe they will be initiated into the mysteries of reincarnation, or perhaps they will meet the pilot of a UFO. But most of the people who make the trek across the mountains expect that they will remain forever young. I remember once going to see Mae West in her shuttered house on the beach at Santa Monica. On a brilliantly blue afternoon the house was as dark as a nightclub. Miss West received me in a circle of candlelight and white satin, and although she was in her late seventies she affected the dress and mannerisms of a coquette. The effect was grotesque but only slightly more exaggerated than the disguises worn by people trying to look anywhere from ten to thirty years younger than their age. In California nobody is middle–aged. For as long as they can afford the cosmetics and the surgery, people pretend that they are still thirty-five; then one day all the systems fail and somebody else vanishes into the gulag of the anonymous old. I'm sure that the desire to obliterate time also has something to do with the weather. The absence of clearly defined seasons helps to sustain the illusion of the evangelical present. Perhaps this is also why people make such a solemn business of sport in California. Among people determined merely to be, and who therefore conceive of the world as a stadium, leisure acquires an importance equivalent to that of work. People get very serious about tennis because from the point of view of a child at play in the fields of the Lord, tennis is as serious as politics or blocks.

I left California because I didn't have the moral fortitude to contend with the polymorphousness of the place. It was too easy to lose myself behind a mask, and I had the feeling that I was wandering in a void, feeding on hallucinatory blooms of the lotus flower. The emptiness frightened me, and so did the absence of culture, of politics in the conventional sense, of art and conversation, of the social contrivances that make it possible to talk to other people about something else besides the degree of their God-consciousness, of all the makeshift laws and patched-together institutions with which men rescue themselves from their loneliness, their megalomania, and the seductions of self-annihilation. Had I been blessed with great genius, like Robinson Jeffers perched upon his rock in Carmel, I might have been able to make something out of nothing. But in San Francisco, as in Los Angeles, I woke up every morning thinking that I had to invent the wheel and discover the uses of fire. I needed the company of other men who had roused themselves from sleep and set forth on the adventure of civilization.

[1979]

II

Northern
California Country

JOHN MUIR

First Glimpse of the Sierra

WHEN I set out on the long excursion that finally led to California, I wandered, afoot and alone, from Indiana to the Gulf of Mexico, with a plant-press on my back, holding a generally southward course, like the birds when they are going from summer to winter. From the west coast of Florida I crossed the Gulf to Cuba, enjoyed the rich tropical flora there for a few months, intending to go thence to the north end of South America, make my way through the woods to the head waters of the Amazon, and float down that grand river to the ocean. But I was unable to find a ship bound for South America—fortunately, perhaps, for I had incredibly little money for so long a trip and had not yet fully recovered from a fever caught in the Florida swamps. Therefore I decided to visit California for a year or two to see its wonderful flora and the famous Yosemite Valley. All the world was before me and every day was a holiday, so it did not seem important to which one of the world's wildernesses I first should wander.

Arriving by the Panama steamer, I stopped one day in San Francisco and then inquired for the nearest way out of town. "But where do you want to go?" asked the man to whom I had applied for this important information. "To any place that is wild," I said. This reply startled him. He seemed to fear I might be crazy, and therefore the sooner I was out of town the better, so he directed me to the Oakland ferry.

So on the 1st of April, 1868, I set out afoot for Yosemite. It was the bloom-time of the year over the lowlands and coast ranges; the landscapes of the Santa Clara Valley were fairly drenched with sunshine, all the air was quivering with the songs of the meadow-larks, and the hills were so covered with flowers that they seemed to be painted. Slow, indeed, was my progress through these glorious gardens, the first of the California flora I had seen. Cattle and cultivation were making few scars as yet, and I wandered enchanted in long, wavering curves, knowing by my pocket map that Yosemite Valley lay to the east and that I should surely find it.

Looking eastward from the summit of the Pacheco Pass one shining morning, a landscape was displayed that after all my wanderings still appears as the most beautiful I have ever beheld. At my feet lay the Great Central Valley of California, level and flowery, like a lake of pure sunshine, forty or fifty miles wide, five hundred miles long, one rich furred garden of yellow compositæ. And from the eastern boundary of this vast golden flowerbed rose the mighty Sierra, miles in height, and so gloriously colored and so radiant, it seemed not clothed with light, but wholly composed of it, like the wall of some celestial city. Along the top and extending a good way down, was a rich pearl-gray belt of snow; below it a belt of blue and dark purple, marking the extension of the forests; and stretching along the base of the range a broad belt of rose-purple; all these colors, from the blue sky to the yellow valley smoothly blending as they do in a rainbow, making a wall of light ineffably fine. Then it seemed to me that the Sierra should be called, not the Nevada or Snowy Range, but the Range of Light. And after ten years of wandering and wondering in the heart of it, rejoicing in its glorious floods of light, the white beams of the morning streaming through the passes, the noonday radiance on the crystal rocks, the flush of the alpenglow, and the irised spray of countless waterfalls, it still seems above all others the Range of Light.   [1868]

JOHN MUIR

Emerson at Yosemite

DURING my first years in the Sierra I was ever calling on everybody within reach to admire them, but I found no one half warm enough until Emerson came. I had read his essays, and felt sure that of all men he would best interpret the sayings of these noble mountains and trees. Nor was my faith weakened when I met him in Yosemite. He seemed as serene as a Sequoia, his head in the empyrean; and forgetting his age, plans, duties, ties of every sort, I proposed an immeasurable camping trip back in the heart of the mountains. He seemed anxious to go, but considerately mentioned his party. I said: "Never mind. The mountains are calling; run away, and let plans and parties and dragging lowland duties all 'gang tapsal-teerie.' We'll go up a cañon singing your own song, 'Good-by, proud world! I'm going home,' in divine earnest. Up there lies a new heaven and a new earth; let us go to the show." But alas, it was too late—too near the sundown of his life. The shadows were growing long, and he leaned on his friends. His party, full of indoor philosophy, failed to see the natural beauty and fullness of promise of my wild plan, and laughed at it in good-natured ignorance, as if it were necessarily amusing to imagine that Boston people might be led to accept Sierra manifestations of God at the price of rough camping. Anyhow, they would have none of it, and held Mr. Emerson to the hotels and trails.

After spending only five tourist days in Yosemite he was led away, but I saw him two days more; for I was kindly invited to go with the party as far as the Mariposa big trees. I told Mr. Emerson that I would gladly go to the Sequoias with him, if he would camp in the grove. He consented heartily, and I felt sure that he would have at least one good wild memorable night around a Sequoia camp-fire. Next day we rode through the magnificent forests of the Merced basin, and I kept calling his attention to the Sugar Pines, quoting his wood-notes, "Come listen what the pine tree saith," etc., pointing out the noblest as kings and high priests, the most eloquent and commanding preachers of all the mountain forests, stretching forth their century-old arms in benediction over the worshiping congregations crowded about them. He gazed in devout admiration, saying but little, while his fine smile faded away.

Early in the afternoon, when we reached Clark's Station, I was surprised to see the party dismount. And when I asked if we were not going up into the grove to camp they said: "No; it would never do to lie out in the night air. Mr. Emerson might take cold; and you know, Mr. Muir, that would be a dreadful thing." In vain I urged, that only in homes and hotels were colds caught, that nobody ever was known to take cold camping in these woods, that there was not a single cough or sneeze in all the Sierra. Then I pictured the big climate-changing, inspiring fire I would make, praised the beauty and fragrance of Sequoia flame, told how the great trees would stand about us transfigured in the purple light, while the stars looked down between the great domes; ending by urging them to come on and make an immortal Emerson night of it. But the house habit was not to be overcome, nor the strange dread of pure night air, though it is only cooled day air with a little dew in it. So the carpet dust and unknowable reeks were preferred. And to think of this being a Boston choice! Sad commentary on culture and the glorious transcendentalism.

Accustomed to reach whatever place I started for, I was going up the mountain alone to camp, and wait the coming of the party next day. But since Emerson was so soon to vanish, I concluded to stop with him. He hardly spoke a word all the evening, yet it was a great pleasure simply to be near him, warming in the light of his face as at a fire. In the morning we rode up the trail through a noble forest of Pine and Fir into the famous Mariposa Grove, and stayed an hour or two, mostly in ordinary tourist fashion—looking at the biggest giants, measuring them with a tape line, riding through prostrate fire-bored trunks, etc., though Mr. Emerson was alone occasionally, sauntering about as if under a spell. As we walked through a fine group, he quoted, "There were giants in those days," recognizing the antiquity of the race. To commemorate his visit, Mr. Galen Clark, the guardian of the grove, selected the finest of the unnamed trees and requested him to give it a name. He named it Samoset, after the New England sachem, as the best that occurred to him.

The poor bit of measured time was soon spent, and while the saddles were being adjusted I again urged Emerson to stay. "You are yourself a Sequoia," I said. "Stop and get acquainted with your big brethren." But he was past his prime, and was now as a child in the hands of his affectionate but sadly civilized friends, who seemed as full of old-fashioned conformity as of bold intellectual independence. It was the afternoon of the day and the afternoon of his life, and his course was now westward down all the mountains into the sunset. The party mounted and rode away in wondrous contentment, apparently, tracing the trail through Ceanothus and Dogwood bushes, around the bases of the Big Trees, up the slope of the Sequoia basin, and over the divide. I followed to the edge of the grove. Emerson lingered in the rear of the train, and when he reached the top of the ridge, after all the rest of the party were over and out of sight, he turned his horse, took off his hat and waved me a last good-by. I felt lonely, so sure had I been that Emerson of all men would be the quickest to see the mountains and sing them. Gazing awhile on the spot where he vanished, I sauntered back into the heart of the grove, made a bed of Sequoia plumes and ferns by the side of a stream, gathered a store of firewood, and then walked about until sundown. The birds, robins, thrushes, warblers, etc., that had kept out of sight, came about me, now that all was quiet, and made cheer. After sundown I built a great fire, and as usual had it all to myself. And though lonesome for the first time in these forests, I quickly took heart again—the trees had not gone to Boston, nor the birds; and as I sat by the fire, Emerson was still with me in spirit, though I never again saw him in the flesh. He sent books and wrote, cheering me on; advised me not to stay too long in solitude. Soon he hoped that my guardian angel would intimate that my probation was at a close. Then I was to roll up my herbariums, sketches, and poems (though I never knew I had any poems), and come to his house; and when

I tired of him and his humble surroundings, he would show me to better people.

But there remained many a forest to wander through, many a mountain and glacier to cross, before I was to see his Wachusett and Monadnock, Boston and Concord. It was seventeen years after our parting on the Wawona ridge that I stood beside his grave under a Pine tree on the hill above Sleepy Hollow. He had gone to higher Sierras, and, as I fancied, was again waving his hand in friendly recognition.   [1871]

SAMUEL LANGHORNE CLEMENS

Roughing It in San Francisco

For a few months I enjoyed what to me was an entirely new phase of existence—a butterfly idleness; nothing to do, nobody to be responsible to, and untroubled by financial uneasiness. I fell in love with the most cordial and sociable city in the Union. After the sage-brush and alkali deserts of Washoe, San Francisco was Paradise to me. I lived at the best hotel, exhibited my clothes in the most conspicuous places, infested the opera, and learned to appear enraptured with music which oftener afflicted my ignorant ear than enchanted it, if I had had the vulgar honesty to confess it. However, I suppose I was not greatly worse than the most of my countrymen in that. I had longed to be a butterfly, and I was one at last. I attended private parties in sumptuous evening dress, simpered and aired my graces like a born beau, and polked and schottisched with a step peculiar to myself—and the kangaroo. In a word, I kept the due state of a man worth a hundred thousand dollars (prospectively,) and likely to reach absolute affluence when that silver-mine sale should be ultimately achieved in the East. I spent money with a free hand, and meantime watched the stock sales with an interested eye to see what might happen in Nevada.

Something very important happened. The property holders of Nevada voted against the State Constitution; but the folks who had nothing to lose were in the majority, and carried the measure over their heads. But after all it did not immediately look like a disaster, although unquestionably it was one. I hesitated, calculated the chances, and then concluded not to sell. Stocks went on rising; speculation went mad; bankers, merchants, lawyers, doctors, mechanics, laborers, even the very washerwomen and servant girls, were putting up their earnings on silver stocks, and every sun that rose in the morning went down on paupers enriched and rich men beggared. What a gambling carnival it was! Gould and Curry soared to six thousand three hundred dollars a foot! And then—all of a sudden, out went the bottom and everything and everybody went to ruin and destruction! The wreck was complete. The bubble left scarcely a microscopic moisture behind it. I was an early beggar and a thorough one. My hoarded stocks were not worth the paper they were printed on. I threw them all away. I, the cheerful idiot that had been squandering money like water, and thought myself beyond the reach of misfortune, had not now as much as fifty dollars when I gathered together my various debts and paid them. I removed from the hotel to a very private boarding house. I took a reporter's berth and went to work. I was not entirely broken in spirit, for I was building confidently on the sale of the silver mine in the east. But I could not hear from Dan, my former reportorial associate at Virginia. My letters miscarried or were not answered.

One day I did not feel vigorous and remained away from the office. The next day I went down toward noon as usual, and found a note on my desk which had been there twenty-four hours. It was signed "Marshall" (another Virginia reporter) and contained a request that I should call at the hotel and see him and a friend or two that night, as they would sail for the east in the morning. A postscript added that their errand was a big mining speculation! I was hardly ever so sick in my life. And I abused myself for leaving Virginia, and entrusting to another man a matter I ought to have attended to myself; I abused myself for remaining away from the office on the one day of all the year that I should have been there. And thus berating myself I trotted a mile to the steamer wharf and arrived just in time to be too late. The ship was in the stream and under way.

I comforted myself with the thought that maybe the speculation would amount to nothing—poor comfort at best—and then went back to my slavery, resolved to put up with my thirty-five dollars a week and forget all about it.

A month afterward I enjoyed my first earthquake. It was one that was called the "great" earthquake, and is doubtless so distinguished till this day. It was just after noon, on a bright October day. I was coming down Third street. The only objects in motion anywhere in sight in that thickly built and populous quarter, were a man in a buggy behind me, and a street car wending slowly up the cross street. Otherwise, all was solitude and a Sabbath stillness. As I turned the corner, around a frame house, there was a great rattle and jar, and it occurred to me that here was an item!—no doubt a fight in that house. Before I could turn and seek the door, there came a really terrific shock; the ground seemed to roll under me in waves, interrupted by violent jogglings up and down, and there was a heavy grinding noise as of brick houses rubbing together. I fell against the frame house and hurt my elbow. I knew what it was now, and from mere reportorial instinct, nothing else, took out my watch and noted the time of day; at that moment a third and still severer shock came, and as I reeled about on the pavement trying to keep my footing I saw a sight! The entire front of a tall four-story brick building in Third street sprung outward like a door and fell sprawling across the street, raising a dust like a great volume of smoke! And here came the buggy—overboard went the man, and in less time than I can tell it the vehicle was distributed in small fragments along three hundred yards of street. One could have fancied that somebody had fired a charge of chair-rounds and rags down the thoroughfare. The street car had stopped, the horses were rearing and plunging, the passengers were pouring out at both ends, and one fat man had crashed half way through a glass window on one side of the car, got wedged fast and was squirming and screaming like an impaled madman. Every door of each house, as far as the eye could reach, was vomiting a stream of human beings; and almost before one could execute a wink and begin another, there was a massed multitude of people stretching in endless procession down every street my position commanded. Never was solemn solitude turned into teeming life quicker.

Of the wonders wrought by "the great earthquake," these were all that came under my eye; but the tricks it did, elsewhere, and far and wide over the town, made toothsome gossip for nine days. The destruction of property was trifling—the injury to it was widespread and somewhat serious.

The "curiosities" of the quake were simply endless. I *could* regale you for weeks, but will limit myself a bit. Gentlemen and ladies who were sick, or were taking a siesta, or had dissipated till a late hour and were making up lost sleep, thronged into the public streets in all sorts of queer apparel, and some without any at all. One woman who had been washing a naked child, ran down the street holding it by the ankles as if it were a dressed turkey. Prominent citizens who were supposed to keep the Sabbath very strictly, rushed out of saloons in their shirt-sleeves, with billiard cues in their hands. Dozens of men with necks swathed in napkins, rushed from barber-shops, lathered to the eyes or with one cheek clean shaved and the other still bearing a hairy stubble. Horses broke from stables, and a frightened dog rushed up a short attic ladder and out on to a roof, and when his scare was over had not the nerve to go down again the same way he had gone up. A prominent editor flew down stairs, in the principal hotel, with nothing on but one brief undergarment—met a chambermaid, and exclaimed: "Oh, what *shall* I do! Where shall I go?"

She responded with naive serenity: "If you have no choice, you might try a clothing-store!"

A certain foreign consul's lady was the acknowledged leader of fashion, and every time she appeared in anything new or extraordinary, the ladies in the vicinity made a raid on their husband's purses and arrayed themselves similarly. One man who had suffered much and growled accordingly, was standing at the window when the shocks came, and the next instant the consul's wife, just out of the bath, fled by with no other apology for clothing than—a bath-towel! The sufferer rose superior to the terrors of the earthquake, and said to his wife: "Now *that* is something *like!* Get out your towel my dear!"

The plastering that fell from ceilings in San Francisco that day, would have covered several acres of ground. For some days afterward, groups of eyeing and pointing men stood about many a building, looking at long zigzag cracks that extended from the eaves to the ground. Four feet of the tops of three chimneys on one house were broken square off and turned around in such a way as to completely stop the draft. A crack a hundred feet long gaped open six inches wide in the middle of one street, and then shut together again with such force, as to ridge up the meeting earth like a slender grave. A lady sitting in her rocking and quaking parlor, saw the wall part at the ceiling, open and shut twice, like a mouth, and then drop the end of a brick on the floor like a tooth. She was a woman easily disgusted with foolishness, and she arose and went out of there. Another lady who was coming down stairs was astonished to see a bronze Hercules lean forward on its pedestal as if to strike her with its club. They both reached the bottom of the flight at the same time,—the woman insensible from the fright. Her child, born some little time afterward, was clubfooted. However, on second thought, if the reader sees any coincidence in this, he must do it at his own risk.

The first shock brought down two or three huge organ-pipes in one of the churches. The minister, with uplifted hands, was just closing the services. He looked up, hesitated, and said: "However, we will omit the benediction!"—and the next instant there was a vacancy in the atmosphere where he had stood.

After the first shock, an Oakland minister exclaimed: "Keep your seat! There is no better place to die than this"—And added, after the third: "But outside is good enough!" He then skipped out at the back door.

Such another destruction of mantel ornaments and toilet bottles as the earthquake created, San Francisco never saw before. There was hardly a girl or a matron in the city but suffered losses of this kind. Suspended pictures were thrown down, but oftener still, by a curious freak of the earthquake's humor, they were whirled completely around with their faces to the wall! There was great difference of opinion, at first, as to the course or direction the quake traveled, but water that splashed out of various tanks and buckets settled that. Thousands of people were made so sea-sick by the rolling and pitching of floors and streets that they were weak and bed-ridden for hours, and some few for even days afterward; hardly an individual escaped nausea entirely.

The queer earthquake—episodes that formed the staple of San Francisco gossip for the next week would fill a much larger book than this, so I will diverge from the subject.

By and by, in the due course of things, I picked up a copy of the Virginia City *Enterprise* one day, and fell under this cruel blow:

Nevada Mines in New York.—G. M. Marshall, Sheba Hurst and Amos H. Rose, who left San Francisco last July for New York City, with ores from mines in Pine Wood District, Humboldt County, and on the Reese River range, have disposed of a mine containing six thousand feet and called the Pine Mountains Consolidated, for the sum of $3,000,000. The stamps on the deed, which is now on its way to Humboldt County, from New York, for record, amounted to $3,000 which is said to be the largest amount of stamps ever placed on one document. A working capital of $1,000,000 has been paid into the treasury, and machinery has already been purchased for a large quartz mill, which will be put up as soon as possible. The stock in this company is all full paid and entirely unassessable. The ores of the mines in this district somewhat resemble those of the Sheba mine in Humboldt. Sheba Hurst, the discoverer of the mines, with his friends corralled all the best leads and all the land and timber they desired before making public their whereabouts. Ores from there, assayed in this city, showed them to be exceedingly rich in silver and gold—silver predominating. There is an abundance of wood and water in the District. We are glad to know that New York capital has been enlisted in the development of the mines of this region. Having seen the ores and assays, we are satisfied that the mines of the District are very valuable—anything but wild-cat.

Once more native imbecility had carried the day, and I had lost a million! It was the "blind lead" over again.

Let us not dwell on this miserable matter. If I were inventing these things, I could be wonderfully humorous over them; but they are too true to be talked of with hearty levity, even at this distant day. Suffice it that I so lost heart, and so yielded myself up to repinings and sighings and foolish regrets, that I neglected my duties and became about worthless, as a reporter for a brisk newspaper. And at last one of the proprietors took me aside, with a charity I still remember with considerable respect, and gave me an opportunity to resign my berth and so save myself the disgrace of a dismissal.

[1875]

NIGEY LENNON

The Society
upon the Stanislaus

IN HIS OWN WAY, Jim Gillis was quite literary. Over the years his little
cabin in the rolling hills of California's mining country had served as a
retreat for a number of city-weary writers, one of whom had been Bret
Harte, who spent a brief period living in the cabin at a time when he was
ill, broke, and discouraged about his future. Jim Gillis had lent Harte twenty
dollars and advised him to try his luck on a San Francisco newspaper, which
Harte did. A few months later, during a visit to San Francisco, Gillis found
out where Harte was living and decided to pay him a friendly visit just to
see how he was getting on. Harte, however, took offense at Gillis's visit; he
assumed that Gillis was merely trying to collect the twenty dollars he had
previously lent him. Consequently, he sent Gillis away rather perfunctorily,
refusing to listen to him when he tried to explain that he had written off
the debt and just wanted to congratulate Harte on the fact that he seemed
to be making a successful career for himself in the city.

Gillis's cabin, on Jackass Hill near Angels Camp, was a few miles away
from the mining towns of Tuttletown and Sonora, surrounded by sighing
pines and in full view of the regal Sierra Nevada mountain range with its
ever-changing light and shadow. Down out of the Sierra tumbled and rolled
the great Stanislaus River, which was to be immortalized in "The Society
Upon the Stanislaus" and other writings of Bret Harte. Twain later recalled
the area as "that serene and reposeful and dreamy and delicious sylvan
paradise."

Twain described Gillis's cabin as follows in the journal he was keeping
at the time: "No planking on the floor; old bunks, pans and traps of all
kinds—Byron, Shakespeare, Bacon, Dickens & every kind of only first class
literature." This last was a reference to Gillis's extensive library, for, as well
as writing a little himself, the elder Gillis was an avid reader. In this he
resembled other California "sourdoughs," for their seemingly rough and
illiterate ranks contained many a self-styled philosopher and idiot savant.

Jim Gillis and Mark Twain shared Gillis's cabin with a miner named Dick
Stoker, whose fictitious cat, "Tom Quartz," was to make an appearance in

Twain's *Roughing It*. Jim Gillis's younger brother William, called Billy by the cabin's various tenants, was also staying in the cabin during the time Twain lived there.

The area surrounding Angels Camp had been a populous mining settlement during the flush period of the 1850s, but by the time Twain took up his abode on Jackass Hill, there was only a handful of dilapidated cabins standing on the spot where twelve or fifteen years earlier a vital, thriving boomtown had been conducting its bustling daily business. This fact made quite an impression on Twain, for it symbolized just how mercurial life and fortune on the Pacific Coast could be. The ghostly ruins of Angels Camp caught Twain's fancy as he loafed and dreamed among them; it seemed to him that the dead mining camp, with its lost and bygone air, suited his present mood exactly.

Jim Gillis, Dick Stoker, and the few remaining miners in the area engaged in what was known as "pocket" mining—a process that was unique to that one little corner of California, at least as far as Twain knew. After spending a few months in the apparent capital of pocket mining, Twain was to claim that it was the most fascinating style of mining he had ever witnessed— perhaps, as he observed, because, due to its extreme uncertainty, pocket mining furnished a large number of victims to the lunatic asylum.

The theory behind pocket mining was that in this particular part of California, gold was scattered at random throughout the soil, and the only thing needed to pinpoint precisely where it lay was a systematic method. The pinpointing was accomplished through a tedious process of panning the soil in random increments. Perhaps a few panfuls of soil, when rinsed with water, would reveal tiny flecks of gold; if so, then the prospector would try samples from either side of the lucky strike to narrow down his field of search. By this process of elimination, the miner would eventually hope to locate the section where the most gold was concentrated. It was by nature extremely time-consuming, and the constant uncertainty of the proceedings was what Twain believed sent the victims to the loony bin. Sometimes a pocket miner could strike one initial shovelful of gold and then never come up with any more after that, no matter how diligently he worked. There were, however, some real reasons for Gillis, Stoker, and the other speculators to keep up their hard work—one strike, for instance, had been made in the area not long before Twain arrived that had totaled $60,000 worth of gold. It had taken two men two weeks to dig out the bonanza. (They had then sold the excavation site for $10,000 to another fellow who, according to Twain, never got fifty dollars out of it afterward.)

Twain was as fascinated as ever with the concept of sudden wealth, but his energy was at a low ebb and he was content to leave the physical work of mining to those with broader shoulders and fewer qualms about labor

The Society upon the Stanislaus | 47

than he. His cabinmates loved to rib him about his lassitude, which was becoming almost legendary among those who knew him. Sometimes Jim Gillis would needle him about the time back in Virginia City when Twain had been reading in bed and his ever-present pipe had gone out. Rather than get up and walk two or three feet to where the matches were sitting, Twain had waited until his roommate, Dan De Quille, had come home a few hours later, whereupon Twain had asked him for a light.

Twain thoroughly enjoyed Jim Gillis's company, and Gillis was even able, on one or two occasions, to persuade his sluggish friend to pitch in and do some mining. On one such occasion—recollected by Albert B. Paine in his biography of Twain—Clemens and Gillis trudged up a hill to a likely site during a chilly, drizzly afternoon. Once they began working, Gillis, who was well versed in the vagaries of pocket mining, became convinced that they were about to make a big strike any minute. Twain was less sure, but arguing took too much effort, so he kept his doubts to himself. His job was to fetch water from a stream that was flowing at the foot of the hill; the water was then used to wash the pans of dirt. As the afternoon progressed, each pan looked more promising than the one before it, but by the time evening began to fall there still had been no payoff, and meanwhile Twain was shivering miserably and his teeth were chattering as the drizzle began to soak through his clothes. Finally he drawled at Gillis, "Jim, I won't carry any more water. This work is too disagreeable."

Poor Gillis was just about to wash out another pan of soil when he received this bombshell. "Bring one more pail, Sam," he said pleadingly.

But Twain flatly refused, explaining that he was freezing and felt like giving up. In vain did Gillis repeat his request in a beseeching tone of voice. "Just one more pail, Sam?"

Twain was adamant. "No, sir, not a drop, not even if I knew there were a million dollars in that pan."

Sadly, Gillis ceased laboring, for he couldn't simultaneously fetch water and wash dirt by himself. After the two men first posted the required thirty-day claim at the site, they then walked back to the cabin.

The weather prevented them from engaging in any more prospecting on the site, and they soon moved on to other locations and forgot about the hillside claim altogether. Meanwhile, the rain had washed away the topsoil in the pan of earth they had left behind them at the claim—the pan which Twain had refused to fetch the water to wash. Under the topsoil in that pan, as it turned out, was a handful of solid gold nuggets.

This was naturally bound to catch the eye of miners more enterprising than Mark Twain. Two Austrians happened along, spied the glittering lure in the pan, and sat down to wait until Gillis's thirty-day claim had expired. As soon as it had, they began panning the surrounding earth with great expectations. Two or three pans of dirt later they struck a pocket of nuggets. By the time they had cleaned out the pocket, they were twenty thousand dollars richer.

Twain was always extremely eloquent in the matter of self-deprecation. It would have been very interesting indeed to hear the names he called himself when he found out that one more lousy pail of water hauled uphill would have freed him from journalistic drudgery for the rest of his life.

In San Francisco, Clemens had been accustomed to dining on scalloped oysters and champagne beneath the gilt chandeliers of elegant, quasi-European restaurants. In Angels Camp the victuals were bound to be considerably less refined. He made the following note in his journal: "Jan. 23, 1865—Angels—Rainy, stormy—Beans & dishwater for breakfast at the Frenchman's; dishwater & beans for dinner, and both articles warmed over for supper."

After a few more days of rain, beans, and dishwater, his grumbling took on a somewhat brighter note: "26th—Tapidaro [he meant tapadera, the leather stirrup covering on a saddle] beefsteak for a change—no use, could not bite it.

"28th—Chili beans & dishwater three times to-day, as usual, & some kind of 'slum' which the Frenchman called 'hash.' Hash be damned."

There was a happy ending, of sorts.

"30th Jan.—Moved to new hotel, just opened—good fare, & coffee that a Christian may drink without jeopardizing his eternal soul."

Twain found the small local population of Angels Camp just as unrefined as the cuisine. Not surprisingly, he was often bored to tears by the local goings-on. "The exciting topic of conversation in this sparse community just at present," he noted sourly in his journal, "(and it always *is* in dire commotion about something or other of small consequence), is Mrs. Carrington's baby, which was born a week ago, on the 14th. There was nothing remarkable about the baby, but if Mrs. C had given birth to an ornamental cast-iron dog big enough for an embellishment for the State-House steps I don't believe the event would have created more intense interest in the community."

The only locals Twain could tolerate were a nearby family with two young and comely daughters, Molly and Nelly Daniels, who were known in the area as "the Chaparral Quails." Twain and Billy Gillis often paid formal calls on the girls, and the foursome sometimes took walks along the deserted trails that disappeared into the hills. On one of these occasions, the party got lost in those hills and came straggling home to the girls' cabin at an hour that was too late to be considered proper. The girls' mother assailed them at the door with a massive outpouring of opinion about heedless rakes such as Clemens, who would stoop so low as to seduce young and innocent girls in cow pastures. Twain wisely refused to involve himself in this one-sided conversation, and walking over to a corner of the cabin, he picked up a guitar that was leaning against the wall and proceeded to sing and play a few folk songs called forth from memory. (Twain always loved indigenous music, especially Negro spirituals, which he had heard from birth.) The girls' mother was so thoroughly enchanted by this impromptu performance that she wound up cooking a late supper for the prodigal Twain, Billy Gillis, and her daughters.

With the exception of the Chaparral Quails, Twain distinctly preferred the company of his cabinmates to that of the locals, however. One of the things he enjoyed the most about living on Jackass Hill was listening to Jim Gillis tell tall tales in front of the fireplace on chilly afternoons and evenings. Gillis would stand there reflectively, with his hands crossed behind him and his back to the fire, and proceed to relate elaborate and ultimately implausible tales, usually featuring Dick Stoker as their hero. Meanwhile Stoker would be sitting quietly in a corner, smoking his pipe and nodding serenely as Gillis painted him in increasingly fantastic lights. One of Gillis's yarns was retold by Twain in *Roughing It*—it was about the remarkable sagacity of Stoker's cat, Tom Quartz. It didn't matter that Stoker did not own a cat and had never owned one; Gillis went on describing the feline's perspicacity in mining as if the animal was still fresh in his mind from yesterday. Another Gillis tale, "The Tragedy of the Burning Shame," was retold by Twain in *Huckleberry Finn*; Twain regretted that he had to clean up the yard considerably to make it fit for publication. "This was a great damage," he mourned in his *Autobiography*. "As Jim told it, inventing it as he went along, I think it was one of the most outrageously funny things I have ever listened to. How mild it is in the book and how pale; how extravagant and how gorgeous in its unprintable form!"

Another California tall tale that Twain used to good advantage was a long, monotonous narrative about a contest between two hayseeds to ascertain which of two frogs could jump the farthest. It was hardly a new story, even though Twain first chanced to hear it in the Mother Lode; in actuality, it dated back to Aristophanes, and in more recent years it had appeared in several Pacific Coast newspapers in various permutations and guises. But when Twain first heard the dull, rambling fable drop ever so slowly from the lips of a loquacious old gent in a decrepit tavern on Jackass Hill, what appealed to him was the manner in which the story was told.

Twain and Jim Gillis, with or without Dick Stoker, were fond of playing billiards or just sitting around the potbelly stove in the dreary old tavern, part of an equally dreary hotel owned by the same Frenchman whom Twain had reviled for doling out the execrable beans and dishwater. The wintry weather was keeping Twain and his friends from getting around much, so they welcomed the chance to play billiards on the tavern's rickety table, or to shoot the breeze with whatever indiscriminate company happened to stop in for a drink.

Twain was always to remember the slanting, battered relic of a pool table in the Angels Camp tavern with great affection. In his old age his fancy sometimes returned to the table's torn felt and undulating surface, and the chipped pool balls and headless cues, the latter with curves in them like parentheses. Once, when Twain and his cabinmates saw their fellow tavern habitué, Texas Tom, rack up a whopping total of seven points during a single inning, they all went mad with admiration and amazement—the table was that difficult to score on.

Another inmate of the decaying saloon was a former Illinois river pilot named Ben Coon, a dim-witted, solemn fellow who dozed by the stove most of the time and was given, when awake, to delivering endless, pointless monologues. Twain and Gillis, bored and bereft of outside influences much of the time, found Coon amusing under the circumstances, and Twain was further tickled by the fact that Coon's run-on narratives never seemed to have a focal point. Later, Twain would write on several occasions about people to whom all details were of equal importance. It is likely that the granddaddy of all these infuriating characters was the self-important Ben Coon.

One raw and dreary afternoon, Ben Coon took his usual seat by the stove and began droning on about a frog belonging to some man named Coleman. Coleman, it seemed, had trained this frog to jump on command, but when he tried to pit it against another frog, the rival's owner secretly loaded Coleman's amphibian with buckshot, weighing it down and causing it to lose the contest. This was a witless enough story, and Coon had in all probability stumbled across it in one of the backwoods weekly newspapers that reached the area at odd intervals, or could even have heard it on the river. But it was Coon's uniquely irritating delivery rather than the yarn itself that struck Twain as noteworthy. He jotted down the bare bones of the story in his notebook, intending to go back to it at some point and write it up more fully. "Coleman with his jumping frog—bet stranger $50—stranger had no frog, & C got him one—in the meantime stranger filled C's frog full of shot & he couldn't jump—the stranger's frog won."

There is no doubt that the period Twain spent in the Mother Lode was extremely fruitful in his development as a writer. The editors of his notebooks and journals (University of California Press, Berkeley) have pointed out that the notebook Twain kept while living in Jim Gillis's cabin on Jackass Hill, despite its brevity, contains material that Twain was to make use of throughout his literary career. None of his other notebooks bears that distinction. (The Mother Lode notebook contains some other irregularities—namely, some abortive attempts at shorthand in the various entries, and a considerable number of French words and phrases. Twain apparently taught himself a fair amount of French while living on Jackass Hill; he practiced it on the Frenchman of the decrepit tavern and the horrible hash.)

In his Mother Lode notebook, Twain set down a number of humorous anecdotes in their sketchiest forms, varying details here and there as if he were trying to see how to best squeeze the humor from the stories. One of these entries, which he called "Report of Prof. G— to accompany Map & Views of the Great Vide Poche Mine, on Mount Olympus, Calaveras Co.," was a full-blown short article written, as the title suggests, in the form of a report by some erstwhile mining expert (very likely Jim Gillis) to an undisclosed committee. Twain may have intended to read it to the nightly gathering in the cabin. He always enjoyed satirizing legalese and judicial language, and this burlesque managed to cram a fair amount of pompous-sounding verbiage into a very limited space. At one point, "Professor G—" was forced to admit that "The map is not absolutely correct. . . . [A]t the time the Prof was drawing it, seated upon a log, he was persistently besieged by piss-ants." The mine's outcroppings were described as containing nearly every mineral known to man—

some soapstone, some brimstone, & even some jackstones, whetstones, 'dobies & brickbats. None of these various articles are found beneath the surface, wherefore the Prof feels satisfied that the [mining] Company have got the world by the ass, since it is manifest that no other organ of the earth's frame could possibly have produced such a dysentery of disorganized & half-digested slumgullion as is here presented.

Although his public humor was developing apace, Twain himself remained absolutely humorless when he himself was the target of satire. Billy Gillis recalled many years later that one of the favorite pastimes in the Gillis cabin during long evenings was a game in which the "boys" implemented a "Hospital for the Insane" on Jackass Hill. A "board of directors" and "resident physician" were appointed, and reports on particular "patients" were made weekly to the committee by the "physician." When Twain's turn as "physician" rolled around, he expressed his grave and fatherly concern about the condition of James N. Gillis,

a companionable young fellow [who] tells some fairly humorous stories. . . . [I]t is sad to know that this young man, who would otherwise be a useful member of society, is hopelessly insane, but such, I am sorry to say, is the truth. He is laboring under the illusion that he is the greatest pocket miner on earth . . . and the only miner having a perfect knowledge of gold-bearing ledges and formations. He is a fairly good pocket hunter and knows a gold nugget from a brass door knob, but there are a dozen boys on the hill who can give him cards and spades and beat him at the game.

Jim Gillis laughed just as hard as the others at this "report." The next week, however, it was his turn to be the "physician," and he addressed himself to the problematic case of inmate Samuel L. Clemens.

One of the most pitiful cases of insanity that has ever fallen under my observation is that of a young man named Samuel L. Clemens, who was committed to this hospital on the thirteenth day of last month, from Angels Camp, Calaveras County. . . . He has, for the past three years, been associated with newspapermen of rare literary ability. He is obsessed with the idea that they are the spokes of a wheel and himself the hub around which they revolve. He has a mania for story telling, and is at the present time engaged in writing one entitled "The Jumping Frog of Calaveras," which he imagines will cause his name to be handed down to posterity from generation to generation as the greatest humorist of all time. This great story of his is nothing but a lot of silly drivel about a warty old toad that he was told by some joker in Angels Camp. Every evening when the inmates are together in the living room, he takes up the manuscript and reads to them a page or two of the story. . . . Then he will chuckle to himself and murmur about "copyrights" and "royalties." If this was the only trouble with Mark Twain, as he dubs himself in his stories, there would be a reasonable hope of the ultimate restoration of his mentality, but the one great hallucination that will forever bar him from the "busy walks of life" is that he was at one time a pilot on one of the great Mississippi River packets. . . . Poor Mark! His nearest approach to being a pilot on the river was when he handled the big steering wheel of a flat boat, freighted with apples from Ohio, which were peddled in towns along the river.

All the "boys" exploded with mirth—all of them, that is, but Samuel Clemens. He was livid with rage. He leaped to his feet and paced back and forth, flinging out fiery sarcasms at Gillis, and calling the others "a lot of laughing jackals." "I appreciate a joke," he sputtered, "and love fun as much as any boy in the world, but when a lot of rotten stuff like Jim Gillis's funny hash is pulled off on me I am ready to cry quits." As a result of Clemens's extreme displeasure, the "asylum" was closed down permanently, although the "boys" continued to take little pokes at Twain just to hear him rage and curse. "Say, Sam, how many barrels of apples could you load onto that flat-bottomed scow?" they would wickedly ask, and then quickly look around for something to hide behind. In his book, *Memories of Mark Twain and Steve Gillis*, Billy Gillis observed that when Twain was angry at someone, instead of talking the incident over in a calm and friendly way, he generally grabbed a drill, pick handle, or any other weapon that came handy and brained the offender with it. Luckily, Twain's rages died down as quickly as they flared up, and then he would be likely to suffer great feelings of remorse, although he often found it difficult to apologize to the wronged party.

Twain apparently never lost his sensitivity to humor aimed in his direction. An old newspaper clipping from the Carson City *Appeal*, dating back to the 1870s or 1880s, reveals a side of Twain that his readers may never have realized existed. The clipping, which reposes in the files of the Mark Twain Papers in Berkeley, contains a farfetched and tongue-in-cheek story about how Twain and Dan De Quille had decided to start a newspaper in Mendocino County during the 1860s. Twain and De Quille had, according to the clipping, taken all the type and other printing equipment "from a recently-defunct newspaper established in San Francisco" with which they had presumably been involved, and had headed off to Mendocino to establish a newspaper there. En route, they had stopped and purchased a small cannon from "a party of emigrants" they met, and had then continued on until they finally were forced to stop for the night in a cheerless wilderness area. Late that night (the story goes on) they were attacked by hordes of marauding Indians, and Twain, thinking quickly, jumped up and loaded the cannon with "a column of nonpareil and a couple of sticks of young spring poetry," along with some other boilerplate rubbish, which, when shot forth from the cannon, blew the oncoming attackers sky-high and just saved the lives of Twain and De Quille by an apostrophe.

Anyone reading this old clipping can see how broad the humor in it is. It starts off in a serious enough tone, but by the time the article's anonymous author has the now-famous Twain writing De Quille a letter, years later, from his home in Hartford, Connecticut, asking De Quille to "make a little pilgrimage to that historic spot, gather the ghostly relics together and plant a table, not too expensive and at your expense, for the memory of the departed," it is impossible not to chuckle at the sly but affectionate pokes some old fellow reporter is taking at Twain. Yet it appears that Twain took the clipping at face value, for scrawled across its length is a message in his handwriting, in purple ink: "Pure imagination—not a fact in it. SLC."

During Twain's stay with Jim Gillis, he frequently visited other parts of the Mother Lode. One place where he and Gillis spent a fair amount of time was Calaveras County. There Gillis continued his pocket mining and Twain, as usual, sat nearby and supervised.

On New Year's Eve in the Calaveras County town of Vallecito, Twain recorded in his notebook that he had seen a "magnificent lunar rainbow," which he glimpsed through a light, pattering rain and that he took to be an auspicious omen of future good fortune. Little did he know that his Mother

Lode experiences were about to change his life in ways he couldn't possibly have foreseen.   [1982]

SAMUEL LANGHORNE CLEMENS

The Celebrated
Jumping Frog of Calaveras County

M R. A. WARD—Dear Sir: Well, I called on good-natured, garrulous old Simon Wheeler, and I inquired after your friend Leonidas W. Greeley,* as you requested me to do, and I hereunto append the result. If you can get any information out of it you are cordially welcome to it. I have a lurking suspicion that your Leonidas W. Greeley is a myth—that you never knew such a personage, and that you only conjectured that if I asked old Wheeler about him it would remind him of his infamous *Jim* Greeley, and he would go to work and bore me nearly to death with some infernal reminiscence of him as long and tedious as it should be useless to me. If that was your design, Mr. Ward, it will gratify you to know that it succeeded.

I found Simon Wheeler dozing comfortably by the barroom stove of the old dilapidated tavern in the ancient mining camp at Angel's, and I noticed that he was fat and bald-headed, and had an expression of winning gentleness and simplicity upon his tranquil countenance. He roused up and gave me good-day. I told him a friend of mine had commissioned me to make some inquiries about a cherished companion of his boyhood named Leonidas W. Greeley—Rev. Leonidas W. Greeley—a young minister of the Gospel, who he had heard was at one time a resident of Angel's Camp. I added that if Mr. Wheeler could tell me anything about this Rev. Leonidas W. Greeley, I would feel under many obligations to him.

Simon Wheeler backed me into a corner and blockaded me there with his chair—and then sat me down and reeled off the monotonous narrative which follows this paragraph. He never smiled, he never frowned, he never changed his voice from the gentle-flowing key to which he turned the initial sentence, he never betrayed the slightest suspicion of enthusiasm—but all through the interminable narrative there ran a vein of impressive earnestness

* The familiar version has "Smiley."—Ed.

and sincerity, which showed me plainly that so far from his imagining that there was anything ridiculous or funny about his story, he regarded it as a really important matter, and admired its two heroes as men of transcendent genius in *finesse*. To me, the spectacle of a man drifting serenely along through such a queer yarn without ever smiling was exquisitely absurd. As I said before, I asked him to tell me what he knew of Rev. Leonidas W. Greeley, and he replied as follows. I let him go on in his own way, and never interrupted him once:

There was a feller here once by the name of *Jim* Greeley, in the winter of '49—or maybe it was the spring of '50—I don't recollect exactly, somehow, though what makes me think it was one or the other is because I remember the big flume wasn't finished when he first come to the camp; but anyway, he was the curiosest man about always betting on anything that turned up you ever see, if he could get anybody to bet on the other side, and if he couldn't he'd change sides—any way that suited the other man would suit *him*—any way just so's he got a bet, *he* was satisfied. But still, he was lucky— uncommon lucky; he most always come out winner. He was always ready and laying for a chance; there couldn't be no solitary thing mentioned but that feller'd offer to bet on it—and take any side you please, as I was just telling you: if there was a horse race, you'd find him flush or you find him busted at the end of it; if there was a dog-fight, he'd bet on it; if there was a cat-fight, he'd bet on it; if there was a chicken-fight, he'd bet on it; why if there was two birds sitting on a fence, he would bet you which one would fly first—or if there was a camp-meeting he would be there reglar to bet on Parson Walker, which he judged to be the best exhorter about here, and so he was, too, and a good man; if he even see a straddle-bug start to go anywheres, he would bet you how long it would take him to get wherever he was going to, and if you took him up he would foller that straddle-bug to Mexico but what he would find out where he was bound for and how long he was on the road. Lots of the boys here has seen that Greeley and can tell you about him. Why, it never made no difference to *him*—he would bet on *anything*—the dangdest feller. Parson Walker's wife laid very sick, once, for a good while, and it seemed as if they warn't going to save her; but one morning he come in and Greeley asked how she was, and he said she was considerable better—thank the Lord for his inf'nit mercy—and coming on so smart that with the blessing of Providence she'd get well yet— and Greeley, before he thought, says: "Well, I'll resk two-and-a-half that she don't, anyway."

Thish-yer Greeley had a mare—the boys called her the fifteen-minute nag, but that was only in fun, you know, because, of course, she was faster than that—and he used to win money on that horse, for all she was so slow and always had the asthma, or the distemper, or the consumption, or something of that kind. They used to give her two or three hundred yards' start, and then pass her under way; but always at the fag-end of the race she'd get excited and desperate like, and come cavorting and spraddling up, and scattering her legs around limber, sometimes in the air, and sometimes out to one side amongst the fences, and kicking up m-o-r-e dust, and raising m-o-r-e racket with her coughing and sneezing and blowing her nose—and always fetch up at the stand just about a neck ahead, as near as you could cipher it down.

And he had a little small bull pup, that to look at him you'd think he warn't worth a cent, but to set around and look onery, and lay for a chance to steal something. But as soon as money was up on him he was a different dog—his under-jaw'd begin to stick out like the for'castle of a steamboat, and his teeth would uncover, and shine savage like the furnaces. And a dog might tackle him, and bully-rag him, and bite him, and throw him over his shoulder two or three times, and Andrew Jackson—which was the name of the pup—Andrew Jackson would never let on but what he was satisfied, and hadn't expected nothing else—and the bets being doubled and doubled on the other side all the time, till the money was all up—and then all of a sudden he would grab that other dog just by the joint of his hind leg and freeze to it—not chaw, you understand, but only just grip and hang on till they throwed up the sponge, if it was a year. Greeley always came out winner on that pup till he harnessed a dog once that didn't have no hind legs, because they'd been sawed off in a circular saw, and when the thing had gone along far enough, and the money was all up, and he come to make a snatch for his pet holt, he saw in a minute how he'd been imposed on, and how the other dog had him in the door, so to speak, and he 'peared surprised, and then he looked sorter discouraged like, and didn't try no more to win the fight, and so he got shucked out bad. He give Greeley a look as much as to say his heart was broke, and it was *his* fault, for putting up a dog that hadn't no hind legs for him to take holt of, which was his main dependence in a fight, and then he limped off a piece, and laid down and died. It was a good pup, was that Andrew Jackson, and would have made a name for hisself if he'd lived, for the stuff was in him, and he had genius— I know it, because he hadn't had no opportunities to speak of, and it don't stand to reason that a dog could make such a fight as he could under them circumstances, if he hadn't no talent. It always makes me feel sorry when I think of that last fight of his'n, and the way it turned out.

Well, thish-yer Greeley had rat-tarriers and chicken cocks, and tom-cats, and all them kind of things, till you couldn't rest, and you couldn't fetch nothing for him to bet on but he'd match you. He ketched a frog one day and took him home and said he cal'lated to educate him; and so never done nothing for three months but set in his back yard and learn that frog to jump. And you bet you he *did* learn him, too. He'd give him a little punch behind, and the next minute you'd see that frog whirling in the air like a doughnut—see him turn one summerset, or maybe a couple, if he got a good start, and come down flat-footed and all right, like a cat. He got him up so in the matter of catching flies, and kept him in practice so constant, that he'd nail a fly every time as far as he could see him. Greeley said all a frog wanted was education, and he could do most anything—and I believe him. Why, I've seen him send Dan'l Webster down here on this floor— Dan'l Webster was the name of the frog—and sing out "Flies! Dan'l, flies," quicker'n you could wink, he'd spring straight up, and snake a fly off'n the counter there, and flop down on the floor again as solid as a gob of mud, and fall to scratching the side of his head with his hind foot as indifferent as if he hadn't no idea he'd done any more'n any frog might do. You never see a frog so modest and straightfor'ard as he was, for all he was so gifted. And when it come to fair-and-square jumping on a dead level, he could get over more ground at one straddle than any animal of his breed you ever see. Jumping on a dead level was his strong suit, you understand, and when it come to that, Greeley would ante up money on him as long as he had a red. Greeley was monstrous proud of his frog, and well he might be, for fellers that had travelled and been everywheres, all said he laid over any frog that ever *they* see.

Well, Greeley kept the beast in a little lattice box, and he used to fetch him down town sometimes and lay for a bet. One day a feller—a stranger in the camp, he was—come across him with his box, and says:

"What might it be that you've got in the box?"

And Greeley says, sorter indifferent like, "It might be a parrot, or it might be a canary, maybe, but it ain't—it's only just a frog."

And the feller took it, and looked at it careful, and turned it round this way and that, and says, "H'm—so 'tis. Well, what's *he* good for?"

"Well," Greeley says, easy and careless, "he's good enough for *one* thing I should judge—he can out-jump any frog in Calaveras county."

The feller took the box again, and took another long, particular look, and give it back to Greeley and says, very deliberate, "Well—I don't see no points about that frog that's any better'n any other frog."

"Maybe you don't," Greeley says. "Maybe you understand frogs, and maybe you don't understand 'em; maybe you've had experience, and maybe you ain't only a amature, as it were. Anyways, I've got *my* opinion, and I'll resk forty dollars that he can out-jump any frog in Calaveras county."

And the feller studied a minute, and then says, kinder sad, like, "Well—

I'm only a stranger here, and I ain't got no frog—but if I had a frog I'd bet you."

And then Greeley says, "That's all right—that's all right—if you'll hold my box a minute I'll go and get you a frog;" and so the feller took the box, and put up his forty dollars along with Greeley's, and set down to wait.

So he set there a good while thinking and thinking to hisself, and then he got the frog out and prized his mouth open and took a teaspoon and filled him full of quail-shot—filled him pretty near up to his chin—and set him on the floor. Greeley he went to the swamp and slopped around in the mud for a long time, and finally he ketched a frog and fetched him in and give him to this feller and says:

"Now if you're ready, set him alongside of Dan'l, with his fore-paws just even with Dan'l's, and I'll give the word." Then he says, "one—two—three—jump!" and him and the feller touched up the frogs from behind, and the new frog hopped off, but Dan'l give a heave, and hysted up his shoulders—so—like a Frenchman, but it wa'nt no use—he couldn't budge; he was planted as solid as an anvil, and he couldn't no more stir than if he was anchored out. Greeley was a good deal surprised, and he was disgusted, too, but he didn't have no idea what the matter was, of course.

The feller took the money and started away, and when he was going out at the door he sorter jerked his thumb over his shoulders—this way—at Dan'l, and says again, very deliberate: "Well—*I* don't see no points about that frog that's any better'n any other frog."

Greeley he stood scratching his head and looking down at Dan'l a long time, and at last he says, "I do wonder what in the nation that frog throw'd off for—I wonder if there ain't something the matter with him—he 'pears to look mighty baggy, somehow," and he ketched Dan'l by the nap of the neck, and lifted him up and says, "Why blame my cats if he don't weigh five pound," and turned him upside down, and he belched out about a double-handful of shot. And then he see how it was, and he was the maddest man—he set the frog down and took out after that feller, but he never ketched him. And—

[Here Simon Wheeler heard his name called from the front-yard, and got up to see what was wanted.] And turning to me as he moved away, he said: "Just set where you are, stranger, and rest easy—I ain't going to be gone a second."

But by your leave, I did not think that a continuation of the history of the enterprising vagabond Jim Greeley would be likely to afford me much information concerning the Rev. Leonidas W. Greeley, and so I started away.

At the door I met the sociable Wheeler returning, and he buttonholed me and recommenced:

"Well, thish-yer Greeley had a yaller one-eyed cow that didn't have no tail only just a short stump like a bannanner, and—"

"O, curse Greeley and his afflicted cow!" I muttered, good-naturedly, and bidding the old gentleman good-day, I departed.

Yours, truly,   MARK TWAIN

CALIFORNIAN, December 16, 1865.

HENRY GEORGE

What the Railroads Will Bring Us

UPON THE PLAINS this season railroad building is progressing with a rapidity never before known. The two companies, in their struggle for the enormous bounty offered by the Government, are shortening the distance between the lines of rail at the rate of from seven to nine miles a day—almost as fast as the ox teams which furnished the primitive method of conveyance across the continent could travel. Possibly by the middle of next spring, and certainly, we are told, before midsummer comes again, this "greatest work of the age" will be completed, and an unbroken track stretch from the Atlantic to the Pacific.

Though, as a piece of engineering, the building of this road may not deserve the superlative terms in which, with American proneness to exaggeration, it is frequently spoken of, yet, when the full effects of its completion are considered, it seems the "greatest work of the age" indeed. Even the Suez Canal, which will almost change the front of Europe and divert the course of the commerce of half the world, is, in this view, not to be compared with it. For this railroad will not merely open a new route across the continent; it will be the means of converting a wilderness into a populous empire in less time than many of the cathedrals and palaces of Europe were building, and in unlocking treasure vaults which will flood the world with the precious metals. The country west of the longitude of Omaha, all of which will be directly or indirectly affected by the construction of the railroad (for other roads must soon follow the first), is the largest and richest portion of the United States. Throughout the greater part of this vast domain gold and silver are scattered in inexhaustible profusion, and it contains besides, in limitless quantities, every valuable mineral known to man, and includes every variety of soil and climate.

The natural resources of this country are so great and varied, the inducements which it offers to capital and labor are so superior to those offered anywhere else, that when it is opened by railroads—placed, as it soon will be, within a few days' ride of New York, and two or three weeks' journey from Southampton and Bremen, immigration will flow into it like pent-up waters seeking their level, and states will be peopled and cities built with a rapidity never before known, even in our central West. In the consideration of the effects of this migratory movement[,] of the economical, social and political features of these great commonwealths shortly to be called into vigorous being, and of the influences which their growth will exert upon the rest of the Union and the rest of the world[,] . . . a boundless and most tempting field for speculation is opened up; but into it we cannot enter, as there is more than enough to occupy us in the narrower range suggested by the title of this article.

What is the railroad to do for *us*?—this railroad that we have looked for, hoped for, prayed for so long?

Much of the matter has been thought about and talked about . . . there are probably but few of us who really comprehend all it will do. We are so used to the California of the stage-coach, widely separated from the rest of the world, that we can hardly realize what the California of the railroad will be. . . .

The sharpest sense of Americans—the keen sense of gain, which certainly does not lose its keenness in our bracing air—is the first to realize what is coming with our railroad. All over the state, land is appreciating—fortunes are being made in a day by buying and parcelling out Spanish ranches; the Government surveyors and registrars are busy; speculators are grappling the public domain by the hundreds of thousands of acres; while for miles in every direction around San Francisco, ground is being laid off into homestead lots. The spirit of speculation, doubles, trebles, quadruples the past growth of the city in its calculations, and then discounts the result, confident that there still remains a margin. And it is not far wrong. The new era will be one of great material prosperity, if material prosperity means more people, more houses, more farms and more mines, more factories and ships. Calculations based upon the growth of San Francisco can hardly be wild. There are men now in their prime among us who will live to see this the second, perhaps the first city on the continent. This, which may sound like the sanguine utterance of California speculation, is simply a logical deduction from the past.

After the first impulse which settled California had subsided, there came a time of stagnation, if not of absolute decay. As the placers one after another were exhausted, the miners moved off; once populous districts were deserted, once flourishing mining towns fell into ruin, and it seemed to superficial observers as though the state had passed the acme of her prosperity. During this period quartz mining was being slowly developed, agriculture steadily increasing in importance, and manufactures gaining a foothold; but the progress of these industries was slow; they could not at once compensate for the exhaustion of the placer mines; and though San Francisco, drawing her support from the whole coast, continued to grow steadily if not rapidly, the aggregate population and wealth of the state diminished rather than increased. Through this period we have passed. Although the decay of portions of mining regions still continues, there has been going on for some time a steady, rapid development of the state at large—felt principally in the agricultural counties and the metropolis, but which is now beginning to make itself felt from one end of the state to the other. To produce this, several causes have combined, but prominent among them must be reckoned the new force to which we principally and primarily look for the development of the future—railroads. . . .

It is not only the metropolis that is hopeful. Sacramento, Stockton and Marysville feel the general impulse. Oakland is laying out, or at least surveying, docks which will cast those of Jersey City, if not of Liverpool, into the shade; Vallejo talks of her coming foreign commerce, and is preparing to load the grain of the Sacramento and Napa valleys into ships for all parts of the world; and San Diego is beginning to look forward to the time when she will have steam communication with St. Louis and New Orleans on the one hand, and China and Japan on the other, and be the second city on the coast. Renewed interest is being taken in mining—new branches of manufacture are being started. . . .

The new era into which our state . . . has already entered [is] without doubt an era of steady, rapid and substantial growth; of great addition to population and immense increase in the totals of the Assessor's lists. Yet we cannot hope to escape the great law of compensation which exacts some loss for every gain. And as there are but few of us who, could we retrace our lives, retaining the knowledge we have gained, would pass from childhood to youth, or from youth into manhood, with unmixed feelings, so we imagine that if the genius of California, whom we picture on the shield of our state, were really a sentient being, she would not look forward now entirely without regret.

The California of the new era will be greater, richer, more powerful than the California of the past; but will she be still the same California whom her

adopted children, gathered from all climes, love better than their own moth-
erlands; from which all who have lived within her bounds are proud to hail;
to which all who have known her long to return? She will have more people;
but among those people will there be so large a proportion of full, true men?
She will have more wealth; but will it be so evenly distributed? She will
have more luxury and refinement and culture; but will she have such general
comfort, so little squalor and misery; so little of the grinding, hopeless
poverty that chills and cramps the souls of men, and converts them into
brutes?

Amid all our rejoicing and all our gratulation, let us see clearly whither
we are tending. Increase in population and in wealth past a certain point
means simply an approximation to the condition of older countries—the
eastern states and Europe. Would the average Californian prefer to "take
his chances" in New York or Massachusetts, or in California as it is and has
been? Is England, with her population of twenty millions to an area not
more than one-third of our state, and a wealth which per inhabitant is six
or seven times that of California, a better country than California to live in?
Probably, if one were born a duke or a factory lord, or to any place among
the upper ten thousand; but if one were born among the lower millions—
how then?

And so the California of the future—the California of the new era—will
be a better country for some classes than the California of the present; and
so too, it must be a worse country for others. Which of these classes will be
the largest? Are there more mill owners or factory operatives in Lancaster-
shire; more brownstone mansions, or tenement-rooms in New York?

With the tendency of human nature to set the highest value on that
which it has not, we have clamored for immigration, for population, as though
that were the one sole good. But if this be so, how is it that the most populous
countries in the world are the most miserable, most corrupt, most stagnant
and hopeless? How is it that in populous and wealthy England there is so
much more misery, vice and social disease than in her poor and sparsely
populated colonies? If a large population is not a curse as well as a blessing,
how was it that the black-death which swept off one-third of the population
of England produced such a rise in the standard of wages and the standard
of comfort among the people?

We want great cities, large factories, and mines worked cheaply, in this
California of ours! Would we esteem ourselves gainers if New York, ruled
and robbed by thieves, loafers and brothel-keepers; nursing a race of savages
fiercer and meaner than any who ever shrieked a war-whoop on the plains;
could be set down on our bay tomorrow? Would we be gainers, if the
cottonmills of Massachusetts, with their thousands of little children who,
official papers tell us, are being literally worked to death, could be trans-

ported to the banks of the American; or the file and pin factories of England, where young girls are treated worse than even slaves on southern plantations, be reared as by magic at Antioch? Or if among our mountains we could by wishing have the miners, men, women and children, who work the iron and coal mines of Belgium and France, where the condition of production is that the laborer shall have meat but once a week—would we wish them here?

Can we have one thing without the other? . . .

. . . [I]t is certain that the tendency of the new era—of the more dense population and more thorough development of the wealth of the state—will be to a reduction both of the rate of interest and the rate of wages, particularly the latter. This tendency may not, probably will not, be shown immediately; but it will be before long, and that powerfully, unless balanced and counteracted by other influences which we are not now considering, which do not yet appear, and which it is probable will not appear for some time yet.

The truth is, that the completion of the railroad and the consequent great increase of business and population, will not be a benefit to all of us, but only to a portion. As a general rule (liable of course to exceptions) those who *have*, it will make wealthier; for those who *have not*, it will make it more difficult to get. Those who have lands, mines, established businesses, special abilities of certain kinds, will become richer for it and find increased opportunities; those who have only their own labor will become poorer, and find it harder to get ahead—first, because it will take more capital to buy land or to get into business; and second, because as competition reduces the wages of labor, this capital will be harder for them to obtain.

What, for instance, does the rise in land mean? Several things, but certainly and prominently this: that it will be harder in [the] future for a poor man to get a farm or a homestead lot. In some sections of the state, land which twelve months ago could have been had for a dollar an acre, cannot now be had for less than fifteen dollars. In other words, the settler who last year might have had at once a farm of his own, must now either go to work on wages for someone else, pay rent or buy on time; in either case being compelled to give to the capitalist a large proportion of the earnings which, had he arrived a year ago, he might have had all for himself. And as proprietorship is thus rendered more difficult and less profitable to the poor, more are forced into the labor market to compete with each other, and cut down the rate of wages. . . .

And so in San Francisco the rise in building lots means that it will be harder for a poor man to get a house and lot for himself, and if he has none that he will have to use more of his earnings for rent; means a crowding of the poorer classes together; signifies courts, slums, tenement-houses, squalor and vice. . . .

To say that "Power is constantly stealing from the many to the few," is only to state in another form the law that wealth tends to concentration. In the new era into which the world has entered since the application of steam, this law is more potent than ever; in the new era into which California is entering, its operations will be more marked here than ever before. The locomotive is a great centralizer. It kills little towns and builds up great cities, and in the same way kills little businesses and builds up great ones. We have had comparatively but few rich men; no very rich ones, in the meaning "very rich" has in these times. But the process is going on. The great city that is to be will have its Astors, Vanderbilts, Stewarts and Spragues, and he who looks a few years ahead may even now read their names as he passes along Montgomery, California or Front streets. With the protection which property gets in modern times—with stocks, bonds, burglar-proof safes and policemen; with the railroad and the telegraph—after a man gets a certain amount of money it is plain sailing, and he need take no risks. Astor said that to get his first thousand dollars was his greatest struggle; but when one gets a million, if he has ordinary prudence, how much he will have is only a question of life. Nor can we rely on the absence of laws of primogeniture and entail to dissipate these large fortunes so menacing to the general weal. Any large fortune will, of course, become dissipated in time, even in spite of laws of primogeniture and entail; but every aggregation of wealth implies and necessitates others, and so that the aggregations remain, it matters little in what particular hands. . . .

Nor is it worth while to shut our eyes to the effects of this concentration of wealth. One millionaire involves the existence of just so many proletarians. It is the great tree and the saplings over again. We need not look far from the palace to find the hovel. When people can charter special steamboats to take them to watering places, pay four thousand dollars for the summer rental of a cottage, build marble stables for their horses, and give dinner parties which cost by the thousand dollars a head, we may know that there are poor girls on the streets pondering between starvation and dishonor. When liveries appear, look out for bare-footed children. A few liveries are now to be seen on our streets; we think their appearance coincides in date with the establishment of the almshouse. They are few, plain and modest now; they will grow more numerous and gaudy—and then we will not wait long for the children—their corollaries.

But there is another side: we are to become a great, populous, wealthy community. And in such a community many good things are possible that are not possible in a community such as ours has been. There have been artists, scholars, and men of special knowledge and ability among us, who could and some of whom have since won distinction and wealth in older and larger cities, but who here could only make a living by digging sand, peddling vegetables or washing dishes in restaurants. It will not be so in the San

Francisco of the future. We shall keep such men with us, and reward them, instead of driving them away. We shall have our noble charities, great museums, libraries and universities; a class of men who have leisure for thought and culture; magnificent theaters and opera houses; parks and pleasure gardens.

We shall develop a literature of our own, issue books which will be read wherever the English language is spoken, and maintain periodicals which will rank with those of the East and Europe. The *Bulletin, Times* and *Alta,* good as they are, must become, or must yield to, journals of the type of the New York *Herald* or the *Chicago Tribune.* The railroads which will carry the San Francisco newspapers over a wide extent of country the same day that they are issued, will place them on a par, or almost on a par in point of time, with journals printed in the interior, while their metropolitan circulation and business will enable them to publish more and later news than interior papers can.

The same law of concentration will work in other businesses in the same way. The railroads may benefit Sacramento and Stockton by making them work-shops, but no one will stop there to buy goods when he can go to San Francisco, make his choice from larger stocks, and return the same day.

But again comes the question: will this California of the future . . . possess still the charm which makes Californians prefer their state, even as it is, to places where all these things are to be found?

What constitutes the peculiar charm of California, which all who have lived here long enough feel? Not the climate alone. Heresy though it be to say so, there *are* climates as good; some that on the whole are better. Not merely that there is less social restraint, for there are parts of the Union— and parts from which tourists occasionally come to lecture us—where there is much less social restraint than in California. Not simply that the opportunities of making money have been better here; for the opportunities for making large fortunes have not been so good as in some other places, and there are many who have not made money here, who prefer this country to any other; many who after leaving us throw away certainty of profit to return and "take the chances" of California. It certainly is not in the growth of local attachment, for the Californian has even less local attachment than the average American, and will move about from one end of the state to the other with perfect indifference. It is not that we have the culture or the opportunities to gratify luxurious and cultivated tastes that older countries afford, and yet those who leave us on this account as a general thing come back again.

No: the potent charm of California, which all feel but few analyze, has been more in the character, habits and modes of thought of her people— called forth by the peculiar conditions of the young state—than in anything else. In California there has been a certain cosmopolitanism, a certain freedom and breadth of common thought and feeling, natural to a community made up from so many different sources, to which every man and woman had been transplanted—all travelers to some extent, and with native angularities of prejudice and habit more or less worn off. Then there has been a feeling of personal independence and equality, a general hopefulness and self-reliance, and a certain large-heartedness and open-handedness which were born of the comparative evenness with which property was distributed, the high standard of wages and of comfort, and the latent feeling of everyone that he might "make a strike," and certainly could not be kept down long. . . .

In a country where all had started from the same level . . . social lines could not be sharply drawn, nor a reverse dispirit. There was something in the great possibilities of the country; in the feeling that it was one of immense latent wealth; which furnished a background of which a better filled and more thoroughly developed country is destitute, and which contributed not a little to the active, generous, independent social tone.

The characteristics of the principal business—mining—gave a color to all California thought and feeling. It fostered a reckless, generous, independent spirit, with a strong disposition to "take chances" and "trust to luck." Than the placer mining, no more independent business could be conceived. The miner working for himself, owned no master; worked when and only when he pleased; took out his earnings each day in the shining particles which depended for their value on no fluctuations of the market, but would pass current and supply all wants the world over. When his claim gave out, or for any reason he desired to move on, he had but to shoulder his pick and move on. Mining of this kind developed its virtues as well as its vices. If it could have been united with ownership of land and the comforts and restraints of home, it would have given us a class of citizens of the utmost value to a republican state. But the "honest miner" of the placers has passed away in California. The Chinaman, the mill-owner and his laborers, the mine superintendent and his gang, are his successors.

This crowding of people into immense cities, this aggregation of wealth into large lumps, this marshalling of men into big gangs under the control of the great "captains of industry," does not tend to foster personal independence—the basis of all virtues—nor will it tend to preserve the characteristics which particularly have made Californians proud of their state.

However, we shall have some real social gains, with some that are only apparent. We shall have more of home influences, a deeper religious sentiment, less of the unrest that is bred of an adventurous and reckless life. We shall have fewer shooting and stabbing affrays, but we will have probably something worse, from which, thank God, we have hitherto been exempt—

the low, brutal, cowardly rowdyism of the great eastern cities. We shall hear less of highway robberies in the mountains, but more, perhaps, of pick-pockets, burglars and sneak thieves.

That we can look forward to any political improvement is, to say the least, doubtful. There is nothing in the changes which are coming that of itself promises that. There will be a more permanent population, more who will look on California as their home; but we would not aver that there will be a larger proportion of the population who will take an intelligent interest in public affairs. In San Francisco the political future is full of danger. As surely as San Francisco is destined to become as large as New York, as certain is it that her political condition is destined to become as bad as that of New York, unless her citizens are aroused in time to the necessity of preventive or rather palliative measures. And in the growth of large corporations and other special interests is an element of great danger. Of these great corporations and interests we shall have many. Look, for instance, at the Central Pacific Railroad Company, as it will be, with a line running to Salt Lake, controlling more capital and employing more men than any of the great eastern railroads who manage legislatures as they manage their workshops, and name governors, senators and judges almost as they name their own engineers and clerks! Can we rely upon sufficient intelligence, independence and virtue among the many to resist the political effects of the concentration of great wealth in the hands of a few? . . .

With our gains and our losses will come new duties and new responsibilities. Connected more closely with the rest of the nation, we will feel more quickly and keenly all that affects it. We will have to deal, in time, with all the social problems that are forcing themselves on older communities (like the riddles of a Sphinx, which not to answer is death), with one of them, the labor question, rendered peculiarly complex by our proximity to Asia. Public spirit, public virtue, the high resolve of men and women who are capable of feeling "enthusiasm of humanity," will be needed in the future more than ever. . . .

Let us not imagine ourselves in a fool's paradise, where the golden apples will drop into our mouths; let us not think that after the stormy seas and head gales of all the ages, *our* ship has at last struck the trade winds of time. The future of our State, of our nation, of our race, looks fair and bright; perhaps the future looked so to the philosophers who once sat in the porches of Athens—to the unremembered men who raised the cities whose ruins lie south of us. Our modern civilization strikes broad and deep and looks high. So did the tower which men once built almost unto heaven.   [1868]

LOUISE CLAPP

The Shirley Letters
from the California Mines

From our Log Cabin, Indian Bar,
April 10, 1852

I HAVE BEEN HAUNTED all day, my dear M., with an intense ambition to write you a letter, which shall be dreadfully commonplace and severely utilitarian in its style and contents. Not but that my epistles are *always* commonplace enough, (spirits of Montagu and Sévigné, forgive me!) but hitherto I have not really *tried* to make them so. Now, however, I *intend* to be stupidly prosy, with malice aforethought, and without one mitigating circumstance, except, perchance, it be the temptations of that above-mentioned ambitious little devil to palliate my crime.

You would certainly wonder, were you seated where I now am, how anyone with a quarter of a soul, *could* manufacture herself into a bore, amid such surroundings as these. The air is as balmy as that of a midsummer's day in the sunniest valleys of New England. It is four o'clock in the evening, and I am sitting on a segar-box outside of our cabin. From this spot not a person is to be seen, except a man who is building a new wing to the "Humboldt." Not a human sound, but a slight noise made by the aforesaid individual, in tacking on a roof of blue drilling to the room which he is finishing, disturbs the stillness which fills this purest air. I confess that it is difficult to fix my eyes upon the dull paper, and my fingers upon the duller pen with which I am soiling it. Almost every other minute, I find myself stopping to listen to the ceaseless river-psalm, or to gaze up into the wondrous depths of the California Heaven; to watch the graceful movements of the pretty brown lizards, jerking up their impudent little heads above a moss-wrought log which lies before me, or to mark the dancing water-shadow on the canvas door of the bakeshop opposite; to follow with childish eyes the flight of a golden butterfly, curious to know if it will crown, with a capital of winged beauty, that column of Nature's carving, the pine stump rising at my feet, or whether it will flutter down (for it is dallying coquettishly around them both,) upon that slate-rock beyond, shining so darkly lustrous through a flood of yellow sunlight; or I lazily turn my head, wondering if I know the blue or red-shirted miner who is descending the precipitous hill behind me. In sooth, Molly, it is easy to be commonplace at all times, but I confess that, just at present, I find it difficult to be utilitary; the saucy lizards—the great, orange-dotted butterflies—the still, solemn cedars—the sailing smoke-wreath and the vaulted splendor above, are wooing me so winningly to higher things.

But, as I said before, I have an ambition that way, and I will succeed. You are such a good-natured little thing, dear, that I know you will meekly allow yourself to be victimized into reading the profound and prosy remarks which I shall make, in my efforts to initiate you into the mining polity of this place. Now you may rest assured that I shall assert nothing upon the subject which is not perfectly correct; for have I not earned a character for inquisitiveness, (and you know that does *not* happen to be one of my failings,) which I fear will cling to me through life, by my persevering questions to all the unhappy miners from whom I thought I could gain any information. Did I not martyrize myself into a human mule, by descending to the bottom of a dreadful pit, (suffering mortal terror all the time, lest it should cave in upon me,) actuated by a virtuous desire to see with my own two eyes the process of underground mining, thus enabling myself to be stupidly correct in all my statements thereupon? Did I not ruin a pair of silk velvet slippers, lame my ankles for a week, and draw a "browner horror" over my already sun-burnt face, in a wearisome walk miles away, to the head of the "ditch," as they call the prettiest little rivulet (though the work of men)—that I ever saw; yea, verily, this have I done for the express edification of yourself, and the rest of your curious tribe, to be rewarded, probably, by the impertinent remark,—"What *does* that little goose, 'Dame Shirley,' think that *I* care about such things?" But madam, in spite of your sneer, I shall proceed in my allotted task.

In the first place, then, as to the discovery of gold. In California, at least, it must be confessed, that in this particular, science appears to be completely at fault;—or, as an intelligent and well-educated miner remarked to us the other day, "I maintain that science is the blindest guide that one could have on a gold-finding expedition. Those men, who judge by the appearance of the soil, and depend upon geological calculations, are invariably disappointed, while the ignorant adventurer, who digs just for the sake of digging, is almost sure to be successful." I suppose that the above observation is quite correct, as all whom we have questioned upon the subject repeat, in substance, the same thing. Wherever Geology has said that gold *must* be, there, perversely enough, it lies not; and wherever her ladyship has declared that it could *not* be, there has it oftenest garnered up in miraculous profusion the yellow splendor of its virgin beauty. It is certainly very painful to a well-regulated mind to see the irreverent contempt, shown by this beautiful mineral, to the dictates of science; but what better can one expect from the "root of all evil?" As well as can be ascertained, the most lucky of the mining Columbuses, have been ignorant sailors; and foreigners, I fancy, are more successful than Americans.

Our countrymen are the most discontented of mortals. They are always longing for "big strikes." If a "claim" is paying them a steady income, by which, if they pleased, they could lay up more in a month, than they could accumulate in a year at home, still, they are dissatisfied, and, in most cases, will wander off in search of better "diggings." There are hundreds now pursuing this foolish course, who, if they had stopped where they first "camped," would now have been rich men. Sometimes, a company of these wanderers will find itself upon a bar, where a few pieces of the precious metal lie scattered upon the surface of the ground; of course they immediately "prospect" it, which is accomplished, by "panning out" a few basinsful of the soil. If it "pays," they "claim" the spot, and build their shanties; the news spreads that wonderful "diggings" have been discovered at such a place,—the monte-dealers, those worse than fiends, rush vulture-like upon the scene and erect a round tent, where, in gambling, drinking, swearing and fighting, the *many* reproduce Pandemonium in more than its original horror, while a *few* honestly and industriously commence digging for gold, and lo! as if a fairy's wand had been waved above the bar, a full-grown mining town hath sprung into existence.

But first, let me explain to you the "claiming" system. As there are no State laws upon the subject, each mining community is permitted to make its own. Here, they have decided that no man may "claim" an area of more than forty feet square. This he "stakes off" and puts a notice upon it, to the effect that he "holds" it for mining purposes. If he does not choose to "work it" immediately, he is obliged to renew the notice every ten days; for without this precaution, any other person has a right to "jump it," that is, to take it from him. There are many ways of evading the above law. For instance, an individual can "hold" as many "claims" as he pleases, if he keeps a man at work in each, for this workman represents the original owner. I am told, however, that the laborer, himself, can "jump" the "claim" of the very man who employs him, if he pleases so to do. This is seldom, if ever, done; the person who is willing to be hired, generally prefers to receive the six dollars *per diem*, of which he is *sure* in any case, to running the risk of a "claim" not proving valuable. After all, the "holding of claims" by proxy is considered rather as a carrying out of the spirit of the law, than as an evasion of it. But there are many ways of *really* outwitting this rule, though I cannot stop now to relate them, which give rise to innumerable arbitrations, and nearly every Sunday, there is a "miners' meeting" connected with this subject.

Having got our gold mines discovered, and "claimed," I will try to give you a faint idea of how they "work" them. Here, in the mountains, the labor of excavation is extremely difficult, on account of the immense rocks which form a large portion of the soil. Of course, no man can "work out" a "claim" alone. For that reason, and also for the same that makes partnerships desirable, they congregate in companies of four or six, generally designating themselves by the name of the place from whence the majority of the members have emigrated; as for example, the "Illinois," "Bunker Hill," "Bay State," etc., companies. In many places the surface-soil, or in mining phrase, the "top dirt," "pays" when worked in a "Long Tom." This machine, (I have never been able to discover the derivation of its name,) is a trough, generally about twenty feet in length, and eight inches in depth, formed of wood, with the exception of six feet at one end, called the "riddle," (query, why riddle?) which is made of sheet-iron, perforated with holes about the size of a large marble. Underneath this cullender-like portion of the "long-tom," is placed another trough, about ten feet long, the sides six inches perhaps in height, which divided through the middle by a slender slat, is called the "riffle-box." It takes several persons to manage, properly, a "long-tom." Three or four men station themselves with spades, at the head of the machine, while at the foot of it, stands an individual armed "wid de shovel and de hoe." The spadesmen throw in large quantities of the precious dirt, which is washed down to the "riddle" by a stream of water leading into the "long-tom" through wooden gutters or "sluices." When the soil reaches the "riddle," it is kept constantly in motion by the man with the hoe. Of course, by this means, all the dirt and gold escapes through the perforations into the "riffle-box" below, one compartment of which is placed just beyond the "riddle." Most of the dirt washes over the sides of the "riffle-box," but the gold being so astonishingly heavy remains safely at the bottom of it. When the machine gets too full of stones to be worked easily, the man whose business it is to attend to them throws them out with his shovel, looking carefully among them as he does so for any pieces of gold, which may have been too large to pass through the holes of the "riddle." I am sorry to say that he generally loses his labor. At night they "pan out" the gold, which has been collected in the "riffle-box" during the day. Many of the miners decline washing the "top dirt" at all, but try to reach as quickly as possible the "bed-rock," where are found the richest deposits of gold. The river is supposed to have formerly flowed over this "bed-rock," in the "crevices" of which, it left, as it passed away, the largest portions of the so eagerly sought for ore. The group of mountains amidst which we are living is a spur of the Sierra Nevada; and the "bed-rock," (which in this vicinity is of slate) is said to run through the entire range, lying, in distance varying from a few feet to eighty or ninety, beneath the surface of the soil. On Indian Bar, the "bed-rock" falls in almost perpendicular "benches," while at Rich Bar, the friction of the river has formed it into large, deep basins, in which the gold, instead of being found, as you would naturally suppose, in the bottom of it, lies for the most part, just below the rim. A good-natured individual bored *me*, and tired *himself*, in a hopeless attempt to make me comprehend that this was only a necessary consequence of the under-current of the water; but with my usual stupidity upon such matters, I got but a vague idea from his scientific explanation, and certainly shall not mystify *you*, with my confused notions thereupon.

When a company wish to reach the bed rock as quickly as possible, they "sink a shaft," (which is nothing more nor less than digging a well,) until they "strike" it. They then commence "drifting coyote holes" (as they call them) in search of "crevices," which, as I told you before, often pay immensely. These "coyote holes" sometimes extend hundreds of feet into the side of the hill. Of course they are obliged to use lights in working them. They generally proceed, until the air is so impure as to extinguish the lights, when they return to the entrance of the excavation, and commence another, perhaps close to it. When they think that a "coyote hole" has been faithfully "worked," they "clean it up," which is done by scraping the surface of the "bed rock" with a knife,—lest by chance they have overlooked a "crevice,"— and they are often richly rewarded for this precaution.

Now I must tell you how those having "claims" on the hills procure the water for washing them. The expense of raising it in any way from the river, is too enormous to be thought of for a moment. In most cases it is brought from ravines in the mountains. A company, to which a friend of ours belongs, has dug a ditch about a foot in width and depth, and more than three miles in length, which is fed in this way. I wish that you could see this ditch. I never beheld a NATURAL streamlet more exquisitely beautiful. It undulates over the mossy roots, and the gray, old rocks, like a capricious snake, singing all the time a low song with the "liquidest murmur," and one might almost fancy it the airy and coquettish Undine herself. When it reaches the top of the hill, the sparkling thing is divided into five or six branches, each one of which supplies one, two, or three "long-toms." There is an extra one, called the "waste-ditch," leading to the river, into which the water is shut off at night and on Sundays. This "race" (another and peculiar name for it) has already cost the company more than five thousand dollars. They sell the water to others at the following rates: Those that have the first use of it pay ten per cent upon all the gold that they take out. As the water runs off from their machine, (it now goes by the elegant name of "tailings,") it is taken by a company lower down; and as it is not worth so much as when it was clear, the latter pay but seven per cent. If any others wish the "tailings," now still less valuable than at first, they pay four per cent on all the gold which they take out, be it much or little. The water companies are constantly in trouble, and the arbitrations on that subject are very frequent.

I think that I gave you a vague idea of "fluming" in a former letter; I will not, therefore, repeat it here, but will merely mention, that the numerous "fluming" companies have already commenced their extensive operations upon the river.

As to the "rockers," so often mentioned in story and in song, I have not spoken of them since I commenced this letter. The truth is, that I have seldom seen them used, though hundreds are lying ownerless along the banks of the river. I suppose that other machines are better adapted to mining operations in the mountains.

Gold mining is Nature's great lottery scheme. A man may work in a claim for many months, and be poorer at the end of the time than when he commenced; or he may "take out" thousands in a few hours. It is a mere matter of chance. A friend of ours, a young Spanish surgeon from Guatemala, a person of intelligence and education, told us that, after "working a claim" for six months, he had taken out but six ounces.

It must be acknowledged, however, that if a person "work his claim" himself, is economical and industrious, keeps his health, and is satisfied with small gains, he is "bound" to make money. And yet, I cannot help remarking, that almost all with whom we are acquainted seem to have *lost*. Some have had their "claims" jumped; many holes which had been excavated, and prepared for working at a great expense, caved in during the heavy rains of the fall and winter. Often after a company has spent an immense deal of time and money in "sinking a shaft," the water from the springs, (the greatest obstacle which the miner has to contend with in this vicinity) rushes in so fast, that it is impossible to work in them, or to contrive any machinery to keep it out, and for that reason only, men have been compelled to abandon places where they were at the very time "taking out" hundreds of dollars a day. If a fortunate or an unfortunate (which shall I call him?) *does* happen to make a "big strike," he is almost sure to fall into the hands of the professed gamblers, who soon relieve him of all care of it. They have not troubled the Bar much during the winter, but as the spring opens, they flock in like ominous birds of prey. Last week one left here, after a stay of four days, with over a thousand dollars of the hard-earned gold of the miners. But enough of these best-beloved of Beelzebub, so infinitely worse than the robber or murderer;—for surely it would be kinder to take a man's life, than to poison him with the fatal passion for gambling.

Perhaps you would like to know what class of men is most numerous in the mines. As well as I can judge, there are upon this river as many foreigners as Americans. The former, with a few exceptions, are extremely ignorant and degraded; though we have the pleasure of being acquainted with three or four Spaniards of the highest education and accomplishments. Of the Americans, the majority are of the better class of mechanics. Next to these, in number, are the sailors and the farmers. There are a few merchants and steamboat-clerks, three or four physicians, and one lawyer. We have no ministers, though fourteen miles from here there is a "Rancho," kept by a man of distinguished appearance, an accomplished monte-dealer and horse-jockey, who is *said* to have been—in the States—a preacher of the Gospel. I know not if this be true; but at any rate, such things are not uncommon in California.

I have spun this letter out until my head aches dreadfully. How tiresome it is to write *sensible* (?) things! But I have one comfort,—though my epistle may not be interesting, you will not deny, dear M., that I have achieved my ambition of making it both commonplace and utilatory.

From our Log Cabin, Indian Bar,
August 4, 1852

We have lived through so much of excitement for the last three weeks, dear M., that I almost shrink from relating the gloomy events which have marked their flight. But if I leave out the darker shades of our mountain life, the picture will be very incomplete. In the short space of twenty-four days, we have had murders, fearful accidents, bloody deaths, a mob, whip-pings, a hanging, an attempt at suicide, and a fatal duel. But to begin at the beginning, as according to rule one ought to do.

I think that even among these beautiful hills, I never saw a more perfect "bridal of the earth and sky," than that of Sunday the eleventh of July. On that morning, I went with a party of friends to the head of the "Ditch," a walk of about three miles in length. I do not believe that Nature herself ever made anything so lovely, as this artificial brooklet. It glides like a living thing, through the very heart of the forest; sometimes creeping softly on, as though with muffled feet, through a wilderness of aquatic plants; some-times dancing gaily over a white pebbled bottom; now making a "sunshine in a shady place," across the mossy roots of the majestic old trees—and anon leaping with a grand anthem, adown the great, solemn rocks, which lie along its beautiful pathway. A sunny opening at the head of the ditch, is a garden of perfumed shrubbery and many-tinted flowers—all garlanded with the prettiest vines imaginable, and peopled with an infinite variety of magnificent butterflies. These last were of every possible color—pink, blue and yellow, shining black splashed with orange, purple fleshed with gold, white, and even green. We returned about three in the evening, loaded with fragrant bundles, which arranged in jars, tumblers, pitcher, bottles and pails, (we are not particular as to the quality of our vases in the mountains, and love our flowers as well in their humble chalices as if their beautiful heads lay against a background of marble or porcelain,) made the dark old cabin, "a bower of beauty for us."

Shortly after our arrival, a perfectly deafening volley of shouts and yells elicited from my companion the careless remark, "that the customary Sabbath-day's fight was apparently more serious than usual." Almost as he spoke, there succeeded a death-like silence, broken in a minute after by a deep groan, at the corner of the cabin, followed by the words, "Why Tom, poor fellow, are you really wounded?" Before we could reach the door, it was burst violently open, by a person who inquired hurriedly for the Doctor— who, luckily, happened at that very moment to be approaching. The man who called him, then gave us the following excited account of what had happened. He said that in a *melé* between the Americans and the foreigners, Domingo—a tall, majestic-looking Spaniard, a perfect type of the novelistic bandit of Old Spain—had stabbed Tom Somers, a young Irishman, but a naturalized citizen of the United States—and that at the very moment, said Domingo, with a *Mejicana* hanging upon his arm, and brandishing threateningly the long, bloody knife with which he had inflicted the wound upon his victim, was parading up and down the street unmolested. It seems that when Tom Somers fell, the Americans, being unarmed, were seized with a sudden panic and fled. There was a rumor, (unfounded, as it afterwards proved) to the effect, that the Spaniards had on this day conspired to kill all the Americans on the river. In a few moments, however, the latter rallied and made a rush at the murderer, who immediately plunged into the river and swam across to Missouri Bar; eight or ten shots were fired at him while in the water, not one of which hit him. He ran like an antelope across the flat, swam thence to Smith's Bar, and escaped by the road leading out of the mountains, from the Junction. Several men went in pursuit of him, but he was not taken, and without doubt, is now safe in Mexico.

In the meanwhile, the consternation was terrific. The Spaniards, who, with the exception of six or eight, knew no more of the affair than I did, thought that the Americans had arisen against them; and our own countrymen equally ignorant, fancied the same of the foreigners. About twenty of the latter, who were either sleeping or reading in their cabins at the time of the *emeute*, aroused by the cry of "Down with the Spaniards!" barricaded themselves in a drinking-saloon, determined to defend themselves as long as possible, against the massacre, which was fully expected would follow this appalling shout. In the bake-shop, which stands next door to our cabin, young Tom Somers lay straightened for the grave, (he lived but fifteen minutes after he was wounded,) while over his dead body a Spanish woman, was weeping and moaning in the most piteous and heart-rending manner.

The Rich Barians, who had heard a most exaggerated account of the rising of the Spaniards against the Americans, armed with rifles, pistols, clubs, dirks, etc., were rushing down the hill by hundreds. Each one added fuel to his rage, by crowding into the little bakery, to gaze upon the blood-bathed bosom of the victim, yet warm with the life, which but an hour before it had so triumphantly worn. Then arose the most fearful shouts of "Down with the Spaniards!" "Drive every foreigner off the river!" "Don't let one of the murderous devils remain." "Oh, if you have a drop of American blood in your veins, it must cry out for vengeance upon the cowardly assassins of poor Tom." All this, mingled with the most horrible oaths and execrations, yelled up, as if in mockery, into that smiling heaven, which in its fair Sabbath calm, bent unmoved over the hell which was raging below.

After a time, the more sensible and sober part of the community succeeded in quieting, in a partial degree, the enraged and excited multitude. During the whole affair I had remained perfectly calm, in truth, much more so than I am now, when recalling it. The entire catastrophe had been so unexpected, and so sudden in its consummation, that I fancy I was stupefied into the most exemplary good behavior. F. and several of his friends, taking advantage of the lull in the storm, came into the cabin and entreated me to join the two women who were living on the hill. At this time, it seemed to be the general opinion, that there would be a serious fight, and they said I might be wounded accidentally, if I remained on the Bar. As I had no fear of anything of the kind, I plead hard to be allowed to stop, but when told that my presence would increase the anxiety of our friends, of course, like a dutiful wife, I went on to the hill.

We three women, left entirely alone, seated ourselves upon a log, overlooking the strange scene below. The Bar was a sea of heads, bristling with guns, rifles and clubs. We could see nothing, but fancied from the apparent quiet of the crowd, that the miners were taking measures to investigate the sad event of the day. All at once, we were startled by the firing of a gun, and the next moment, the crowd dispersing, we saw a man led into the log cabin, while another was carried, apparently lifeless, into a Spanish drinking-saloon, from one end of which, were burst off instantly several boards, evidently to give air to the wounded person. Of course, we were utterly unable to imagine what had happened; and to all our perplexity and anxiety, one of the ladies insisted upon believing that it was her own husband who had been shot, and as she is a very nervous woman, you can fancy our distress. It was in vain to tell her—which we did over and over again—that that worthy individual wore a *blue* shirt, and the wounded person a *red* one; she doggedly insisted that her dear M. had been shot, and having informed us confidentially and rather inconsistently that "she should never see him again, never, never," plumped herself down upon the log in an attitude of calm and ladylike despair, which would have been infinitely amusing, had not the occasion been so truly a fearful one. Luckily for our nerves, a benevolent individual, taking pity upon our loneliness, came and told us what had happened.

It seems that an Englishman, the owner of a house of the vilest description, a person, who is said to have been the primary cause of all the troubles of the day, attempted to force his way through the line of armed men which had been formed at each side of the street. The guard very properly refused to let him pass. In his drunken fury, he tried to wrest a gun from one of them, which being accidentally discharged in the struggle, inflicted a severe wound upon a Mr. Oxley, and shattered in the most dreadful manner the thigh of Señor Pizarro, a man of high birth and breeding, a *porteño* of Buenos Ayres. This frightful accident recalled the people to their senses, and they began to act a little less like madmen, than they had previously done. They elected a Vigilance Committee, and authorized persons to go to the Junction and arrest the suspected Spaniards.

The first act of the Committee was to try a *Mejicana*, who had been foremost in the fray. She has always worn male attire, and on this occasion, armed with a pair of pistols, she fought like a very fury. Luckily, inexperienced in the use of fire-arms, she wounded no one. She was sentenced to leave the Bar by day-light, a perfectly just decision, for there is no doubt that she is a regular little demon. Some went so far as to say, she ought to be hung, for she was the *indirect* cause of the fight. You see always, it is the old, cowardly excuse of Adam in Paradise: "The *woman* tempted me, and I did eat." As if the poor, frail head, once so pure and beautiful, had not sin enough of its own, dragging it forever downward, without being made to answer for the wrong-doing of a whole community of men.

The next day, the Committee tried five or six Spaniards, who were proven to have been the ringleaders in the Sabbath-day riot. Two of them were sentenced to be whipped, the remainder to leave the Bar that evening; the property of all to be confiscated to the use of the wounded persons. Oh Mary! Imagine my anguish when I heard the first blow fall upon those wretched men. I had never thought that I should be compelled to hear such fearful sounds, and, although I immediately buried my head in a shawl, nothing can efface from memory the disgust and horror of that moment. I had heard of such things, but heretofore had not realized, that in the nineteenth century, men could be beaten like dogs, much less that other men, not only could sentence such barbarism, but could actually stand by and see their own manhood degraded in such disgraceful manner. One of these unhappy persons was a very gentlemanly young Spaniard, who implored for death in the most moving terms. He appealed to his judges in the most eloquent manner—as gentlemen, as men of honor; representing to them that to be deprived of life, was nothing in comparison with the never-to-be-effaced stain of the vilest convict's punishment—to which they had sentenced him. Finding all his entreaties disregarded, he swore a most solemn oath, that he would murder every American that he should chance to meet alone, and as he is a man of the most dauntless courage, and rendered desperate by a burning sense of disgrace, which will cease only with his life, he will doubtless keep his word.

Although in my very humble opinion and in that of others more competent to judge of such matters than myself, these sentences were unnecessarily severe, yet so great was the rage and excitement of the crowd, that the Vigilance Committee could do no less. The mass of the mob demanded fiercely the death of the prisoners, and it was evident that many of the Committee took side with the people. I shall never forget how horror-struck I was (bombastic as it *now* sounds) at hearing no less a personage than the Whig candidate for representative say, "that the condemned had better fly for their lives, for the Avenger of Blood was on their tracks!" I am happy to say, that said very worthy, but sanguinary individual, "The Avenger of Blood!" represented in this case by some half dozen gambling rowdies, either changed his mind or lost scent of his prey; for the intended victims slept about two miles up the hill, quite peacefully until morning.

The following facts, elicited upon the trial, throw light upon this unhappy affair: Seven miners from Old Spain, enraged at the cruel treatment which their countrymen had received on the "Fourth," and at the illiberal cry of "Down with the Spaniards," had united for the purpose of taking revenge on seven Americans whom they believed to be the originators of their insults. All well armed, they came from the Junction, where they were residing at the time, intending to challenge each one his man, and in fair fight, compel their insolent aggressors to answer for the arrogance which they had exhibited more than once towards the Spanish race. Their first move on arriving at Indian Bar was to go and dine at the Humboldt, where they drank a most enormous quantity of champagne and claret. Afterwards, they proceeded to the house of the Englishman, whose brutal carelessness caused the accident which wounded Pizarro and Oxley, when one of them commenced a playful conversation with one of his countrywomen. This enraged the Englishman, who instantly struck the Spaniard a violent blow, and ejected him from the shanty. Thereupon ensued a spirited fight, which, through the exertion of a gentleman from Chili, a favorite with both nations, ended without bloodshed. This person knew nothing of the intended duel, or he might have prevented, by his wise counsels, what followed. Not suspecting for a moment anything of the kind, he went to Rich Bar. Soon after he left, Tom Somers, who is said always to have been a dangerous person when in liquor, without any apparent provocation, struck Domingo, (one of the original seven) a violent blow, which nearly felled him to the earth. The latter, a man of "dark antecedents" and the most reckless character, mad with wine, rage and revenge, without an instant's pause, drew his knife and inflicted a fatal wound upon his insulter. Thereupon followed the chapter of accidents which I have related.

On Tuesday following the fatal Sabbath, a man brought the news of the murder of a Mr. Bacon, a person well known on the river, who kept a ranch about twelve miles from Rich Bar. He was killed for his money, by his servant, a negro, who not three months ago was our own cook. He was the last one anybody would have suspected capable of such an act.

A party of men, appointed by the Vigilance Committee, left the Bar immediately in search of him. The miserable wretch was apprehended in Sacramento and part of the gold found upon his person. On the following Sunday he was brought in chains to Rich Bar. After a trial by the miners, he was sentenced to be hung at four o'clock in the evening. All efforts to make him confess proved futile. He said, very truly, that whether innocent or guilty, they would hang him; and so he "died and made no sign," with a calm indifference, as the novelists say, "worthy of a better cause." The dreadful crime and death of "Josh," who having been an excellent cook, and very neat and respectful, was a favorite servant with us, added to the unhappiness which you can easily imagine that I was suffering under all these horrors.

On Saturday evening about eight o'clock, as we sat quietly conversing with the two ladies from the hill—who, by the way, we found very agreeable additions to our society, hitherto composed entirely of gentlemen—we were startled by the loud shouting, and rushing close by the door of the cabin, which stood open, of three or four hundred men. Of course, we feminines, with nerves somewhat shattered from the events of the past week, were greatly alarmed.

We were soon informed that Henry Cook, *vice* "Josh" had, in a fit of delirium tremens, cut his throat from ear to ear. The poor wretch was alone when he committed the desperate deed, and in his madness, throwing the bloody razor upon the ground, he ran part of the way up the hill. Here he was found almost senseless, and brought back to the Humboldt, where he was very nearly the cause of hanging poor "Paganini Ned"—who returned a few weeks since from the valley,—for his first act on recovering himself, was to accuse that culinary individual of having attempted to murder him. The mob were for hanging our poor "Vatel" without judge or jury, and it was only through the most strenuous exertions of his friends, that the life of this illustrious person was saved. Poor Ned! It was forty-eight hours before his cork-screws returned to their original graceful curl; he threatens to leave us to our barbarism and no longer to waste his culinary talents upon an ungrateful and inappreciative people. He has sworn "war to the knife" against Henry, who was formerly his most intimate friend, as nothing can persuade him that the accusation did not proceed from the purest malice on the part of the suicide.

Their majesties the mob, with that beautiful consistency which usually distinguishes those august individuals, insisted upon shooting poor Harry— for said they, and the reasoning is remarkably conclusive and clear, "a man so hardened as to raise his hand against his *own* life, will never hesitate to murder another!" They almost mobbed F. for binding up the wounds of the unfortunate wretch and for saying that it was possible he might live. At last, however, they compromised the matter, by determining, that if Henry should recover, he should leave the Bar immediately. Neither contingency will probably take place, as it will be almost a miracle if he survives.

On the day following the attempted suicide, which was Sunday, nothing more exciting happened than a fight and the half-drowning of a drunken individual in the river, just in front of the Humboldt.

On Sunday last, the thigh of Señor Pizarro was amputated; but alas, without success. He had been sick for many months with chronic dysentery, which after the operation returned with great violence, and he died at two o'clock on Monday morning with the same calm and lofty resignation which had distinguished him during his illness. When first wounded, believing his case hopeless, he had decidedly refused to submit to amputation, but as time wore on he was persuaded to take this one chance for his life, for the sake of his daughter, a young girl of fifteen, at present at school in a convent in Chili, whom his death leaves without any near relation. I saw him several times during his illness, and it was melancholy indeed, to hear him talk of his motherless girl who, I have been told, is extremely beautiful, talented and accomplished.

The state of society here has never been so bad as since the appointment of a Committee of Vigilance. The rowdies have formed themselves into a company called the "Moguls," and they parade the streets all night, howling, shouting, breaking into houses, taking wearied miners out of their beds and throwing them into the river, and in short, "murdering sleep," in the most remorseless manner. Nearly every night they build bonfires fearfully near some rag shanty, thus endangering the lives, (or I should rather say the property—for as it is impossible to sleep, lives are emphatically safe) of the whole community. They retire about five o'clock in the morning; previously to this blessed event posting notices to that effect, and that they will throw any one who may disturb them into the river. I am nearly worn out for want of rest, for truly they "make night hideous" with their fearful uproar. Mr. O——, who still lies dangerously ill from the wound received, on what we call the "fatal Sunday," complains bitterly of the disturbance; and when poor

Pizarro was dying, and one of his friends gently requested that they would be quiet for half an hour and permit the soul of the sufferer to pass in peace, they only laughed and yelled and hooted louder than ever, in the presence of the departing spirit, for the tenement in which he lay, being composed of green boughs only, could of course shut out no sounds. Without doubt if the "Moguls" had been sober, they would never have been guilty of such horrible barbarity as to compel the thoughts of a dying man to mingle with curses and blasphemies; but alas! they were intoxicated, and may God forgive them, unhappy ones, for they knew not what they did. The poor, exhausted miners, for even well people cannot sleep in such a pandemonium, grumble and complain, but they—although far outnumbering the rioters—are too timid to resist. All say "it is shameful; something ought to be done; something *must* be done," etc. and in the meantime the rioters triumph. You will wonder that the Committee of Vigilance does not interfere; it is said that some of that very Committee are the ringleaders among the "Moguls."

I believe I have related to you everything but the duel—and I will make the recital of this as short as possible, for I am sick of these sad subjects, and doubt not but you are the same. It took place on Tuesday morning at eight o'clock, on Missouri Bar, when and where that same Englishman who has figured so largely in my letter, shot his best friend. The duelists were surrounded by a large crowd, I have been told, foremost among which stood the Committee of Vigilance! The man who received his dear friend's fatal shot, was one of the most quiet and peaceable citizens on the Bar. He lived about ten minutes after he was wounded. He was from Ipswich, England, and only twenty-five years of age, when his own high passions snatched him from life. In justice to his opponent, it must be said, that he would willingly have retired after the first shots had been exchanged, but poor Billy Leggett, as he was familiarly called, insisted upon having the distance between them shortened, and continuing the duel until one of them had fallen.

There, my dear M., have I not fulfilled my promise of giving you a dish of horrors? And only think of such a shrinking, timid, frail thing, as I *used* to be "long time ago," not only living right in the midst of them, but almost compelled to hear if not see the whole. I think that I may without vanity affirm, that I have "seen the elephant." "Did you see his tail?" asks innocent Ada J., in her mother's letter. Yes, sweet Ada, the "entire Animal" has been exhibited to my view. "But you must remember, that this is California," as the new comers are so fond of informing *us*! who consider ourselves "one of the oldest inhabitants" of the golden State.

And now dear M., *A Dios*. Be thankful that you are living in the beautiful quiet of beautiful A., and give up "hankering arter" (as you know what dear creature says—) California, for believe me, this coarse, barbarous life would suit you, even less than it does your sister.

WILL IRWIN

Old Chinatown

FROM the moment when you crossed the golden, dimpling bay, whose moods ran the gamut of beauty, from the moment when you sailed between those brown-and-green headlands which guarded the Gate to San Francisco, you heard always of Chinatown. It was the first thing which the tourist asked to see, the first thing which the guides offered to show. Whenever, in any channel of the Seven Seas, two world-wanderers met and talked about the city of Many Adventures, Chinatown ran like a thread through their reminiscences. Raised on a hillside, it glimpsed at you from every corner of that older, more picturesque San Francisco which fell to dust and cinders in the great disaster of 1906. From the cliffs which crowned the city, one could mark it off as a sombre spot, shot with contrasting patches of green and gold, in the panorama below. Its inhabitants, overflowing into the American quarters, made bright and quaint the city streets. Its examplars of art in common things, always before the unillumined American, worked to make San Francisco the city of artists that she was. For him who came but to look and to enjoy, this was the real heart of San Francisco, this bit of the mystic, suggestive East, so modified by the West that it was neither Oriental nor yet Occidental—but just Chinatown.

It is gone now—gone with the sea-gray city which encircled it. The worse order changeth, giving place to better; but there is always so much in the worse order which our hearts would have kept! In a newer and stronger San Francisco rises a newer, cleaner, more healthful Chinatown. Better for the city—O yes—and better for the Chinese, who must come to modern ways of life and health if they are to survive among us. But where is St. Louis Alley, that tangle of sheds, doorways, irregular arcades and flaming signs which fell into the composition of such a marvelous picture? Where is the dim reach of Ross Alley, that romantically mysterious cleft in the city's walls? Where is Fish Alley, that horror to the nose, that perfume to the eye? Where are those broken, dingy streets, in which the Chinese made art of rubbish?

I hope that some one will arise, before this generation is passed, to record that conquest of affection by which the Californian Chinese transformed themselves from our race-adversaries to our dear, subject people.

Theirs will be all the glory of that tale, ours all the shame. In the dawn of the mining rush, the little, trading Cantonese began to appear in California. The American, the Celt, the Frenchman came for gold—gold washed out of the hills—uncounted millions. Gold brought the Chinaman also; but his ideas were modest. The prospect of two, four, five dollars a day was enough for him, who had made only ten cents a day at home. He asked simply to do menial work at a menial's wage. Beside our white pioneers, he took his part in the glorious episode of the Pacific conquest. He, with them, starved on the desert, died on the trails, faced Indian bullets and arrows. Wherever the report of gold called into being a new camp, he struggled in behind the whites, built his laundry, his cook-house or his gold rocker, girded up his pig-tail, and went to work. In his own spirit of quiet heroism, he shared all the hardships of our giant men—shared in everything they held except for dissipations and their reward of glory. For glory, he had to wait half a century.

That curious, black episode of early Western civilization, the Chinese persecution, followed hard upon their first arrival. Why this thing began, what quality in the Chinese nature irritated our pioneers beyond all justice and sense of decency, remains a little dim and uncomprehended to this generation. They were an honest people—honest beyond our strictest ideas. They attended to their own business and did not interfere with ours. Their immoralities, their peculiar and violent methods of adjusting social differences, affected only themselves. Not for thirty years was there reason for believing them a danger to American working-men. But the fact remains. Our pioneers cut off their sacred pig-tails, cast them forth disgraced, beat them, lynched them. Professional agitators made them a stock in trade. By the power of reiteration, this honest people came to figure in the public mind as a race of thieves, this cleanly people—inventors of the daily bath—as "dirty" and "diseased," this heroic people, possessed of a passive fortitude beside which our stoicism is cowardice, as poltroons. With a dignity all their own, they suffered and went about their business, though death lay at the end.

The day came when the Chinese themselves nearly justified the professional labor agitator. The romantic, unsettled period of the gold rush passed into history; the age of bonanza farming followed; the state buckled down to stable industry. But two and three and five dollars a day was still a lure to the Canton man. Their number increased with every Pacific steamer. Even yet they were no real menace to American labor—the state at any time might have swallowed up fifty thousand more without harming a single white workingman—but that menace lifted itself in the immediate future. Ripples from the black Dennis Kearney outrages, the shameful Montana massacres, reached Washington. Congress passed the Exclusion Law. When that happened, there vanished the last logical objection to the Californian Chinese.

A gradual change passed over the spirit of California. We were a long time learning that human souls, different but equal, souls softened by forty centuries of highly moral civilization, lay under those yellow skins, under those bizarre customs and beliefs. The Chinaman, being a gentleman, gives himself forth but charily. I think that we first glimpsed the real man through our gradual understanding of his honesty. American merchants learned that none need ever ask a note of a Chinaman in any commercial transaction. His word is his bond. Precedent, as well as race characteristic, makes it so.

The newer generation of Californians grew up with baby-loving, devoted Chinese servants about them. The Sons and Daughters of the Golden West did not, indeed, draw their first sustenance from yellow breasts, as the Southerner has drawn it from black ones. That mystic bond was lacking. But a Chinese man-servant had watched at the cradle above most of them, rejoiced with the parents that there was a baby in the house, laughed to see it laugh, hurried like a mother at its cry. A backyard picture in any of the old Californian mansions included always the Chinese cook, grinning from the doorway on the playing babies.

This Chinese cook was a volunteer nurse; for him, the nursery was heart of the house. He was the consoler and fairy-teller of childhood. He passed on to the babies his own wonder tales of flowered princesses and golden dragons, he taught them to patter in sing-song Cantonese, he saved his frugal nickels to buy them quaint little gifts; and as the better Southerner, despising the race, loves the individual negro through this very association of childhood, so the Californian came to love the Chinaman that he knew. In his ultimate belief, indeed, he outstripped the Southerner; for he came first to a tolerance of the race and then to an admiration.

. . . On the night which I am recalling, a certain observation upon the Chinese crystallized in my mind. Out of his mental difference from us, his oblique thinking as contrasted with our straight reasoning, his subtlety as contrasted with our directness, his commercial honesty as contrasted with our comparative commercial dishonor, his gentility as contrasted with our rudeness; further, out of our wholly unnecessary persecution and race hatred, he has come to a superior contempt of us and our ways. Certain broad spirits among them look across the race line and regard us as human beings; certain humble personages among them, such as the old family retainers whom I have mentioned already, develop a curious, dog-like affection. But in the main, they feel a passive contempt. We were to them a medium of commerce when we stopped at the stores to buy, meddlers when we interfered with lotteries, fan-tan games, plague, highbinder wars and other affairs which were none of our business, plain pests when we swept down upon them with uniforms and patrol wagons, but always Things—never persons. You passed them on the streets; they turned out for you; but they glanced at you no more than they glanced at the innumerable sleek cats sunning themselves in the doorways. You might pick a specially beautiful or interesting Chinaman and stare at him all day; he would notice you no more than a post—unless you pulled a camera on him. A Chinese father would, indeed, soften if you stopped to pay court to the baby in his arms; it was too much to expect that he would refuse tribute from anything in the earth below or the air above to the pride of his heart and the hope of his immortal salvation. That, it seemed to me, was the only point at which your Chinese willingly granted intercourse to the despised race.

But on that night, when the punk-sticks and the pocket altars burned at every corner and before every sweet-meat stand, when all the alleys were canopied over for the use of the priests, when every window glowed soft from the sacrificial lights within; on that night, when horror and mystery held the air—then you paid court to no Chinese baby. Approach him, and his father drew him sharply away; persist, and his bearer would hurry off on his slipping, high-soled shoes in panicky run. Pidgin English brought no answer to your most polite inquiries. The children imitated their elders; the big brother or sister, caring for little Ah Wu or tiny Miss Peach Blossom of the lily feet, scattered fearfully from the foreign touch. We, inferior, incomprehending, were brothers to the powers of the air. Only this I noticed— your money was still welcome at the stores. Perhaps it was right to take devil tribute.

It seems that there is no Lent, no Day of Atonement, in the Chinese calendar. All religious festivals are also feast days. Even on that night, men turned from fighting the devils to make holiday. Every restaurant held its banquet, every wealthy home its reception.

What is it which makes one picture of life linger in memory while others, and more marvelous ones, fade out? As vivid as though its bright impression was still dancing on my retina, I remember a dinner party which I saw that night. Perhaps I had with me a friend, whose identity is the one thing which has gone from me, but whose strong and stimulating pull on my mind lingers in this rise of memory to a permanent thing; perhaps that was one of those nights of youth when the world is right and life dances down before you, and all your powers are multiplied by some golden number of the gods. At any rate this picture remains, while greater and brighter things linger only as blurred outlines.

It was on the top floor of the old Man Far Low Restaurant on Dupont street, a show place it is true, but also the great café of the rich and dissolute. That floor, running clear through the block, was a succession of private dining rooms, divided one from the other by pictured, scroll-work screens. Carved woods and painted lanterns decked the walls; the tables were of black teak, delicately and minutely inlaid. The guests sat not on chairs, but upon square stools of the same teak wood. From the front apartment, you stepped out upon a balcony made into a little Chinese garden. This looked upon the dark stretch of Dupont street. At the rear was another balcony, a small, undecorated thing; and from that you saw first Portsmouth Square with its gilded caravel set to remember Robert Louis Stevenson; further on the city buildings, topped by the masts and spars of Adventure Ships in from Pacific voyagings; and still further the golden delights of the great bay. One who came to enjoy the Man Far Low must buy at least tea and sweet-meats. The tea, poured from the crack between two bowls, one inverted over the other, was of a light lemon yellow, and in taste no more than hot water slightly flavored by an aromatic herb. Color and taste were deceptive; it would kill sleep for a night. One ate the sweetmeats—picked ginger, preserved nuts, plums and citron—from the end of a spindly tin fork. When the guest had finished, the waiter stood at the head of the stairs and bawled something in Cantonese. That was the check; the cashier, sitting in round cap and horn spectacles at the desk below, knew by it how much to collect.

That night, however, the Chinese occupied it; a great, expensive dinner, costing its tens of dollars a plate, was proceeding in the front apartment. At the biggest table sat a dozen Chinese men-about-town, very dignified as to dress, for they wore the long, silk tunic of ravishing neutral tint which is dress coat and a frock coat both to a Chinese gentleman. With each man sat his woman—not at the table, but just behind, so that she had to reach caressingly over his shoulder to get at the hundred viands in their toy porcelain bowls. When her lord's appetite failed, she fed him with her plaything hands; when he wanted a cigarette, she lighted it for him between her own rouged lips. One of these women, I remember, had a homely, irregular face, with a broad mouth, but with an illumination and expression in her features exceptional among Chinese women—they tend to the brain-less, doll type. A soubrette sauciness showed in her every gesture, but you felt that it was a measured impudence which knew its convenient bounds. Musicians, squatted on a woven straw couch in the corner, were tormenting a moon fiddle, a sam yin and a gong. In the rests of that sound, which I shall not call music, she would lean forward and throw out a remark; and the company, already a little gone with rice brandy, would laugh mightily.

Presently, the feast having reached the stage when food is less to the feaster than drink, they began to play "one-two." I must explain that game, so simple and so appealing to the convivial. You challenge a partner. If he accepts, you throw out from your closed hand any number of fingers from one to four and call off in a loud tone of voice the proper number of fingers.

He throws out the same number of fingers and calls the number after you. But at last you call out, craftily, any one number, and throw out a different number of fingers. And if, by calling that number after you, he shows that he has failed to watch your hand, he has lost; and he must drink a cup of rice brandy as a forfeit. He who first becomes drunk is "it." It goes faster and faster, until all the table is playing it in pairs. "Sam!" "Sam!" "See!" "See!" "Yee!" "Yee!" "Sam!" "Sam!" Then a howl of Oriental laughter, more crackling and subdued than ours; for the proponent, on "Sam" (three) has thrown forward only two fingers, and the opponent, falling into the trap, has thrown out three. So he is caught, and down his throat goes the forfeit.

And as they drank and played, and played and drank, something deep below the surface came out in them. Their shouts became squalls; lips drew back from teeth, beady little eyes blazed; their very cheek bones seemed to rise higher on their faces. I thought as I watched of wars of the past; these were not refined Cantonese, with a surface gentility and grace in life greater than anything that our masses know; they were those old yellow people with whom our fathers fought before the Caucusus was set as a boundary between the dark race and the light; the hordes of Ghengis Khan; the looters of Atilla.

The "its" fell out one by one, retired with some dignity to the straw couch and to sleep. She of the saucy, illuminated face crept close to her lord and whispered in his ear—she, like all her kind, was taking the moment of intoxication to ply her business; and the debauch was nearly over. Only when I was out on the street, and purged somewhat from the impression of Tartar fierceness which that game of "one-two" had given me, did this come into my mind: there had been not one unseemly or unlovely act in all that debauch of young bloods and soiled women, not one over-familiar gesture. Tartar though they had shown themselves, they had remained still Chinese gentlemen and—may I say it of women in their class?—Chinese ladies.

These pretty and painted playthings of men furnished a glimpse into Frank Norris's Third Circle, the underworld. We shall never quite understand the Chinese, I suppose; and not the least comprehensible thing about them is the paradox of their ideas and emotions. On the anomalies of Chinese courage, for example, one might write a whole treatise. A Chinese pursued by a mob never fights back. He lies down and takes his beating with his lips closed. If he is able to walk when it is done, he moves away with a fine, gentlemanly scorn for his tormentors. To take another instance; at Steveston, in the mouth of the Frazer River, the white and Indian fisherman struck. The owners, supported by the Canadian militia, decided to man the boats with Oriental cannery laborers. The Japanese jumped at the chance. The Chinese, to a man, refused to go out on the river. They were afraid of it. Yet a Chinese merchant condemned to death by the highbinders, aware that the stroke may come at any time from any alley, walks his accustomed way through the streets without looking to right or left. So it goes, all through their characters. Nothing fits our rules.

By the same token, underneath their essential courtesy, fruit of an old civilization, underneath their absolute commercial honor, underneath their artistic appreciation of the grace in life, runs a hard, wild streak of barbarism, an insensibility in cruelty, which, when roused, is as cold-blooded and unlovely a thing as we know.

Chinatown, the Tenderloin for all the Western Chinese, lived not only by tea and rice and overalls and cigars and tourists, but also by the ministry to dissipation. It had gathered to itself the tough citizens, and especially the gamblers. Gambling is a darling sin to all the race; take his fan-tan counters and his pie-gow blocks away, and he will bet on the number of seeds in an uncut orange. With most, it is a mere diversion. Your efficient, quiet houseboy, no more trouble about the place than a well ordered cat, will go into Chinatown on Saturday night, have his little whirl at fan-tan, smoke, perhaps, his one pipe of opium, and return in the morning none the worse for his social diversion. Others get the passion of it into their blood. One hears continually of this or that Chinese laborer, who, having saved for fifteen years to go back to China and live on his income, has dropped into a fan-tan house on the eve of his departure, lost his whole pile in one night, and returned, with a great surface indifference, to begin a life of service over again. Fat and powerful waxed the keepers of gambling houses. They came to be controlling factors in the vicious side of Chinatown; and they gathered under them all the priests of vice into one alliance of crime and graft. Those who traded in slave girls, those who ran the cheap, internicine politics of the ward, those who lived by blackmail, and especially those gentlemen of fortune known as highbinders, whose reason for being was paid murder, lived and moved in the shadow of the gambling game.

. . . Doubtless I am following here the newspaper fashion and dwelling too much upon this criminal aspect of the Quarter. If so, it is because the crime was so picturesque, because it expressed so clearly the difference of this civilization from its parent Orient and its adopted Occident. I am not quite done with it, either, for I must speak of the slave trade.

The world knows from Christian missionaries how little the careless and criminal, among the Chinese at home, value a girl baby. The sale of such children is an established custom—born of the low esteem in which women are held and of the terrible Chinese famines. Those Californian Chinese, who were degraded enough to stoop to such things, sold these babies into pure shame and the ruin of souls. So small was the supply, owing to the difficulty of smuggling women past Federal inspection, that prices were high; it paid a coolie woman to bear female children. A girl four years old, past the delicate stage of infancy, would bring from fifteen hundred to two thousand dollars as a speculation. At thirteen or fourteen, when she was of age to begin making returns to her owner, her price was three thousand. Slavery it was, literal and hopeless; and that in face of the Fourteenth Amendment. The Federal authorities tried to break it up. Pretty generally, they failed. The trouble lay in the Chinese contempt for our courts. Snatch a girl from a brothel, and what happened? A slave from babyhood, kept in ignorance of any other world than that of her brothel, she believed the word of her keeper when he said that white men want girls only to pickle their eyes and eat their brains. First, one must win her from that idea. Then, the master would always bring action in the courts through certain white attorneys unscrupulous enough to take such cases. Chinese witnesses would be found to go upon the stand and swear that this girl was a daughter or niece of the master; and the poor girl, the moment she faced her master in court, would fall into the cowed custom of a lifetime, quail before his eye, and swear falsely that these witnesses told the truth—that she wanted to go back to her "uncle." This system, shameful in our eyes—though indeed there are institutions just as cold-blooded and evil in our own social structure—existed from the first day of Chinatown; exists, I make no doubt, to-day.

From a woman, and she a pretty, fair-spoken Scotch maiden, this slave trade took its hardest blow. Donaldine Cameron was a girl stripling of twenty when she came to take charge of the Presbyterian Mission, which concerns itself especially with the lives and souls of Chinese women. She says herself that she inherited her tastes and talents from a line of Scotch parsons grafted on a line of sheep-stealing Camerons. The spirit in her led her straight to the slave trade. First, as all her predecessors had done, she tried the police and the courts. She found the police inefficient or venal, the courts ineffective. She saw girl after girl, who had welcomed rescue in the beginning, crumple up on the witness stand and swear herself back into Hell.

Nevertheless, Miss Cameron kept on, raiding and fighting in the courts. In a warfare of ten years, she won a kind of Fabian victory. She usually lost her girl in the end, but before that end she had cost the owner dear in smashed doors, valuable property kept idle, disturbance of business, and the heavy fees which cheap white attorneys used to exact from the Chinese. Playing her desperate lone hand, she reduced the traffic by about one-half.

Our lives in old San Francisco were all tinged a little with romance; but I can think of no life among us which so quivered with adventure as hers. Would that I could convey the quaint, workaday style in which this soncy Scotch gentlewoman related her adventures—the material of a dime novel, the manner of a housewife telling about her marketing. During one raid, she met at the door of the brothel some unforeseen barrier which delayed the attack. As she waited for the axman, she looked through the latticed window upon a confusion of painted, flowered, Chinese women, all squalling together. From this group, a girl disentangled herself and came running, her arms outstretched, toward the raiders. It was the girl they had come to rescue; and by this fatal slip, born of over-eagerness, she revealed that she was first cause of the raid. The slave master perceived it, too; before Miss Cameron's eyes he knocked her down and dragged her by the hair through a sliding panel, which opened at his touch. When at last Miss Cameron gained entrance, she found a dozen passages leading confusingly from this secret door; the inmates had lost themselves in the Third Circle. She never saw that girl again; but months later the underground gossip of Chinatown brought Miss Cameron the end of the tale. The master, down there in the bowels of the earth, had beaten her to death in presence of his other cowering women.

This piece of artistic detail from another of her raids which failed: The inmates had rolled into a trap door under a bed, and escaped into the underworld. So orderly and so deserted was the place that she wondered, at first glance, whether she had not made a mistake. Then she noticed a samesin in the corner, and perceived that its strings still quivered and gave forth a dying sound—showing how recently it had dropped from the lily hands of the lily woman.

One of the slave girls in the mission was an orphan, sold as a baby; she had never known any life but that of the brothel. Neither had she any education save in certain primitive arts of woman, any religion except a superstitious fear of her masters. "If you escape from us down to Hell," they had told her, "we will drag you up by the hair. If you escape to Heaven, we will drag you down by the feet."

A certain man, a Christianized Chinese as it turned out later, used to visit that house. He singled out this girl, talked to her apart of the life outside, showed her that she was a slave and a prisoner, informed her of the white woman who lived only to rescue such as she.

"When he spoke of a white woman," said this girl, "I was much afraid, because they had told me that the whites were devils who wanted to get me just to eat my brains. Though I knew nothing different, I had always been discontented with my kind of life, and had been wishing for something else—I never knew what. After he went away from me, I thought about all this. I fell into such a melancholy and longing for the open world that I was ready to take my chances with the white woman being a witch. I could think of nothing but escape.

"When this man visited me again, I told him that I would trust the white woman. He advised me then to wear some secret token so that they might know whom to rescue; because if they failed, and my master knew that I had brought on the raid, they might abuse me afterward. We agreed on a lily-flower over my left ear. He told me also to fight and cry when they carried me away—"

Well, Miss Cameron smashed that door and snatched from the arms of her slave master the girl with the lily over her ear. All the way down the stairs, she kicked and fought; but when they got her alone in the carriage, she said: "Why didn't you come for me before?" This was one of the few girls who ever stood by her guns on the stand. She kept her freedom; and the last I heard of her she was getting ready to marry that Chinese who first told her about Miss Cameron.   [1908]

GERALD HASLAM

Sojourner

A FTERNOONS he liked to face the gradually lowering sun, to feel it smooth his ridged and canyoned face, soothe his sightless eyes. Lulled by its warmth, he registered shrill voices of children from the playground and allowed them to evoke the one shrill voice he'd not heard for more than half-a-century, that he could never again hear but would never cease listening for. Beyond, just over the levee, sucked the great river, the Sacramento. During such somnolent moments he imagined it was the mighty Shuang sweeping past.

So, so far away, all of it: his land, his life, his people, yet never deserted. He carried all within where he could often return, especially on long, warm afternoons.

He had traveled to this heathen land originally in search of the golden dream. Since his older brother had occupied their ancestral home when their parents died, Wing Nu had set out in search of his own best opportunities, first as a laboring peasant in the fields of others until great floods had destroyed crops and forced him to eke out subsistence cutting wood in Fukien's nearly denuded hills.

Tied to no man, he had been young, sinewy, and clever, clever enough to realize that his abilities would be wasted in Fukien unless nature itself changed dramatically, something he neither expected nor bothered to hope for. He could do any job and do it well, and he could both read and write a bit, but what was the point if work promised no improvement in his conditions?

He had heard, of course, of the mountains of gold across the sea. Rumors of great fortunes spread where poor men gathered, gossip of kinsmen who had migrated and, within a week, gathered enough gold to return home rich beyond the dreams of the emperor. For a woodcutter, however, the very trip to the mountains of gold was hopelessly expensive.

Gnawing himself within, he had stalked the lanes of his village seeking a loan, but could arrange none. Then he had seen the posted sign: "Laborers wanted for California in the United States of America. There is much work. Food and housing supplied. Wages are generous. There is no slavery. You will be treated considerately. All is nice.

"The ship is going soon and will take all who can pay for their passage. Persons having property can have it sold for them by my agents or borrow money for passage against it from me. I cannot take security on your wife or children but if you are a good worker, I will loan you passage money which you repay from your wages in California.

"The ship is substantial and convenient."

The poster was signed "Ah Chang," and an address in Fuchou was listed below the name. Wing Nu read the poster to himself, then read it aloud to other men gathered around. He reread the part that began, "If you have no money. . . .," and the men gathered round him chattered excitedly. He had no money, but he was a good worker and an educated man. He would climb those mountains of gold.

Voices, voices, voices:

"What else could I do? Crops had failed and floods had ruined our field. There was no wood left to cut in the hills. What else could I do?"

Lu Ng, laborer, Sacramento, California, 1854

"I remember the mornings on the river at home, the sounds of women calling to one another, the laughter of children. I miss them most."

Ying Nu, laborer, Auburn, California, 1856

"My father sold me when I was nine. He had no choice."

Jade Ping, prostitute, San Francisco, California, 1858

From downstream the old man heard the hoarse hoot of a steamer's whistle and he strained his ears for the slap-slap of its wheel churning through the water. Before his eyes had dimmed he had much enjoyed pausing in his work to watch the large white ships that plied the Sacramento, and had been amused at the sometimes rude gestures and shouts passengers made at the lone man waving toward them from a field. These Americans, he had thought, so immature, so uncertain, so frightened.

Like the red-faced man who had confronted him at Silva's Bar on the Consumnes River. "I don't give a good goddamn what the law says," the

Yankee had growled to the constable, "I say when American miners quit, these goddamn chinks gotta quit too. They got no goddamn business workin' longer'n white men. It ain't natural!"

"Well," chuckled the constable, whose main occupation appeared to be avoiding mayhem to himself while breaking up fights, "seems like to me, Jake, it was you told me a Chinaman couldn't work as long or as hard as an American whenever these boys come to the diggin's. Said they was too little and weak and dumb. I recollect you sayin' how these little fellers'd burn out in no time."

Wing Nu stood impassively before the two men, lightly holding a spade. He understood enough of their difficult tongue to know he was in danger, and he was prepared to defend himself.

"I don't know why a bunch of goddamn Chinee pirates can come from nowheres and dig American gold and take it back to their king or who-the-hell-ever."

"These here little fellers all pay the foreign miners' tax, Jake. And look what they're scrubbin' dust from. Why you boys finished with this bar months ago, claimed it was played out." The constable's arm gestured at the pile of tailings on which the Chinese worked. "Hell, they're workin' second-hand gold."

"First-hand or second, the boys deputized me to come stop these damn chinks from workin' overtime and to make 'em observe the sabbath like Christians. Hell's fire, ain't no human bein' can work like these heathens. There's somethin' wrong with 'em. They don't have feelin's like normal folks. They ain't human, and we can't have 'em workin' when we ain't."

The constable rocked on his heels. "Wellsir, I disremember you boys holdin' any church service on the sabbath."

The big man's neck swelled like a horned toad. "This ain't no damned joke! The new miners' law at Silva's Bar is that no goddamn chink works longer'n us Americans work or they'll all lose a hell of a lot more than their pigtails."

Still grinning, the constable had turned toward Wing Nu, who acted as captain of the Fukinese miners. "You heard 'im, Chinaman. No more work until I say so." Wing had merely nodded, his gaze straight and unblinking. He had to acquiesce but he did not want these Americans to think they intimidated him. In fact, they reminded him of a Northern Chinese he had met on the boat to California. The man, expensively dressed and traveling on the upper deck, had spat that Wing and the other Fukinese were barbarians and had laughed at their plight. When the Northerner's remark was translated for him, Wing had struck the man. These Yankees, however, were too numerous and too well armed, so Wing Nu kept his counsel.

Three weeks later, carrying only what they could secret on their persons, all 71 Fukinese miners were driven from Silva's Bar by a mob of drunken heathens. The volunteer fire department marching band and drum corps had accompanied the grim procession, and their presence probably saved many Chinese lives, for the music lightened the mood of the drunken Yankees, who contented themselves with cutting queues and a few slaps and punches to keep Wing Nu and his friends moving.

Voices, voices, voices:

"We had saved enough so that all four of us could return to Canton rich men, but a Yankee bandit stole it from us in broad daylight. When we complained to the sheriff, he laughed."

Yu Wang, laborer, Reno, Nevada, 1866

"They are in many respects a disgusting element of the population but not wholly unprofitable."

Editorial, **Record-Avalanche**, Silver City, Idaho, June 23, 1867

"No one bothered me, except when they were drunk. Most people left me alone, and I avoided them. I became a Christian."

Au Li, herbalist, Mariposa, California, 1871

From the labor contractor's office across the street, the old man heard voices of laborers returning from the fields, piling from wagons in mid-afternoon, then drifting in small groups toward saloons or camps or the park where Wing Nu rested. Many of them spoke tongues he did not understand—Spanish, Portuguese, Italian—and they smelled unlike the people he knew well. But he did understand their toil and their fatigued relief at the workday's end.

Despite the congratulations and cries of envy from other Fukinese laborers, there had been little triumph in Wing Nu's step that first morning following his return to Mr. Schmidt's farm outside Stockton. True, he had visited his small village in Fukien, a rare enough occurrence in itself. Moreover, he had married and sired a son there, the cause of great celebration among his fellows.

But a more harsh and immediate reality made it impossible for him to rejoice: he was back in California while his wife and son remained in China. One part of him acknowledged his good fortune, while another ached for his wife and little brown bundle he feared he would never again see.

At least he knew they would be well cared for. Each month he turned most of his wages over to the *hui kuan*, his clan, which in turn forwarded it to his village. The question of whether he would ever see his family again was entirely up to him. He would work. He would save. Some day he would return to his village a wealthy and respected man.

It would take a great fortune, though, to accomplish that, as he had learned on his first visit home. With nearly 1,500 American dollars he had saved or won gambling, Wing Nu had assumed he could return and remain. But his money had disappeared more quickly than he had imagined possible.

Conditions had changed and the entire country seemed to be run by soldiers and petty officials. He had been forced to pay-off a minor magistrate and the man's lackeys in order to leave the port. Then his aging uncle had to be rescued from bankruptcy. He loaned his older brother a substantial sum. When all was done, he had barely enough money left to marry, buy a small house, and provide for his family when he finally returned, far too soon, to the gambling halls and whore houses and opium dens of America.

Back in California, he knew his next fortune would come more slowly than his first. There was no more gold to be dug. He would now dig another man's vegetables or irrigate another man's fields. On the boat taking him from those he loved, he had fantasized that one day his son would join him and help accumulate wealth for the family.

That had only been a dream and, standing in the searing sunlight of a San Joaquin Valley morning, his comrades still teasing and praising him, everything and everywhere else seemed unreal. The ache in his loins was real, the ache in his heart was too. In front of him, heat waves shimmered from Mr. Schmidt's fields, and Wing Nu strode forward certain in his secret self that he would never see his wife and son again, not in this world anyway. That realization was his first death.

Voices, voices, voices:

"I liked working on the farm. It was good work, outdoors, with animals. If only my family could have been with me, then I could have been truly happy."

Lin Ho, laborer, Fresno City, California, 1879

"We cut through mountains for the railroad, chipping stone, blasting it, hauling it away. We spanned rivers. It was hard, but I was young and strong. Afterwards I was able to return home."

Pyau Ng, merchant, Kwantung, China, 1881

"They killed my brother and they tried to kill me. I was beaten. My queue was cut. I was stripped and my clothes were thrown into the stream. They left me to die, but I did not die."

Woo Soo, laborer, Rock Springs, Wyoming, 1885

Caught in a dragon's bowels, Wing struggled with the bulky sacks of laundry, sweating, almost unable to breathe. No longer young, the tough toil wearied him. His eyes had so dimmed that he could not do the farm work he preferred and, forced into this humid basement to earn a living, he could no longer hear birds sing or feel breeze on his skin. Another part of him died then.

Nonetheless, he toiled, struggling through hissing, grinding mechanical monsters. Through the bragging of fellow-workers, through the steam that seemed to enter and sap him, he labored. He was trapped in these bowels, but it had been the only job the *hui kuan* could arrange for him, and he had to work. That much was certain.

Each evening he bumped through crowded streets to the small alleyway cafe where Fukinese workers gathered to eat and talk about home, then he would move on to his tiny room, usually too exhausted to even read the newspaper the restaurateur saved for him each day. Less frequently, he would visit a fantan parlor, more for companionship than gambling. For the same reason he would occasionally patronize one of the bordellos so available in Chinatown. Somehow, even they brought little joy.

Although he had plenty of people to talk to in the city, plenty of people who could understand his feelings and hopes, he felt trapped here. All his life he had loved the outdoors. Now only once a week or so could he wander to the new park being built near the levee on the town's west edge and gaze across the river at the open land beyond. Those were the best times of all.

Voices, voices, voices:

"It is quite simple. We provide entertainment for lonely men. In exchange, we earn a profit. Occasionally we must protect our interests, but we are not violent men."

Lin Jay, Tong leader, San Francisco, California, 1893

"Cities are filthy, but what choice have I? I cannot operate my business without customers. Besides, I can speak a civilized tongue again here, and perhaps begin a family."

Yang Lee, laundryman, Los Angeles, California, 1899

"I am strongly of the opinion that, but for the presence of the Chinese, California would not now have more than one-half or two-thirds of her present population; Chinese labor has opened up many avenues and new industries for white labor, made many kinds of business possible."

Alva Griffin, State Senator, Sacramento, California, 1903

Meeting Mr. Reily had been one joy of his late years. Retired like himself, Reily also had no family and few friends, and he was also blind. Every sunny day, the old Irishman's servant deposited him on a bench in the town's square—it was there the old men met—and he would sun, chatting with Wing Nu as the outer heat fought their dimming inner fires, two travelers near journeys' end.

Each had trouble understanding the other at first, although both spoke English, "or so we thought," chuckled Mr. Reily. Both were immigrants—each regaling the other with tales of his youth, of strange green lands and long-dead friends—but Reily's fortune had been considerably better than Wing's: he owned a restaurant and a home and several rentals. Still, aging and alone save for his servant, ignored if not disdained except by those coveting his property, his emptiness was no less. For him, too, the golden dream had come to dust.

While Wing yearned for the wife and child he'd not touched for over fifty years, Reily—who'd never married, pined for a girl he'd left in Ireland half-a-century before, "gone dead in the convent these twenty-seven years," and for the children they'd never had. Rich or poor, loneliness was the same.

But the two men did not mire themselves in maudlin memories. Each having acknowledged the pain of estrangement, they found many lively topics to discuss, conversing through most afternoons, laughing frequently about episodes from their lives or those of others, debating points of religion or philosophy or politics, resolving nothing. It was the fray they enjoyed, the respect each paid the other's ideas. Those conversations were the liveliest moments either man experienced any more.

Passersby often noted with amusement the two old men who had never seen one another animatedly debating in near-incomprehensible accents the doctrine of Original Sin or farm labor practices. From a distance, in fact, it was difficult to notice their physical differences, and their tones revealed little.

Voices, voices, voices:

"No greater scourge in the history of mankind has been recorded. The heathen mongol must be stopped. He breeds like an animal and soon Christianity and Democracy will be dead. If the Chinaman is allowed to resume his invasion, the White Race faces mongrelization."

> Benjamin Franklin Burns, Congressman, Washington, D.C.
> October 9, 1906

"All we do is sit. No family here. Just as old men. Just us. I only hope to return home some day. Some day . . ."

> Ko Yip, retired, Seattle, Washington, 1914

"Edward, my son, returned home from school crying yesterday. He said a gang of bullies had chased him and called him 'Ching-chong Chinaman.' We're going to move to a better neighborhood."

> Mrs. Lin Chen, housewife, San Francisco, California, 1918

The aging man trudged the stairs to his room, resting every few steps, his breath seeming to grow shorter each day. Fumbling his key into the lock, Wing Nu snapped the door open, entered, then closed it. Evening had come. He felt the slight chill and heard the sounds of night begin to replace those of day, traps and carriages rattling by on the street below, and even a few automobiles.

He slumped to his bed and sat for several moments before stretching out. It had been a full day for an old man far away from home. Yet, and only fatigue prompted such a question, where was home? He had lived three-quarters of his life in California. He knew its rivers and fields better than he had ever known Fukien's. With his wife dead and his son disappeared, his only true friend remained here in Sacramento.

It was no question, really. America had tolerated and used Wing Nu; it had never accepted him. Only dreams of Fukien motivated him. He was Fukien: it dwelled within him, as tangible as the bed on which he rested, and soon his third death would free him from this tiny room, this alien town. Then the *hui kuan* would transport his body back home, to the soil that had given him life. Then, at last, he could rest.

Still, lying in darkness, nearly asleep, hearing familiar sounds from the street, smelling familiar odors, feeling a familiar breeze, it was difficult separating places, as though there were only one place with many names, one life with many journeys, and he—this weary sojourner—was about to begin another. [1983]

WARREN HINCKLE

A Social
History of the Hippies

A N ELDERLY SCHOOL BUS, painted like a fluorescent Easter egg in orange, chartreuse, cerise, white, green, blue, and, yes, black, was parked outside the solitary mountain cabin, which made it an easy guess that Ken Kesey, the novelist turned psychedelic Hotspur, was inside. So, of course, was Neal Cassady, the Tristram Shandy of the Beat Generation, prototype hero of Jack Kerouac's *On the Road*, who had sworn off allegiance to Kerouac when the beat scene became menopausal and signed up as the driver of Kesey's fun and games bus, which is rumored to run on LSD. Except for these notorious luminaries, the Summit Meeting of the leaders of the new hippie subculture, convened in the lowlands of California's High Sierras during an early spring weekend last month, seemed a little like an Appalachian Mafia gathering without Joe Bananas.

Where was Allen Ginsberg, father goddam to two generations of the underground? In New York, reading his poetry to freshmen. And where was Timothy Leary, self-styled guru to tens or is it hundreds of thousands of turned-on people? Off to some nowhere place like Stockton, to preach the gospel of Lysergic Acid Diethylamide to nice ladies in drip dry dresses.

The absence of the elder statesmen of America's synthetic gypsy movement meant something. It meant that the leaders of the booming psychedelic bohemia in the seminal city of San Francisco were their own men—and strangely serious men, indeed, for hippies. Ginsberg and Leary may be Pied Pipers, but they are largely playing old tunes. The young men who make the new scene accept Ginsberg as a revered observer from the elder generation; Leary they abide as an Elmer Gantry on their side, to be used for proselytizing squares, only.

The mountain symposium had been called for the extraordinary purpose of discussing the political future of the hippies. Hippies are many things, but most prominently the bearded and beaded inhabitants of the Haight–Ashbury, a little psychedelic city-state edging Golden Gate Park. There, in a daily street-fair atmosphere, upwards of fifteen thousand unbonded girls and boys interact in a tribal, love-free, free-swinging, acid-based type of society where, if you are a hippie and you have a dime, you can put it in a parking meter and lie down in the street for an hour's suntan (thirty minutes for a nickel) and most drivers will be careful not to run you over.

Speaking, sometimes all at once, inside the Sierra cabin were many voices of conscience and vision of the Haight–Ashbury—belonging to men who, except for their Raggedy Andy hair, paisley shirts, and pre-mod western Levi jackets, sounded for all the world like Young Republicans.

They talked about reducing governmental controls, the sanctity of the individual, the need for equality among men. They talked, very seriously, about the kind of society they wanted to live in, and the fact that if they wanted an ideal world they would have to go out and make it for themselves, because nobody, least of all the government, was going to do it for them.

The utopian sentiments of these hippies were not to be put down lightly. Hippies have a clear vision of the ideal community—a psychedelic community, to be sure—where everyone is turned on and beautiful and loving and happy and floating free. But it is a vision that, despite the Alice in Wonderland phraseology hippies usually breathlessly employ to describe it, necessarily embodies a radical political philosophy: communal life, drastic restriction of private property, rejection of violence, creativity before consumption, freedom before authority, de-emphasis of government and traditional forms of leadership.

Despite a disturbing tendency to quietism, all hippies *ipso facto* have a political posture—one of unremitting opposition to the Establishment which insists on branding them criminals because they take LSD and marijuana, and hating them, anyway, because they enjoy sleeping nine in a room and three to a bed, seem to have free sex and guiltless minds, and can raise healthy children in dirty clothes.

The hippie choice of weapons is to love the Establishment to death rather than protest it or blow it up (hippies possess a confounding disconcern about traditional political methods or issues). But they are decidedly and forever outside the Consensus on which this society places such a premium, and since the hippie scene is so much the scene of those people under twenty-five that *Time* magazine warns will soon constitute half our population, this is a significant political fact.

This is all very solemn talk about people who like to skip rope and wear bright colors, but after spending some time with these fun and fey individuals you realize that, in a very unexpected way, they are as serious about what they're doing as the John Birch Society or the Junior League. It is not improbable, after a few more mountain seminars by those purposeful young men wearing beads, that the Haight–Ashbury may spawn the first utopian collectivist community since Brook Farm.

That this society finds it so difficult to take such rascally looking types seriously is no doubt the indication of a deep-rooted hang-up. But to comprehend the psychosis of America in the computer age, you have to know what's with the hippies.

[KEN KESEY—I]
Games People Play, Merry Prankster Division

Let us go, then, on a trip.

You can't miss the Tripmaster: the thick-necked lad in the blue and white striped pants with the red belt and the golden eagle buckle, a watershed of wasted promise in his pale blue eyes, one front tooth capped in patriotic red, white and blue, his hair downy, flaxen, straddling the incredibly wide divide of his high forehead like two small toupees pasted on sideways. Ken Kesey, Heir Apparent Number One to the grand American tradition of blowing one's artistic talent to do some other thing, was sitting in a surprisingly comfortable chair inside the bus with the psychedelic crust, puffing absentmindedly on a harmonica.

The bus itself was ambulatory at about fifty miles an hour, jogging along a back road in sylvan Marin County, four loudspeakers turned all the way up, broadcasting both inside and outside Carl Orff's *Carmina Burana*, and filled with two dozen people simultaneously smoking marijuana and looking for an open ice cream store. It was the Thursday night before the Summit Meeting weekend and Kesey, along with some fifteen members of the turned-on yes men and women who call him "Chief" and whom he calls the "Merry

Pranksters" in return, was demonstrating a "game" to a delegation of visiting hippie firemen.

Crossing north over the Golden Gate Bridge from San Francisco to Marin County to pay Kesey a state visit were seven members of The Diggers, a radical organization even by Haight–Ashbury standards, which exists to give things away, free. The Diggers started out giving out free food, free clothes, free lodging, and free legal advice, and hope eventually to create a totally free cooperative community. They had come to ask Kesey to get serious and attend the weekend meeting on the state of the nation of the hippies.

The dialogue had hardly begun, however, before Kesey loaded all comers into the bus and pushed off into the dark to search for a nocturnal ice cream store. The bus, which may be the closest modern man has yet come to aping the self-sufficiency of Captain Nemo's submarine, has its own power supply and is equipped with instruments for a full rock band, microphones, loud-speakers, spotlights, and comfortable seats all around. The Pranksters are presently installing microphones every three feet on the bus walls so every-body can broadcast to everybody else all at once.

At the helm was the Intrepid Traveler, Ken Babbs, who is auxiliary chief of the Merry Pranksters when Kesey is out of town or incommunicado or in jail, all three of which he has recently been. Babbs, who is said to be the model for the heroes of both Kesey novels, *One Flew Over the Cuckoo's Nest* and *Sometimes a Great Notion*, picked up a microphone to address the guests in the rear of the bus, like the driver of a Grayline tour: "We are being followed by a police car. Will someone watch and tell me when he turns on his red light."

The law was not unexpected, of course, because any cop who sees Kesey's bus just about *has* to follow it, would probably end up with some form of professional D.T.'s if he didn't. It is part of the game: the cop was now playing on their terms, and Kesey and his Pranksters were delighted. In fact, a discernible wave of disappointment swept across the bus when the cop finally gave up chasing this particular U.F.O. and turned onto another road.

The games he plays are very important to Kesey. In many ways his intellectual rebellion has come full circle; he has long ago rejected the struc-tured nature of society—the foolscap rings of success, conformity, and ac-ceptance "normal" people must regularly jump through. To the liberated intellect, no doubt, these requirements constitute the most sordid type of game. But, once rejecting all the norms of society, the artist is free to create his own structures—and along with any new set of rules, however personal, there is necessarily, the shell to the tortoise, a new set of games. In Kesey's case, at least, the games are usually fun. Running around the outside of an insane society, the healthiest thing you can do is laugh.

It helps to look at this sort of complicated if not confused intellectual proposition in bas-relief, as if you were looking at the simple pictures on Wedgwood china. Stand Successful Author Ken Kesey off against, say, Successful Author Truman Capote. Capote, as long as his game is accepted by the system, is free to be as mad as he can. So he tosses the biggest, most vulgar ball in a long history of vulgar balls, and achieves the perfect idiot synthesis of the upper middle and lower royal classes. Kesey, who cares as much about the system as he does about the Eddie Cantor Memorial Forest, invents his own game. He purchases a pre-'40's International Harvester school bus, paints it psychedelic, fills it with undistinguished though lovable individuals in varying stages of eccentricity, and drives brazenly down the nation's highways, high on LSD, watching and waiting for the cops to blow their minds.

At the least, Kesey's posture has the advantage of being intellectually consistent with the point of view of his novels. In *One Flew Over the Cuckoo's Nest*, he uses the setting of an insane asylum as a metaphor for what he considers to be the basic insanity, or at least the fundamentally bizarre illogic, of American society. Since the world forces you into a game that is both mad and unfair, you are better off inventing your own game. Then, at least, you have a chance of winning. At least that's what Kesey thinks.

[KEN KESEY—II]
The Curry Is Very Hot;
Merry Pranksters Are Having Pot

There wasn't much doing on late afternoon television, and the Merry Pranksters were a little restless. A few were turning on; one Prankster amused himself squirting his friends with a yellow plastic watergun; another staggered into the living room, exhausted from peddling a bicycle in ever-diminishing circles in the middle of the street. They were all waiting, quite patiently, for dinner, which the Chief was whipping up himself. It was a curry, the recipe of no doubt cabalistic origin. Kesey evidently took his cooking seriously, because he stood guard by the pot for an hour and a half, stirring, concentrating on the little clock on the stove that didn't work.

There you have a slice of domestic life, February, 1967, from the swish Marin County home of Attorney Brian Rohan. As might be surmised, Rohan is Kesey's attorney, and the novelist and his *aides de camp* had parked their bus outside for the duration. The duration might last a long time, because Kesey has dropped out of the hippie scene. Some might say that he was pushed, because he fell, very hard, from favor among the hippies last year when he announced that he, Kesey, personally, was going to help reform the psychedelic scene. This sudden social conscience may have had something to do with beating a jail sentence on a compounded marijuana charge, but when Kesey obtained his freedom with instructions from the judge "to preach an anti-LSD warning to teenagers" it was a little too much for the Haight–Ashbury set. Kesey, after all, was the man who had turned on the Hell's Angels.

That was when the novelist was living in La Honda, a small community in the Skyline mountain range overgrown with trees and, after Kesey invited the Hell's Angels to several house parties, overgrown with sheriff's deputies. It was in this Sherwood Forest setting, after he had finished his second novel with LSD as his co-pilot, that Kesey inaugurated his band of Merry Pranksters (they have an official seal from the State of California incorporating them as "Intrepid Trips, Inc."), painted the school bus in glow sock colors, announced he would write no more ("Rather than write, I will ride buses, study the insides of jails, and see what goes on"), and set up funtime housekeeping on a full-time basis with the Pranksters, his wife and their three small children (one confounding thing about Kesey is the amorphous quality of the personal relationships in his entourage—the several attractive women don't seem, from the outside, to belong to any particular man; children are loved enough, but seem to be held in common).

When the Hell's Angels rumbled by, Kesey welcomed them with LSD. "We're in the same business. You break people's bones, I break people's heads," he told them. The Angels seem to like the whole acid thing, because today they are a fairly constant act in the Haight–Ashbury show, while Kesey has abdicated his role as Scoutmaster to fledgling acid heads and exiled himself across the Bay. This self-imposed Elba came about when Kesey sensed that the hippie community had soured on him. He had committed the one mortal sin in the hippie ethic: *telling* people what to do. "Get into a responsibility bag," he urged some four hundred friends attending a private Halloween party. Kesey hasn't been seen much in the Haight–Ashbury since that night, and though The Diggers did succeed in getting him to attend the weekend discussion, it is doubtful they will succeed in getting the novelist involved in any serious effort to shape the Haight–Ashbury future. At thirty-one, Ken Kesey is a hippie has-been.

[KEN KESEY—III]
The Acid Tests—From Unitarians to Watts

Kesey is now a self-sufficient but lonely figure—if you can be lonely with dozens of Merry Pranksters running around your house all day. If he ever gets maudlin, which is doubtful, he can look back fondly on his hippie memories, which are definitely in the wow! category, because Ken Kesey did for acid roughly what Johnny Appleseed did for trees, and probably more.

He did it through a unique and short-lived American institution called the Acid Test. A lot of things happened at an Acid Test, but the main thing was that, in the Haight–Ashbury vernacular, everyone in the audience got zonked out of their minds on LSD. LSD in Pepsi. LSD in coffee. LSD in cake. LSD in the community punch. Most people were generally surprised, because they didn't know they were getting any LSD until it was too late. Later, when word got around that this sort of mad thing was happening at Acid Tests, Kesey sometimes didn't give out LSD on purpose, just so people wouldn't know whether they did or did not have LSD. Another game.

The Acid Tests began calmly enough. In the early versions Kesey merely gave a heart-to-heart psychedelic talk and handed LSD around like the Eucharist, which first happened at a Unitarian conference in Big Sur in August of 1965. He repeated this ritual several times, at private gatherings in his home in La Honda, on college campuses, and once at a Vietnam Day Committee rally at Berkeley. Then Kesey added the Grateful Dead, a pioneer San Francisco rock group, to his Acid Tests and, the cherry on the matzos, the light show atmospheric technique of projecting slides and wild colors on the walls during rock dances. This combination he called "trips." Trip is the word for an LSD experience, but in Kesey's lexicon it also meant kicks, which were achieved by rapidly changing the audience's sensory environment what seemed like approximately ten million times during an evening by manipulating bright colored lights, tape recorders, slide projectors, weird sound machines, and whatever else may be found in the electronic sink, while the participants danced under stroboscopic lights to a wild rock band or just played around on the floor.

It was a fulgurous, electronically orgiastic thing (the most advanced Tests had closed circuit television sets on the dance floor so you could see what you were doing), which made psychedelics very "fun" indeed, and the hippies came in droves. Almost every hippie in the Bay Area went to at least one Acid Test, and it is not exceeding the bounds of reasonable speculation to say that Kesey may have turned on at least ten thousand people to LSD during the twenty-four presentations of the Acid Test. (During these Tests the Merry Pranksters painted everything including themselves in fluorescent tones, and bright colors became the permanent in-thing in psychedelic dress.)

Turning so many unsuspecting people on to LSD at once could be dangerous, as the Pranksters discovered on a 1965 psychedelic road show when they staged the ill-fated Watts Acid Test. Many of the leading citizens of Watts came to the show, which was all very fine except that whoever put the LSD in the free punch that was passed around put in too much by a factor of about four. This served to make for a very wild Acid Test, and one or two participants "freaked out" and had a very hard time of it for the next few days.

After the California legislature played Prohibition and outlawed LSD on October 6, 1966, Kesey wound up the Acid Test syndrome with what was billed as a huge "Trips Festival" in San Francisco. People who regularly turn on say the Trips Festival was a bore: it embodied all the Acid Test elements except acid and, happily for the coffers of Intrepid Trips, Inc., attracted a huge crowd of newspapermen, narcotics agents and other squares, but very few hippies. The Merry Pranksters slyly passed out plain sugar cubes for the benefit of the undercover agents.

Suddenly San Francisco, which for a grown-up city gets excited very easily, was talking about almost nothing but "trips" and LSD. Hippies, like overnight, had become fashionable.

If you are inclined to give thanks for this sort of thing, they go to the bad boy wonder of Psychedelphia, disappearing there over the horizon in his wayward bus.

[HISTORIAN CHESTER ANDERSON—I]
The Ghosts of Scenes Past, or
How We Got Here from There

Like Frederick J. Turner and Arnold Toynbee, Chester Anderson has a theory of history. His theory is psychedelic, but that is perfectly natural since he is a veteran acid head. Anderson, a thirty-five-year-old professional bohemian who looks forty-five, considers himself the unofficial historian of the psychedelic movement and has amassed enough footnotes to argue somewhat convincingly that the past fifteen years of social change in the United States—all the underground movements, and a significant part of the cultural changes—have been intimately connected with drugs.

If he is going to press his argument all the way, he may have to punch it out with Marshall McLuhan, who no doubt would assert that such phenomena as hippie colonies are nothing but a return to "tribal" culture, an inevitable reaction to our electronic age. And any social historian worth his salt will put it that every society has found some way to allow the sons and daughters of its middle class to drop out and cut up (most hippies, by the way, are from middle-class stock, so what's the difference from, say, the Teddy Boys?). Maybe lots, maybe none. But there is no disputing the cultural and artistic flip-flops this country has gone through in the last decade. The jazz musicians' vogue meant something. So did the Beat Generation. So, we suppose, did Pop Art, and Rock and Roll, and so, of course, the hippies.

If, in briefly tracing the derivation of the hippies from their seminal reasons in the intellectual uneasiness of the early 1950's, we chance to favor the testimony of Chester Anderson, it is only because he was there.

That was some bad year, 1953. There was a war on in Korea, a confusing, undefined war, the first big American war that wasn't the one to end all wars, because the aftermath of World War II had blown that phobia. And now the Bomb was with us, and with it the staccato series of disturbing headline events that stood for the Cold War; college was the only escape from the draft, but eggheads were becoming unpopular; Stevenson had lost the election and the Rosenbergs had been executed. It was all gloom, gloom, and dullsville, and if you were young and intellectual you were hard-pressed to find a hero or even a beautiful person. The only really alive, free thing, it seemed, was jazz—and the arrival of the long playing record had sparked a jazz renaissance, and with it the first drug heroes: most kids sympathized with Gene Krupa's marijuana busts, the agony of Lady Day's junk hangup was universal, and Charlie Parker had his own drugstore.

Lady Day's way wasn't the way of the new generation, Chester Anderson will be quick to tell you, because she was on "body" drugs. Whatever else body drugs—heroin, opium, barbiturates, alcohol, tranquilizers—may do, they eventually turn you off, and contemporary heads like to be turned on— i.e., senses intensified, stimulated rather than depressed. "Head" drugs, which do the latter, are both cheaper and easier to get than body drugs, and come in approximately eighteen varieties in three different classifications—natural drugs like marijuana, hashish, peyote, morning glory seeds, Hawaiian wood rose seeds, and certain types of Mexican mushrooms; artificial psychedelics like mescaline, LSD, psilocybin and psilocin, and whatever the ingredient is that makes Romilar cough syrup so popular with young heads; and synthetic stimulants which, used in large doses by heads, are known as "speed"—dexedrine, benzedrine, and methedrine.

But in the early 1950's there wasn't such a complete psychedelic medicine shelf to choose from, and the culturally disenchanted pioneers who began to settle new colonies in New York's Village and San Francisco's North Beach had to make do with pot. In a climate dominated by Dwight Eisenhower in the newspapers and Ed Sullivan on television, they also began to turn on to the pacifist, humanist philosophies of Asia—particularly Buddhism, most especially Zen—while Christianity as a workable concept became more meaningless, despite the exemplary efforts of such men as Brother Antoninus and Thomas Merton. American churchmen seemed to have neither the patience nor the fortitude to deal with people who were, well, *unsettled*. Folk music, which had been slowly dying, perked up a little, and there was a new interest in fresh, tuned-in poetry. As the '50's approached middle age and McCarthy went on the rampage, the few signs of life in a stagnant society centered around the disoriented peace movement, the fledgling civil rights movement, the young political Left, jazz and folk music, poetry, and Zen. Most of these followers were, of course, taking pot, while the rest of the country remained on booze and sleeping pills.

(If, in memory of the 85th anniversary of Anthony Trollope's death, we may be permitted an aside to the reader, it would be to say that one of the things that is considered original, but is in fact not, about the hippies is the concept of "dropping out" of society. Without adopting the histrionics of Hogarth crusading against the masses drinking gin, it is true that alcohol is an opiate which serves to help tens of millions of busy businessmen and lethargic housewives to "drop out" of any essential involvement in life and remain political and artistic boors. But alcohol is legal so nobody cares. If pot and LSD were ever legalized, it would be a mortal blow to this bohemia. Hippies have a political posture essentially because of the enforced criminality of their daily dose, and if taking LSD meant no more in society than the commuter slugging down his seventh martini, the conspiratorial magic would go out of the movement.)

Meanwhile, in San Francisco, Allen Ginsberg remembers an evening in 1955 which could stand as well as any for the starting point of what was to become the most thorough repudiation of America's middlebrow culture since the expatriates walked out on the country in the 1930's. The vanguard of what was to be the Beat Generation had gathered at the 6 Gallery on Fillmore Street for a poetry reading moderated by Kenneth Rexroth, a respectable leftish intellectual who was later to become the Public Defender of the beats. Lawrence Ferlinghetti was in the audience, and so were Kerouac and his then sidekick, Neal Cassady, listening to Michael McClure, Phil Lamantia, Gary Snyder, and Philip Whalen read their poetry. Ginsberg was there too, and delighted everyone with a section of the still unfinished "Howl," better known to beats as the Declaration of Independence.

Two distinct strains in the underground movement of the '50's were represented at this salient gathering. One was a distinctly fascist trend, embodied in Kerouac, which can be recognized by a totalitarian insistence on action and nihilism, and usually accompanied by a Superman concept. This strain runs, deeper and less silent, through the hippie scene today. It is into this fascist bag that you can put Kesey and his friends, the Hell's Angels, and, in a more subtle way, Dr. Timothy Leary.

The other, majority, side of the beats was a cultural reaction to the existential brinkmanship forced on them by the Cold War, and a lively attack on the concurrent rhetoric of complacency and self-satisfaction that pervaded the literary establishment all the way from the *Atlantic Monthly* to Lionel

Trilling. Led by men like Ginsberg and Ferlinghetti, the early beats weighed America by its words and deeds, and found it pennyweight. They took upon themselves the role of conscience for the machine. They rejected all values and when, in attempting to carve a new creative force, they told America to "go fuck itself," America reacted, predictably, with an obscenity trial.

The early distant warnings of the drug-based culture that would dominate the Haight–Ashbury a decade later were there in the early days of North Beach. Marijuana was as popular as Coke at a Baptist wedding, and the available hallucinogens—peyote and mescaline—were part of the beat rebellion. Gary Snyder, poet, mountain climber, formal Yamabushi Buddhist, and a highly respected leader of the hippie scene today, first experimented with peyote while living with the Indian tribe of the same name in 1948; Ginsberg first took it in New York in 1951; Lamantia, Kerouac and Cassady were turned on by beat impresario Hymie D'Angolo at his Big Sur retreat in 1952. And beat parties, whether they served peyote, marijuana or near beer, were rituals, community sacraments, setting the format for contemporary hippie rituals.

But the psychedelic community didn't really begin to flourish until late 1957 and 1958 in New York, and for that story we take you to Chester Anderson in the Village.

[HISTORIAN CHESTER ANDERSON—II]
Was the Kingston Trio Really Red Guards?

On Thanksgiving Day, 1957, Chester Anderson was turned on to grass by a bongo-playing superhippie who went by the code name of Mr. Sulks. Grass, if you don't know and don't have an underground glossary handy, is translated marijuana, and from that day forward, Anderson, who once studied music at the University of Miami so he could write string quartets like Brahms, became a professional Turn-On and migrated with bohemia, east to west to east to west, from the Village to North Beach back to the Village to the Haight–Ashbury, where he can be found today—a prototype of the older psychedelic type who mixes with the drifting, turning on kids to form the central nervous system of any body of hippies.

The first psychedelic drug to reach the Village in any quantity was peyote, an obscure hallucinatory cactus bud used by Indians in religious ceremonies. Peyote was cheap and plentiful (it can still be ordered by mail from Laredo at $10 for 100 "buttons") and became highly touted—Havelock Ellis and Aldous Huxley recommended it. The only problem with peyote was that it tasted absolutely terrible, and, as peyote cults sprang up, peyote cookbooks came out with recipes for preparing the awful stuff in ways that would kill the taste. "Man," Chester recalls a head telling him at the time, "if I thought it'd get me high, I'd eat shit." As with most new head drugs, the taking of peyote was treated as a quasi-religious event. The first time Chester took it, he did so with great ritual before a statue of the Buddha.

Peyote was the thing in late 1957, and by the summer of 1958 mescaline, the first synthetic psychedelic, was widely distributed. The heads reacted like unwed mothers being handed birth control pills—they were no longer dependent on nature. Turn-ons could be *manufactured*!

According to Chester's files, LSD didn't arrive in any large, consumer-intended supply in the Village until the winter of 1961–62, and not in the Bay Area until the summer of 1964, but by that time something unusual had happened to America's psychedelic gypsies: they had become formal enemies of the State. Massive harassment by the cops in San Francisco, by the coffee-house inspectors in New York, had let the heads and the young middle-class types who came in caravan proportions, to test the no-more-teachers, no-more-books way of bohemian life, to view the Establishment as the bad guy who would crush their individuality and spirituality in any way he could. This is the derivation of whatever political posture the hippies have today. It will be significant, of course, only if the Haight–Ashbury scene doesn't go the way of the Beat Generation—assimilated by a kick-hungry society. For the serious, literary Beats, it was all over but the shouting when the Co-existence Bagel Shop became a stop on sightseeing tours.

In 1962, the Village was pulsating with psychedelic evangelism. LSD was so cheap and so plentiful that it became a big thing among heads to turn on new people as fast as they could give LSD away.

Pot, also, was being used more widely than ever by middle-class adults, and spread from the urban bohemias to the hinterlands by small folk music circles that were to be found everywhere from Jacksonville, Florida, to Wausau, Wisconsin. At the same time, almost the entire Village was treating LSD like it was a selection on a free lunch counter, and a scruffy folknik called Bobby Dylan was beginning to play charitable guest sets in the Washington Square coffeehouses. "Things," Chester said, "were happening more rapidly than we knew."

What was happening, Mr. Jones, was that folk music, under the influence of early acid culture, was giving way to rock and roll. Rock spread the hippie way of life like a psychedelic plague, and it metamorphosed in such rapid fashion from the popularity of folk music, that a very suspicious person might ask if seemingly safe groups like the Kingston Trio were not, in fact, the Red Guards of the hippie cultural revolution.

There was a rock and roll before, of course, but it was all bad seed. The likes of Frankie Avalon, Fabian, and Elvis Presley sent good rock and roll musicians running to folk music. Then absolutely the world's greatest musical blitz fell and the Beatles landed, everywhere, all at once. The impact of their popular music was analogous to the Industrial Revolution on the nineteenth century. They brought music out of the juke box and into the street. The Beatles' ecstatic, alive, electric sound had a total sensory impact, and was inescapably participational. It was "psychedelic music." "The Beatles are a trip," Chester said. Whether the Beatles or Dylan or the Rolling Stones actually came to their style through psychedelic involvement (Kenneth Tynan says a recent Beatles song "Tomorrow Never Knows" is "the best musical evocation of LSD I've ever heard") is not as important as the fact that their songs reflect LSD values—love, life, getting along with other people, and that this type of involving, turn-on music galvanized the entire hippie underground into overt, brassy existence—particularly in San Francisco.

Drug song lyrics may, in fact, be the entire literary output of the hippie generation. The hippies' general disregard for anything as static as a book is a fact over which Chester Anderson and Marshall McLuhan can shake hands. For acid heads are, in McLuhan's phrase, "post-literate." Hippies do not share our written, linear society—they like textures better than surfaces, prefer the electronic to the mechanical, like group, tribal activities. Theirs is an ecstatic, do-it-now culture, and rock and roll is their art form.

[THE MERCHANT PRINCES—I]
Dr. Leary—Pretender to the Hippie Throne

The suit was Brooks Brothers '59, and the paisley tie J. Press contemporary, but the bone-carved Egyptian mandala hanging around his neck, unless it was made in occupied Japan, had to be at least two thousand years old. Dr. Timothy Leary, B.A. University of Alabama, Ph.D. University of California, LSD Cuernavaca, and 86'd Harvard College, was dressed up for a night on the town, but as his devotees say of this tireless proselytizer of the psychedelic cause, it was work, work, work. Tonight Leary was scouting somebody else's act, a Swami's at that, who was turning on the hippies at the Avalon Ballroom by leading them in an hour-long Hindu chant without stopping much for breath. The Avalon is one of the two great, drafty ballrooms where San Francisco hippies, hippie-hangers-on, and young hippies-to-be congregate each weekend to participate in the psychedelic rock and light shows that are now as much a part of San Francisco as cable cars and a lot noisier.

This dance was a benefit for the new Swami, recently installed in a Haight–Ashbury storefront, with a fair passage sign from Allen Ginsberg whom he had bumped into in India. The hippies were turning out to see just what the Swami's *schtick* was, but Dr. Leary had a different purpose.

He has a vested, professional interest in turning people on, and here was this Swami, trying to do it with just a chant, like it was natural childbirth or something.

The word professional is not used lightly. There is a large group of professionals making it by servicing and stimulating the hippie world—in the spirit of the Haight–Ashbury we should refer to these men as merchant princes—and Timothy Leary is the pretender to the throne.

Dr. Leary claims to have launched the first indigenous religion in America. That may very well be, though as a religious leader he is Aimee Semple McPherson in drag. Dr. Leary, who identifies himself as a "prophet," recently played the Bay Area in his LSD road show, where he sold $4 seats to lots of squares but few hippies (Dr. Leary's pitch is to the straight world), showed a technicolor movie billed as simulating an LSD experience (it was big on close-ups of enlarged blood vessels), burned incense, dressed like a holy man in white cotton pajamas, and told everybody to "turn on, tune in, and drop out."

In case you are inclined to make light of this philosophic advice you should not laugh out loud. Because Dr. Leary is serious about his work, he can not be dismissed as a cross between a white Father Divine and Nietzsche, no matter how tempting the analogy. He has made a substantial historical contribution to the psychedelic scene, although his arrest records may figure more prominently than his philosophy in future hippie histories.

Since, something like Eve, he first bit into the sacred psychedelic mushroom while lounging beside a swimming pool in Cuernavaca, he has been hounded by the consequences of his act. Since Dr. Leary discovered LSD, he has been booted out of Harvard for experimenting a little too widely with it among the undergraduate population, asked to leave several foreign countries for roughly the same reasons, and is now comfortably if temporarily ensconced in a turned-on billionaire friend's estate near Poughkeepsie, New York, while awaiting judicial determination of a thirty-year prison sentence for transporting a half-ounce of marijuana across the Rio Grande without paying the Texas marijuana tax, which has not been enforced since the time of the Lone Ranger.

If he were asked to contribute to the "L" volume of the World Book Encyclopedia, Dr. Leary would no doubt sum up his work as "having turned on American culture," though his actual accomplishments are somewhat more prosaic. Together with Richard Alpert, who was to Dr. Leary what Bill Moyers was to President Johnson, Leary wrote an article in May, 1962, in, surprise, *The Bulletin of the Atomic Scientists*. The article warned that in event of war, the Russians were likely to douse all our reservoirs with LSD in order to make people so complacent that they wouldn't particularly care about being invaded, and as a civil defense precaution we ought to do it ourselves first—you know, douse our own reservoirs—so that when the reds got *their* chance the country would know just what was coming off. It was back to the old drawing board after that article, but Alpert and Dr. Leary made their main contribution to the incredibly swift spread of LSD through the nation in 1964 by the simple act of publishing a formula for LSD, all that was needed by any enterprising housewife with a B-plus in high school chemistry and an inclination for black market activity. Dr. Leary's religious crusade has been a bust, convert-wise, and not so salutary financially, either, so he announced recently that he was dropping out, himself, to contemplate his navel under the influence. It would be easier to take Dr. Leary seriously if he could overcome his penchant for treating LSD as a patent snake-bite medicine.

An enlightening example of this panacea philosophy is found back among the truss ads in the September, 1966, issue of *Playboy*. In the midst of a lengthy interview when, as happens in *Playboy*, the subject got around to sex, Dr. Leary was all answers. "An LSD session that does not involve an ultimate merging with a person of the opposite sex isn't really complete," he said, a facet of the drug he neglected to mention to the Methodist ladies he was attempting to turn on in Stockton, California. But this time, Dr. Leary was out to turn on the *Playboy* audience.

The following selection from the interview is reprinted in its entirety. Italics are *Playboy*'s.

PLAYBOY: We've heard some women who ordinarily have difficulty achieving orgasm find themselves capable of multiple orgasms under LSD. Is that true?
LEARY: In a carefully prepared, loving LSD session, a woman will inevitably have several hundred orgasms.
PLAYBOY: Several *hundred?*
LEARY: Yes. Several hundred.

After recovering from that intelligence, the *Playboy* interviewer, phrasing the question as diplomatically as possible, asked Dr. Leary if he got much, being such a handsome LSD turn-on figure. Dr. Leary allowed that women were always falling over him, but responded with the decorum of Pope Paul being translated from the Latin: "Any charismatic person who is conscious of his own mythic potency awakens this basic hunger in women and pays reverence to it at the level that is harmonious and appropriate at the time."

Dr. Leary also said that LSD is a "specific *cure* for homosexuality."

The final measurement of the tilt of Dr. Leary's windmill, his no doubt earnest claim to be the prophet of this generation, must be made by weighing such recorded conversations against his frequent and urgent pleas to young people to "drop out of politics, protest, petitions and pickets" and join his "new religion" where, as he said recently:

"You have to be out of your mind to pray."

Perhaps, and quite probably so.

[THE MERCHANT PRINCES—II]
Where Dun & Bradstreet Fears to Tread

Allen Ginsberg asked ten thousand people to turn towards the sea and chant with him. They all did just that, and then picked up the papers and miscellaneous droppings on the turf of Golden Gate Park's Polo Field and went contentedly home. This was the end of the first Human Be-In, a gargantuan hippie happening held only for the joy of it in mid-January. The hippie tribes gathered under clear skies with rock bands, incense, chimes, flutes, feathers, candles, banners, and drums. Even the Hell's Angels were on their good behavior—announcing that they would guard the sound truck against unspecified evil forces. It was all so successful that the organizers are talking about another be-in this summer to be held at the bottom of the Grand Canyon with maybe two hundred thousand hippies being-in.

The local papers didn't quite know how to treat this one, except for the San Francisco *Chronicle*'s ace society editor Frances Moffat, who ran through the crowd picking out local socialites and taking notes on the fashions.

Mrs. Moffat's intense interest reflects the very in, very marketable character of San Francisco Hippiedom. Relatively high-priced mod clothing and trinket stores are as common in the Haight–Ashbury as pissoirs used to be in Paris. They are run by hippie merchants for square customers, but that doesn't mean that the hippies themselves aren't brand name conscious. Professing a distaste for competitive society, hippies are, contradictorily, frantic consumers. Unlike the beats, they do not disdain money. Indeed, when they have it, which with many is often, they use it to buy something pretty or pleasureful. You will find only the best hi-fi sets in hippie flats.

In this commercial sense, the hippies have not only accepted assimilation (the beats fought it, and lost), they have swallowed it whole. The hippie culture is in many ways a prototype of the most ephemeral aspects of the larger American society; if the people looking in from the suburbs want change, clothes, fun, and some lightheadedness from the new gypsies, the hippies are delivering—and some of them are becoming rich hippies because of it.

The biggest Robber Baron is dance promoter Bill Graham, a Jewish boy from New York who made it big in San Francisco by cornering the hippie bread and circuses concession. His weekend combination rock and roll dances and light shows at the cavernous, creaky old Fillmore Auditorium on the main street of San Francisco's Negro ghetto are jammed every night. Even Andy Warhol played the Fillmore. Although Graham is happy providing these weekend spiritual experiences, he's not trying to be a leader. "I don't want to make cadres, just money," he said. Graham's cross-town competitor is Chet Helms, a rimless-glasses variety hippie from Texas who has turned the pioneer, non-profit San Francisco rock group called The Family Dog into a very profit-making enterprise at the Avalon Ballroom.

A side-product of the light show dances, and probably the only other permanent manifestation of hippie culture to date, is the revival in a gang-busters way of Art Nouveau poster art. Wes Wilson, who letters his posters in 18, 24 and 36 point Illegible, originated the basic style in posters for the Fillmore dances. Graham found he could make as much money selling posters as dance tickets, so he is now in the poster business, too.

The posters, at $1 apiece, as common as window shades in the Haight–Ashbury, demand total involvement from the reader, and are thus considered psychedelic manifestations of the existential, non-verbal character of hippie culture.

Haight Street, the Fifth Avenue of Hippiedom, is geographically parallel to Golden Gate Park but several blocks uphill, where rows of half vacant store fronts once indicated the gradual decline of a middle-class neighborhood. But all that changed, dramatically, during the past eighteen months. Haight Street now looks like the Metropolitan Opera Company backstage on the opening night of *Aida*. The stores are all occupied, but with mercantile ventures that might give Dun & Bradstreet cause to wonder. Threaded among the older meat markets, discount furniture stores, laundromats, and proletarian bars are a variety of leather goods shops, art galleries, mod clothing stores, and boutiques specializing in psychedelic paraphernalia like beads, prisms, and marijuana pipes, and of course there is the Psychedelic Shop itself.

The Psychedelic Shop is treated as a hippie landmark of sorts, but the Haight–Ashbury scene was percolating long before the Thelin brothers, Ron and Jay, stuffed a disconcertingly modern glass and steel store front full of amulets, psychedelic books, a large stock of the underground press, and some effete gadgetry for acid heads. The hippie phenomena began to metamorphose from a personal to a social happening around the fall of 1965 after the kids at Berkeley turned on to LSD, Ken Kesey started holding Acid Tests, and The Family Dog staged its first dance.

Instrumental in spreading the word was the *Chronicle*'s highly regarded jazz critic, Ralph J. Gleason. Gleason is read religiously by hippies. Besides explaining to his square readers what is happening, he is also the unofficial arbitrator of good taste in the Haight–Ashbury community. Gleason was quick to tell Ken Kesey, in print, when he was out of line, and did the same for Dr. Leary. Gleason's writings tuned in other members of the *Chronicle* staff, and the extensive, often headline publicity the newspaper gave to the hippie scene (Kesey's return from a self-imposed Mexican exile was treated with the seriousness of a reasonably large earthquake) helped escalate the Haight–Ashbury population explosion.

So there is plenty of business for the hippie merchants, but some of them, like the Thelin brothers, are beginning to wonder where it will all lead. At the prodding of The Diggers, the Thelins are considering making the store a non-profit cooperative that will help "the kids get high and stay high" at low cost. They may also take the same steps with *The Oracle*, the Haight–Ashbury monthly tabloid. The majority of the hip merchants, however, are very comfortable with the ascending publicity and sales, and have as little vision of what they are helping create than did Alexander Bell when he spilled acid on himself.

[EMMETT GROGAN—I]
Will the Real Frodo Baggins Please Stand Up?

Except for the obvious fact that he wasn't covered with fur, you would have said to yourself that for sure there was old Frodo Baggins, crossing Haight Street. Frodo Baggins is the hero of the English antiquarian J. R. R. Tolkien's classic trilogy, *Lord of the Rings*, absolutely the favorite book of every hippie, about a race of little people called Hobbits who live somewhere in pre-history in a place called Middle Earth. Hobbits are hedonistic, happy little fellows who love beauty and pretty colors. Hobbits have their own scene and resent intrusion, pass the time eating three or four meals a day and smoke burning leaves of herb in pipes of clay. You can see why hippies would like Hobbits.

The hustling, heroic-looking fellow with the mistaken identity was Emmett Grogan, kingpin of The Diggers and the closest thing the hippies in the Haight–Ashbury have to a real live hero. Grogan, twenty-three, with blond, unruly hair, and a fair, freckled Irish face, has the aquiline nose of a leader, but he would prefer to say that he "just presents alternatives." He is in and out of jail seventeen times a week, sometimes busted for smashing a cop in the nose (Grogan has a very intolerant attitude toward policemen), sometimes bailing out a friend, and sometimes, like Monopoly, just visiting. The alternatives he presents are rather disturbing to the hippie bourgeoisie, since he thinks they have no business charging hippies money for their daily needs and should have the decency to give things away free, like The Diggers do, or at least charge the squares and help out the hippies.

Grogan has a very clear view of what freedom means in society ("Why can't I stand on the corner and wait for nobody? Why can't everyone?") and an even clearer view of the social position of the hippie merchants ("They just want to expand their sales, they don't care what happens to people here; they're nothing but goddamn shopkeepers with beards").

Everyone is a little afraid of Grogan in the Haight–Ashbury, including the cops. A one-man crusade for purity of purpose, he is the conscience of the hippie community. He is also a bit of a daredevil and a madman, and could easily pass for McMurphy, the roguish hero in Kesey's novel set in an insane asylum. There is a bit of J. P. Donleavy's *Ginger Man* in him, too.

A few weeks ago, out collecting supplies for The Diggers' daily free feed, Grogan went into a San Francisco wholesale butcher and asked for soup bones and meat scraps. "No free food here, we work for what we eat," said the head butcher, a tattooed Bulgar named Louie, who was in the icebox flanked by his seven assistant butchers. "You're a fascist pig and a coward," replied Grogan, whom Louie immediately smashed in the skull with the blunt side of a carving knife. That turned out to be a mistake, because the seven assistant butchers didn't like Louie much, and all jumped him. While all those white coats were grunting and rolling in the sawdust, a bleeding Grogan crawled out with four cardboard boxes full of meat.

This was a typical day in Dogpatch for Grogan, who has had his share of knocks. A Brooklyn boy, he ran away from home at fifteen and spent the next six years in Europe, working as a busboy in the Alps, and, later, studying film making in Italy under Antonioni. Grogan had naturally forgotten to register for the draft, so when he returned to the United States he was in the Army four days later. That didn't last long, however, because the first thing Grogan had to do was clean the barracks. His idea of cleaning barracks was to throw all the guns out the window, plus a few of the rusty beds, and artistically displeasing footlockers. Then he began painting the remaining bed frames yellow. "I threw out everything that was not esthetically pleasing," he told the sergeant.

Two days later Grogan was in the psychiatric ward of Letterman Hospital in San Francisco where he stayed for six months before the authorities decided they couldn't quite afford to keep him. That was shortly after an Army doctor, learning of his film training, ordered Grogan to the photo lab for "work therapy." It was a "beautiful, tremendously equipped lab," Grogan recalls, and since it wasn't used very much, he took a picture of his own big blond face and proceeded to make 5000 prints. When the doctors caught up with him, he had some 4700 nine by twelve glossies of Emmett Grogan neatly stacked on the floor, and all lab machines: driers, enlargers, developers were going like mad, and the water was running over the floor. "What did you do *that* for?" a doctor screamed.

Grogan shrugged. "I'm crazy," he said.

He was released a little later, and acted for a while with the San Francisco Mime Troupe, the city's original and brilliant radical theater ensemble. Then last fall, when the Negro riots broke out in San Francisco and the National Guard put a curfew on the Haight–Ashbury, The Diggers happened. "Everybody was trying to figure how to react to the curfew. The SDS came down and said ignore it, go to jail. The merchants put up chicken posters saying 'for your own safety, get off the street.' Somehow, none of those ideas seemed right. If you had something to do on the streets, you should do it and tell the cops to go screw off. If you didn't, you might as well be inside."

Something to do, to Grogan, was to eat if you were hungry, so at 8 P.M., at the curfew witching hour, he and an actor friend named Billy Landau set up a delicious free dinner in the park, right under the cops' noses, and the hippies came and ate and have been chowing down, free, every night since. The Haight–Ashbury has never been quite the same.

[EMMETT GROGAN—II]
A Psychedelic *Grapes of Wrath*

Every Bohemian community has its inevitable coterie of visionaries who claim to know what it is all about. But The Diggers are, somehow, different. They are bent on creating a wholly cooperative subculture and, so far, they are not just hallucinating, they are doing it.

Free clothes (used) are there for whoever wants them. Free meals are served every day. Next, Grogan plans to open a smart mod clothing store on Haight Street and give the clothes away free, too (the hippie merchants accused him of "trying to undercut our prices"). He wants to start Digger farms where participants will raise their own produce. He wants to give away free acid, to eliminate junky stuff and end profiteering. He wants cooperative living to forestall inevitable rent exploitation when the Haight–Ashbury becomes chic.

Not since Brook Farm, not since the Catholic Workers, has any group in this dreadfully co-optive, consumer society been so serious about a utopian community.

If Grogan succeeds or fails in the Haight–Ashbury it will not be as important as the fact that he has tried. For he is, at least, providing the real possibility of what he calls "alternatives" in the down-the-rabbit-hole-culture of the hippies.

Grogan is very hung up on freedom. "Do your thing, what you are, and nothing will ever bother you," he says. His heroes are the Mad Bomber of New York who blissfully blew up all kinds of things around Manhattan over thirty years because he just liked to blow things up, and poet Gary Snyder, whom he considers the "most important person in the Haight–Ashbury" because instead of sitting around sniffing incense and talking about it, he went off to Japan and became a Zen master. "He did it, man."

This is an interesting activist ethic, but it remains doubtful just what the hippies will do. Not that many, certainly, will join Grogan's utopia, because utopias, after all, have a size limit.

The New Left has been flirting with the hippies lately, even to the extent of singing "The Yellow Submarine" at a Berkeley protest rally, but it looks from here like a largely unrequited love.

The hip merchants will, of course, go on making money.

And the youngsters will continue to come to the Haight–Ashbury and do—what?

That was the question put to the hippie leaders at their Summit Meeting. They resolved their goals, but not the means, and the loud noise you heard from outside was probably Emmett Grogan pounding the table with his shoe.

The crisis of the happy hippie ethic is precisely this: it is all right to turn on, but it is not enough to drop out. Grogan sees the issue in the gap "between the radical political philosophy of Jerry Rubin and Mario Savio and psychedelic love philosophy." He, himself, is not interested in the war in Vietnam, but on the other hand he does not want to spend his days like Ferdinand sniffing pretty flowers.

This is why he is so furious at the hip merchants. "They created the myth of this utopia; now they aren't going to do anything about it." Grogan takes the evils of society very personally, and he gets very angry, almost physically sick, when a pregnant fifteen-year-old hippie's baby starves in her stomach, a disaster which is not untypical in the Haight–Ashbury, and which Grogan sees being repeated ten-fold this summer when upwards of two hundred thousand migrant teen-agers and college kids come, as a psychedelic *Grapes of Wrath*, to utopia in search of the heralded turn-on.

The danger in the hippie movement is more than overcrowded streets and possible hunger riots this summer. If more and more youngsters begin to share the hippie political posture of unrelenting quietism, the future of activist, serious politics is bound to be affected. The hippies have shown that it can be pleasant to drop out of the arduous task of attempting to steer a difficult, unrewarding society. But when that is done, you leave the driving to the Hell's Angels.   [1967]

LIONEL ROLFE

Why Norman
Is Still on the Bus

I'VE ALWAYS WONDERED what Benjamin Bufano's St. Francis of Assisi might have thought of that strange night back in 1966 when Ken Kesey's Merry Pranksters reveled for several hours in front of the Longshoremen's Hall in San Francisco, shortly before departing to Los Angeles in their Day-Glo–painted bus. The great sculptor's rendition of the gentle, animal-loving Catholic saint looked enigmatic to me through the dope-hazed stroboscopic madness of that crazy evening that has lingered in my mind as a time-frozen snapshot of the era. I remembered the outlandish costumes of Kesey and the Pranksters, the ugly and pervasive noise of the acid rock sounds of the Grateful Dead, as well as the startling sight of a phalanx of women dancing topless, and the cops who hovered as if they were about to pounce, but then didn't. Just as Kesey had intended, they had become part of the bizarre proceedings. The Merry Pranksters was an apt name.

Kesey had just finished telling the court, suddenly sounding as chaste as an old Baptist maiden lady, that his new Acid Tests, of which this was one, would be LSD-free. The LSD experience without the LSD, he announced—which everyone knew was a big joke. The joke was for the benefit of the courts, where Kesey was facing various marijuana charges. Another big prank. Too big a prank. For after the San Francisco Acid Test, Kesey had to escape to Mexico. The idea was that the Pranksters would drive the bus south, holding Acid Tests all the way down the coast into Mexico, where eventually they would rendezvous with the fugitive from justice. LSD was not yet illegal—it would be in a few more months, but not quite yet. No doubt one of the reasons it did become illegal were the various Acid Tests conducted by the Pranksters as they headed south, especially the four in Los Angeles, and in particular the Acid Test in L.A.'s Watts, where LSD-spiked Kool-Aid—so-called Electric Kool-Aid—left a number of innocents so freaked out they had to be hospitalized. Kesey's Pranksters without Kesey were as outrageous as McMurphy, the main character in Kesey's 1962 novel, *One Flew Over the Cuckoo's Nest.*

A couple of years later Tom Wolfe (again, the journalist, not the real novelist) published *The Electric Kool-Aid Acid Test,* his best-seller based on Kesey's adventures with his Merry Pranksters aboard their 1939 Day-Glo–painted former church bus. I was one of thousands who rushed out to buy the book. Then the following year, which was 1969, I was brought full circle back to that original night under St. Francis' nose. A fellow from Filmways invited me in to discuss doing something to do with Kesey's thousands of hours of movie footage, which because of misfocusing and overexposure and other amateur problems had boiled down to half an hour of usable footage. Wolfe's book had already been published, so everyone was aware of the existence of "The Movie," shot by Kesey's Pranksters during their initial trip across the country. The studio wanted someone who would work with Kesey, a writer who could devise a script that could be shot around the usable footage. We talked a long time—yes, I was anxious to work on the film. Certainly I had heard of Kesey. The Filmways executive warned me that Kesey was difficult to work with—in fact, a number of other writers already had failed. But the Filmways executive thought I might be successful with Kesey, just as he no doubt had thought the others would.

I think he meant what he said, however, for he viewed me as a more bona fide hippy than his other writers, with their fancy digs in Malibu and the Hollywood Hills. And, of course, I had done LSD, yes, and I had followed the doings of those priests of LSD such as Timothy Leary and Ken Kesey. I had read and been deeply impressed by Kesey's novels. The executive said he would hire me when Kesey got back, for no one was quite sure where he was at that moment, except that he was on the road in the Day-Glo bus. He had gone with a whole truckload of the studio's equipment to do what, no one was precisely sure. As happens so often in such flaky deals, the executive finally called me back and said that the studio was dropping out of the whole project—they had come to the conclusion that Kesey was simply impossible.

I spent much of that psychedelic decade traveling between Los Angeles and San Francisco, as did many of my generation. Gas was cheap, and the big old American cars we drove were, if nothing else, reliable and comfortable. The psychedelic tide carried us, the remnants of the late beatnik coffeehouse scene in the early sixties, to and fro between Los Angeles and San Francisco. When the waves were out, we invariably found ourselves in Los Angeles, waiting for the next tide that would carry us to the Jerusalem that San Francisco was for us. In those days, we native Angelenos saw ourselves as the pikers when the psychedelic revolution overtook us: everything was happening up north, it seemed. With hindsight, it now seems as if that may not have been quite the truth. For down here we were reading Aldous Huxley's *Doors of Perception*, in part, no doubt, because we were all impressed by the fact that the great British author who adopted the Southland as his native home for more than the last two decades of his life went out on his deathbed in his Hollywood Hills home under the influence of LSD—notes of which were dutifully kept by his widow, Laura Huxley. Kesey and Leary may have been the gurus of the psychedelic movement, but it is doubtful that they would have found so many followers had it not been for the impact of Huxley's slim but potent little volume.

One day not long ago Jeanne Morgan, the first wife of my old coffeehouse buddy, *Free Press* founder and proprietor Art Kunkin, left a note for me at Chatterton's Bookstore on Vermont Avenue. She was going to meet Norman Hartweg at the House of Pies coffeeshop across from the bookstore to talk about old times. Would I like to join them? Hartweg had been one of Kesey's Merry Pranksters. In fact, much of Wolfe's book, since Wolfe himself never actually was on the bus, was based on material taped by Hartweg: Hartweg had been a major character in *The Electric Kool-Aid Acid Test* as well, and his was, in a sense, the ultimate story of what happened to much of the writing talent of my generation in Los Angeles. He was the great writer who might have been; today he lives in obscurity in a tiny, dingy little apartment in North Hollywood. Hartweg survived Kesey's various acid tests as well as the notorious stoned driving of Neal Cassady. The irony of Hartweg's life today is that he is a paraplegic, confined to a wheelchair as a result of a broken back sustained in an auto accident that occurred right after he left Kesey's bus in Los Angeles in 1967.

When Kesey approached him in 1964, however, Hartweg was riding high. He was a columnist at the *Free Press*, which had just started at the Fifth Estate coffeehouse on Sunset Boulevard. Hartweg also lived at the Fifth Estate, in a cheap basement apartment that had no windows. He had recently won an award for his play *The Pit*, which the prestigious *Tulane Drama Review* not only published, but gave him an award for. The play was being performed all over the country—eventually it would be produced on public television in Boston. Hartweg was deeply involved in a small theater called Theatre Event in Hollywood on Kenmore Avenue, located in what was then The Bridge coffeehouse (today the Deja Vu). He had also directed the West Coast premier of Genet's *The Maze*. Through the rumor mill, he had also heard that the *New Republic* was considering him for a position as drama critic. But he threw all this up, which included giving away his personal library, to go off and become one of Kesey's Merry Pranksters.

Hartweg wouldn't have been interested in Kesey's proposal that he abandon all of this in Los Angeles and come up to his place in the redwoods (just south of San Francisco) had it not been for the mention of the legendary Neal Cassady's name. For Neal Cassady was none other than the Dean Moriarty of Kerouac's *On the Road*, a book that Hartweg considered to be one of his biggest influences.

The chance of being around Cassady was one that Hartweg couldn't resist. Their introduction, however, was not entirely auspicious. Cassady's first love, as one of the Merry Pranksters, was cars and driving. He was a whiz with old cars—and the bus was one of the oldest. He was a whiz at fixing it, and a whiz at driving. In Tom Wolfe's book there are some memorable descriptions of the Pranksters' first cross-country trip, some truly terrifying moments with Cassady, his mind blowing on too many mics of LSD, maneuvering the old vehicle down the slopes of the great mountains without benefit of brakes.

Hartweg had a similar hair-raising experience when he first met Cassady. They had gone for a drive in the country around Kesey's home and again Cassady was at the wheel. And all the time he was driving, especially down one long winding curve coming out of the hills, Cassady kept up an incessant patter about the bus and old cars and anything else that crossed his mind, looking not at the road but directly at the terrified Hartweg. Hartweg saw the truck coming up the grade, but he was also sure Cassady had not. At the last moment, as the bus approached the truck, Cassady looked back to the road, fishtailed the old bus out of the truck's path along the edge of the road, and without comment looked back again at Hartweg, his patter resuming where it had left off a second before.

Back at La Honda, where Kesey lived, the famed author suddenly appeared before his guest, as if he knew that Hartweg needed an explanation, saying, "Cassady doesn't have to think anymore." By which, Hartweg presumed, he was supposed to believe that Cassady had moved on to everhigher and more noble plains of pure thought, helped, of course, by the large doses of acid he had taken.

There was a lot of history behind Hartweg's journey to meet the prototype Dean Moriarty. In the early fifties, Hartweg had written a play called *Joe Brown*, which was performed and won a prize in Oklahoma. "The play recorded my distress at just discovering racial prejudice," Hartweg told me on the occasion of a second meeting in another coffeeshop across from the North Hollywood library. He laughed at himself as he told me about it. "I thought this was really good stuff. I was going to write plays against war and mob violence and see if I couldn't straighten some of these things out." He also read *On the Road*, which had a tremendous impact on him, introducing him not only to the fantastic character of Moriarty, but also to the fact that marijuana was used elsewhere besides the black ghettos.

Not long after this he ended up in the army and found himself stationed in Denver, which was extraordinary luck. He thought he could go searching for Moriarty's famous lost drunken father on Larimer Street, as described in *On the Road*. But Larimer had changed. It had gone uptown; the old slum part of town was undergoing urban renewal. As if to make up for the fact, however, the fates smiled kindly on Hartweg. He was assigned to work in the library of an army hospital, and mostly what he did was read. "There were five or six souls of my ilk on the post," he says. "We made up the 'Beat contingent.' We went out and got the obligatory bongo drums, berets, and Miles Davis records and had a good time. We managed to survive the army that way. We all wanted to be writers, but we also all had trouble finishing anything." One of his buddies, a fellow named Kent Chapman, was from California and knew Venice well. In fact, Chapman had been portrayed as a Venice Beat in Larry Lipton's best-selling *The Holy Barbarians*, and that impressed Hartweg no end.

Chapman introduced Hartweg to names he had never heard of—writers such as Malcolm Lowry and Christopher Isherwood, and the Vedanta Society. The latter was what originally got Hartweg interested in going to the West Coast after the army, "for I heard there was this whole Eastern trip submerged on the West Coast."

The first thing Hartweg did on being mustered out in 1960 was to head for Los Angeles, where he looked up his old friend Chapman. The two of them rented an apartment in Hollywood for $40 a month. The fascination with the "Eastern thing" persisted, and no doubt through the influence of Huxley and other writers, whom Hartweg read avidly, drugs were mixed into the brew of Eastern mysticism developing on the West Coast. At first, Hartweg says, "Marijuana provided a pleasant way to draw and write that also made you think that what you were doing was terrific. You felt warm and relaxed and euphoric." So when Hartweg first decided to take Kesey up on his offer, to meet Moriarty, he thought that he would find the Pranksters "into the Tibetan thing." What he found, instead, was not the "Tibetan" (meaning lots of flies buzzing around a meditating wise man), but Kesey's own rather odd kind of Americana—among the Day-Glo mania at La Honda were the Hell's Angels, all the movie-making gear, the sound equipment, and all the other paraphernalia of Kesey's northern loony bin environment. The only real "Eastern thing" around La Honda was Kesey's rampant anti-intellectualism, as revealed in his statement to Hartweg about the nobleness of Cassady's dope dementia.

From 1964 to 1967 was an "extraordinary time in human history," Hartweg proclaims. "Leaders sprang up all over the place from the grass roots.

They came in all types, colors, and descriptions. They gave names to things for people. That's still what I'm most interested in now, and physics of that phenomenon—what it was that happened then. It doesn't exist now. Many of the same people are around, but they're doing different things, or maybe even the same things. But the leaders and the clusters are gone."

Hartweg looked me squarely in the eye. "That's what the lamentation over coffeehouses and the sixties was all about when we met the first time with Jeanne Morgan. About how it's all gone, and how we wish it were back again," he said. I nodded my agreement that indeed this might be true. I wasn't convinced by all that Hartweg said, but I also felt that his must have been the most archetypical sixties writer's story ever to come out of the Los Angeles coffeehouse scene. Which meant, naturally, that despite talent and intelligence, even brilliance, he ultimately produced very little. Hartweg explained the process precisely. He said that the whole generation of young painters, writers, and musicians stopped being painters, writers, and musicians as a result of the psychedelic revolution. In his case, this voyage began with his leaving Los Angeles to join Kesey and the Pranksters. Basically, Hartweg insisted, his generation left their arts and went off into two different directions. One group went into radical politics, and the other into psychedelics. "There just wasn't much writing or painting going on if you were going to be doing the other things."

There is some sense of this parting of the generational ways in Wolfe's description of the meeting between Kesey and Kerouac in *The Electric Kool-Aid Acid Test*. Here was the most important writer of the fifties in the same room with Kesey, who looked as if he were going to be the best writer of the sixties. And although it was as if Kesey had picked up the banner that Kerouac had wearily put down, in Wolfe's description, there was no rapport between the two men. Neither had much to say to the other.

To this day Hartweg shares Kesey's militant anti-intellectualism, which was, of course, a hallmark of the psychedelic generation. Hartweg will hardly even admit to himself that he was, and in fact remains, a hero worshipper of Kesey. Hartweg argues that it would be pointless to say what he felt, or feels today, about Kesey, the man who snatched him out of his developing career and former life, even though he admits what he thinks indirectly. "Kesey was an enormously powerful personality," he says, "and he was also huge. He's not that tall, but he had neck muscles like oil field wire lines; he was a collegiate heavyweight wrestler aiming at going to the Olympics, which he never did. Now, if you take an unsure person and run him across a huge man like that with a powerful personality who is dead sure of what he believes, you will find circles of insecure people around him, trying to figure out if they agree with him or not, sort of like the way little fish latch onto the side of a whale." Later, Hartweg insists that in actual fact Kesey did not seek out followers, that "he did not expect worship at all, that he simply one day looked around and realized he had acquired a lot of people who centered their identity on his, most of whom were underfoot, who were making it harder and harder for him to move." On the other hand, I pointed out, it was his money that supported all these people, to which Hartweg replied with what I thought was an unconvincing response, namely that if "someone wasn't really contributing by doing his or her thing, they would eventually be kicked out."

Hartweg eventually left the Merry Pranksters on his own. After the well-publicized Acid Tests in Los Angeles, some of the Pranksters continued south with Kesey on his Mexican sojourn, and others just "scattered." It was in the process of scattering that the accident occurred that more than any of his previous experiences with the Los Angeles coffeehouse scene or Kesey's Pranksters changed the rest of Hartweg's life. Yet even the crash that ultimately brought down Hartweg's writing career seemed to me a logical culmination for an archetypical Los Angeles coffeehouse experience. The sheer velocity of that generation could only end in a crash. Hartweg and his old friend Evan Engber, and famed Prankster Marge the Barge, piled into an ancient, uninsured automobile and headed out to New York. Hartweg drove the first leg of the journey, to Las Vegas. It was three in the morning when they arrived in town. They all had a quick sandwich, and then Hartweg curled up in the right front seat and went to sleep. He doesn't even remember who was actually driving after that. "Halfway out in the desert we banged into something. I don't know exactly what happened, except that I was thrown out and my back was broken. The other two sustained only slight injuries and bruises."

For a year after that, Hartweg lay in a hospital bed in his native Ann Arbor, Michigan, which gave him a lot of time to think. One of the things he thought about the most was his goal of wanting to be a writer. He came to the conclusion that it wasn't so much he wanted to be a writer as that he was in love with the idea of others' thinking he was one. Except for a few brief book reviews and articles, he's hardly written a thing since then. Instead, he spent the next ten years trying to regain his sanity after the turmoil of the sixties.

He went back to the University of Michigan, where he had already earned a master's degree in the sixties, figuring he would check things out "with the people who do philosophy for a living." He entered the doctoral degree program and also got a job teaching at the university—"They gave me easy stuff to teach like symbolic logic." After three years there he only had to write a dissertation to earn his doctorate. But he found he had nothing to write about. "The philosophy professors knew nothing either—only how to articulate the dilemmas." He now believes that the best answer to the old philosophical questions is the proverbial Zen reply, which is to hit anyone who asks such questions with a big stick, and then run away giggling. "I decided that anybody who giggles is probably all right," he said, giggling.

Hartweg also pretty much abstains from marijuana, alcohol, and other drugs these days, with the exception of coffee and cigarettes. He's adamantly opposed to cocaine and speed and thinks that LSD is really only appropriate for those whose situation is so hopeless that "They might as well try blasting powder. But then it's still very risky. You might get blown up. People are in loony bins to this day from it." He described some of the scenes from the sixties in San Francisco's Haight-Ashbury so vividly, you almost wonder that he's not totally against drugs. "You'd find those dismal crash pads with people in terribly desiccated states, dark hollows around their eyes, still saying 'wow' and 'groovy.' They came out from Des Moines to San Francisco to wear flowers in their hair, but they found only sharks who said they could score a kilo. Suddenly, instead of consciousness-raising, it had become drug dealing, and it was scummy."

Yet despite his disavowal of drugs, the psychedelic way of looking at things is still there—one might even suggest that it is these very attitudes that effectively prevented him from finding his way back to the typewriter. He explains that he just doesn't take words, or for that matter his own beliefs and thoughts, very seriously. He paraphrases that old sixties shaman Marshall McLuhan, who said, "Words have just become reality probes." "You try them out to see what works," says Hartweg. "You throw them away when they don't work. Words just aren't engraved in stone anymore. Don't look for the meaning of words, look for their use."

For a while, Hartweg and I engaged in a bit of debate over the meaning of great writing. He still retains the very sixties notion that says there is nothing but everyone's subjective truth, and hence no one statement is really more valid than another because there really is no such thing as truth. I argued that Mark Twain's works, for instance, have survived because their author had the breadth of vision that made his works immortal. But neither of us was convincing the other. To Hartweg, my statement was no more true and no more false than his or anyone else's statement. After fifteen minutes of that, my head started to hurt.

Hartweg even refused to see any significance in his coming home again to Los Angeles in 1977, after his decade of soul-searching in Michigan. He admits that he had a "whole mess of California stuff still hanging over my head undone." He admitted that he "wanted to see what had become of the underground newspapers, the coffeehouses." And you certainly could sense his disappointment as he discovered "every spit, every scrap" gone. "It was like an organism that had grown," he said, "lived its life, and then decomposed back into the initial elements from which it had sprung. The places were still there—Venice, the Pacific Ocean, a whole mess of the individuals." But the group consciousness was gone.

Hartweg had originally come to Los Angeles in 1960 only to check out the scene for a couple of weeks before going to New York to settle down. But he stayed. "You can spend 25 years in L.A. never buying a six-pack of Coke because at any moment you may be leaving for New York." Before he came back to L.A. for the last time in '77, he had checked out New York once again. But he found the mobs and its nastiness and tension "inhuman. It was like finding good things in postwar Berlin. If you have to be there, fine, make the most of it." At that point in his life, however, it wasn't for him. Thus he came West.

There was one brief moment after his arrival back in town when it looked as if some of the old gang would materialize. Art Kunkin and Paul Krassner hired him to be the editor of a new *Realist* that Larry Flynt, of the *Hustler* empire, was planning to resurrect. But then Flynt got shot, either by the Mafia or the CIA, and Kunkin, Krassner, and Hartweg were on the streets again.

He still wanted to settle in. He drove up and down the old streets with names like Alvarado Street and Hollywood Boulevard, so he could renew "the tapes" and destroy the old mystique of L.A. that he had built up in his mind since he left it the last time in '67. He sat down with maps to figure out where the city's backbone, where its nervous system was. He even went out to look at the power lines and foundries. He read books on the unstable geology underneath. And he sat high on the top of the Hollywood Hills so he could contemplate the city as it really was, not as his own personal self, or the mystique, had made it seem.

He seemed pleased to report that the same "muscle layers" were there— the big retail stores, the jammed freeways, the phone company, the service clubs. But he noted that the culture signified nothing. The art and writing of the seventies, which had gone on in his absence, affected no one. "In the mid-fifties and sixties art mattered," he said. "It had an effect. There was a great arch of the artistic, political, and Bohemian, all linked in one great swirl. It made a difference. But nowadays the fleas aren't jumping. They're not biting the dog. The exciting issues that enflame the human spirit are gone. Things still happen—important things like the sun coming up, the tide coming in, the flowers growing. But the fleas just ain't jumping."

Like a lot of other people in town, Hartweg has been having a tough time surviving in the Reagan depression of 1982. Just finding work is tough— today he runs a one-man office for a man who sells drilling equipment to Texas oil fields. He's glad to have the job, which, from the trade journals spread all over his apartment, you can tell he takes seriously. He's getting his rent paid. He will concede, with what seems some wistfulness, that there are some new signs of a cultural awakening beginning in Los Angeles again. Hartweg is a firm believer in the notion that art needs some oppression to give it impetus, and that's just beginning to happen now. For him, and for many of his generation, there was a spurt, an eruption, and then the futility of the dreary seventies and early eighties when little was written, less was painted, and ultimately nothing was said.   [1984]

FRANK ROBERTSON

Hippies
Without a Home

ALTHOUGH most of San Francisco's flower children have long since wilted back into straight society, in some Northern California towns it is still possible to find people and places that make you feel as though you were smack in the middle of Golden Gate Park in 1968. Walking down the main street of a town such as Monte Rio or Guerneville, along the Russian River in Sonoma County, you may still be confronted by extremely hirsute men begging for spare change. In the checkout line of the Guerneville Safeway you can overhear mothers (with food stamps) scolding children who have names like Virgo, Season, Starshine, or Mantra ("Mantra, please shut up for mother, okay?") When Country Joe McDonald headlined at a Guerneville nightclub recently, he advertised himself with the slogan: "Let's bring back the sixties, man!" This may have been an unnecessary exhortation around Guerneville, where the sixties have never really been away.

So it was probably inevitable that in the ongoing Sonoma County debate over the social value of building a multimillion-dollar condominium complex in Guerneville, one often heard argument among local old-timers is that the condos will be a blessing because they will help drive out the "hippies," a term that in Guerneville is often construed to mean "people on welfare."

In the late sixties Guerneville held a singular attraction for people who wanted to tune in, turn on, and drop out: the cheap rents of the many vacant summer houses and cabins left over from Guerneville's heyday as a resort. But this was before the real estate market in California became a new version of the California gold rush, it was before the Bay Area housing crunch, and

Hippies Without a Home | 129

it was before San Francisco's gay community discovered Guerneville, where gay people have invested heavily in resorts, businesses, and real estate. It was also before Guerneville got a new sewer system, which opened the door for real estate investors such as Paul Wang, the Berkeley architect who recently bought the largest moribund river resort in the area, a seventeen-acre parcel known as Ginger's Rancho. Here Wang proposed to build Dubrava Village, a "package" community of beachfront hotel rooms, a new restaurant and bar, boutiques, and 91 "garden town house" condominiums—a project that called for an environmental impact report, a zoning change, an amendment to the county plan, and a series of public meetings on the merits of the project.

Meanwhile, the site of Guerneville's first planned condo community is a vacant beach, a padlocked ramshackle riverside bar and restaurant, about 500 second-growth redwood trees (which the developer has promised not to cut), and the remains of several dozen dilapidated summer cabins that until last year housed several dozen of the area's welfare hippies.

When the hippies were evicted, their most immediate option was simply to move down the road to other decaying resorts, places that also are, like a lot of commercial property in Guerneville, up for sale. When a locally notorious low-rent slum called Sycamore Court was sold in the summer and the tenants there put out, it was just one more piece of a pattern. In Guerneville the sixties are being replaced by the eighties, which means that for the area's disenfranchised longhairs, the center is not holding. The local health food store was bought last year by a gay businessman and activist, Leonard Matlovich (the ex-air force sergeant who was on the cover of *Time* magazine in 1975 for the then untenable position of being both gay and in the service), who replaced yogurt and sprouts with an eclectic retail blend of pizza, Sunday brunch, and video games. The Monte Rio food co-op went out of business in December. The official counterculture paper, the *Sonoma County Stump* (which had struggled from week to week since 1971 to serve loyal readers with an odd mix of antinuke protest reports, essays on wave power, local poetry, and hagiographical interviews with sixties holy men such as Tim Leary), published its last issue in January. The same week that the *Stump* folded, a local auto repairman (who had moved to Guerneville from Hollywood) explained to the county planning commission that one reason he knew that the time was right for condo development in Guerneville was that his clientele was no longer primarily made up of people driving old Volkswagens. The planning commission approved the condominiums.

When the old neighborhood goes condo, where can an aging hippie mellow out? In Guerneville the question has yet to be completely answered, but early indications point to the street and the great outdoors. There have been recent stories in the local press about people living in tents in Sonoma

County public parks. There have been some instances along the Russian River beaches of people setting up permanent camp—permanent, that is, until a property owner or a neighbor complains and the sheriff asks the gypsies to leave. There is Cazadero, to the northwest, where, if you have the right connections, you might find a place in the woods to pitch a tepee or erect a yurt. There is sometimes official relief—during the recent rains, the Red Cross set up a temporary storm shelter in the local Veterans Memorial Building to house the flood victims, many of whom were residents of the town's old low-rent summer resorts. "Some of them lost everything," said a Red Cross volunteer dryly.

There was a TV on in the Red Cross shelter one Sunday, and noticeable among the homeless men gathered around it to watch *NFL Today* were those dressed in army fatigue jackets, bell-bottom jeans, shoulder-length Buffalo Bill coifs, and a prodigious amount of facial hair; there were also a lot of receding hairlines and beer bellies. Whether peace and love will survive the eighties remains to be seen, but it doesn't look like they are on the supply side.

If anything remains invulnerable from those years when everyone was trying to get his head together and dig where you were coming from, it may be the distinctly cosmic approach to language. As the editor of the *Stump*, discussing the paper's demise, wrote in the last editorial: "The *Stump* is coming to an end, but the energy that fueled it is here, ready to make the transition to another form, about to recycle itself into something new that none of us can quite identify as yet. It's an exciting and somewhat scary leap into unknown possibilities."

Far out. [1982]

KATE COLEMAN

Country Women

T HE "BACK-TO-THE-LAND" movement, beginning in the late '60s, struck me as a bore. Worse, it seemed a cop-out on the part of counterculture people, a white flight on the Left, leaving the rest of us radical activists to fight the war, racism and night-stick-wielding police intent on cracking our city skulls.

Still, in the early '70s, when Sheena-of-the-Jungle urges overtook me or

I sought an idyllic respite to soothe the political depression in every joint and bone, I deigned to visit my country cousins in Mendocino County and the Santa Cruz Mountains. God, how I railed, when I returned, at the sexism I found in the country.

The women I knew were reverting to the Stone Age. The feminist revolution was as far removed from the country as artsy-fartsy films: an alien-import culture not adaptable to clean rural air, redwood trees, mountains and homegrown veggies. I saw the same old role-split: the men and their cars and trucks, the women and their cooking and canning; the hairy male arm chopping wood, erecting fencing; the female hand dragging a dirty-faced kid. How I pitied my sisters, becoming the barefoot, swollen-bellied communers with nature who gave up newspapers and politics because country life extracted all their time.

City chauvinism dies a slow death. News from rural areas is scant. Changes, no doubt, occur out there, but because populations are sparse, the phenomenon seems less noteworthy. I sat up and took note recently when, after radical fugitive Susan Saxe was apprehended, it was revealed that she had been hiding out for years in lesbian-feminist farming communities. I was further forced to alter my stereotypical views when I came across *Country Women*, a publication produced by rural feminists for the last five years and having one of the largest circulations (10,000 at its peak, but, like *Playboy*, God forgive me, passed on to other eyes) of any feminist publication in the country. All these changes afoot—and in the stunning Mendocino Coast area that I have been visiting for years. A community of ardent feminists live up there, and I never knew it!

The magazine was founded by a handful of women situated on Albion Ridge, a spine of land running back and up from Highway One and the rock-strewn Pacific Coast. One of the first sites in the country settled by "back-to-the-land" experimentors, the area has always been marked by a tolerance toward freaks, communards and welfare scammers. To this day, the core of the Mendocino County feminist community lives in the little fishing town of Albion and up on the ridge of the same name, though the original group has expanded as far north as Fort Bragg. These are also pockets of feminist farmers inland near Willits, in Garberville and in the tiny town of Philo on Highway 128, which cuts inland from the coast to Highway 101. In all, there are perhaps 50 local women who have worked on the magazine in one capacity or another or who relate to the *Country Women* collectives as affinity groups. My first fantasies envisioned an army of 50 feminists kicking redneck ass in local bars. While this is not the case, I'm impressed that their numbers grew from an original few, testimony to the need of those women for one another and to the power of feminism itself.

City Chauvinist Hits the Ridge

The coast is mantled this morning with its usual foggy shroud a
south from my digs in Little River to Albion. Once inland on the
however, the fog thins to wisps and strands. I drive down a rutted,
dirt lane past the usual junk cars and finally stop in front of a two-,
octagonal, cedar barn that is one of the most beautiful structures I have ever
seen. This is no hippie shack. It houses the economic mainstay of this feminist
farming collective: prize-winning Nubians and the rarer, exotic-looking (because they are seemingly without ears) La Mancha goats.

Carmen emerges from her one-room structure to meet me. There are
currently about four women living on Carmen's 40-acre parcel of pasture
and woods, with two more women expected. Although some live in the
original farm house, a couple have or are in the process of erecting their
own teepee and cabin.

I go with Carmen this morning on her farming rounds as we talk of the
origins of the magazine and feminist community here. On our route through
the secluded farm, I ooh and ah like the novice I am as Carmen carries out
her prosaic chores. The does—the Nubians are dun-colored, the La Mancha
piebald—step on my feet and on each other in order to get next to Carmen,
who talks to them in a tone not too different from the one she uses with
me. After feeding the females, we move on to her prize-winning males. She
cleans the troughs and inspects the sturdy pens erected by the women. Her
nose wrinkles at the smell. When the female goats are in heat and the males
go into a rutting period, Carmen tells me, the males urinate into their beards.
"It's disgusting," she says. At such time she dons rubber overalls because
she can't stand the lingering male aromas left on her clothes and her body.
For a brief moment I harbor the notion that such repugnance is predicated
on her militant feminism, but her obvious pride in her bearded Billys—
particularly the snow-white Nubian—quickly dispels this suspicion.

Everywhere, it seems, are cats, Muscovy ducks, barred rock hens, Rhode
Island hens, runty dogs and even the honk of a nearby peahen. Once Carmen
had sheep on the land as well. The women cleared an acre of land of brush
and then fenced in the whole area as grazing pasture—"back-breaking work,"
she says—but the sheep were eventually sold off. The cost of hay made the
operation prohibitive.

I confess I am charmed watching the slim-hipped, 32-year-old former
Vassar student doing her farm chores, but I see the drudgery demanded by
her commitment. The magazine, too, extracts a lot of Carmen's time, for
she is a permanent member of the editorial collective (and one of the original
founders). I want to know the genesis of it all—the magazine, the feminist
community and Carmen herself.

We make our way back to Carmen's modest cabin that sits beside a magnificent flower and vegetable garden. The women on this particular farm are all vegetarians, so what they grow on this plot and on the other garden adjacent to the original farm house is vital. There is obviously an aesthete at work here too, for the flowers are every bit as lovingly cultivated as the food. Inside, while I sip strong coffee laced with goat's milk, my stomach growling for a fresh egg, we talk.

Country Women, the soft-spoken, dark-eyed Carmen explains, was born out of a consciousness-raising group started by Carmen's then-lover, Jeanne, who was armed with nothing more than her reading of Shulamith Firestone's powerful book, *The Dialectic of Sex*. (I am appreciative of that fact, because it was and is *the* feminist work that had the most profound influence on my own thinking.)

The two lovers had lived together in Berkeley, but their upper flat was so crowded by the five big dogs, seven cats and a baby goat that they made the leap to the country in 1968, finally settling on the present 40-acre parcel.

"Jeanne and I were lesbians," Carmen says, "but we were not feminists at all then. We just assumed that a commune meant a mixed commune of men and women. So for two years we had the most sleazy array of men living here. They resented our authority, but we put up with it." The men were also bumping up against the women's ownership of the land. Carmen's father was a lawyer for Aramco, and her early years were spent in Saudi Arabia, where her father was based. Schooled in Europe and then at Vassar, Carmen became an orphan-heiress in 1966 when both her parents were killed in a car crash. The money for the farm's purchase and all subsequent investments (including the $17,000 for the cedar barn built by women) has come out of her dwindling inheritance.

After a few short months of their consciousness-raising group, Carmen and Jeanne "booted the men off the land." "We realized we didn't need them," Carmen says, her thin face breaking triumphantly into a smile. ("Oh," my own Joan of Arc voice moans, "not to need them anymore! How wonderful! How many sleazy men have *I*. . . .") Jeanne and Carmen eventually split up, Jeanne moving inland to a sheep-raising farm. Though the two women are no longer lovers, they remain friends.

The power of that original consciousness-raising group spread to all of its members like a prairie fire. The impetus came quickly, original members theorize, because of these two avowed lesbians. Other groups sprang up in the area within six months of the first one, but they did not go so far. Certainly they did not arrive at anything as concrete as a magazine.

Carmen surmises that the influence of herself and Jeanne was such that they belied the sexual-role stereotype. The two of them were undoubtedly so damned competent and self-sufficient it must have been a complete revelation to the other women. Jeanne's and Carmen's new-found militant feminism both forced the other women to reflect on their own internalized role expectations and provided support for the troubling changes they were all about to embark upon. The effect, the women say, was electrifying.

It was this original charge that impelled the women to start the magazine. Though inexperienced in publishing, they were consumed with the desire to *do something* about what they had learned and were learning—propagandize, if you will, a new religion. They wanted to share and celebrate the changes they were all experiencing, and, they reasoned correctly, there were many rural women who were as isolated from feminist thought as they were. *Country Women* was born.

The magazine continues to reflect those original concerns. The practical section in each issue offers a prodigious and overwhelming amount of lore and how-to's on everything related to farming and country life: building houses and barns, plumbing, car repair, black-smithing. Contributors to this section (articles are solicited from readers all over the country) share their expertise and lace their prose with predictable feminist encouragement. The rest of each issue is organized around a concept or idea of concern to women. "Spirituality," "Class," "Sexuality," "Women Working," "Children's Liberation," "Politics," "Food" are some of the past titles.

The writing in these pages tends to be amateurish, confessional and seemingly devoid of editing. It is endlessly pep-talky: "Organize farmer's markets . . . teach-ins . . . Food Days"; defiant: "Fat is beautiful!"; or wallowing, in turn—"I know I shouldn't feel so upset . . . But I still feel sick with old hurt and anger . . . A lot of my feelings about money simply come from never having enough of it. . . ."

Cloying stuff; yet, with all its imperfections, the magazine has a devoted readership throughout the country and in parts of Canada as well. It could never have survived these five years if *Country Women* were not addressing the needs of rural women. But more than just individual women, the magazine is responsible to a readership rarely reached by other publications: a network of militant lesbian communes in the Ozarks, Oregon, upstate New York, New England and several Middle Eastern Seaboard states. These women tend to be overlooked amid the currents of alternative lifestyles and radical politics. They are also militant about keeping a low profile, wishing to be ignored by the Establishment so they can live out their experiments in private.

Reforging Lives

I don't wish to overemphasize the fact that lesbianism dominates the feminism in Mendocino County and, more specifically, the magazine itself.

Nevertheless, it's certainly significant, because it was lesbianism, originally rooted in Carmen's and Jeanne's relationship, that provided the protective, sisterly umbrella under which these women were far freer to break out of conventional roles as helpmates, mothers and lovers. The absence of men, of male orientation, even though the choice was theirs, forced these women to do for themselves what they had never done before, changing their whole outlook in the process.

There were times among these country women when I felt they sawed off the limb between men and themselves. But none of them had regrets. Rather, many tended to view themselves as a modest vanguard, a small group of people who had somehow managed to reforge their whole lives.

Harriet is a striking example—a model, if you will, of how a feminist community and lesbian peer group can act as a catalyst for change. This 34-year-old mother of two children split up with her husband and afterwards became a lesbian. Harriet, one of the more forceful personalities on the magazine and in the community, often strikes me as some ideological cheerleader for her new lifestyle, yet something in her manner leaves me unconvinced.

Perhaps it is the similarity in our backgrounds—L.A., Jewish, middle-class. They still stick out all over her, despite a healthy patina of politics—feminist, lefty and otherwise. She remains, or so it struck me, feminine and maternal, the kind of woman who listens sympathetically and then gives you the good swift metaphorical kick in the ass you need to get going. Why this should be puzzling to me in a lesbian is obviously *my* problem, but Harriet's dramatic life changes don't seem to grow from her personality the way, say, Carmen's do, to cite just one of the women whose sexual and political choices struck me as less cerebral than Harriet's.

Harriet, too, had undeniably great decisions to make. Splitting up with her second husband was far less momentous than her decision to relinquish the custody of her male child to his father (her daughter by her first husband remains with her in the bosom of the female society). But she still was emphatically influenced in both decisions by the feminist platoon close by.

Reluctant to discuss these matters fully with me, she nevertheless spoke freely—if prosaically—in *Country Women* about the difficulty of the decision to give up her son, Eli, to his father, Michael.

Plagued at that time with guilt feelings of failing as a "homestead wife and mother" and recognizing that her marriage was on the skids, Harriet wrote that the "choice was clear." Recalling her state of mind then, she wrote: "Imagining Michael get in the truck and drive away with my curly-haired baby next to him definitely brought tears to my eyes, but the thought of Michael getting into the truck and driving away with Allison [her daughter] tugging at my skirt, Eli in my arms and mounds of diapers waiting to be washed seized my whole body with terror. No, no, no, my insides screamed. Luckily," she adds breezily, "my feminist consciousness and supporting friends were able to help me rationally interpret those screams in a way that allowed me to let go of the image of being a 'good mother' and thereby let go of Eli."

But Harriet *is* concerned with being a good mother. She points to her daughter's picture in one of several structures on her land (her daughter was away on a visit). At another time, Harriet and her current lover braved hand-numbing cold as they worked to finish a barn to house her daughter's horse. Is this so different, I wonder, from the Harriet of before, the teacher of ghetto kids in Los Angeles? "I hated it," she says. "I wanted to make sensitive little Jewish poets out of them."

Harriet proudly shows off the buildings she's constructed; the stained-glass windows of exotic birds and flowers that she made with her own hands; the drought-withered garden where she was, until recently, growing her own vegetables; the chickens; the eggs; and the recounting of her treks to the city to buy up windows to truck back and sell.

I think she might have done it all—with or without a man—but Harriet believes the significance in her life is the giant strides she made from heterosexuality to lesbianism, from femme roles to omni-roles. "My own concept of myself is to be self-sufficient," she asserts, adding with pride: "I can build a house, raise my own food, gut, skin, butcher, clean and tan a deer." Harriet has made her choices, though the stridency associated with the newly converted is mitigated by her humor and earthiness.

Separatism and Pluralism

Once that stridency in this community was much harsher when it came to heterosexual women than today; pluralism regarding sexuality and living preferences is now manifest in the community and the magazine. In the past, however, it made some hetero feminists paranoid and unsure of themselves.

Arlene, an easy-going former career woman (an assistant fashion editor at *Teen Magazine* and an assistant advertising manager of another firm) is a case in point. Although a career woman in New York, Arlene was no feminist when she arrived in the Mendocino area seven years ago with her lover, David, to try their luck in a small farming collective. Converted quickly to the feminism around her, she enlisted as an original member of *Country Women*'s editorial collective, even as she and David continued to live and love together.

"David suddenly became invisible to a lot of women who had known us both," says the former fashion editor who now wears faded, shapeless long skirts, warm men's shirts and "sensible" shoes and socks. "At the grocery store or the post office they would act as if he weren't there at all." Arlene blames herself for being too intimidated to confront the issue more directly at the time. Instead, she left the magazine, feeling bruised; yet, as the separatist stance softened, she came back into the fold, resuming work on the magazine in the capacity of office manager. She and David also work together and live on the premises of Aquarius Electronics, a firm on Albion Ridge producing bio-feedback machines and small computers, an honest-to-God cottage-type industry set in the midst of a pygmy forest.

Within the covers of *Country Women* one sees ads for "dykes only" communes around the country, for "lesbians with female children only," along with other, blander, "women's refuge" offerings. And, though the Mendocino area women have made a conscious decision to keep their magazine's door open to all feminists, regardless of their sexuality, I could understand Arlene's former discomfort, especially when I'd slink off at night to the sexist bar in Caspar, where men were in abundance and still—ah Lordy, that I should sell out so—call women "chicks."

Most of the feminists in the area—but by no means all—prefer the company of each other. Although the magazine draws these women together for what seem like never-ending meetings, they visit with each other frequently as cronies or lovers. There are occultish festivals celebrating solstices or full moons (often mixed with peyote ingestion and bacchanalian overtones), women-only music and dance nights at a local coffee house. While some of the women expressed their distaste for the mystical gatherings, many still travel the ridge road for group dinners, coffee klatches or, on the more serious side, meetings to help one another with farming, car mechanics or building problems.

The pioneer spirit is impressive, but there is also the undeniable element of a community in-grown. It is a society in which every woman knows every other woman's business—whether it be financial difficulties, class background or the taking on or shedding of a lover. Relationships between the women lovers tend to be "serially monogamous," according to one woman, which means faithful during the courtship and romance period, branching out and changing partners when the thrill is gone; and the fact of women loving women does little to mitigate the jealousy or pains that one finds in *any* sexual relationship.

Sage, Class and Money

Despite the cohesiveness of the women on the issue of feminism, their politics don't fall into line as readily. From half-mumbled comments from some of the women, I begin to detect some resentment, some paranoia, on the classic questions of class and land ownership. They all look rather poor to me; they're all busting ass to make a go of things. But some of the women come from wealth, middle-class-with-resources, and some of them don't. Some women own their land; others have scrounged a place on someone else's land, scurrying around to make the rent or to work in exchange for rent.

There are some women in the community who feel that feminists who own land should open up their land to the use of Third World and poor working women. One such woman—I shall call her Sage—a tall, open-faced former political activist from San Diego, with a blonde "Dutch boy" hair cut, sees her role in the Mendocino community as the self-appointed scourge of women with class privileges, as she calls them. This surprisingly cheery radical, who wears over-sized men's pants held up with red suspenders, lectures me on the class make-up of the other women in the community and how important it is for these women to show more consciousness toward other oppressed sisters. Despite these women being "land rich, but money poor," as Sage describes it, they still have resources, and, moreover, they made the decision to be downwardly mobile, accepting the lower income potential in the country in order to enjoy the blessings of nature, or whatever—doing all this and eschewing material comforts, at the same time that the Third World and working poor are seeking just the opposite.

It's hard for me to understand just exactly what Sage wants from these bourgeois landowners, but I do see the repercussions of her arguments among the landowning women themselves. They are sensitive to the charges, worried about schisms in the community, and even reluctant that mention be made of their backgrounds in a magazine article. Laney (not her real name) was very upset when she found out I intended to identify her father's profession. A friend of hers told me that Laney has become extremely sensitive on the subject because of the recent discussions about social class, and also because she has been taking flack on her "privileged background" for many years before that while working in leftist causes. That, plus the fact that Laney owns one of the biggest "feminist" chunks of land around (a 100-acre sheep-ranching farm) in conjunction with her parents, makes her the most susceptible to the land redistribution mutterings.

Seeing this issue debated in the magazine, one realizes the publication acts as a sounding board, a symposium. Carmen *is* taking steps to collectivize the ownership of her farm, but it comes less, I suspect, from class concerns than it does from her desire to share more fully the burdens of farming, which up to now have fallen squarely on her shoulders. While acknowledging her fears that she might lose the land eventually, she hopes to ensure, contractually, her right to live on and use the land for the rest of her life.

"It's risky," she concedes, "but I want to be able to get away sometimes."

Carmen is certainly correct about the question of time for her and other women. It is remarkable that the women have found time to do the magazine at all, so busy are they with the money scramble—even those who own their own land. In the collectives money is not pooled. Each woman is responsible for paying her own way in addition to sharing chores. What impossibly few jobs are available in the Mendocino area are primarily tourist-related and low-paying—i.e., waitressing or maid service. The feminists who have these jobs are champing at the bit to change.

Curly-haired Nancy, who grew up near Mohave Desert military bases, considers herself lucky to work as a typesetter in a non-union print shop for $3.50 an hour. She is happy, too, living in a converted old house overlooking the coastal cliffs of Little River, paying $175 a month for her New Yorky-efficiency apartment. Each working day, Nancy hitchhikes the nearly 12 miles to Fort Bragg to go to work. Afterwards she hitchhikes to editorial or issue collective meetings, usually held beyond Little River, in Albion, and arrives home near midnight, exhausted. Her fridge has no meat or fish and few luxury foods at all. Too costly. A car is out of the question, even an old clunker.

Changes are afoot in this community, even where money may not exactly be a problem. Laney, who has been running a sheep farm, has told others of her intention to get out of the business in hopes of pursuing a writing career (she should have talked to me, I told her friends, on the economic advantages of *that*!). Recently, almost half of Laney's flock was killed by marauding dogs; while she and Tami (the latter lives on her land in exchange for caretaking and other farm chores) saved a few of them. Laney reportedly is discouraged with the enterprise after many years of trying.

Carmen, too, is wearying of what she calls "the shit work" in farming and her inability to make more than a subsistence living at it. She is looking for a way to earn money that will give her more leisure to do her painting.

Small farms, Carmen maintains, cannot make it. "It costs $15,000," she says with irritation, "for a Grade-A milk parlor." After her investment of $17,000 for her goat barn, another $15,000—the additional money for cement floors, stainless steel receptacles, sinks and the like—is beyond her means. It seems a shame, and I immediately agree with her when she argues that it would make far more sense for an inspector to visit periodically and check the quality of her goats' milk. But they don't do that; the laws demand, instead, the initial huge outlay of money.

Because of this, Carmen cannot sell her goat milk in a store. "I have to bootleg my milk house to house," she says, while I envision her with a yoke across her frail shoulders. In fact, neighbors and friends more usually come to *her* door to buy.

And there are other costs. The price of feed goes up all the time, particularly during a drought. Moreover, the feed for her goats is not grown in
the area and must be trucked in. Nevertheless, when I witness the delivery
of 12 tons of sweet-smelling alfalfa for her La Manchas and Nubians—and,
as I watch the shirtless male truckers heave the bales from the enormous
diesel truck onto the conveyer belt that reaches up to the second story of
her octagonal barn—I see Carmen's face breaking into a huge smile of satisfaction. She says, "I just love the smell of it, and it makes me feel good
to see it stacked up there in the loft so neatly."

The Beat Goes On

Just when I think there is a consensus among the women that farming
stinks, 24-year-old Tami, a blond and freckled former physical education
instructor from Los Angeles, belies the trend. Sturdy, muscular, cute in a
Norman Rockwellish way, this relative newcomer to the country (she was
one of the lucky drifters to the area who did find a berth on Laney's farm)
is ga-ga over farming in an ardent capitalist style and dreams of owning and
running her own farm.

She's taken to farming as if she slept all her life in a hayloft. I watch her
one day wielding a short scalpel on a hapless male lamb—on his testicles,
that is—as Harriet and I assist in holding the miserable creature down. The
white underflesh is bared. The poor male's eyes roll. His body trembles all
over even as he struggles, while I moan in sympathy and Tami blithely
assures me that cutting off their balls doesn't hurt them as much as I think
it does, because these pre-pubescent rams have a higher threshold of pain
than their struggles indicate. She reaches up into the incision, digs around,
and voilà: a short tug and there they are, the twin membranous bloody sacs,
cast aside on the dusty ground. (Sometimes, Tami informs me, they feed
the scrota to the pig they are raising, a newsy tidbit making me blanch with
the domestic cannibalism of it all.)

I am surprised, watching Tami's sure hand applying a purplish antibiotic
to the open incision, to find she has learned this cutting procedure only
recently. "I love working with animals," Tami says wistfully, as she strokes
the neck of her dazed victim, "but it's an expensive hobby. I have problems
of self-worth when I'm not getting a paycheck and am doing so much work."
The lamb shakes itself, rises and scampers clumsily to the other end of the
pen, where it wedges itself among the woolly bodies of the other sheep who
have witnessed his ignominy. To rectify the money/self-respect problem,
Tami went to sheep-shearing school this past year and is hoping soon to
make a living at it. Currently, she explains, there is only one shearer on the
Mendocino coast, so there is definitely a need for her skills; but, she points

out, as if admonishing herself, she must learn to shear quickly while keeping the fleece in one piece (hacked pieces don't sell on the wool market).

Such initiative as Tami's is continually spawned by this community of women and is reflected in the magazine as well. I understand a little of the reticence of these women to offend each other politically or any other way, because they have a built-in system of mutual support. Recently, for example, women from Carmen's farm and from the more "working-class" collective on which Sage lives banded together to form a carpentry collective. Again, it was trying to meet the challenges of earning a living and having that sense of self-worth.

The forming of a carpentry collective is politically significant as well as practical: it is the working manifestation of these women's feminism. One hears the area's denizens frequently talk about "continuing internal life changes," their desire to share these and their proudly won country skills with other women. It is as if they view their collective lives as a test tube. Yet they keep to themselves, and their impact on the area as a whole is imperceptible (at least in the relatively short time of my visit). Rather, it seems their discoveries are limited to those who are seeking it anyway in the pages of the magazine, or to those like me, who stumble upon them.

One long-time resident in the area, a 65-year-old administrator of a private social services organization in Fort Bragg, is critical of the *Country Women* feminists: "All the advancements of women in rural areas in recent years are the result of affirmative action programs *and* the law—not from consciousness-raising groups or magazines." Moreover, she blames the women for "polarizing some of the opinion of the community. Our experience with them is that a large part of them are lesbians." Mrs. X of Fort Bragg doesn't want anything to do with that. "The impression in the area is that they're a breed apart." Gay rights, she points out, receives little sympathy in most rural areas because of the innate conservatism of country residents.

But Betty Goodman, on the other hand, the bespectacled proprietor of the Gallery Book Shop in Mendocino, gives the feminists high marks on both their magazine and their lifestyle. "They've established high ideals. They've proved it can be done, and they've done it with a lot of hard work. I've seen these gals when they're so tired—staying up pulling the goat kids through birthing . . . distributing the magazine, too. . . ." She sighs at their efforts. "Part of my generation here is so tired of the other young people who have come up here to sit on the streets and ask for spare change, all the while complaining about the way things are. Those women aren't like that. They're trying to learn, and they're so determined and work so hard at it."

They are not the legions of earthshakers I anticipated. Nor are they the apathetic dropouts I feared. They have a kind of integrity to themselves and their ideals that is sometimes abrasive to me but that I nevertheless respect, even as I bristle under their attempts to control what I say about them. Their constant "internal life changes" smack of "Me Generation," and yet, they *have* come a long way against incredible economic and social odds.

Why do they keep at it, I wonder, with all the poverty and hard work? It comes down to the land, the beauty of the area itself and the ways in which their very lives seem crafted as an aesthetic object. Nancy speaks of living in the area as a "privilege." There is an undeniable spectacular grace to life that you see when you drive to town for supplies and see the jolt of eye-searing blue or aquamarine on the pallette of the Pacific Ocean as it crashes against sheer, jutting cliffs. And there are the time-stolen walks through fields of swaying bleached grasses, making garlands of them to put in the country windows; or the strolls through the nearby centuries-old pygmy forest with its shrunken, gnarled, but strangely appealing, trees.

My fantasies of living in this rarefied environment stop with a shudder at the endless toil. "But don't you see there's still an incredible amount of freedom that all of us have?" one remonstrated. Another said, "You pay a price to live and work in the country, but it's worth every sacrifice. We have everything we need here."

Even country-styled feminism!   [1978]

HENRY MILLER

The Oranges
of the Millennium

THE LITTLE COMMUNITY of one, begun by the fabulous "outlander," Jaime de Angulo, has multipled into a dozen families. The hill (Partington Ridge) is now nearing the saturation point, as things go in this part of the world. The one big difference between the Big Sur I encountered eleven years ago and that of today is the advent of so many new children. The mothers here seem to be as fecund as the soil. The little country school, situated not far from the State Park, has almost reached its capacity. It is the sort of school which, most unfortunately for our children, is rapidly disappearing from the American scene.

In another ten years we know not what may happen. If uranium or some other metal vital to the warmongers is discovered in these parts, Big Sur will be nothing but a legend.

Today Big Sur is no longer an outpost. The number of sightseers and visitors increases yearly. Emil White's "Big Sur Guide" alone brings swarms of tourists to our front door. What was inaugurated with virginal modesty threatens to end as a bonanza. The early settlers are dying off. Should their huge tracts of land be broken up into small holdings, Big Sur may rapidly develop into a suburb (of Monterey), with bus service, barbecue stands, gas stations, chain stores and all the odious claptrap that makes Suburbia horrendous.

This is a bleak view. It may be that we will be spared the usual horrors which accompany the tides of progress. Perhaps the millennium will be ushered in before we are taken over!

I like to think back to my early days on Partington Ridge, when there was no electricity, no butane tanks, no refrigeration—and the mail came only three times a week. In those days, and even later when I returned to the Ridge, I managed to get along without a car. To be sure, I did have a little cart (such as children play with), which Emil White had knocked together for me. Hitching myself to it, like an old billy goat, I would patiently haul the mail and groceries up the hill, a fairly steep climb of about a mile and a half. On reaching the turn near the Roosevelts' driveway, I would divest myself of everything but a jock-strap. What was to hinder?

The callers in those days were mostly youngsters just entering or just leaving the service. (They're doing the same today, though the war ended in '45.) The majority of these lads were artists or would-be artists. Some stayed on, eking out the weirdest sort of existence; some came back later to have a serious go at it. They were all filled with a desire to escape the horrors of the present and willing to live like rats if only they might be left alone and in peace. What a strange lot they were, when I think on it! Judson Crews of Waco, Texas, one of the first to muscle in, reminded one—because of his shaggy beard and manner of speech—of a latter-day prophet. He lived almost exclusively on peanut butter and wild mustard greens, and neither smoked nor drank. Norman Mini, who had already had an unusual career, starting as in Poe's case with his dismissal from West Point, stayed on (with wife and child) long enough to finish a first novel—the best first novel I have ever read and, as yet, unpublished. Norman was "different" in that, though poor as a church mouse, he clung to his cellar, which contained some of the finest wines (native and foreign) anyone could wish for. And then there was Walker Winslow, who was then writing *If a Man Be Mad*, which turned out to be a best seller. Walker wrote at top speed, and seemingly without interruption, in a tiny shack by the roadside which Emil White had built to house the steady stream of stragglers who were forever busting in on him for a day, a week, a month or year.

In all, almost a hundred painters, writers, dancers, sculptors and musicians have come and gone since I first arrived. At least a dozen possessed genuine talent and may leave their mark on the world. The one who was an unquestionable genius and the most spectacular of all, aside from Varda, who belongs to an earlier period, was Gerhart Muench of Dresden. Gerhart belongs in a category all by himself. As a pianist he is phenomenal, if not incomparable. He is also a composer. And in addition, a scholar, erudite to the finger tips. If he had done no more for us than to interpret Scriabin—and he did vastly more, all without result, alas!—we of Big Sur ought be forever indebted to him.

Speaking of artists, the curious thing is that few of this stripe ever last it out here. Is something lacking? Or is there too much . . . too much sunshine, too much fog, too much peace and contentment?

Almost every art colony owes its inception to the longing of a mature artist who felt the need to break with the clique surrounding him. The location chosen was usually an ideal one, particularly to the discoverer who had spent the better years of his life in dingy holes and garrets. The would-be artists, for whom place and atmosphere are all important, always contrive to convert these havens of retreat into boisterous, merry-making colonies. Whether this will happen to Big Sur remains to be seen. Fortunately there are certain deterrents.

It is my belief that the immature artist seldom thrives in idyllic surroundings. What he seems to need, though I am the last to advocate it, is more first-hand experience of life—more bitter experience, in other words. In short, more struggle, more privation, more anguish, more disillusionment. These goads or stimulants he may not always hope to find here in Big Sur. Here, unless he is on his guard, unless he is ready to wrestle with phantoms as well as bitter realities, he is apt to go to sleep mentally and spiritually. If an art colony is established here it will go the way of all the others. Artists never thrive in colonies. Ants do. What the budding artist needs is the privilege of wrestling with his problems in solitude—and now and then a piece of red meat.

The chief problem for the man who endeavors to live apart is the idle visitor. One can never decide whether he is a curse or a blessing. With all the experience which these last few years have provided, I still do not know how, or whether, to protect myself against the unwarranted intrusion, the steady invasion, of that prying, curious-minded species of "homo fatuoso" endowed with the annoying faculty of dropping in at the wrong moment.

To seek a hide-out more difficult of access is futile. The fan who wants to meet you, who is *determined* to meet you, if only to shake your hand, will not stop at climbing the Himalayas.

In America, I have long observed, one lives exposed to all comers. One is expected to live thus or be regarded as a crank. Only in Europe do writers live behind garden walls and locked doors.

In addition to all the other problems he has to cope with, the artist has to wage a perpetual struggle to fight free. I mean, find a way out of the senseless grind which daily threatens to annihilate all incentive. Even more than other mortals, he has need of harmonious surroundings. As writer or painter, he can do his work most anywhere. The rub is that wherever living is cheap, wherever nature is inviting, it is almost impossible to find the means of acquiring that bare modicum which is needed to keep body and soul together. A man with talent has to make his living on the side or do his creative work on the side. A difficult choice!

If he has the luck to find an ideal spot, or an ideal community, it does not follow that his work will there receive the encouragement he so desperately needs. On the contrary, he will probably find that no one is interested in what he is doing. He will generally be looked upon as strange or different. And he *will* be, of course, since what makes him tick is that mysterious element "X" which his fellow-man seems so well able to do without. He is almost certain to eat, talk, dress in a fashion eccentric to his neighbors. Which is quite enough to mark him out for ridicule, contempt and isolation. If, by taking a humble job, he demonstrates that he is as good as the next man, the situation may be somewhat ameliorated. But not for long. To prove that he is "as good as the next man" means little or nothing to one who is an artist. It was his "otherness" which made him an artist and, given the chance, he will make his fellow-man other too. Sooner or later, in one way or another, he is bound to rub his neighbors the wrong way. Unlike the ordinary fellow, he will throw everything to the winds when the urge seizes him. Moreover, if he *is* an artist, he will be compelled to make sacrifices which worldly people find absurd and unnecessary. In following the inner light he will inevitably choose for his boon companion poverty. And, if he has in him the makings of a great artist, he may renounce everything, even his art. This, to the average citizen, particularly the good citizen, is preposterous and unthinkable. Thus it happens now and then that, failing to recognize the genius in a man, a most worthy, a most respected, member of society may be heard to say: "Beware of that chap, he's up to no good!"

The world being what it is, I give it as my candid opinion that anyone who knows how to work with his two hands, anyone who is willing to give a fair day's work for a fair day's pay, would be better off to abandon his art and settle down to a humdrum life in an out of the way place like this. It may indeed be the highest wisdom to elect to be a nobody in a relative paradise such as this rather than a celebrity in a world which has lost all sense of values. But this is a problem which is rarely settled in advance.

There is one young man in this community who seems to have espoused the kind of wisdom I refer to. He is a man with an independent income, a man of keen intelligence, well educated, sensitive, of excellent character, and capable not only with his hands but with brain and heart. In making a life for himself he has apparently chosen to do nothing more than raise a family, provide its members with what he can, and enjoy the life of day to day. He does everything single-handed, from erecting buildings to raising crops, making wines, and so on. At intervals he hunts or fishes, or just takes off into the wilderness to commune with nature. To the average man he would appear to be just another good citizen, except that he is of better physique than most, enjoys better health, has no vices and no trace of the usual neuroses. His library is an excellent one, and he is at home in it; he enjoys good music and listens to it frequently. He can hold his own at any sport or game, can vie with the toughest when it comes to hard work, and in general is what might be called "a good fellow," that is, a man who knows how to mix with others, how to get along with the world. But what he also knows and does, and what the average citizen can not or will not do, is to enjoy solitude, to live simply, to crave nothing, and to share what he has when called upon. I refrain from mentioning his name for fear of doing him a disservice. Let us leave him where he is, Mr. X, a master of the anonymous life and a wonderful example to his fellow-man.

While in Vienne (France) two years ago I had the privilege of making the acquaintance of Fernand Rude, the *sous-préfet* of Vienne, who possesses a remarkable collection of Utopian literature. On leaving, he presented me with a copy of his book, *Voyage en Icarie*,* which is the account of two workers from Vienne who came to America just a hundred years ago to join Étienne Cabet's experimental colony at Nauvoo, Illinois. The description given of American life, not only at Nauvoo but in the cities they passed through—they arrived at New Orleans and left by way of New York—is worth reading today, if only to observe how essentially unchanged is our American way of life. To be sure, Whitman was giving us about this same time (in his prose works) a similar picture of vulgarity, violence and corruption, in high and low places. One fact stands out, however, and that is the inborn urge of the American to experiment, to try out the most crack-brained schemes having to do with social, economic, religious and even sex relations.

* The title is taken from the book of the same name by Étienne Cabet wherein the latter describes his (imaginary) Utopia. A remarkable work in this, that though Communistic in the romantic sense, it is an accurate blueprint of the totalitarian governments we now have.

Where sex and religion were dominant, the most amazing results were achieved. The Oneida Community (New York), for example, is destined to remain as memorable an experiment as Robert Owen's in New Harmony (Indiana). As for the Mormons, nothing comparable to their efforts has ever been undertaken on this continent, and probably never will again.

In all these idealistic ventures, particularly those initiated by religious communities, the participants seemed to possess a keen sense of reality, a practical wisdom, which in no way conflicted (as it does in the case of ordinary Christians) with their religious views. They were honest, law-abiding, industrious, self-sustaining, self-sufficient citizens with character, individuality and integrity, somewhat corroded (to our present way of thinking) by a Puritan sobriety and austerity, but never lacking in faith, courage and independence. Their influence on American thought, American behavior, has been most powerful.

Since living here in Big Sur I have become more and more aware of this tendency in my fellow-American to experiment. Today it is not communities or groups who seek to lead "the good life" but isolated individuals. The majority of these, at least from my observation, are young men who have already had a taste of professional life, who have already been married and divorced, who have already served in the armed forces and seen a bit of the world, as we say. Utterly disillusioned, this new breed of experimenter is resolutely turning his back on all that he once held true and viable, and is making a valiant effort to start anew. Starting anew, for this type, means leading a vagrant's life, tackling anything, clinging to nothing, reducing one's needs and one's desires, and eventually—out of a wisdom born of desperation—leading the life of an artist. Not, however, the type of artist we are familiar with. An artist, rather, whose sole interest is in creating, an artist who is indifferent to reward, fame, success. One, in short, who is reconciled from the outset to the fact that the better he is the less chance he has of being accepted at face value. These young men, usually in their late twenties or early thirties, are now roaming about in our midst like anonymous messengers from another planet. By force of example, by reason of their thoroughgoing nonconformity and, shall I say, "nonresistance," they are proving themselves a more potent, stimulating force than the most eloquent and vociferous of recognized artists.

The point to note is that these individuals are not concerned with undermining a vicious system but with leading their own lives—on the fringe of society. It is only natural to find them gravitating toward places like Big Sur, of which there are many replicas in this vast country. We are in the habit of speaking of "the last frontier," but wherever there are "individuals" there will always be new frontiers. For the man who wants to lead the good life, which is a way of saying *his own life*, there is always a spot where he can dig in and take root.

But what is it that these young men have discovered, and which, curiously enough, links them with their forebears who deserted Europe for America? That the American way of life is an illusory kind of existence, that the price demanded for the security and abundance it pretends to offer is too great. The presence of these "renegades," small in number though they be, is but another indication that the machine is breaking down. When the smashup comes, as now seems inevitable, they are more likely to survive the catastrophe than the rest of us. At least, they will know how to get along without cars, without refrigerators, without vacuum cleaners, electric razors and all the other "indispensables" . . . probably even without money. If ever we are to witness a new heaven and a new earth, it must surely be one in which money is absent, forgotten, wholly useless.

Here I should like to quote from a review of *Living the Good Life*, by Helen and Scott Nearing.* Says the editor: "What we are trying to suggest is that the solution for a cluttered, frustrated existence is not merely in moving to the country and attempting to practise 'the simple life.' The solution is in an attitude towards human experience which makes simple physical and economic arrangements almost a moral and esthetic necessity. It is the larger purpose in life which gives to its lesser enterprises—the obtaining of food, shelter and clothing—their essential harmony and balance. So often people dream of an ideal life "in community," forgetting that a "community" is not an end in itself, but a frame for higher qualities—the qualities of the mind and the heart. Making a community is not a magic formula for happiness and good; making a community is the result of the happiness and the good which people already possess in principle, and the community, whether of one family or several, is the infinitely variable expression of the excellences of human beings, and not their cause. . . ."

Digging in at Big Sur eleven years ago, I must confess that I had not the least thought or concern about the life of the community. With a population of one hundred souls scattered over several hundred square miles, I was not even conscious of an existent "community." My community then comprised a dog, Pascal (so named because he had the sorrowful look of a thinker), a few trees, the buzzards, and a seeming jungle of poison oak. My only friend, Emil White, lived three miles down the road. The hot sulphur baths were three miles farther down the road. There the community ended, from my standpoint.

I soon found out how mistaken I was, of course. It was no time before

* From *Manas*, Los Angeles, March 23, 1955.

neighbors began popping up from all sides—out of the brush, it seemed—and always laden with gifts, as well as the most discreet and sensible advice, for the "newcomer." Never have I known better neighbors! All of them were endowed with a tact and subtlety such as I never ceased to marvel at. They came only when they sensed you had need of them. As in France, it seemed to me that I was once again among people who knew how to let you be. And always there was a standing invitation to join them at table, should you have need of food or company.

Being one of those unfortunate "helpless" individuals who knew nothing but city ways, it wasn't long before I had to call upon my neighbors for aid of one kind or another. Something was always going amiss, something was always getting out of order. I hate to think what would have happened had I been left entirely to my own resources! Anyway, with the assistance that was always willingly and cheerfully extended, I received instruction in how to help myself, the most valuable gift that can be offered. I discovered all too quickly that my neighbors were not only extremely affable, helpful, generous in every way, but that they were far more intelligent, far wiser, far more self-sufficient than I had fatuously thought myself to be. The community, from being at first an invisible web, gradually became most tangible, most real. For the first time in my life I found myself surrounded by kind souls who were not thinking exclusively of their own welfare. A strange new sense of security began to develop in me, one I had never known before. In fact, I would boast to visitors that, once a resident of Big Sur, nothing evil could possibly happen to one. I would always add cautiously: "But one has first to prove himself a good neighbor!" Though they were addressed to my visitor, I meant these words for myself. And often, when the visitor had departed, I would repeat them to myself like a litany. It took time, you see, for one who had always lived the jungle life of the big city to realize that he too could be "a neighbor."

Here I must say flatly, and not without a bad conscience, that I am undoubtedly the worst neighbor any community could boast of. That I am still treated with more than mere tolerance is something which still surprises me.

Often I am so completely out of it all that the only way I can "get back" is to look at my world through the eyes of my children. I always begin by thinking back to the glorious childhood I enjoyed in that squalid section of Brooklyn known as Williamsburg. I try to relate those squalid streets and shabby houses to the vast expanse of sea and mountain of this region. I dwell on the birds I never saw except for the sparrow feasting on a fresh pile of manure, or a stray pigeon. Never a hawk, a buzzard, an eagle, never a robin or a hummingbird. I think of the sky which was always hacked to pieces by roof-tops and hideous smoking chimneys. I breathe again the air that filled the sky, an atmosphere without fragrance, often leaden and oppressive, saturated with the reek of burning chemicals. I think of the games we played in the street, ignorant of the lure of stream and forest. I think, and with tenderness, of my little companions, some of whom later went to the penitentiary. Despite it all, it was a good life I led there. A wonderful life, I might say. It was the first "Paradise" I knew, there in that old neighborhood. And though forever gone, it is still accessible in memory.

But *now*, now when I watch the youngsters playing in our front yard, when I see them silhouetted against the blue white-capped Pacific, when I stare at the huge, frightening buzzards swirling lazily above, circling, dipping, forever circling, when I observe the willow gently swaying, its long fragile branches drooping ever lower, ever greener and tenderer, when I hear the frog croaking in the pool or a bird calling from the bush, when I suddenly turn and espy a lemon ripening on a dwarfish tree or notice that the camellia has just begun to bloom, I see my children set against an eternal background. They are not even *my* children any longer, but just children, children of the earth . . . and I know they will never forget, never forsake, the place where they were born and raised. In my mind I am with them as they return from some distant shore to gaze upon the old homestead. My eyes are moist with tears as I watch them moving tenderly and reverently amid a swarm of golden memories. Will they notice, I wonder, the tree they were going to help me plant but were too busy then having fun? Will they stand in the little wing we built for them and wonder how on earth they ever fitted into such a cubicle? Will they pause outside the tiny workroom where I passed my days and tap again at the windowpane to ask if I will join them at play—*or must I work some more*? Will they find the marbles I gathered from the garden and hid so that they would not swallow them? Will they stand in reverie at the forest glade, where the little stream prattles on, and search for the pots and pans with which we made our make-believe breakfast before diving into the woods? Will they take the goat path along the flank of the mountain and look up in wonder and awe at the old Trotter house teetering in the wind? Will they run down to the Rosses, if only in memory, to see if Harrydick can mend the broken sword or Shanagolden lend us a pot of jam?

For every wonderful event in my golden childhood they must possess a dozen incomparably more wonderful. For not only did they have their little playmates, their games, their mysterious adventures, as did I, they had also skies of pure azure and walls of fog moving in and out of the canyons with invisible feet, hills in winter of emerald green and in summer mountain upon mountain of pure gold. They had even more, for there was ever the unfathomable silence of the forest, the blazing immensity of the Pacific, days drenched with sun and nights spangled with stars and—"Oh, Daddy, come quick, see the moon, it's lying in the pool!" And besides the adoration of the neighbors, a dolt of a father who preferred wasting his time playing with them to cultivating his mind or making himself a good neighbor. Lucky the father who is merely a writer, who can drop his work and return to childhood at will! Lucky the father who is pestered from morn till sundown by two healthy, insatiable youngsters! Lucky the father who learns to see again through the eyes of his children, even though he become the biggest fool that ever was!

"The Brothers and Sisters of the Free Spirit called their devotional community-life 'Paradise' and interpreted the word as signifying the quintessence of love."*

Looking at a fragment of "The Millennium" (by Hieronymus Bosch) the other day, I pointed out to our neighbor, Jack Morgenrath, (formerly of Williamsburg, Brooklyn) how hallucinatingly real were the oranges that diapered the trees. I asked him why it was that these oranges, so preternaturally real in appearance, possessed something more than would oranges painted, say, by Cézanne (better known for his apples) or even by Van Gogh. To Jack it was simple. (Everything is quite simple to Jack, by the way. It's part of his charm.) Said Jack: "It's because of the ambiance." And he is right, absolutely right. The animals in this same triptych are equally mysterious, equally hallucinating, in their super-reality. A camel is always a camel and a leopard a leopard, yet they are altogether unlike any other camels, any other leopards. They can hardly even be said to be the camels and leopards of Hieronymus Bosch, magician though he was. They belong to another age, an age when man was one with all creation . . . "when the lion lay down with the lamb."

Bosch is one of the very few painters—he was indeed more than a painter!—who acquired a magic vision. He saw through the phenomenal world, rendered it transparent, and thus revealed its pristine aspect.† Seeing the world through his eyes it appears to us once again as a world of indestructible order, beauty, harmony, which it is our privilege to accept as a paradise or convert into a purgatory.

The enchanting, and sometimes terrifying, thing is that the world can

* *The Millennium of Hieronymus Bosch*, by Wilhelm Fränger (Chicago: University of Chicago Press, 1951), page 104.

† "The human mind has drawn a net of logical relationships and practical ingenuity over the phenomenal world with which it is confronted; and so, by this intellectual and material domination of the world, it has removed itself to an infinite distance from the created world in which it once had a purely natural share. It was this natural world in which the Brethren of the Free Spirit saw the meaning of life." (*The Millennium of Hieronymus Bosch*, page 152.)

be so many things to so many different souls. That it can be, and is, all these at one and the same time.

I am led to speak of the "Millennium" because, receiving as many visitors as I do, and from all parts of the globe, I am constantly reminded that I am living in a virtual paradise. ("And how did you manage to find such a place?" is the usual exclamation. As if *I* had any part in it!) But what amazes me, and this is the point, is that so very few ever think on taking leave that they too might enjoy the fruits of paradise. Almost invariably the visitor will confess that he lacks the courage—imagination would be nearer the mark— to make the necessary break. "You're lucky," he will say—meaning, to be a writer—"you can do your work anywhere." He forgets what I have told him, and most pointedly, about the other members of the community—the ones who really support the show—who are not writers, painters or artists of any sort, except in spirit. "Too late," he probably murmurs to himself, as he takes a last wistful glance about.

How illustrative, this attitude, of the woeful resignation men and women succumb to! Surely every one realizes, at some point along the way, that he is capable of living a far better life than the one he has chosen. What stays him, usually, is the fear of the sacrifices involved. (Even to relinquish his chains seems like a sacrifice.) Yet everyone knows that nothing is accomplished without sacrifice.

The longing for paradise, whether here on earth or in the beyond, has almost ceased to be. Instead of an *idée-force* it has become an *idée fixe*. From a potent myth it has degenerated into a taboo. Men will sacrifice their lives to bring about a better world—whatever that may mean—but they will not budge an inch to attain paradise. Nor will they struggle to create a bit of paradise in the hell they find themselves. It is so much easier, and gorier, to make revolution, which means, to put it simply, establishing another, a different, status quo. If paradise were realizable—this is the classic retort!— it would no longer be paradise.

What is one to say to a man who insists on making his own prison?

There is a type of individual who, after finding what he considers a paradise, proceeds to pick flaws in it. Eventually this man's paradise becomes even worse than the hell from which he had escaped.

Certainly paradise, whatever, wherever it be, contains flaws. (Paradisiacal flaws, if you like.) If it did not, it would be incapable of drawing the hearts of men *or* angels.

The windows of the soul are infinite, we are told. And it is through the eyes of the soul that paradise is visioned. If there are flaws in your paradise, open more windows! Vision is entirely a creative faculty: it uses the body and the mind as the navigator uses his instruments. Open and alert, it matters little whether one finds a supposed short cut to the Indies—or discovers a new world. Everything is begging to be discovered, not accidentally, but intuitively. Seeking intuitively, one's destination is never in a beyond of time or space but always here and now. If we are always arriving and departing, it is also true that we are eternally anchored. One's destination is never a place but rather a new way of looking at things. Which is to say that there are no limits to vision. Similarly, there are no limits to paradise. Any paradise worth the name can sustain all the flaws in creation and remain undiminished, untarnished.

If I have entered upon a vein which I must confess is one not frequently discussed here, I am nevertheless certain that it is one which secretly engages the minds of many members of the community.

Everyone who has come here in search of a new way of life has made a complete change-about in his daily routine. Nearly every one has come from afar, usually from a big city. It meant abandoning a job and a mode of life which was detestable and insufferable. To what degree each one has found "new life" can be estimated only by the efforts he or she put forth. Some, I suspect, would have found "it" even had they remained where they were.

The most important thing I have witnessed, since coming here, is the transformation people have wrought in their own being. Nowhere have I seen individuals work so earnestly and assiduously on themselves. Nor so successfully. Yet nothing is taught or preached here, at least overtly. Some have made the effort and failed. Happily for the rest of us, I should say. But even these who failed gained something. For one thing, their outlook on life was altered, enlarged if not "improved." And what could be better than for the teacher to become his own pupil, or the preacher his own convert?

In a paradise you don't preach or teach. You practice the perfect life— or you relapse.

There seems to be an unwritten law here which insists that you accept what you find and like it, profit by it, or you are cast out. Nobody does the rejecting, please understand. Nobody, no group here, would crave such authority. No, the place itself, the elements which make it, do that. It's the law, as I say. And it is a just law which works harm to no one. To the cynical-minded it may sound like the same old triumph of our dear status quo. But the enthusiast knows that it is precisely the fact that there is no status quo here which makes for its paradisiacal quality.

No, the law operates because that which makes for paradise can not and will not assimilate that which makes for hell. How often it is said that we make our own heaven and our own hell. And how little it is taken to heart! Yet the truth prevails, whether we believe in it or not.

Paradise or no paradise, I have the very definite impression that the people of this vicinity are striving to live up to the grandeur and nobility which is such an integral part of the setting. They behave as if it were a privilege to live here, as if it were by an act of grace they found themselves here. The place itself is so overwhelmingly bigger, greater, than anyone could hope to make it that it engenders a humility and reverence not frequently met with in Americans. There being nothing to improve on in the surroundings, the tendency is to set about improving oneself.

It is of course true that individuals have undergone tremendous changes, broadened their vision, altered their natures, in hideous, thwarting surroundings—prisons, ghettos, concentration camps, and so on. Only a very rare individual elects to *remain* in such places. The man who has seen the light follows the light. And the light usually leads him to the place where he can function most effectively, that is, where he will be of most use to his fellow-men. In this sense, it matters little whether it be darkest Africa or the Himalayan heights. God's work can be done anywhere, so to say.

We have all met the soldier who has been overseas. And we all know that each one has a different story to relate. We are all like returned soldiers. We have all been somewhere, spiritually speaking, and we have either benefited by the experience or been worsted by it. One man says: "Never again!" Another says: "Let it come! I'm ready for anything!" Only the fool hopes to repeat an experience; the wise man knows that *every* experience is to be viewed as a blessing. Whatever we try to deny or reject is precisely what we have need of; it is our very need which often paralyzes us, prevents us from welcoming a (good or bad) experience.

I come back once again to those individuals who came here full of needs and who fled after a time because "it" was not what they hoped to find, or because "they" were not what they thought themselves to be. None of them, from what I have learned, has yet found it or himself. Some returned to their former masters in the manner of slaves unable to support the privileges and responsibilities of freedom. Some found their way into mental retreats. Some became derelicts. Others simply surrendered to the villainous status quo.

I speak as if they had been marked by the whip. I do not mean to be cruel or vindictive. What I wish to say quite simply is that none of them, in my humble opinion, is a whit happier, a whit better off, an inch advanced in any respect. They will all continue to talk about their Big Sur adventure for the rest of their lives—wistfully, regretfully, or elatedly, as occasion dictates. In the hearts of some, I know, is the profound hope that their children will display more courage, more perseverance, more integrity than they themselves did. But do they not overlook something? Are not their children, as the product of self-confessed failures, already condemned? Have they not been contaminated by the virus of "security"?

The most difficult thing to adjust to, apparently, is peace and contentment. As long as there is something to fight, people seem able to brave all manner of hardships. Remove the element of struggle, and they are like fish out of water. Those who no longer have anything to worry about will, in desperation, often take on the burdens of the world. This not through idealism but because they must have something to do, or at least something to talk about. Were these empty souls truly concerned about the plight of their fellow-men they would consume themselves in the flames of devotion. One need hardly go beyond his own doorstep to discover a realm large enough to exhaust the energies of a giant, or better, a saint.

Naturally, the more attention one gives the deplorable conditions outside the less one is able to enjoy what peace and liberty he possesses. Even if it be heaven we find ourselves in, we can render it suspect and dubious.

Some will say they do not wish to *dream* their lives away. As if life itself were not a dream, a very real dream from which there is no awakening! We pass from one state of dream to another: from the dream of sleep to the dream of waking, from the dream of life to the dream of death. Whoever has enjoyed a good dream never complains of having wasted his time. On the contrary, he is delighted to have partaken of a reality which serves to heighten and enhance the reality of everyday.

The oranges of Bosch's "Millennium," as I said before, exhale this dreamlike reality which constantly eludes us and which is the very substance of life. They are far more delectable, far more potent, than the Sunkist oranges we daily consume in the naive belief that they are laden with wonder-working vitamins. The millennial oranges which Bosch created restore the soul; the ambiance in which he suspended them is the everlasting one of spirit become real.

Every creature, every object, every place has its own ambiance. Our world itself possesses an ambiance which is unique. But worlds, objects, creatures, places, all have this in common: they are ever in a state of transmutation. The supreme delight of dream lies in this transformative power. When the personality liquefies, so to speak, as it does so deliciously in dream, and the very nature of one's being is alchemized, when form and substance, time and space, become yielding and elastic, responsive and obedient to one's slightest wish, he who awakens from his dream knows beyond all doubt that the imperishable soul which he calls his own is but a vehicle of his eternal element of change.

In waking life, when all is well and cares fall away, when the intellect is silenced and we slip into reverie, do we not surrender blissfully to the eternal flux, float ecstatically on the still current of life? We have all experienced moments of utter forgetfulness when we knew ourselves as plant, animal, creature of the deep or denizen of the air. Some of us have even known moments when we were as the gods of old. Most every one has known *one* moment in his life when he felt so good, so thoroughly attuned, that he has been on the point of exclaiming: *"Ah, now is the time to die!"* What is it lurks here in the very heart of euphoria? The thought that it will not, can not last? The sense of an ultimate? Perhaps. But I think there is another, deeper aspect to it. I think that in such moments we are trying to tell ourselves what we have long known but ever refuse to accept—that living and dying are one, that all is one, and that it makes no difference whether we live a day or a thousand years.   [1957]

CYRA MC FADDEN

The Serial

11. A CHANGE OF PACE

When the news of Kate's and Harvey's separation reached Martha, the friend whose Mount Tam wedding they'd attended a few months before, it really got to her. Her gut reaction, as she told her new husband Bill, was "You gotta be kidding!"

The split, however, was for real. Several people all confirmed it, though there was some confusion about whether Harvey was living with a fourteen-year-old female mainliner or a male hairdresser.

Martha was cool about that part: different strokes and like that. But she felt really paranoid about the breakup of the marriage, because if the Holroyds couldn't make it, who could? They'd seemed so *together* together. And Martha was genuinely fond of them both, even if they were heavily into that whole suburban materialistic bag.

Reciting Rod McKuen to the Boston ferns in her Fairfax Canyon A-frame, baking whole-grain pumpernickel and reading *Jonathan Livingston Seagull* to the children (they knew it by heart but clamored for it anyway), Martha did some deep thinking about marriage. After five of them, she felt she had some insight on the subject, and one thing she had learned, while she was paying her dues, was that marriage was this dynamic process. You had to stay really in touch with yourself if you were going to relate to the other person's feelings instead of just ego-tripping.

Bill said you shouldn't judge anybody else until you'd walked a mile in his hiking boots, but Martha couldn't help wondering, nonetheless, if the Holroyds' separation wasn't one more spin-off from Watergate. Not that she thought the CIA had sent Kate obscene tape recordings or anything—she wasn't *that* paranoid—but her own last marriage had deteriorated rapidly when Nixon finally resigned. Almost immediately, she and her ex had realized that they didn't have anything else to talk about.

While life, too, was a process, and all experience was good if you took the cosmic overview, Martha knew from personal experience that failure *felt* like a bummer at the time. She knew she ought to call Kate and invite her to dinner, or at least encourage her to dump on her and get her feelings right up front where Martha could help her work through them.

She kept procrastinating, though, because the Holroyd bit threatened her, in view of her own new permanent commitment, and she thought she'd better get clear on the whole shtick herself before she got involved. After all, she and Bill were still getting inside each other's heads, a high-energy trip that didn't leave a lot of space for outside interaction.

Consequently, Martha was particularly freaked out when she learned accidentally that Harvey was now involved with Carol, Kate's friend and Martha's own.

The first time she saw them together; picking out a Camembert at The Cheese Store in Old Brown's, she didn't put it together; lots of people were into Camembert, so maybe it was no big thing. Certainly Carol was dressed to kill, in a forties dress from Foxy Lady and the platforms Martha had admired in the window of Wanda's Boutique/Footique the week before, but Carol always dressed like a Pointer Sister anyway. And they were both laid back. Harvey even invited Martha to drop by his condo on the Greenbrae canal some afternoon and feed the ducks.

The next time she encountered the two of them, at the new Saturday Night Movie series in that funky old Odd Fellows Hall on Throckmorton, Martha just figured Harvey's hairdresser lover had already seen *Payday*. If he and Carol were getting it on, wouldn't they be keeping a low profile? Anyway, it had always been Martha's impression that Harvey didn't like Carol. You didn't go to bed with someone you couldn't even *relate* to.

Finally, however, she saw Harvey and Carol practically crawling all over each other in the parking lot in front of Caruso's one Saturday afternoon. There they were, squashed together in the driver's seat of Harvey's familiar Volvo with the bumper sticker that read "I'd Rather Be Sailing."

Martha wound her way back up Scenic deeply upset. Thank God it wasn't her problem, because after all those years of unhappy marriages to psychotics, all of whose self-images were based on destroying hers, she'd earned the right to just look after Numero Uno. But she was burned at Carol. Sisterhood was powerful, for sure, but it ought to stop short, in Martha's view, of incest.

She and Bill rapped about the whole thing in depth that night over the cioppino. It was a somewhat fragmented conversation, because Tamalpa, Martha's four-year-old from her second marriage, kept throwing clams at Bill's son Gregor from his last permanent commitment, and a lot of the time was necessarily devoted to an open discussion of sibling rivalry and the extended-family concept. Nonetheless, Bill convinced Martha that she should probably tell Kate, because if you weren't part of the solution, you were part of the problem. How could Kate deal with the realities of her particular time and space if she didn't know what they were?

Martha agreed to call Kate as soon as she'd scraped the tomato sauce out of the natural Iranian rug from Rezaian's that was the only positive carry-over from her last domestic interlude, but she wasn't very happy about the prospect. What if Kate somehow blamed her? Like subconsciously?

Fortunately, she didn't have to cope right away; the Maginnises, who lived next door and whose kids went to the same alternative nursery school as hers and Bill's, were coming over for coffee. By the time Martha got the kids to stop trying to mug each other and settled them in front of their respective easels for their regular half hour of free expression, it was time to grind the French roast for the Chemex.

Martha was looking forward to some stimulating adult conversation, since it was hard to keep your mind alive when you spend most of your life with people three feet high. While she was standing at the sink digging the play-dough out of her demitasse cups, she also had a flash that made her feel a lot more integrated about Kate, Harvey and that whole scene. If anybody could tell her whether or not she should be upfront with Kate or take part in the cover-up, it was Naomi Maginnis. Naomi, a heavy-duty intellectual, was practically Martha's guru. . . .

12. DEALING WITH THE WHOLE CHILD

Kate's friend Martha and her husband Bill shared with their Fairfax next-door neighbors a total commitment to the nurturing of the whole child, so they had a lot in common even though Martha was a college dropout while Naomi Maginnis had two master's degrees from Mills, one in sociology and one in batik.

It just went to show that intellectual heavies could be beautiful in spite of all those smarts. Naomi, for instance, was a model mother. Unlike Martha herself, she never shouted at her kids, never blew her cool with them and never came on like a parent figure. Look at the way she was now persuading her youngest, John Muir Maginnis, to stop swinging on Martha's drapes.

"John-John," Naomi was saying, "I shouldn't engage in that form of activity if I were you. Your actions might be subject to misinterpretation, don't you agree?"

John-John stared at her balefully. "I don' give a shit," he said, and instead began to beat Tamalpa, Martha's four-year-old daughter, over the head with his Playskool carpenter's awl. It was just amazing the way children worked out their hostilities among themselves if you didn't interfere with their natural instincts.

Serving the coffee and her homemade whole-wheat baklava, Martha thought about the way parents in Marin raised their young. The contrast to her own oppressively regimented childhood made her feel truly optimistic about the future of humanity in the hands of Consciousness III. If, like Tamalpa and John-John, she had been permitted as a child to "act out" when she felt like it, Martha was pretty sure she wouldn't have spent all those years in psychoanalysis. Her shrink had told her that her own father, as she'd described him, was practically a casebook example of an anal retentive.

It did worry her, occasionally, that her oldest daughter, Debbie, had gone all through high school in Marin without learning to write a grammatical sentence and without knowing where Europe was. (Debbie got Europe mixed up with Eureka.) But Martha had discussed the whole thing with Debbie's counselor on more than one occasion and had found him terrifically *simpático*; he'd pointed out to her that the written word was on its way out, that what was most important was that Debbie learn to function in the here/now, and that Martha must want her daughter to be happy.

Martha hadn't heard from Debbie since she ran off to Zihuatanejo with a dirt-bike racer, so she didn't know whether Debbie was really, *really* happy or not. But she was glad she had a chance to parent all over again with Tamalpa, Gregor and Che.

She sat down beside Naomi on her new natural linen sofa from Mc-Dermott's (Martha was getting back to natural fibers and earthy colors, because your environment was terrifically important to your inner serenity), and started to ask her, as she'd planned to do earlier, about whether or not she should tell Kate about Harvey's new liaison. Naomi was the person to give her the straight dope, because while she didn't know either of the Holroyds, she not only belonged to Mensa but was fantastic at conceptualizing.

But John-John sort of blew it by picking up his father's coffee cup and dumping the scalding French roast methodically down his pant leg, which caused Jason, who usually didn't overreact like that, to scream. So they had to drop everything else for the moment and explain the pleasure/pain principle to him, and Martha had to get a sponge and mop up the coffee from the natural linen, a little nostalgic for the old Naugahyde sofa it had replaced. Of course she wouldn't have plastic in her house anymore, because it was so *synthetic*, but sometimes she missed it.

Jason was superintelligent, too, however (he had a Ph.D. in Medieval Studies from Cornell and was currently teaching night classes in bonehead English at the College of Marin), so he naturally dealt with John-John calmly once he stopped writhing. "John," he said, "I can only surmise that your impulsive gesture, in pouring hot coffee on your father, was the result of some instinctual aversion to the use of stimulants—an admirable course of action in the abstract but a painful one in actuality. I feel we should discuss the question of how one chooses the form of protest he employs as a vehicle for his convictions. It's difficult to entertain an honest difference of opinion on the rational level when one is suffering from third-degree burns, can you understand that?"

John-John gave him the finger, snatched Martha's baklava off her plate and began to pull Gregor's hair. Martha thought it really spoke volumes for the Maginnises that he was so uninhibited.

Finally, although the intrusion of the children continued to be a problem throughout the evening, Martha and Bill brought the conversation around to what Martha should do about Kate. Was it more authentic to tell her that Harvey was getting it on with Carol, whom Kate thought of as her best friend, or just to cop out?

Naomi resolved the issue definitively once she'd gently restrained Gregor from kicking her repeatedly in the calf of her Danskin leotard. "Look, Martha," she said, "while my opinion is necessarily 'off the wall,' as you'd put it, I should think that your dilemma, as you've articulated it, has wider implications. . . . John-John, Mummy finds it unpleasant to be poked in the eye like that. . . . I myself feel that absolute honesty must always take precedence, in an enlightened community, over crasser, more pragmatic considerations. Otherwise we simply recreate the hypocrisy of our times, with all its disastrous and perhaps irrevocable consequences.

"I, for one, would want to know if Jason were betraying me in that particularly squalid fashion . . ." Naomi paused meaningfully . . . "so I could *kill* the son-of-a-bitch."

Martha was just zapped. Naomi *always* got right down to the nitty-gritty. "Wow," she said, "you're right. You're right, you know? Really." As soon as the Maginnises went home, if they ever did, she was determined to call Kate, painful duty though it was, and give her the word. . . .   [1976]

III

Southern California Country

JACK SMITH

Harry's Bar, Century City

PERHAPS what made the winning entry seem fresh and appealing was that it abandoned the usual Hemingway locales—the bullrings and battlefields of Spain, the bistros of Paris, the cafés and piazzas of Italy, the green hills of Africa—and brought him improbably to a place he undoubtedly never saw—the San Fernando Valley:

"Outside it was raining. It does not rain inside, south of Ventura Boulevard. The rain ran down the little brown hills, past the condos and the wine bistros and the off-ramps where the Caltrans carabinieri waited.

"In the Galleria it was fine. If you have been to the Galleria, then you know how it is. Sometimes clean and warm and bright. Sometimes clean and warm and cold, and the fine strong girls from the valley with their lovely clean legwarmers and tight miniskirts and soft pretzels. Sometimes Jennifer and Andrea and Kimberley. Sometimes Megan.

"She had been there as long as the concrete, longer than Sears, and she understood how it is when you do not know what it is you want to buy until you have forgotten and bought a Blasters album, only she did not know it then. She had just had her toes done.

" 'Darling,' she said. 'Like, awesome.' She looked very young and fresh and stonewashed. At the sight of her my stomach went hollow and empty.

" 'You are a bitchen girl, a tubular girl,' I told her. . . .

"She smiled through her Sony Walkman. 'Like, you know, tell me everything at once. . . .' "

The author turned out to be Lynda Leidiger. She lives in North Hollywood and works for the Auto Club. The news was telephoned to her.

Forty minutes later she walked into Harry's Bar—a very excited blonde young woman in a peppermint striped jersey dress. She looked very young and fresh and stonewashed, and my stomach went hollow and empty.

Everyone cheered.   [1983]

RICHARD REEVES

Vulnerable

IT WAS midafternoon when I arrived at Los Angeles International Airport on October 23, 1978, but the sky was already dark. Driving home along the Pacific Ocean, I could see black to the north and west—boiling clouds of smoke coming off the Santa Monica Mountains. By six o'clock, I was standing in front of my house, in Pacific Palisades, watching waves of orange flame break over the mountains. Houses in the path of the waves exploded silently just before the flames reached them. I counted eight—puffs of bright gas, and then the houses were gone. By seven o'clock, I was packing the car—family photograph albums and insurance policies first—and listening to a radio report of tires melting as people tried to escape the fire in automobiles. At eight o'clock, the winds—the fierce desert winds called Santa Anas—suddenly died down, and the waves of fire spent themselves north of Sunset Boulevard, five blocks away. In places, the fire had been moving at fifty miles an hour.

My first earthquake was on New Year's Day of 1979. A friend and I were having a late lunch in a little place called the Inn of the Seventh Ray, in Topanga Canyon. There was a heavy jolt, and the floor vibrated. I thought a truck had hit the building. But the floor did not stop vibrating, as it would have if the building had been struck. I was confused. Actions seemed to be taking place in slow motion. People pushed chairs and tables aside, stood up, and began running toward the door. I realized that there was a sound— a steady roaring, as if a freight train were coming into the room. Outside, I still heard the sound and felt the vibration. Stones were clattering down a hillside into the roadway. The next day's Los Angeles *Times* reported that the quake was "small"—4.6 on the Richter scale. It had lasted less than ten seconds, and there were twenty smaller aftershocks. While it was happening, there was no way of knowing that this thing would be judged small by instruments at the California Institute of Technology.

I had already begun to wonder whether God intended for people to live in Los Angeles. Certainly He never meant for millions of them to live there. One of the first Europeans who saw the place—Father Juan Crespi, a Spanish missionary who passed through in August of 1769—wrote that the area was beautiful and a perfect place for a mission settlement. But he also noticed the signs of alternating drought and "great floods," and felt earthquake after earthquake, "which astonishes us." The men who followed Crespi defied God, defied nature, living in air they regularly poisoned, rerouting the rivers, levelling the hills, filling the canyons, building thousands and thousands of homes among the gnarled little trees and bushes—the "brush" in brush-fires—that burn periodically and so make room for new growth, on slopes that continually slide back into canyons, above earthquake fault lines veined deep into the earth. Now I knew: Nature wanted Los Angeles back.

"There would be very few people in Los Angeles if they had to live with the energy, the wood, and the water that are naturally here," Richard Lillard, a retired professor of American studies and English at California State University, Los Angeles, told me not long ago. "Everything is imported. Four-fifths of the water in Los Angeles comes from other places—from as far away as four hundred and forty-four miles to the north. Nature has been pushed further here—a long way indeed—than almost anyplace on earth." Lillard has spent a professional life-time thinking and writing about the ecology of Southern California, and in 1966 he put his thoughts together in a book titled "Eden in Jeopardy." He wrote then, "Southern California speeds from one brilliant improvisation to another, valuing means, neglecting ends . . . the sun never rises and sets twice on the same landscape."

We sat talking last summer on the deck of Lillard's house, in the Hollywood Hills, overlooking, on a rare clear day, thirty miles of Los Angeles and the Pacific Ocean. "The city is a triumph of American genius and greed," he said. "What we're looking at was once a grassy plain. There were deer and antelope out there, and the Los Angeles River flowed through. It's been rerouted, of course, but it flowed through there"—he pointed to West Hollywood—"and nature remembers. There was a big rain in 1969, the spring of '69, and water began coming up near houses on Melrose and La Cienega. The original springs under La Cienega had begun to rise again."

West Hollywood is on the "City" side of Los Angeles, between the Pacific and forty miles of the Santa Monica Mountains. The Hollywood Hills are part of the southern slope of the Santa Monicas, a range with peaks that reach up to three thousand feet. To the north of the Santa Monicas is "the Valley"—the San Fernando Valley, flatland that stretches more than ten miles to the San Gabriel Mountains and was desert before water was pumped to it from farther north. When we talked about Los Angeles, we were talking about the basin of the Los Angeles River—roughly a thousand square miles between the San Gabriels and the sea, from Malibu in the north to Long Beach in the south. Politically, the area is a collage of cities—the City of

Los Angeles, Santa Monica, Beverly Hills, and others—and communities scattered through the southern part of Los Angeles County. Perhaps six million people live in that basin.

"This is a city built by Yankee ingenuity," Lillard said. "The mud flats at the end of the continent were turned into harbors, marinas were dredged, the hills were levelled and nicked, and the canyons filled in. The water is imported. Even the air is imported, by the Santa Anas from the desert. Otherwise, no one could breathe the air that civilization has brought to the basin. The changes in nature have made us all vulnerable. The '61 fire, the Bel Air fire, almost got me in Beverly Glen—my deck furniture was smoldering from the heat—but the flames stopped about twenty feet from the house. Up there"—he pointed to the hills—"that's been bulldozed and filled; it's held up by cement pylons, but the earth still has a tendency to obey the law of gravity. We haven't had 'the storm of the century' yet—that's a geologists' term. The last one was in the eighteen-eighties. A lot of water will come—twelve inches in twenty-four hours, say. It would tear out half of what you and I are looking at right now."

John D. Weaver is also a Los Angeles writer, the author of a book on the city titled "El Pueblo Grande." He and his wife, Harriett, are active in the Federation of Hillside and Canyon Associations, a conglomeration of citizen groups that monitors hillside development in thirty-one communities. Standing behind his house, in Sherman Oaks, recently, Weaver pointed to the west and said, "That ridge over there is above Stone Canyon. That's where the Bel Air fire started in 1961. They think a bulldozer backfired or struck a spark. There were—let's see if I can remember. Harriett, how many acres burned in the Bel Air fire?"

Harriett Weaver is considered one of Los Angeles' experts on brushfires. She has many titles, among them chairperson of the Mayor's Brush Clearance Committee. "Six thousand and ninety acres burned," she said. "Four hundred and eighty-four homes were destroyed, and the total property loss was about twenty-five million dollars." She continued, "The fires are a natural part of the ecological system. Dead growth has to burn off to continue the life cycle of the chaparral on these hills. The problem came with urbanization in the middle of the brush. A third of the city is in brush. In Los Angeles County, they joke that they don't need fire maps, because the whole thing would be red—'extremely hazardous.' We were just asking for it. The deadwood underneath the green that you see out there is soaked with resin and oils. It literally explodes. An acre of brush is the fuel equivalent of fifteen hundred to two thousand gallons of gasoline. Ernie Hanson, a fire chief in Los Angeles, got a lot of attention a few years ago by calculating that a hundred acres of brush five feet high can produce the same amount of heat as the atomic bomb that was dropped on Hiroshima."

I asked Mrs. Weaver about the fire I had seen in Mandeville Canyon, in the Santa Monicas, on October 23, 1978.

She said that it had burned sixty-one hundred acres. Another fire that day, fifteen miles to the north, had burned twenty-five thousand three hundred and eighty-five acres between Agoura and Malibu. The two fires together damaged or destroyed two hundred and seventy houses and caused forty million dollars' worth of property damage. Two persons were killed in the Agoura fire. "The thing that was remarkable about October 23rd was the speed with which the fires moved," Mrs. Weaver said. "It all happened within twenty-four hours, and the Santa Anas were above thirty-five miles an hour. If the wind hadn't died down, there wouldn't have been a prayer of keeping the Mandeville fire from jumping Sunset Boulevard." I had been standing on the other side, the south side, of Sunset. "Someday there will be a holocaust in this town," she added.

John Weaver said, "Not too far from our house, they built some houses that sold for around two hundred thousand dollars." He pointed again to the ridge west of us. "That view was a selling point. They didn't tell the buyers that they're planning to cut the top off the ridge and use the dirt to fill that little canyon—that they want to flatten out the view to build more houses. They're taking fifty feet off the top of the ridge and putting a hundred and sixty-five feet of fill in the canyon." He pointed to a slope and said, "Those homes down there will be flooded out unless the area gets adequate drainage. That's how it works."

"Floods and landslides are a real problem in the hills," Mrs. Weaver said. "A house half a block down the street lost its front yard in the last rain, and the whole thing is likely to go anytime. The brush is important—you need to leave enough to hold the hills against erosion but not enough to form a fire canopy. Worst of all, the developers cut out the toe of hills to get in that extra house. Much of the soil here is clay, and sooner or later, usually when they're wet, the geological planes slide out like cards from a deck. People aren't aware of the dangers—particularly people from the East. That's who they sell these houses to."

The Weavers talked on about the danger of slides, showing me clippings from the Los Angeles Times. In one story, about slides in Tarzana during April of 1978, John O. Robb, chief of the city's Grading Division, the section of the Department of Building and Safety that regulates the preparation of land for development, was quoted as saying that homeowners might be responsible for much of their own trouble. "One problem is educating hillside homeowners to maintain their property," Robb said. "Many mudslides have been caused by stopped drains and the overwatering of plants and other kinds of neglect."

"Overwatering of plants?" I said. "Are the hills that unstable?"

"They can be," John Weaver said. "You have to be careful of gopher holes, too."

He showed me some Polaroid snapshots a neighbor had taken of a house in a nearby canyon which had been caved in by a mudslide in March of 1978. "They've put the house back together now," he said. "You'd come out from New York and buy that house tomorrow. It looks fine. What you wouldn't know is that Los Angeles is not at peace with nature—that's why we get these periodic punishments. It's a man-made city, a tribute to rapacity and tenacity. There were people who could make money by putting a city here—the last place there should have been one. Hell, most of Los Angeles was just a swath of desert between great harbors in San Francisco and San Diego."

The next day, I went over to Tarzana, four miles west of Sherman Oaks, to meet a friend of the Weavers', Irma Dobbyn, who is also active in the Federation of Hillside and Canyon Associations. "They're building in steeper and steeper territory," Mrs. Dobbyn said. "Let me show you something." She took me out to her patio and pointed. We were looking at a bare beige pyramid that was flat-topped and terraced. "They've scraped that down to put in fifty-five houses," she said.

"How long will it look like that?" I asked.

"Probably only about three years," she said. "Plants can be slapped on, and they grow very quickly, with our twelve-month season. These pine trees"—she pointed at thirty-foot-high Aleppo and Monterey pines behind her house—"were planted when we came here, fifteen years ago."

We got into my car and drove around the corner to Conchita Way, a street of two-hundred-thousand-dollar homes. "You see the cracks in the streets," she said. "The city would come out to patch them when we complained that something was very wrong out here. They said everything was fine, and let the building continue. Then heavy rains came in the spring of 1978, and houses started coming down in April. Mudslides. The Smith house, up there, broke in half and started down the hill. That empty lot a little lower down was a rabbi's house; it just toppled on its front into the street. The Palmers there are suing for the damages to their house. Two men owned that vacant one next door. I think they just walked away from it when the cracks started appearing. That one"—she pointed to another vacant lot—

"went in an earlier slide, eight or ten years ago. They're building there again now. See the foundation?"

The rabbi's name, I found out, was Michael Roth. "It looked like a normal house to us," Roth told me when I called on him. "There was a little hill behind us, but it's not there anymore. I was in Philadelphia when it happened, and my daughter called me and said, 'I don't want you to be shocked. If you watch the news on television tonight, you might see a house in the street. It's yours.' " The Roths are suing. "We're suing them all," he said. "The developer, the city, everybody."

Mrs. Dobbyn, like the Weavers, had pointed out earthmovers clanking along on the ridge that forms the base of Mulholland Drive, the long, winding road dividing the City and the Valley. Lil Melograno, who is an assistant to the area's city councilman and also a realtor, took me along the ridge, which is the peak line of the Santa Monicas. "There are a hundred and twenty-six acres in the tract," she said as we walked along terraces carved in the crumbly beige clay. "It's a pretty steep slope—parts of it might be as much as fifty per cent—and the city is allowing ninety-three houses. The developers originally wanted four hundred and thirty-eight houses, but we cut them down. That's what the Federation and people like me do. The lots start at three hundred thousand dollars apiece, so, with houses, the cost of most of the properties will be well over a million dollars. The developers cut fifty feet from the mountaintop over there and about a hundred feet here. The fill dumped in the canyon will eventually be two hundred and eighty-five feet deep. The city says it'll be a safe development, but no one knows for sure. No one has enough knowledge or control over the elements, the geology. We can't keep up with the technology of earthmoving and building. In the last fifteen years, the developers have learned to carve the mountains up into flatlands. These are just flatland developments with a view." The view was truly spectacular. In places, we were overlooking both the City and the Valley—Beverly Hills to the south, Studio City to the north.

"That's called Benedict Hills," Mrs. Melograno said after we had driven a few miles west along Mulholland. We were gazing out over hundreds of pseudo-Tudor homes. "Prices start at four hundred and fifty thousand dollars, but we got him down to three hundred and forty. They're still building."

"It's a nice setting," I said, and she looked at me strangely.

"It used to be a lot nicer," she said. "They moved six million cubic yards of earth here beginning in 1970. There was a mountain there." She pointed into the air above a cluster of thirty houses. "They cut off a hundred and sixty-five feet of it to get more houses in. That's when the mudslides began.

I spent one Christmas Eve shovelling mud out of the house of a friend. There's not much that the city can do. We don't do any testing work ourselves. We evaluate the reports of private geologists. We have to take their word, and, of course, most of them are hired by the developers. The only way to stop this would be for the city to buy the land, and it doesn't have the money."

"Is there corruption involved?" I asked. "Is somebody making enormous amounts of money here?"

"No," she said. "I don't think there's much of that. Basically, it's the American way—that attitude that a man has a right to do whatever he pleases with his own property. Even if it's dangerous for him and for everybody else. And it *is* dangerous. Anyone who wants to live on a hillside here faces the same hazards—fire, water, and earth. People are willing to take the chance because there's peace and quiet, they're still closer to nature, and the air is cleaner up here. They accept the chance that something will happen. They live with danger."

"Are you one of them?" I asked.

"Yes."

The flight to the hills was no doubt another attempt to outwit nature. The air is cleaner because many of the hillside homes are above the smog that sometimes blankets the flatlands of both the City and the Valley. The day Mrs. Melograno and I stood on Mulholland Drive—September 12th— was one of the worst days for breathing in Los Angeles history. The city was alive with "Stage 2" smog alerts. The day was one of eight consecutive Stage 2 days—a record unmatched since 1955—and admissions to local hospitals because of chronic lung disorders were increasing by fifty per cent a day. The basin is routinely in a state of inversion; that is, a pool of stagnant, humid air is trapped above the city by a lid of warmer, drier air that forms north of Hawaii and drifts eastward until it is trapped by the Santa Monicas and the San Gabriels. Pollution, particularly from automobiles, pumps into the stagnant mass until ocean breezes or Santa Anas wash away the whiskey-colored gases. The hills, however, are usually above the inversion level, which often reaches only three hundred feet above sea level.

As I drove west along Mulholland Drive after talking to Mrs. Melograno, I watched helicopters chattering toward Sepulveda Pass, a cut through the Santa Monicas. They dropped, quite accurately, columns of water on a brushfire climbing up the hills along the San Diego Freeway. The fire was stopped after it had covered ten acres. Los Angeles is very good at that sort of thing. It has to be. Disaster—"holocaust," Harriett Weaver had said—is always near. "Disaster control" has real meaning here, and the city office charged with that function is the Office of Civil Defense, in City Hall East—or, rather, under City Hall East. I drove down four levels below the ground, parked my car, and then took an elevator down another level before being admitted—by buzzer—through eight-foot-high steel vault doors that lead to the office of the director, Michael J. Regan. He is a pudgy Irishman, sixty-two years old, who was a patrolman in the Los Angeles Police Department for twenty-one years and then police chief of a small town called Arvin. In 1970, he came to his present job. He told me that he had been the first police officer at the scene of a "killer slide" in Pacific Palisades, down the street from my house. That was in 1956, when part of the palisade overlooking the Pacific Coast Highway had slid over the roadway—something like that happens every couple of weeks in the winter, with houses and patios hanging over the highway—and pushed a small foreign car almost into the Pacific. "You never saw two people as scared or muddy as the two men in that car," Regan said. "The next day, a highway inspector was on the slope. He was signalling that everything was O.K. when a second slide came and buried him. Killed him."

As we talked, two women carrying rolled maps under their arms walked through Regan's office.

"We're really talking about ongoing preparations for an earthquake," one said.

"It's like a bomb," the other said. "If it drops, everything is gone. If we predict it and it doesn't happen, no one will pay attention the next time."

"Earthquake," Regan said, shaking his head. "That's what the public worries about. But for us it's not so bad. There's nothing you can do about the first shock. But then you can race in and save people before the aftershocks hit. Floods are the thing we worry about most—they're the scariest. There's not a heck of a lot you can do about flash floods, and there's no warning. The ones we get push around boulders the size of vans. And a lot of people are living in certain flood paths."

He paused, and continued, "I'm not sure it makes a big difference. Darned near everybody living in Los Angeles is vulnerable to something. Flood, fire, slides, earthquake. If you live in Bel Air or Brentwood, you could be in a firestorm canyon. People living in houses on stilts—I just shake my head. People in Tujunga, Sunland—they're in a natural flood path."

"What about you?" I asked.

"Me, too," he said. "I live in Verdugo Hills. A flood would wash me off. An earthquake would flip me off. You can't think about it too much. You'd shudder all the time, because you know these things are going to happen again."

Earthquakes are certainly going to happen again. There were four around Los Angeles in June of this year. What the city is worried about is a big one, and that is what the women I saw were working on that day, with the city's Task Force on Earthquake Prediction. No one is yet sure whether there actually is a science of earthquake prediction—the Chinese reportedly predicted a large quake in 1976 and evacuated hundreds of thousands of citizens from the threatened area before tremors began—but the need for such capability is obvious. The "General Background" section of the Task Force's October, 1978, Consensus Report began:

> In mid-February, 1976, the U.S. Geological Survey announced the discovery of a major uplift of the earth covering a large area that is centered approximately on the San Andreas fault in Southern California. Because of its large size and its alignment along a segment of the San Andreas fault that is known to have been "locked" since Southern California's last great earthquake, in 1857, scientists expressed the concern that the "Palmdale Bulge," or "Southern California Uplift," may foreshadow the next great earthquake in the region. . . .
>
> In mid-March, 1976, the U.S. Geological Survey noted the potential significance of the Southern California Uplift, and issued a warning: "If an earthquake similar to that in 1857 occurred today in the region about thirty miles north of Los Angeles, the probable losses in Orange and Los Angeles Counties alone are estimated as follows: 40,000 buildings would collapse or be seriously damaged. 3,000 to 12,000 people would be killed. 12,000 to 48,000 people would be hospitalized. $15 billion to $25 billion in damage would occur. Failure of one of the larger dams could leave 100,000 homeless, and tens of thousands dead."

If such a disaster occurred, Los Angeles might be run from a complex of rooms visible through a glass wall behind Michael Regan's desk. The emergency-operations center is encased in concrete, and it contains food, water, generators, and dormitories designed to sustain three hundred people for two weeks. "This is supposed to withstand a war," Regan said. It looked as if it could. The heart of the center is a cross-shaped "war room." One arm of the cross (Regan's office) would be the working area of the mayor and the chiefs of the Police and Fire Departments and their staffs. The other arm, interestingly, is reserved for the press, on the theory that what is most important—the operations center has already been used for fire and rain emergencies—is providing a panicked public with quick, accurate information. The main room, twenty-eight by fifty feet, lined with glass walls, maps, charts, and blackboards marked "Status" and "Deployment," is essentially a communications center, filled with twenty-button telephones and radio consoles, including a setup to commandeer every municipal radio frequency.

The Fire Department's Operations Control Division headquarters is down a long hall. It is an even more impressive room, two stories high, looking very much like the set of the television series "Star Trek." Under a flashing "Quiet" light, men wearing white shirts, black pants, and ties sit in five-foot-high rust-colored leather swivel chairs before peach-and-cream-colored keyboards, screens, and microphone consoles. Towering over them are two huge maps, and display panels with flashing, moving colored lights that monitor equipment and personnel deployment. It was one of the most extraordinary rooms I have ever seen, but several people told me it does not work very well—the equipment, they said, is always breaking down.

Aboveground, the manipulation of the landscape was proceeding as usual. KFWB, an all-news radio station, was reporting that North Hollywood homeowners were protesting plans by MCA, Incorporated, to level three hills to provide flatland for parking and movie sets at its Universal City Studios. The company wanted to level sixty-seven acres, providing enough fill to cover a football field to a depth of eleven hundred and twenty-five feet. MCA, it was reported, was willing to give each of the homeowners six thousand dollars for their acquiescence. But one resident, identified as Billie Varga, was quoted as saying, "The hill we're on is going to go if they take down that one over there." Billie Varga said she was worried about "slide creep"—the geological phenomenon that Harriett Weaver had likened to cards sliding out of a deck.

A month later, I was driving north along the Pacific Coast Highway to visit Helen Funkhouser, a seventy-six-year-old woman who had moved back into the Santa Monica Mountains after losing her home in the Agoura fire of October 23, 1978. KFWB was reporting that twenty-seven hundred acres were burning near Pasadena. I passed a steel wall being constructed in what used to be one lane of the highway. The wall is supposed to hold back the crumbling, sliding palisades above Malibu. Then I turned into Kanan-Dume Road, past a sign that said:

KANAN-DUME ROAD
SLIDE REMOVAL AREA
UP TO 20 MIN DELAYS
8:30 A.M. TO 4 P.M.
WEEKDAYS

Mrs. Funkhouser is an impressive woman. She was a state legislator in New Hampshire before coming to California, in 1961, with her husband, James, a chemistry professor. They were reading in the ten-foot-wide mobile-home units they had bought to replace their house—two were attached, to give them twenty feet of width—when I arrived at their isolated homesite, just north of Malibu, almost at the point where the Santa Monicas meet the Pacific. "We beat the fire by five minutes," Mrs. Funkhouser said. "We lost everything. Paintings, books, antiques. But Jim did manage to get his cello.

We thought we would be safe, because we had built a system literally pouring water on every bit of the house and property, but they say the temperature of the fire was between twenty-five hundred and three thousand degrees. Here. This was my chicken-cooking pot." Jim Funkhouser handed me a flattened blob of aluminum. "It takes a certain kind of person to live here," she said. "We came back. We all came back. We're damn fools, but the trees come back, and so do we. It's a constant battle. Nature keeps trying to take over here. But it's beautiful, and it's where we want to be."

[1979]

WILLIAM IRWIN THOMPSON

Looking for History in L.A.

A T THE END of the eighteenth century it was the rage to journey to ruins and graveyards and meditate upon the prospect these stones held out to mortal man. Now, as the twentieth century declines, it is the rage to journey to Los Angeles and meditate upon the prospect that city holds out to the rest of the nation. Unlike the gravestone, Los Angeles seems to have become a marker of just how far we can go and stay this side of history. . . . The fear is a popular one, for in the past few years a host of Easterners have made the journey to Los Angeles to study the nature of its threat to urban civilization. All these new books and articles have contributed to our dread of things to come, but still something is missing. If one is concerned with the strange goings-on out at the edge of history, then it would seem natural that he should wonder just what the whole *idea of history* becomes for people who live at the edge.

As one who grew up in Los Angeles and as one who always wished to escape it for "a real life back east," I have become astonished to find that I cannot let go of Los Angeles even though I live away from it. Other expatriates I know from Southern California have settled into comfortably civilized lives in Boston and New York, and I would think my fascination with Los Angeles almost pathological were it not for the fact that so many Easterners share it. The only people more obsessed with Los Angeles than the residents themselves are the people who don't live there. If no man is an island, it would seem that in our era of urbanization he is automatically a resident of a suburb of L.A. Those expatriates from Southern California who succeed in shutting Los Angeles out of their minds do so because they are past-oriented and turning their backs on the future is a posture that comes naturally to them. They recognize the sense of dread that emanates from the city at the edge, but they hope the future will overlook them and that they will be able to make it all the way to the end of their lives undisturbed. But even in turning away from Los Angeles they reveal the rich fantasy life of the L.A. man and turn Eastern life into a caricature of fashion that proves them not to the manner born. Like Oscar Wilde, that Anglo-Irishman in a world of real Englishmen and real Irishmen, the expatriate can only achieve identity at the cost of self-distorting excess.

For those whose fantasies are about the future rather than the past, Los Angeles is an inevitable subject of speculation, if only for the simple reason that fantasy can live a richer life in the West than in the East. In the East the burden of tradition, power, and religion is so great that the fantasy has little room in which to realize itself. . . . In Los Angeles it is much harder to distinguish between personal fantasy and social reality because the realization of fantasy is one of our dominant cultural traits—from Disneyland to Sacramento. It would be a simple matter if one could say that all fantasy is bad, and, therefore, that the East is right and the West is wrong; but like all dualistic arrangements, the human predicament seems to cut at right angles across the cosmic division between good and evil. Fantasy is good and bad, just as the lack of it is good and bad. . . . The average citizen who has escaped the dreariness of the village mentality of the South or the Midwest has encountered in Southern California the freedom to find himself, or lose himself. Most people are frightened by the possibilities of this new freedom, and as they sense themselves slipping away from the traditional American culture of work into the new culture of pleasure, they recoil from the edge and have fantasies of "the real thing" that is "just like back east." And these fantasies make the guilt they feel for their own self-indulgence easier to live with.

But these fantasies of tradition are not limited to Hollywood or Orange County. When Chancellor Dean McHenry of the new University of Santa Cruz gestured to the barren rolling hills and said that there was to be another Amherst, another Bryn Mawr, another Swarthmore, he was demonstrating how even a university campus can turn out to be a movie set. McHenry went on to say that "There will be traditions." Friends at UCSC tell me that there are high teas and a high table.

This form of the realization of fantasy is not restricted to one sector of the Southern California way of life; it is all-pervasive. Los Angeles restaurants and their parking lots are such million-dollar structures because they are palaces of fantasy in which the upward-moving individual comes to act out a self-mythology he has learned from a hero of the mass media. Often enough the establishments of La Cienega Boulevard's Restaurant Row are fantasies of history in their very architecture. Within a few blocks one can move from an old English inn to a Tahitian hut, a Mediterranean villa, a Japanese garden, and such sentimentalizations of the past as "The Gay Nineties" and "The Roaring Twenties." On certain nights some restaurants pass out balloons, hats, and noisemakers so that the guests may fantasy that they are enjoying themselves. Disneyland is not an anomaly contained by Anaheim, but a gathering and concentration of the Southern California world view.

. . . Orange County is the preeminent example of the new posturban landscape, and, as every paranoid Eastern liberal knows, Orange County is the capital of California Right Wing extremism. The lower-middle classes fled the South and the Midwest for the airplane-defense jobs during the war, and with Korea and the new aerospace industry they kept up the wars in their Pacific lake to keep those jobs coming. They had come to Southern California for space and weather, and in the crowded, smog-infested tracts around the defense plants, they found neither, but learned to forget both in their newly acquired swimming pools and sports cars.

Now as one moves through this shattered landscape in which the mountains are invisible from the exhausts of four and a half million cars and the orange trees have been eliminated for real estate speculation, how is he to gain any sense of history except through the artificial monuments he sees nearby in Disneyland or, in the even more Right Wing Crystal Palace, Knott's Berry Farm—where Philadelphia's Independence Hall has been duplicated brick by brick? Since there is no history to be seen or experienced in any meaningful way, the citizen must grab onto time and hold on for all he is worth. He must nourish an inner fantasy landscape in which he figures larger than he does in life, or suffer the risk of losing himself utterly. It is for this reason that Southern Californians imagine ivy-covered, leaf-strewn squares, and villages clustered around white frame New England churches, and, lacking them in reality, create them in the plastic towns to which they go to find themselves.

Frivolous as all this realization of fantasy may seem, its role in the individual's consciousness (or unconsciousness) is an important aspect of his social and political behavior. A culture's idea of history is related to its present, and in Southern California the idea of history is iconically enshrined in Anaheim. The idea of history is a shattered landscape in which the individual moves through a world of discontinuities: Mississippi riverboats, medieval castles, and rocket ships equally fill the reality of a single moment. When children could not articulate their problems, the psychologist Erik Erikson used to observe them at play with the toys in his office; inevitably they would act out their fantasies. Disneyland is such a place. But the essential question of this Southern California idea of history is: What happens to the individual who grows up with it? What is life like for a person who moves through the shattered landscape of the megalopolis in which time, tradition, and history are scrambled? What sense of identity does the citizen have when the city he lives in is without a significant image? For the image of the city is not simply a matter of beautification; it is a matter of giving to the individual the basic ontological security of knowing where he is in life. . . . When the megalopolis is too vast to be perceived meaningfully, the individual projects, against the chaos of his world, a new mythopoeic simplification. Whether the myth is Right Wing, Black Nationalist, or the Cal Tech freshman's millenarian science fiction myth of space (or my own fantasy of pipesmoking Ivy League professors with knowledge and wisdom shining out of their eyes), the myth is a fiery signature of a new reality making a special covenant with the individual. Man simply cannot tolerate the stress of an absence of order; if the urban sprawl is without order, he will see patterns in it even if these patterns are paranoid signs of a conspiracy.

Oedipa Maas, the mirror image of Oedipus Rex and the heroine of Thomas Pynchon's brilliant novella, *The Crying of Lot 49*, searches throughout Southern California for her inheritance from her big daddy lover, and as she becomes increasingly lost, she begins to see the signs of the Trystero underground network of postal communication on the trash cans of the state. She searches for an inheritance from a past that is dead, discovers an imagined system of communication in a land where human communications fails, and finds in the rubbish of the state the fertile decay for her own ambiguous regeneration. Pynchon's profound novel is the story as well of every Southern California Right Winger who reads everywhere about him the signs of an underground Communist conspiracy, but the real tragedy of the novella comes from the fact that these caricatures also describe the scientific perception of nature. Myths are simplifications of reality, but so are scientific laws, for they magnetize the infinite information of the universe into the fields of their own formulaic descriptions; what is objectively outside the field of our consciousness if literally inconceivable. If we wish smugly to put down the imaginative perceptions of Oedipa Maas, we will also have to take apart the relationship between imagination and reality in the quantum theory of Werner Heisenberg. Because mind is a contribution to reality, the more mind one has, the more he sees in reality, and madmen, poets, and physicists are all of a company apart from readers of ticker tapes and scholarly journals. In his comic parodies of knowledge in an age of data processing, Pynchon has brilliantly succeeded in relating science to the artist's vision of tragedy and human ambiguity. *The Crying of Lot 49*, like Nathanael West's *Day of the Locust* before it, is worth volumes of sociology, and in focusing on a heroine who is cut off from familial identifications, Pynchon has recognized just how the connective tissue of history breaks down at the edge.

. . . In Los Angeles one can change his house, job, wife, and religion pretty much as he likes. If one lives in an Irish ghetto and misses Mass once, the family has the priest bearing down on him. In Los Angeles the family situation is loosened because the extended family is back wherever the nuclear family came from, and as the nuclear family grows up, it is likely to remain loose by spinning off its new families into widely separated suburban towns. But even with the nuclear family further fragmentation seems to be developing in the new pattern of life in the Southern California megalopolis, where the Eleventh Commandment is: "Thou shalt not grow old."

A slightly upper-middle-class young engineer moves into a "Singles" either before he marries or just after his first divorce. (One must remember that the divorce rate in California is twice that of the nation, or one out of every *two* marriages.) Because all his friends and acquaintances are related to his previous marriage, the young divorcé needs a place for what the developers call "interim living"—a place where he may begin a new life with new friends in a "community atmosphere." This sense of community is necessary because, more likely than not, the family that could help him over the difficult period of divorce (or intimidate him out of ever seeking one) is somewhere back in the vast expanse of the Midwest that lies behind Southern California in space and time. But if the young engineer has never married and has his twelve thousand a year and more to himself, then he is in a position to entertain, with Corvettes and Chivas Regal, the bikini-clad girls who decorate the pool of his apartment-club complex. In some "Singles," if the girls are sufficient architectural contributions to the landscaping of the pool their rent is lower than that of the young professional men who can quite easily and willingly make up the difference. After the young engineer samples the offerings of his female neighbors, he nearly doubles his income by getting married and moving up to an accelerated phase of consumption: two cars, stereos, appliances, and perhaps a boat. When this program is stopped by the pregnancy of the wife (if this is desired, and it is not in many cases, for indebtedness can postpone pregnancy indefinitely), the engineer moves out with his wife to a tract house in a newly opened "Planned Community." And here he begins the child-bearing phase of life by joining *sub-urban* civilization.

A "Planned Community" is another new concept in real estate development like the "Singles." Rather than bulldozing the trees and putting up house after house in four basic styles, the developers now include concrete-embedded artificial lakes for boating, golf courses, swimming pools, tennis courts, teen-age clubhouses, and advertise that life becomes a permanent vacation when one lives in this instant community. If the extra payments over the mortgage that one pays for all the facilities become too much, along with all the other payments, then the wife returns to work and the children grow up in age sets and derive their norms from their own generational peer group. With the approach of adolescence and the driver's license, the children have a mobility of several hundred miles and one foreign country, Mexico. As the children go off to one of the universities, state colleges, or local junior colleges (and the peripheral dropout life that clusters around each in varying degrees of hippiness), the engineer and his wife (if it is the same wife) are free to return to the joys of urban society. He moves back into the city and takes up residence in a luxury condominium in which the Minoan bathroom is a positive shrine to the glories of the flesh that are fast slipping beyond his middle-aged reach. Once he has tasted the nouveau elegance of the forty-million-dollar cultural shopping plaza downtown at the Music Center, and forgotten his days of Little League and Boy Scouts, and once the frantic sexuality of the middle-age period has quieted down, he is free to move away from condominiums, key clubs, and topless restaurants to the retirement community of Leisure World.

But more than likely a Californian of some years' standing could not live with all the aged Midwesterners who have come to Leisure World to get in on the California scene with the last chance they have. Not having had the courage to get up and leave sooner, those who have waited docilely for retirement to free them from Ogallala and Wichita are not likely to prove the best companions for one who has lived with his top down all his life. But for those who have come to Leisure World from the traditional ways of American life, a room in the two-story, three-generational home in a small town will never seem better than Leisure World. With bowling green, swimming pool, hobby rooms, closed-circuit TV station, classes, shops and regular meetings of the Kansas Club, guilt-ridden immigrants to this new world can indulge their fantasies by talking about the good old days in another country.

The effect of this new pattern of life is to separate in space and time within the megalopolis the critical periods of life. No longer need a person carry the burden of a single identity from the cradle to the grave. He is free to change lives and wives as often as he has the energy. I imagine that the way McLuhan would describe this pattern is that the individual is no longer a novel, but a television set: at the flip of a channel he changes his program. Disneyland itself is a kind of television set, for one flips from medieval castles to submarines and rockets as easily as one can move, in downtown Los Angeles, from the plaza of the Mexican Olvera Street to Little Tokyo, to the modern Civic Center with its new pavilion for the performing arts.

But these discontinuities of history are no longer to be contained by Disneyland and Southern California. As the SST jet brings us closer to what the city planner Constantinos Doxiadis calls "Ecumenopolis," the Los Angelization of the past becomes quite possible. Even now as one looks out of the window of his Boeing 720 on the L.A.-to-Boston run, it seems as if he were flipping channels on a continental TV set: California tracts, Southwestern desert, a drink, and then it's Rocky Mountains, Green Iowa, the Finger Lakes, the Hudson, and then back, in time as well as space, to Boston. In the old days the difficulty of travel preserved the integrity of widely separated cultures. Now the cultures are being scrambled together, and the traditions of the fathers seem irrelevant to the lives of the sons, whether the sons are in Watts, Vietnam, or Nigeria. What Los Angeles is experiencing is the future for us all. The violent juxtaposition of aerospace technology and neo-tribal politics contains the thesis and antithesis of the new planetary culture; hopefully, the synthesis will be contained in the coming twenty-first century.

In the meantime more people will lose their way than find themselves in this new world. As they become lost, they will fall into the artificial subcultures of Right Wing Americanism, Black Nationalism, Maoism, hippiedom, and the cults of the flying saucer contactees. Lacking the strong connective tissue of tradition, the individual can entertain in his fantasy life various possible identities. Since nothing is to stop him from acting out his fantasies, he can flip from identity to new identity, changing jobs and communities, as he makes his odyssey through the vast Mediterranean world of Southern California. Since one lives in generational ghettos, there is no continuity in generational exchanges of knowledge. There is only the community of those who share one's historical moment, for these are the only ones who can be trusted to be a genuine part of one's world. The young mother in a new tract may find that the average age of her entire neighborhood is under thirty. She will find many other pregnant wives to talk with, but she will not find any older "Jewish mothers" to give her a larger kind of sympathy.

Living in a generational ghetto becomes like living on a campus where there are no teachers other than one's fellow students. Since all too often the best teachers are one's fellow students, this is not necessarily for the worst. There is a good deal more wisdom in Bob Dylan than in Robert Welch. Nevertheless, this new discontinuous life-rhythm helps traditional wisdom to disappear; which means that, negatively, the young are doomed to repeat history because they are ignorant of it; and, positively, that the young can react more quickly to the accelerated process of technological change. The imaginations of the older generation are bogged down by the economic and technical arrangements of a previous epoch.

. . . Precisely because the California Miracle was made by government intervention into the private sector through the railroads, the defense industries, and FHA housing, our elders from the Old World have become frightened at the prospects of the metacapitalistic, technological society and have regressed into a caricatured version of the past. Precisely because there is no real tradition, the elders create fantasies of mother, country, God (who is really Uncle Sam in more heavenly attire), private property, flag and family, and on and on in the litany of the atavist. Significantly, the entrance to Disneyland is through a nostalgic, garter-sleeved, soda-fountained, marble-topped, apothecary-jarred small town. The small town in the midst of the scrambled past and the idealized future is there to ease the shock and dispel the fears of those who are about to encounter the meaning of Southern California in its most concentrated form. The older generation may not take LSD, but when they go to Disneyland, they are taking real trips through heightened space and time. The Gothic cathedral summed up the world view of the medieval town; Disneyland is the technological cathedral of Southern California. If this sounds flippant and journalistically clever, but not really true, then the foreigner to California should visit Lincoln Savings and Loan's "Great Moments with Mr. Lincoln," or see Bell Telephone's 360-degree vision of "America the Beautiful," or get on General Electric's "Carousel of Progress," or ultimately take Monsanto's "Adventure Through Inner Space." The fantasies of the hippies, at least, are in better taste than those of the middle classes they have left behind, for it is in the small-town setting that the sanctimonious Babbitts of Lincoln Savings and Loan run a coin-operated Lincoln concession in which a mechanical effigy of President Lincoln recites a speech for those who sit in the dim religious light of the theater. To preserve the dignity of the apparition, the usherette asks, in prayerful tones, that the solemnity of the occasion be respected and that no photograph be taken. This request, no doubt, helps the Lincoln souvenir gift shop which awaits the visitor upon the completion of his patriotic trip. Ironically enough, the speech chosen by our capitalist guardians of the past is one that warns us of the dangers of civil war.

The impact of the scrambling of history in Los Angeles was first noticed by Nathanael West in his novel, *The Day of the Locust*. His "Sargasso of the Imagination" is now Disneyland. It was Walt Disney's insight that one could make a fortune, not by making movies with a studio lot, but by charging admission. But West's artistic prophecies point up another quality of Los Angeles fantasy life: the longer one lives at this edge of history, the more his vatic nerves begin to tremble. People who come here suddenly feel like making apocalyptic prophecies. Normal intellectuals who would be quite embarrassed to do anything of the sort back east suddenly find themselves filling up with a dreadful noise. . . . But the prospect is not totally bleak; or, at least, if the worst happens, there still is the chance that after apocalypse the millennium of "The Age of Aquarius" will appear over the ashes of the previous order. In the culture of the black man and the "white Negro" one can catch a glimpse of the culture of the twenty-first century.

The businessman mistakes the black man when he sees in Watts only an unemployed people cut off from the appliances of American life. Watts may be far from white suburbia, but this distance has given it room in which to create. Because the realization of fantasy is so integral a part of the Southern California way of life, Watts is as different from Harlem as Los Angeles is from New York. Under the permissive sun the black man is as free as the white to act out his fantasies, "don robes, and go out and change the world." The riot of 1965 called Watts into existence, for it gave to an indistinct slurb in the Los Angeles sprawl the boundary, shape, and form of a new cultural identity. Karl Marx has said that "Force is the midwife of every old society pregnant with a new one." Now that force has brought Watts into existence, the easy realization of fantasy that Los Angeles allows has given it space in which to express itself in more sublimated forms. The first anniversary of the 1965 riot was a community bonfire, which has since grown into the annual Watts festival of the arts. Now as one moves around in Watts he senses an ethos and the beginnings of what may become a real culture that the black man is creating for himself, and for us.

. . . Undoubtedly, some of the new possibilities are the usual Hollywood movie-set landscape, and it is quite possible that second-generation black men, being human, are not necessarily going to do better than second-generation dust-bowlers did with their Disneylands and Knott's Berry Farms. Nevertheless, there is no reason to think that all of the experiments will fail. The revival of Swahili may seem ridiculous, but it is no more ridiculous than the revival of Irish was at the turn of the century. It seemed to many an Englishman (and Irishman as well) that Dublin had little to offer in the face of London and Paris, and the revival of Irish and Gaelic games only tended to strengthen his conviction of Irish primitiveness. But the nativistic movement that contained these clumsy gropings toward a revitalization of industrial civilization was still large enough to contain the work *in English* of Yeats, Synge, Joyce, O'Casey, and O'Connor. There is no reason to doubt, but there is much reason to hope, that what Dublin did for Great Britain, Watts could do for America. Certainly the enervated culture of white suburbia could stand the stimulation that a black nativistic movement could contribute, and if civil war on the San Andreas Fault does not ruin the chances, the black man may make Los Angeles a far greater city. But most likely, as happened before in Ireland, the cultural renaissance and the revolution will go on at once, and "there will be time to murder and create."

The Irish had a national culture of centuries' duration to sustain their resurgence, but the American black man finds himself in the place where he has neither Africa nor America. For this reason the Muslims call for the traditional promised land in a separate black nation in the South. The idea is unthinkable, but so was the dismemberment of the British Empire contained in the founding of the Irish Free State; it was force and an anarchy which made moderate, peaceful government impossible that made it thinkable. If apocalypse does not hurl us back to another Stone Age, and if we allow our fantasies of the future to impinge upon the present, then the triumph of the *Protestant Ethic and the Spirit of Capitalism* in bourgeois, national, and industrial culture will be replaced by the triumph of a new religious sensibility in a miscegenetic, Pythagorean, and planetary culture. In which case, the American black man, with his lack of a nation, is not behind us, but ahead of us. The whites, exulting in the work ethic, always saw the black man as the preindustrial past; it never occurred to them that he could be the post-industrial future. Now as we move from the industrial technology of meaningless work to the Pythagorean science of meaningful play, and Homo Ludens replaces Homo Faber, we are witnessing the creation of a new culture. For the black men who were left out of the old society, and for the whites who have dropped out, there are the roles of storied folk and leisured aristocrat in the new medieval order—an order in which the unemployed and the leisured share the common humanity that remains after one has subtracted the job from one's identity. As black revolutionary and white fascist, hippie and radical, technocrat and rugged individualist move toward apocalypse and/or the millennium, one thing remains certain: Los Angeles will remain at the edge of our history and will be thrust up to its hilt in the future of this country.   [1971]

CAREY MC WILLIAMS

The Discovery
of Los Angeles

COMING TO, so to speak, in Los Angeles in the spring of 1922, after that brief season of fun and frolic in Denver, was a jarring and, for a time, painful experience. Suddenly I found myself in a strange new city that was changing every hour on the hour; I was broke, without prospects or connections, and with essentially one skill: I could type. But I soon got a job in the business office of the Los Angeles *Times*, and there I stayed—for seven years. Fortunately I was able to arrange a work schedule which permitted me to hold what was in effect a full-time job by working afternoons, weekends, and a portion of the early night shift. So I was able to attend the University of Southern California, first Liberal Arts and then the Law School, from which I graduated in 1927.

For an informal but revealing "education" in the ways of laissez–faire capitalism, I had come to the right place at precisely the right time. In the Southern California of the 1920s, the whole saga of frontier growth and westward expansion, the storybook version of the American Dream, was given its penultimate staging in a semitropical setting at the western edge of the continent. Concentrated in time and space, the reenactment accelerated at such a pace that it attracted worldwide interest and attention. The various phases of economic development—pastoral, agricultural, "cottage" industries, industrialization, urbanization, postindustrial—came in such rapid succession that the region's growth seemed staged or contrived, like an outdoor pageant or a motion picture being shot on location.

The Great Los Angeles Boom of the 1920s was just getting under way when I arrived. Other great cities—London, Paris, Constantinople, Athens, Cairo, Peking, Moscow, Tokyo, New York—had evolved as historic entities over long periods of time. Los Angeles emerged out of nowhere, without much of a past. The first hundred years were a kind of prehistory in which it moved from pueblo to cow town to hick town at a leisurely pace. San Francisco was a famous city from the moment gold was discovered, but Los Angeles slumbered on for decades. Then suddenly, beginning in the 1920s, it achieved great-city status through a process of forced growth based on booster tactics and self-promotion. Initially growth was stimulated by luring latter-day "pioneers" seeking low-cost retirement in pleasant circumstances, to a new kind of "frontier" where the sun shone most of the time and winter was another name for summer. But residential expansion required water, which was in short supply. So, using control of limited water resources as a key pressure, the city extended its domain; outlying communities were forced to merge with Los Angeles or face annexation. In the process, highly productive orchards, citrus groves and produce fields had to make way for unplanned and often jerry-built subdivisions, and much of the beauty and charm of the region was lost or impaired.

The first major step in the city's "water imperialism" was its raid on the water resources of Owens Valley, some 230 miles distant, carried out by a series of maneuvers (given fictional treatment in Robert Towne's film *Chinatown*), some of which were tainted with force, fraud, and deception. The desecration of this beautiful valley on the east side of the High Sierras was justified in terms of "the greatest good for the greatest number," which turned out to mean maximum quick profits for the promoters of Greater Los Angeles. Then, as the Los Angeles area continued to expand—hundreds of subdivisions were spawned between 1922 and 1928—more water was needed for *future* growth, so the city reached out to tap Colorado River supplies and, later, began to draw water from the Central Valley, with far-ranging consequences.

As the boom of the 1920s gained momentum, the new media—radio and motion pictures—projected an image of Los Angeles that attracted worldwide attention. Aggressive national advertising and promotion campaigns drew more and more people to the region. The accelerating influx was "good for business," since it stimulated the growth of industry and kept wages low. The expansion of the motion picture industry and the discovery of important oil fields helped fuel the boom, as did the opening of new industries; the first tire-manufacturing plants, for example, date from 1919. After 1915 auto travel to California increased as thousands of tourists and visitors swept into the region, including many Middle Western farm families that had decided to rent or sell their farms and move west. The growth of the state societies— a unique Southern California phenomenon—accurately mirrored this significant shift in population. Some of the societies had huge memberships; the annual picnic of the Iowa Society, usually held in Long Beach, seldom failed to attract thousands of transplanted Iowans. In retrospect, the spectacular growth of the region can be seen as the first phase in the development of what is now known as the Sun Belt.

As luck would have it, I had gone to work for the institution that more than any other was responsible for the phenomenal growth of Southern California. General Harrison Gray Otis, publisher of the Los Angeles *Times*, had been the moving force in the city's first boom at the turn of the century. The second, that of the 1920s, was masterminded by his son-in-law, Harry Chandler, who succeeded him as publisher. From the time he stepped into the shoes of General Otis until his death in 1944, Harry Chandler was, beyond all doubt, the city and the region's most influential resident. He was the generalissimo of the forces that engineered the great postwar boom. As part of its expansionist strategy, the *Times* would publish any and all kinds of advertising and then worry about collecting for it. So those of us in the legal and credit departments engaged in a round-the-clock feud with an army of deadbeats, con men, fly-by-night promoters, "business opportunity" crooks, bad-check artists, noisy tent-style evangelists, proprietors of cheap dance halls, flashy oil promoters of the C. C. Julian type, and not a few realtors who later became civic leaders and multimillionaires, all desperate for advertising but usually unable or unwilling to pay for it. What water was to the region, advertising space in the *Times* was to them.

For a time I had responsibility for accounts in the old dilapidated Music and Arts Building, a relic of the boom of the 1880s, located a block or so from the *Times*. Its "studios" housed a constantly changing swarm of voice teachers, "masseurs," swamis, mind readers, graphologists, yogis, ballet dancers, faith healers, spiritualists, fake publishers, dubious literary and theatrical agents, so-called talent scouts, and other exotic types drawn from the ends of the earth to the "bright spot" that was Los Angeles: the new city of the future. This battered hulk of a building, with its wide corridors which made bizarre twists and turns, might have been fairly described as a museum of two-bit predators out to con the ignorant and fleece the innocent. Indeed, few vantage points offered such an excellent close-up view as my work provided of the armies of men and women on the make who had surged into Los Angeles in search of fame, fortune, easy money, and instant success. Of course, this view was somewhat distorted—it focused on the seamy side of the boom—but it strongly reinforced my misgivings about the "prosperity" of the Harding-Coolidge-Hoover years. How could a society be truly prosperous that spawned such a vicious economic underworld, that despite appearances caused so much unadvertised hardship and unreported financial loss? Nathanael West's *The Day of the Locust* (first published in May, 1939) offers a classic picture of the "underside" of Hollywood and the motion picture industry—the American Dream in disarray—but the counterpart could be found in most phases of the region's mushroom development; the surface was bright and pleasing. But the nether side was often dark and ugly.

To say that my first reactions to Los Angeles were negative would be a gross understatement. I loathed the place. It lacked form and identity; there was no center. By contrast to its never-ending spread and sprawl, Denver was a beautifully structured small city. Those rows of rococo mansions on Capitol Hill stood as monuments to the fortunes in silver and gold made in Cripple Creek and Leadville; they reflected pride, position, wealth. The elegant ladies who buzzed around the city in the winter months in handsome electric coupés knew exactly who they were and what they represented and so did everyone else. But Los Angeles was a city of strangers, of milling marauders staring at one another without a glint of recognition. There were never many "first families," in the historic sense, and tidal waves of newcomers had pushed most of them into the background so that civic leadership was up for grabs.

To Louis Adamic, Los Angeles in the 1920s was the "Enormous Village," and that about describes it, a village in outlook, civic feeling, and even appearance. Westwood was yet to be; in the spring, after the rains, the area between La Brea and Beverly Hills would be ablaze with wild mustard growing in what were then open fields. Hollywood was still a village and San Fernando Valley largely undeveloped. On my first night in Los Angeles I attended a benefit concert staged by motion picture stars in a circus tent on a vacant lot at Sunset and Vine. The affair exuded the atmosphere of a small-town shindig; I remember that the actor Wallace Reid played a strident trombone solo. The city's best-known residents in 1922 were Aimee Semple McPherson, who was to open Angelus Temple in 1923, and the Reverend Robert Shuler, a hellfire-and-brimstone parson with a large radio following. Aimee opted for love and kindness, while Shuler flayed fornicators and other sinners. Protestant fundamentalism was the dominant religious force; Catholics were a largely unnoticed constituency with little political clout; and the Jewish influx was just starting. Revivalism went hand in hand with comically corrupt boom-town politics. Social organization was rudimentary; Los Angeles, in the 1920s, had the finest murders ever, from Clara Phillips and her not-so-gentle hammer to the Black Dahlia and William Desmond Taylor cases. Slight wonder, then, that it should have inspired some of the best private-eye fiction. The city had more newspapers then than now, but even so the press could not keep up with the crazy pace of events. As the columnist Lee Shippey once remarked, in Los Angeles "tomorrow isn't another day, it's another town." It surely was in the 1920s.

Gradually I began to acquire a relish for this strange new scene. Long before the end of the decade, I came to feel that I had a ringside seat at a year-round circus. As more and more visitors felt a compulsion to jot down their impressions for the folks back home, the fame of Los Angeles spread far and wide. The new world of motion pictures attracted universal interest. Then, too, the city became a source of marvelous news stories for the national and world press: the disappearance of Sister Aimee, the gaudy murders, and the tribulations of Fatty Arbuckle, Charles Chaplin, and Mabel Normand. Still later, of course, the spectacular increase in wealth, power, and population invited a new and more serious interest. The flow of visitors—and investors—was stepped up. More and more Americans had been to Southern California or were planning a visit or had a cousin who lived there. By the end of the decade, Los Angeles was perhaps the most highly publicized, talked about, city in the world. It was a "now" city that piqued curiosity and interest, a city without a past whose emergence coincided with new modes of transportation (the automobile and the airplane) and new forms of communication (motion pictures and radio); it was, in fact, destined to become the media capital of the world. The effect of this upsurge of interest and attention was to create a growing market for "L.A." stories which those of us who were just beginning to write were only too happy to supply.

The range of interesting subject matter was fantastic. It was in Southern California that I first acquired a reporter's interest in religious cults and occult movements. The "psychic" world was even fruitier then than it is today. I found it impossible to keep track of the new cults, occult sciences, and religions. In the words of Annie Besant, who had settled in Ojai in 1926,

Southern California had "an incomparable multiplicity and diversity of faiths." In that year Los Angeles had seven separate churches of the American Theosophical Association and twenty-nine affiliates of the National Spiritualists Association. Hamlin Garland, the distinguished American novelist, and his circle of friends were then receiving nightly messages, or so they thought, from Henry James, Sir Arthur Conan Doyle, Dwight L. Moody, and Walt Whitman. I interviewed Garland—a handsome grandfatherly type with snow-white hair—a number of times and often took long walks with him in Griffith Park.

In the 1920s, Francis Grierson, author of *The Valley of Shadows* (1909), a book about Illinois on the eve of the Lincoln–Douglas debates that had drawn high praise from Edmund Wilson, Theodore Spencer, Bernard de Voto, and Van Wyck Brooks, came to live in Los Angeles and aroused much local interest with his piano improvisations and "messages" from the dead. Zona Gale, Edwin Markham, Sara Teasdale, Mary Austin, and others were fascinated by his personality, interested in his writings, and tried to help him. I found him to be a most intriguing figure, part genius, part faker. As Van Wyck Brooks once said, he was "a strange fish, quite unlike anything in American literature." After a distinguished career in Europe as a concert pianist, appearing at court circles from Moscow to London, Grierson had helped make San Diego a center for psychic and occult phenomena in the late 1880s but was soon forced to leave under a cloud of scandal. Among his books was *Psycho-Phone Messages*, which created quite a stir when published in Los Angeles in 1921. At a concert which Zona Gale arranged for him in 1927, he suddenly slumped over the keyboard, quite dead. So far as I could learn, none of his devotees received psycho-phone messages from him. Even Upton Sinclair got caught up in the Los Angeles enthusiasm of those years for "vibration messages" and wrote a book about them: *Mental Radio* (1930). In such a lush setting, I soon began to tap the abundant supply of fascinating characters and lively subjects for magazine articles. At first I contributed to California magazines, of which there were a surprising number in those days—*The Overland Monthly, The Argonaut, The Dumbook, Hesperian, Game and Gossip, Sports and Vanities*, San Francisco *Review*, and *Saturday Night*—and then began to write articles and reviews for the Los Angeles *Times*, the San Diego *Union*, and national publications.

But I had other and better reasons for being pleased that I had come to live in Los Angeles. I soon came to know an interesting group of intellectuals: painters, writers, bookmen, designers, architects, and journalists, most of whom had arrived in Southern California at about the same time I did. In sober fact, we became the first "bohemians" of modern Los Angeles. Included were Jake Zeitlin, the bookdealer; Paul Jordan Smith, literary editor of the Los Angeles *Times*; Arthur Millier, its art critic; Phil Townsend Hanna, editor of *Westways*; Will Connell, the photographer; Lloyd Wright, the son of Frank Lloyd Wright; Merle Armitage, the impresario; Hildegarde Flanner, a fine poet; Kem Weber, the designer; Louis Adamic; Herbert Klein, the journalist and author; José Rodriquez, the musicologist and radio commentator; S. MacDonald Wright, the painter (brother of Willard Huntington Wright, "S. S. Van Dine"); Lawrence Clark Powell, librarian and critic; Duncan Aikman, then West Coast correspondent for the Baltimore *Sun*; the architects Richard Neutra, R. W. Schindler and Harwell Harris; Ward Ritchie, the printer; and others. I became indebted to this group for many insights about Southern California, its culture, history and folkways. For a time some of us published *Opinion*, one of the better little magazines of the period, which we usually put together at dinner meetings at René and Jean's French restaurant, where you could get a good meal for seventy-five cents. Also some of us formed Primavera Press, which brought out quite an interesting list of first-rate books, mostly about California. The nascent bohemia of Los Angeles was hardly comparable to the Left Bank in Paris or New York's Greenwich Village, but even so we managed to strike a few sparks.

As a young lawyer with literary interests I was a sucker for fine bookshops, of which there were not many in Los Angeles in the 1920s. As part of my coverage of the local "literary scene" for the weekly *Saturday Night*, I met a young poet from Texas, Jake Zeitlin, shortly after his arrival in Los Angeles in 1925. At that time he managed to eke out a living, of a sort, by peddling rare books. We became great friends, and a few years later I helped him organize the first of several bookstores—At the Sign of the Grasshopper it was called—near the Los Angeles Public Library; later he had a shop around the corner on Westlake Park. Today Jake is California's dean of rare-book dealers, and his Red Barn bookstore on La Cienega Boulevard is world-famous. You never knew just whom you might meet in Jake's shops: Aldous Huxley, Hugh Walpole, Edward Weston, D. H. Lawrence, or some young poet who had just hitchhiked his way to Los Angeles.

At about the same time, I also met Stanley Rose, another Texan. A country boy from Matador, Texas, Stanley had run away from home to enlist in the Army in World War I. At the war's end he cleverly feigned mysterious psychiatric disorders and managed to spend a year or more in a delightful facility near Stanford University, where he acquired a taste for reading and a fondness for books. He too peddled books for a time in Los Angeles, primarily risqué items which he hawked in the studios. As with Jake, I lent Stanley a hand in organizing the two stores he operated, one on Vine near Hollywood Boulevard, the other next door to Musso-Frank's restaurant. Both were favorite meeting places for writers: Bill Saroyan, George Milburn, Erskine Caldwell, Louis Adamic, William Faulkner, Nathanael West, Frank Fenton (*A Place in the Sun*), John Fante, Jo Pagano, Jim Tully, Owen Francis, and others, and also for actors and directors. Both shops were hangouts for Hollywood writers and artists (many painters)—"intellectuals," if you will—in much the same way that Jake's shops were in downtown Los Angeles.

Stanley was a superb storyteller and a very funny man whose generosity was proverbial. In the late afternoons, as he began to warm up for the evening with a few drinks, he would hold court in the store, entertaining whoever happened to drop in, and the performance would invariably continue into the early morning hours in the back room at Musso's. At one time Stanley had been part owner of the Satyr Book Store on Vine Street. His two associates in this enterprise managed to induce him to take the rap for a pornographic item the three of them had published in violation of the copyright. The two associates were married: Stanley was not; and, besides, they glibly assured him that a jail sentence would not be imposed. Always amiable, Stanley entered a plea of guilty, drew sixty days in the cooler, and promptly sent for me. I arranged to secure his release and induced his associates to buy out his interest. The two of us then organized the first of his bookstores, directly opposite the Satyr shop on Vine Street. After a few drinks, Stanley would now and then emerge from the store and, to the amusement of his customers, swagger to the curb, shake his fist at his two former associates across the street, and hurl eloquent Texas curses at them. Uneducated but of great native charm, he was forever being lured on expensive hunting and fishing trips by wealthy actors, writers and directors on their promises to buy large libraries of books, which of course they never did; they merely wanted him along as court jester. Stanley dressed like a Hollywood swell, spoke like the Texas farm boy he never ceased to be, and carried on as Hollywood's unrivaled entertainer and easiest touch until his death in 1954. We were close friends during all the years he held court in the two bookshops which have long since become part of the legend of Hollywood.

Like other "bohemian" intellectuals, I had little active interest in politics in the 1920s. I kept inveighing, in my diary, against "a crazy money-mad world, formless and chaotic" which, paraphrasing La Fontaine, was endurable only to those of stout stomach and a sinful heart. I had only the most limited contact with any "left" politics, although some of the newspaper and magazine pieces I wrote were often rebellious in tone and content. In 1924 I met Upton Sinclair for the first time and wrote a piece about him which reflected my admiration. But there was not much of a socialist movement in Los Angeles in the 1920s; an earlier prewar movement, which had shown surprising strength, had been crushed after the dynamiting of the Los Angeles *Times* on October 1, 1910. Shortly after I came to Los Angeles, Sinclair had tried to address an outdoor meeting of striking longshoremen at Liberty Hills in San Pedro and had been arrested along with several hundred people. All he had managed to say before being arrested was, "This is a delightful climate . . ." But by then, 1923, the open-shop movement was in full swing and organized labor throughout California was on the defensive. On August 23, 1927, I had lunch with Sinclair in a huge dank, dreary, nearly empty cafeteria in Long Beach where Upton was then living, the day Sacco and Vanzetti were executed. I can still see the huge ominous headline: "Sacco and Vanzetti To Die!" I was supposed to interview Sinclair about his novel *Oil*, which had just been published, but we spent the entire afternoon talking about the executions in Boston. At the time I was more concerned with the literary ferment of the 1920s than with politics or causes, although I never doubted the innocence of the two anarchists. But listening to Upton gave me an uneasy feeling that the executions had a deeper and graver significance than most Americans realized.

The university or "formal" phase of my education, which proved to be largely irrelevant, was concluded in 1927. I was not well matched to the kind of institution I attended. The University of Southern California was then as it is today a famous football factory, and I did not play football. But I cannot say that the time I spent there did me any harm and I have fond memories of the place. I wrote editorials for the *Daily Trojan*, which were sassy enough to keep the editor in hot water most of the time, and edited the college literary magazine. But this phase of my education failed to provide much by way of guidance to the "world" of the 1920s which was soon to be snuffed out. Of more lasting impact were my explorations of the Southern California milieu and the emerging new city of Los Angeles, the influence of rebel writers of the period, and the more or less chance discovery of the "outsider" or "maverick" strain in American letters represented by Ambrose Bierce. A major influence in this informal or accidental phase of my "education" was H. L. Mencken.   [1978]

CAREY MC WILLIAMS

"Don't Shoot Los Angeles"

NO SINGLE ASPECT of Southern California has attracted more attention than its fabled addiction to cults and cultists. "I am told," said Mrs. Charles Steward Daggett in 1895, "that the millennium has already begun in Pasadena, and that even now there are more sanctified cranks to the acre than in any other town in America." Writing in 1921, John Steven McGroarty said that "Los Angeles is the most celebrated of all incubators of new creeds, codes of ethics, philosophies—no day passes without the birth of something of this nature never heard of before. It is a breeding place and a rendezvous of freak religions. But this is because its winters are mild, thus luring the pale people of thought to its sunny gates, within which man can give himself over to meditation without being compelled to interrupt himself in that interesting occupation to put on his overcoat or keep the fire going." "Los Angeles is full of people with queer quirks," observed Julia M. Sloane in 1925, "and they aren't confined to gardeners. I haven't had a hairdresser who wasn't occult or psychic or something." "Every religion, freakish or orthodox, that the world ever knew is flourishing today in Los Angeles," wrote Hoffman Birney in 1930. "This lovely place, cuckoo land," wrote the editors of *Life*, "is corrupted with an odd community giddiness . . . nowhere else do eccentrics flourish in such close abundance. Nowhere do spiritual or economic panaceas grow so lushly. Nowhere is undisciplined gullibility so widespread." "Here," wrote Bruce Bliven in 1935, "is the world's prize collection of cranks, semi-cranks, placid creatures whose bovine expression shows that each of them is studying, without much hope of success, to be a high-grade moron, angry or ecstatic exponents of food fads, sun-bathing, ancient Greek costumes, diaphragm breathing and the imminent second coming of Christ." Uniformly, these aberrant tendencies have been attributed to the climate. But are there other, and less hackneyed explanations?

The first eccentric of Southern California was a Scotsman by the name of William Money, who arrived in Los Angeles around 1841. Married to a Mexican woman, Money was a quack doctor, an economic theorist, and the founder of the first cult in the region. Known to local residents as "Professor Money," "Doctor Money," and "Bishop Money," he had been born, so he contended, with four teeth and "the likeness of a rainbow in the eye." It is significant that Money should have been the first person to write and to publish a book in the region, *The Reform of the New Testament Church*. Later, in 1858, he issued a dissertation in Spanish entitled, *A Treatise on the Mysteries of the Physical System and the Methods of Treating Diseases by Proper Remedies*. Of the 5,000 patients he had treated, only four, he said, had died. The cult that he founded was called "The Reformed New Testament Church of the Faith of Jesus Christ" and was pretty largely made up of "native Californians." He once prepared a map of the world entitled "William Money's Discovery of the Ocean." On this map San Francisco, a community that he detested, was shown poised on a portion of the earth that he predicted would soon collapse, precipitating the city into the fiery regions. Living in a weird oval structure in San Gabriel, the approaches to which were guarded by two octagonal edifices built of wood and adobe,

Money was the leading Los Angeles eccentric from 1841 until his death in 1880. He died with "an image of the Holy Virgin above his head, an articulated skeleton at his feet, and a well-worn copy of some Greek classic within reach of his hand."

Bishop Money was a typical Southern California eccentric: he was born elsewhere, he came to the region in middle life, his aberrations were multiform, and he founded a cult. As an eccentric, however, he was in advance of his time, an exceptional figure. Southern California evidenced few manifestations of cultism between 1850 and 1900. The hordes of newcomers who came after 1880 were a god fearing, highly respectable, conservative lot. In 1894 a visitor reported that 2,000 Easterners were spending their winters in Pasadena, that they were all regular church communicants, and that there was "not a grog shop in town." The publication of the W.C.T.U., *The White Ribbon*, was issued in Pasadena, where, as throughout Southern California, the dry sentiment was exceedingly strong. When J. W. Shawham started a "wet" newspaper in Pasadena in 1888, the local historian laconically notes that "he was a drinking fellow: he didn't last long." In 1888 the Pasadena *Standard* published a battle song of the W.C.T.U.:

> Rise, Pasadena! march and drill
>   To this your bugle rally—
> A Church or school on every hill,
>   AND NO SALOON IN THE VALLEY.
>
> Stand firm in rank, but do not boast
>   Too soon your victory's tally;
> You 'hold the fort' for all the coast
>   FOR NO SALOON IN THE VALLEY.
>
> The siege is on, the bombs aflight!
>   Let no true soldier dally;
> For truth and right, for HOME we fight,
>   AND NO SALOON IN THE VALLEY.

The truth of the matter was well expressed by Charles Frederick Holder when he described Pasadena in 1889 as "a city built rapidly yet without a vestige of the rough element that is to be found in the new cities of the inter-oceanic region. This is due to the fact that Pasadena has been built up by wealthy, refined, and cultivated people from the great cities of the East; and, while without maturity in years, she possesses all that time can bring, especially as regards the social ties that bind and mould communities." As long as the tide of migration was made up of such people, there was no opportunity for the visionary or the faith-healer or the mystic. But, as the region grew in wealth and fame, it began to attract some strange characters.

1. THE PURPLE MOTHER

The first major prophetess of the region was unquestionably Katherine Tingley. Born in New England in 1847, three times married, Mrs. Tingley lived in almost total obscurity for the first forty years of her life. When she was forty, she moved to New York, where, through her interest in spiritualism, she came to know the theosophist William Quan Judge, over whom she soon acquired an extraordinary influence. Much talk began to be heard in theosophical circles about the emergence of a mysterious disciple, referred to by Judge as "The Promise," "The Veiled Mahatma," "The Light of the Ledge," and "The Purple Mother." Shortly after Judge's death, Katherine Tingley was revealed as The Purple Mother. Although she had never been west, Mrs. Tingley had, since childhood, dreamed of "building a White City in a Land of Gold beside a Sunset Sea." Raising a considerable sum of money in the East, she established the Point Loma Theosophical Community near San Diego in 1900.

The community was an extraordinary apparition to appear in the complacent middle-class village of San Diego. It consisted of forty buildings, with "a harmonious blending of architectural lines, partly Moorish, partly Egyptian, with something belonging to neither." One of the main structures, called The Homestead, had ninety rooms and a great dome of opalescent green. Still another building, The Aryan Temple, had an amethyst Egyptian gateway. When visitors approached the colony, a bugler hidden behind the Egyptian gates sounded the note of their arrival. It was not long before some 300 bizarre devotees, representing 25 different nationalities, had taken up residence in the colony. When a person entered the colony it was customary to present Mrs. Tingley with a sizable "love offering." The Purple Mother ruled the colony with the utmost despotism. "From changing the milk-bottles of the newest baby to laying the last shingle on a bungalow," wrote one observer, "her desire equals a Czar's edict."

On the lovely 500-acre Point Loma tract soon appeared a School of Antiquity, a Theosophical University, a Greek Theater, a Raja Yoga College, and the Iris Temple of Art, Music, and Drama. Still later an opera house was acquired in San Diego, where the Point Loma yogis, appearing in Grecian costumes, lectured the natives on the subtle dialectics of theosophy. In its early years, Point Loma possessed an atmosphere described as "like ozone—like poppy-scented champagne." Wearing strange costumes, the residents of the colony raised chickens, vegetables, and fruits, and cultivated silkworms. During the years of Mrs. Tingley's residence, Point Loma was the headquarters for the branch of the theosophical movement which she headed and which claimed a membership of 100,000 followers scattered throughout the world. Not only did theosophists from all over the world visit Point Loma, but the emphasis placed on music attracted visitors from far and wide. Madame Modjeska, visiting the colony, called it "a second Bayreuth."

Needless to say, the appearance of this exotic colony in Southern California greatly disturbed the boosters of the period who regarded it as "bad advertising." General Harrison Gray Otis was convinced that weird orgies were being enacted at Point Loma. He was particularly incensed by stories of a sacred dog, called Spot, who was supposed to be the reincarnation of one of Mrs. Tingley's deceased husbands. Under such headlines as "Outrages at Point Loma Exposed by an 'Escape,'" "Startling Tales from Tingley," sensational stories began to appear in the Los Angeles *Times*. General Otis contended that Point Loma was a "spookery"; that Mrs. Tingley exercised a hypnotic influence on the colonists and fed the children so skimpily that they became "ethereal"; that "the most incredible things happen in that lair"; that purple robes were worn by the women and khaki uniforms by the men; and that, at midnight, the pilgrims "in their nightrobes, each holding a torch," went to a sacred spot on the Point Loma peninsula where "gross immoralities were practiced by the disciples of spookism." For once, however, General Otis had met his weight in wildcats. Mrs. Tingley promptly sued the *Times* for libel, and after years of litigation, eventually collected a handsome judgment.

It was through Point Loma that the yogi influence reached Southern California. Attracting thousands of visitors to the region, some of whom purchased real estate, the colony soon ceased to be regarded as heretical. Unfortunately Mrs. Tingley became involved in a serious scandal in 1923, as a result of which she abandoned Point Loma and went to Europe. One of the first couples to settle at Point Loma, Dr. and Mrs. George F. Mohn lived for some years in the Homestead before Mrs. Mohn first suspected that the Purple Mother was exerting a powerful influence on her husband. Whatever the nature of the influence, it was unquestionably persuasive; Dr. Mohn contributed $300,000 to the colony. Mrs. Mohn thereupon sued Mrs. Tingley for alienation of affections and a jury returned a verdict in her favor for $75,000.

After Mrs. Tingley's appearance in Southern California, the region acquired a reputation as an occult land and theosophists began to converge upon it from the four corners of the earth. One of these early colonists was Albert Powell Warrington, a retired lawyer from Norfolk, Virginia, who arrived in Los Angeles in 1911. Purchasing a fifteen-acre tract in what is now the center of Hollywood, he established Krotona, "the place of promise." The particular site had been selected, according to Warrington, because "not only does the prevailing breeze from off the nearby Pacific give physical tone to the surroundings, but a spiritual urge seems to be peculiar to all this section." The hills and groves around Krotona were, it seems, "magnetically impregnated."

At its heyday, Krotona boasted an Occult Temple, a psychic lotus pond, a vegetarian cafeteria, several small tabernacles, a large metaphysical library, and a Greek Theater. Grouped around the central buildings, were the dwellings of the colonists, described as a people whose faces had "a consciously sanctified look." Krotona was the headquarters of the Esoteric School, the Order of the Star of the East, and the Temple of the Rosy Cross. Under the direction of Dr. F. F. Strong of Tufts College and W. Scott Lewis of Los Angeles, research was conducted "in the subtler fields of physics and chemistry, psychology and psychic phenomena." Like Point Loma, the architecture was Moorish-Egyptian. At one time, Warrington rented a hall on Hollywood Boulevard where courses were given in Esperanto, the Esoteric Interpretation of Music and Drama, and the Human Aura. Krotona, in fact, "became a considerable factor in the commercial life of Hollywood."

At Krotona lived the mystic Phil Thompson who founded the science of "stereometry," a science of nature based upon a three dimensional geometric alphabet. Thompson demonstrated the science by a form on which he had worked for fifteen years. The form was made up of more than a million pieces of wood which he had fitted together. More than three tons of good redwood lumber went into the creation of this singular contraption. A charming man from County Down, Thompson was the author of *The Great Weaver* and *Letters of a Lunatic to Passing Shadows*. At one time his work attracted the attention of Albert Einstein and Dr. Robert Millikan. He died a few years ago at the Hondo "poor farm" in Los Angeles. Another resident of Krotona for many years was the writer Will Levington Comfort. "Krotona," writes his daughter, "in its circle of hills above Hollywood, was like some mystical birthplace of his soul and it welcomed him like a prodigal son." At Krotona, also, lived a remarkable woman, Wilhelmina L. Armstrong, who, under the pen-name of Zamin ki Dost, wrote eighteen of the superb stories collected in Mr. Comfort's *Son of Power*. Miss Armstrong, who spent many years in India, was the author of *Incense of Sandalwood* (1904), a rare collector's item.

The story of Krotona has been well told, in novel form, by Jane Levington Comfort (*From These Beginnings*, 1937). While most residents of Hollywood have never heard of the place, Krotona left a definite cultural imprint on Southern California. It was at Krotona in 1918 that Christine Wetherill Stevenson, a wealthy Philadelphian, sponsored an outdoor production of Sir Edwin Arnold's *The Light of Asia* which ran for thirty-five nights. It was this production which led to the creation of the Theater Arts Alliance in 1919, out of which eventually came the Hollywood Bowl concerts of today. Mrs. Stevenson was also responsible for the production of the *Pilgrimage*

Play in 1920, long since institutionalized by the boosters as one of the major tourist attractions of Los Angeles.

By 1920 Hollywood had begun to encroach upon Krotona and Dr. Warrington decided to lead the faithful to Ojai Valley, a section of Southern California thoroughly impregnated with occult and psychic influences. It is the home of Edgar Holloway, the Man from Lemuria, who claims to have flown to Ojai some years ago in a great flying fish. The real genesis of Ojai as an occult center, however, may be traced to thè publication in the early 'twenties of a magazine article by Dr. Hrdlicka predicting the rise of "a new sixth sub-race." It seems that psychological tests given in California schools had revealed the existence of a surprising number of child prodigies; ergo, California was the home of the new sub-race. Once this revelation was made, writes the biographer of Annie Besant, "theosophists all over the world turned their eyes toward California" as the Atlantis of the Western Sea. Among those who came to California was Mrs. Besant, who, "acting on orders of her Master," purchased 465 acres in the Ojai Valley as a home for the new sixth sub-race. And to Ojai, she brought Krishnamurti, "the new Messiah." Throughout the 'twenties, the annual encampments in Ojai were widely reported in the Southern California press, as thousands of people, mostly elderly neurotic women, trouped to Ojai to worship the Messiah. Ojai is, today, the center of all esoteric influences in the region. The Ojai Valley theosophists, however, do not get along well with those of Point Loma. Bitter enmity existed between Annie Besant and Katherine Tingley, the former referring to the latter as "a professional psychic and medium" and "a clever opportunist."

2. NEW THOUGHT AND KINDRED INFLUENCES

> *Some one made the careless remark before we came, that there wasn't any religion in Los Angeles, and we hadn't been here a week before the Persian who rents a room opposite us asked Uncle Jim if he were a Christian, and when we were on the car going to Whittier, a lady handed each of us a leaflet with a solemn question on it, and afterwards asked him if he'd read it, and if he were a Christian; now, if that isn't religion I don't know what is.*
> —FROM *Uncle Jim and Aunt Jemimy*
> *in Southern California* (1912)

Just as theosophy migrated to Southern California, so other strange faiths have been imported. Originally the New Thought movement was centered in New England; in fact, it was called "the Boston craze." But, like all metaphysical and religious movements, New Thought traveled westward. From Boston it moved to Hartford, then to New York, and finally spread westward to Chicago, Kansas City, and St. Louis. First appearing on the west coast in San Francisco, it did not reach Los Angeles until after the World's Fair in 1915. A day at the San Francisco Fair was given over to New Thought, and George Wharton James, the omnipresent, delivered a lecture on "California—the Natural Home of New Thought."

Following the fair, the New Thought leaders began to arrive in Los Angeles: Annie Rix Militz, who established the University of Christ; Fenwicke Holmes, who founded the Southern California Metaphysical Institute; and Eleanor M. Reesberg, who organized the Metaphysical Library. During these years, New Thought studio-lecture rooms sprang up throughout the city and the Metaphysicians' May Day Festival became an annual civic event. Among the pioneers of the movement was the Rev. Benjamin Fay Mills. Under his leadership, the Los Angeles Fellowship was a flourishing institution from 1904 to 1911, with over 1,000 members, a large organizational apparatus, and its own orchestra, schools, and magazine. In 1915, alas! Reverend Mills abandoned New Thought, left California, and died, a few years later, in Grand Rapids, a sound Presbyterian.

These two imported movements, theosophy and New Thought, constitute the stuff from which most of the later creeds and cults have been evolved. Since Southern California was the world center of both movements—theosophy from 1900; New Thought since 1915—it not only attracted adherents of these creeds from all over the world, but it became a publishing center from which issued a steady flow of magazines, newspapers, and books devoted to mysticism, practical and esoteric. The mystical ingredients came from Point Loma, the practical money-mindedness from the New Thought leaders. Of nearly a hundred books catalogued in the Los Angeles Public Library under the heading "New Thought," over half have been published in Southern California. I once attempted to examine these items, but abandoned the effort after a try at the first volume indexed: *Scientific Air Possibilities With the Human* by Zabelle Abdalian, "Doctor of Airbodiedness."

On meeting in Southern California, strangers are supposed to inquire, first, "Where are you from?" and, second, "How do you feel?" Invalidism and transiency have certainly been important factors stimulating cultism in the region. In Los Angeles, wrote Mark Lee Luther, "a vast amount of therapeutic lore was to be had for nothing in Westlake Park. The elderly men and women, hailing chiefly from the Mississippi watershed, who made this pleasance their daily rendezvous, were walking encyclopedias of medical knowledge. They seemed to have experienced all ailments, tried all cures.

Allopathy, homeopathy, osteopathy, chiropractic, faith-healing and Christian Science, vegetarianism and unfried food, the *bacillus bulgaricus* and the internal bath had each its disciples and propagandists." The number of food and body cults in Southern California has never been reckoned. In the early 'thirties, there were over 1,000 practicing nudists in Los Angeles, and three large nudist camps: Fraternity Elysia; the Land of Moo, over the entrance to which appeared the saucy slogan, "In All the World, No Strip Like This"; and, in the hills of Calabasas, a mysterious retreat called Shangri-la. The existence of a large number of transients and visitors has always stimulated the cult-making tendency. It should be remembered that, for the last twenty-five years, Los Angeles has had, on an average, about 200,000 temporary residents.

More than invalidism, however, underlies the widespread belief in faith-healing and magic cures. As a result of intensive migration, the growth of medical science has been retarded in Southern California. Much of the early medicine of the region was a combination of folk-healing, quackery, and superstition. Chinese herb doctors still did a lively business when I first arrived in Los Angeles in 1922. For years all the institutions of medical learning and most of the hospitals were concentrated in the northern part of the state. As late as 1870, Southern California had only one doctor in attendance at the annual meeting of the State Medical Society, and a local society was not formed until 1888. The vacuum created in the medical art was filled by Chinese herb doctors, faith-healers, quacks, and a miscellaneous assortment of practitioners. As a consequence, the unorthodox medical sciences got an early foothold in Southern California. Of eight schools of osteopathy in the United States in 1909, two were located in Los Angeles. Today, of 1,580 osteopaths in the state, all but 500 are in Los Angeles; of 3,655 licensed chiropractors, 2,052 are in Los Angeles. Osteopaths, chiropractors, and naturopaths were so powerful by 1922 that they were able to carry an initiative measure under which they have their own regulatory setup. Anti-vivisection, and similar initiative measures, always get a heavy vote in Southern California, a region that, to this day, lacks a real school of medicine. In such an environment it was, of course, foreordained, that a Messiah would some day emerge. The first local Messiah was a poor, uneducated, desperately ambitious widow by the name of Aimee Semple McPherson.

3. SISTER AIMEE

Aimee, who was "not so much a woman as a scintillant assault," first appeared in California at San Diego in 1918. There she began to attract attention by scattering religious tracts from an airplane and holding revival meetings in a boxing arena. That Mrs. McPherson's first appearance should have been in San Diego is, in itself, highly significant. In San Diego she unquestionably heard of Katherine Tingley, from whom she probably got the idea of founding a new religious movement on the coast and from whom she certainly got many of her ideas about uniforms, pageantry, and show-manship.

Furthermore, San Diego has always been, as Edmund Wilson once said, "a jumping off place." Since 1911 the suicide rate of San Diego has been the highest in the nation; between 1911 and 1927, over 500 people killed themselves in San Diego. A haven for invalids, the rate of sickness in San Diego in 1931 was 24% of the population, whereas for the whole country the sick rate was only 6%. Chronic invalids have always been advised to go to California, and once there, they drift to San Diego. From San Diego there is no place else to go; you either jump into the Pacific or disappear into Mexico. Seventy percent of the suicides of San Diego have been put down to "despondency and depression over ill health." Curiously enough, Southern California has always attracted victims of so-called "ideational" diseases like asthma, diseases which are partly psychological and that have, as Wilson pointed out, a tendency to keep their victims moving away from places under the illusion that they are leaving the disease behind. But once they acquire "a place in the sun" in California, they are permanently ma-rooned.

From San Diego, Mrs. McPherson came to Los Angeles in 1922 with her Four Square Gospel: conversion, physical healing, the second coming, and redemption. She arrived in Los Angeles with two minor children, an old battered automobile, and $100 in cash. By the end of 1925, she had collected more than $1,000,000 and owned property worth $250,000. In the early 'twenties, as Nancy Barr Mavity has pointed out (in an excellent bi-ography of Mrs. McPherson), "Los Angeles was the happy hunting ground for the physically disabled and the mentally inexacting . . . no other large city contains so many transplanted villagers who retain the stamp of their indigenous soil. . . . Most cities absorb the disparate elements that gravitate to them, but Los Angeles remains a city of migrants," a mixture, not a compound.

Here she built Angelus Temple at a cost of $1,500,000. The Temple has an auditorium with 5,000 seats; a $75,000 broadcasting station; the classrooms of a university which once graduated 500 young evangelists a year; and, as Morrow Mayo pointed out, "a brass band bigger and louder than Sousa's, an organ worthy of any movie cathedral, a female choir bigger and more beautiful than the Metropolitan chorus, and a costume wardrobe comparable to Ziegfeld's." Founding a magazine, *The Bridal Call*, Mrs. McPherson established 240 "lighthouses," or local churches, affiliated with Angelus Temple. By 1929 she had a following of 12,000 devoted members in Los Angeles and 30,000 in the outlying communities. From the platform of Angelus Temple, Sister Aimee gave the Angelenos the fanciest theological entertainment they have ever enjoyed. I have seen her drive an ugly Devil around the platform with a pitchfork, enact the drama of Valley Forge in George Washington's uniform, and take the lead in a dramatized sermon called "Sodom and Gomorrah." Adjutants have been praying, night and day, for thirteen years in the Temple. One group has been praying for 118,260 hours. While Mrs. McPherson never contended that she could heal the sick, she was always willing to pray for them and she was widely known as a faith-healer. A magnificent sense of showmanship enabled her to give the Angelus Temple throngs a sense of drama, and a feeling of release, that probably did have some therapeutic value. On state occasions, she always appeared in the costume of an admiral-of-the-fleet while the lay members of her entourage wore natty nautical uniforms.

On May 18, 1926, Sister Aimee disappeared. Last seen in a bathing suit on the beach near Ocean Park, she had apparently drowned in the Pacific. While Los Angeles went wild with excitement, thousands of templites gathered on the beach to pray for her deliverance and return. A specially chartered airplane flew over the beach and dropped flowers on the waters. On May 23, an overly enthusiastic disciple drowned in the Pacific while attempting to find her body. A few days later, a great memorial meeting was held for Sister at Angelus Temple, at which $35,000 was collected. Three days later, the mysterious Aimee reappeared at Agua Prieta, across the border from Douglas, Arizona.

Her entrance into Los Angeles was a major triumph. Flooded with requests from all over the world, the local newspapers and wire services filed 95,000 words of copy in a single day. Airplanes showered thousands of blossoms upon the coach that brought Sister back to Los Angeles. Stepping from the train, she walked out of the station on a carpet of roses. A hundred thousand people cheered while she paraded through the streets of the city, accompanied by a white-robed silver band, an escort of twenty cowboys, and squads of policemen. The crowd that greeted her has been estimated to be the largest ever to welcome a public personage in the history of the city. As she stepped on the platform at Angelus Temple, the people in the crowded auditorium were chanting:

> *Coming back, back, back,*
> *Coming back, back, back,*
> *Our sister in the Lord is coming back.*
> *There is shouting all around,*
> *For our sister has been found;*
> *There is nothing now of joy or peace we lack.*

The jubilation, however, did not last long. Working hard on the case, the newspapers soon proved that the kidnaping story, which she had told on her return, was highly fictitious. In sensational stories, they proceeded to trace her movements from the time she disappeared, through a "love cottage" interlude at Carmel with a former radio operator of the Temple, to her reappearance in Arizona. Following these disclosures, she was arrested, charged with having given false information designed to interfere with the orderly processes of the law, and placed on trial. Later the charges against her were dropped. During the trial, thousands of her followers gathered daily in the Temple and shouted:

> *Identifications may come,*
> *Identifications may go;*
> *Goggles may come,*
> *Goggles may go;*
> *But are we downhearted?*
> *No! No! No!*

Sister's trial was really a lynching bee. For she had long been a thorn in the side of the orthodox Protestant clergy who stoked the fires of persecution with memorials, petitions, and resolutions clamoring for her conviction. No one bothered to inquire what crime, if any, she had committed (actually she had not committed any crime). It was the fabulous ability with which she carried off the kidnaping hoax that so infuriated the respectable middle-class residents of Los Angeles. Miss Mavity writes that, in her opinion, it is "improbable that Aimee ever deliberately sought to harm another human being." Although I heard her speak many times, at the Temple and on the radio, I never heard her attack any individual or any group and I am thoroughly convinced that her followers always felt that they had received full value in exchange for their liberal donations. She made migrants feel at home in Los Angeles, she gave them a chance to meet other people, and she exorcised the nameless fears which so many of them had acquired from the fire-and-brimstone theology of the Middle West.

Although she managed to maintain a fairly constant following until her death in 1945 from an overdose of sleeping powder, she never recovered from the vicious campaign that had been directed against her in 1926. The old enthusiasm was gone; the old fervor had vanished. She was no longer "Sister McPherson" in Los Angeles, but merely "Aimee." In many respects, her career parallels that of Katherine Tingley: both were highly gifted women with a great talent for showmanship, both had lived in poverty and obscurity until middle-age, both founded cults, and both were ruined by scandal. In 1936 the Four Square Gospel had 204 branch organizations and a total membership of 16,000. More than 80% of her followers were city residents, mostly lower-middle-class people—small shopkeepers, barbers, beauty-parlor operators, small-fry realtors, and the owners of hamburger joints. Never appealing to the working class, as such, she had an enormous fascination for the uprooted, unhappy, dispirited *lumpenproletariat*. Over the years, many of her followers moved into the area around Angelus Temple, where they still reside.

4. MIGHTY I AM

The outstanding cult movement in Southern California in the 'twenties, the Four Square Gospel was succeeded by still fancier cults in the 'thirties. By any standard of the conceivable, the I AM cult is the weirdest mystical concoction that has ever issued from the region. It is a witch's cauldron of the inconceivable, the incredible, and the fantastic. Stated in objective terms, the tenets of the cult constitute a hideous phantasm. Originating in Los Angeles, the cult spread across the nation, with centers in Chicago, New York, West Palm Beach, Washington, Philadelphia, Boston, Cleveland, Denver, Salt Lake City, Fort Worth, and Dallas; enrolled 350,000 converts; and deposited in the hands of its creators the rather tidy sum of $3,000,000.

The creators of the cult, Guy W. Ballard and his wife Edna Ballard, came to Los Angeles from Chicago around 1932. Paperhanger, stock salesman, and promoter, Ballard had been obsessed, since his childhood in Newton, Kansas, with visions of gold and jewels. Indicted in Illinois in 1929, for a gold-mine promotion, he had fled westward. A professional medium, his wife had edited a spiritualist magazine, *The Diamond*, in Chicago. After coming to Los Angeles, Ballard, under the nom de plume of Godfrey Ray King, published a treatise in 1934 entitled *Unveiled Mysteries*, which sets forth the doctrine of the Mighty I AM Presence.

The deity of the cult, it seems, is the Ascended Master Saint Germain. While on a hiking trip near Mt. Shasta in Northern California, Ballard relates that Saint Germain, appearing out of the void, tapped him on the shoulder and offered him a cup filled with "pure electronic essence." After drinking the essence and eating a tiny wafer of "concentrated energy," Ballard felt himself surrounded by "a White Flame which formed a circle about fifty feet in diameter." Enveloped in the flame, he and Saint Germain set forth on a trip around the world in the stratosphere, visiting "the buried cities of the Amazon," France, Egypt, Karnak, Luxor, the fabled Inca cities of antiquity, the Royal Tetons, and Yellowstone National Park. Wherever they journeyed, they found rich treasures: jewels of all kinds, Spanish pirate gold, rubies, pearls, diamonds, emeralds, amethysts, gold bullion, casks of silver, the plunder of antiquity. Fantastic as this revelation may sound, *Unveiled Mysteries* began to sell like hot cakes at $2.50 a copy. Soon the Ballards were able to secure radio time. The "love gifts" poured in so rapidly, that they took over a large rambling tabernacle from the top of which a blazing neon light flashed word to all Los Angeles of the Mighty I AM Presence.

And then the Ballards began to sell things: a monthly magazine called *The Voice of the I AM*; various books, *The Magic Presence*, the *I AM Discourses*, the *I AM Adorations, Affirmations*, and *Decrees*, and the *Ascended Master Discourses*. Photographs of Ballard, "our beloved messenger," sold for $2.50; phonograph records, which recorded "the music of the spheres" and lectures of Ballard, sold for $3; a "Chart of the Magic Presence" brought $12, a steel engraving of the "Cosmic Being, Orion, better known as the Old Man of the Hills," retailed for $2; the "Special I AM Decree binder" was listed at $1.25; I AM rings at $12; a special electrical device, equipped with colored lights, called "Flame in Action," sold, in varying sizes, for $50 and $200; and, finally, a "New Age Cold Cream" preparation was available for the faithful. When Mrs. Ballard was later convicted in the federal court in Los Angeles, an audit of the books revealed that over $3,000,000 had been collected in sales, contributions, and "love offerings."

The meetings of this cult were unlike anything of the sort I have witnessed in Los Angeles. Buxom middle-aged usherettes, clad in flowing evening gowns, with handsome corsages of orchids and gardenias, bustled around at the morning services in a tabernacle that literally steamed with perfume. Although sex is taboo in the I AM creed—it tends to divert "divine energy"— it would be difficult to imagine a ritual in which sexual symbolism figured as prominently as it does in Master Saint Germain's revelation. Basically the cult has two symbols, wealth and energy. Great emphasis is placed on words such as "energy," "wealth," "jewels," "riches," and "power." The faithful are promised power by which they can acquire wealth, gold, radios, hotels, automobiles, jewels, and innumerable luxuries. A key word in the affirmations, chants, and adorations is "blasted" by the dynamic energy of Saint Germain's "purple light" and the "atomic accelerator." A talented appropriator, Ballard had lifted ideas at random from a dozen sources in putting this strange creed together (the sources are documented in an interesting volume: *Psychic Dictatorship in America* by Gerald B. Bryan, published in Los Angeles in 1940). One of the sources that Ballard used was a series of articles which William Dudley Pelley had published in 1929, entitled "Seven Minutes in Eternity," written while Pelley was a resident of Sierra Madre, near Pasadena. It is not by chance, therefore, that the I AM cult has Hitlerian overtones, with such auxiliary organizations as "the Minute Men of Saint Germain" and "the Daughters of Light." By the time an I AM audience repeat a chant the fourth time, they are shouting with all the frenzy of a mob of Nazis yelling *Sieg Heil!* Will some future historian regard this Buck Rogers phantasy as the first cult of the atomic age?

5. MANKIND UNITED

In 1875, a group of men, whose names must be forever unknown, succeeded in establishing contact with a superhuman race of little men with metallic heads who dwell in the center of the earth. With the aid of these supermen, The Sponsors propose to eradicate war and poverty from the earth. Such is the basic revelation of Mankind United, a cult movement launched by Arthur Bell in 1934. Once 200,000,000 people have joined the organization, Mankind United will be in a position to insure that no mortal will have to work more than 4 hours a day, 4 days a week, 8 months a year, to earn a salary of not less than $3,000 a year. Pensions of $250 a month will be paid all who have worked 11,000 hours or have reached the age of sixty. Bell promised each of his followers a $25,000 home, equipped with radio, television, unlimited motion pictures, and an "automatic local-type correspondence machine." The homes were also to be equipped with automatic news and telephone recording equipment; automatic air-conditioning; with fruit trees, vegetable gardens, hot houses, athletic courts, swimming pools, fountains, shrubbery, and miniature waterfalls. While traveling some years before the war in China and Japan, "and certain countries in Europe," Bell had discovered 100,000,000 gardeners who were anxious to spend the rest of their lives gardening in America for Mankind United.

In exchange for these promised luxuries, members were asked to surrender their worldly possessions on joining the secret order. Throughout a network of affiliated organizations—the Universal Service Corporation, the International Institute of Universal Research, and the International Legion of Vigilantes—the leaders of Mankind United received $97,500 in 1939 from the sale of Arthur Bell's revelation. Between 1934 and 1941, more than 14,000 Californians joined the cult, most of whom were "either elderly persons or individuals who had suffered severe economic losses." Arthur Bell claimed to have possession of a ray machine so powerful that its beams, once released, would knock out the eyesockets of people thousands of miles distant (a notion based upon an article which Dr. R. M. Langer, of the California Institute of Technology, had contributed to *Collier's* in 1940). Using the principle of the ray machine, power plants would be created capable of exterminating 1,000,000 people at a single blast (the atomic bomb killed 100,000 at Hiroshima). Claiming to be omnipotent, Bell told a California legislative committee that, if he wished, he could go into a trance and be whisked off to the far corners of the earth. On one occasion he went to sleep in San Francisco and woke up aboard a British merchant vessel in mid-Atlantic. Shortly after the attack on Pearl Harbor, the leaders of the cult, most of whom were anti-war, were convicted of violating the sedition statutes.

Certain basic themes appear in both the I AM and Mankind United cults. In both movements there is a marked emphasis upon energy and power: symbolized by the ray machine in Mankind United and by the "mystic purple light" of the I AM cult. Both cults reflect a psychoneurotic preoccupation with the symbols of material wealth, luxury, and ease of living. Splendor and release, power and wealth, are to come, in both cases, through the intervention of a Messiah who possesses the magic formula. There are villains in both cults: hidden rulers, destructive forces, static elements that must be blasted into eternity. Sired by Buck Rogers and Superman, they are nevertheless profoundly symptomatic of the unrest, the suppressed fury, and the preoccupation with violence and power of certain classes in our society. The revelation of Arthur Bell contains this significant passage:

The middle classes of people, who have always constituted the backbone of every nation, have been held in bondage throughout the centuries, primarily because of the fact that they have been penny wise and pound foolish in devoting their full time to performing the world's work, and in taking so little time for ascertaining the reasons for their ceaseless bondage.

The character, Tod, in the late Nathanael West's brilliant novel, *The Day of the Locust*, spends his nights at the different Hollywood churches, drawing their worshipers:

He visited the "Church of Christ, Physical," where holiness was attained through the constant use of chest-weights and spring grips; the "Church Invisible" where fortunes were told and the dead made to find lost objects; the "Tabernacle of the Third Coming," where a woman in male clothing preached the "Crusade Against Salt"; and the "Temple Modern" under whose glass and chromium roof, "Brain-Breathing," the Secret of the Aztecs, was taught. As he watched these people writhe on the hard seats of their churches, he thought of how well Alessandro Magnasco would dramatize the contrast between their drained-out, feeble bodies and their wild, disordered minds. He would not satirize them as Hogarth or Daumier might, nor would he pity them. He would paint their fury with respect, appreciating its awful, anarchic power and aware that they had it in them to destroy civilization.

One Friday night in the "Tabernacle of the Third Coming," a man near Tod stood up to speak. Although his name most likely was Thompson or Johnson and his home town Sioux City, he had the same counter-sunk eyes, like the heads of burnished spikes, that a monk by Magnasco might have. He was probably just in from one of the colonies in the desert near Soboba Hot Springs where he had been conning over his soul on a diet of raw fruits and nuts. He was very angry. The message he had brought to the city was one that an illiterate anchorite might have given decadent Rome. It was a crazy jumble of dietary rules, economics and Biblical threats. He claimed to have seen the Tiger of Wrath stalking the walls of the citadel and the Jackal of Lust skulking in the shrubbery, and he connected these omens with "thirty dollars every Thursday and meat eating." Tod didn't laugh at the man's rhetoric. He knew it was unimportant. What mattered were his hearers. They sprang to their feet, shaking their fists and shouting. On the altar someone began to beat a bass drum and soon the entire congregation was singing "Onward Christian Soldiers."

In Los Angeles, I have attended the services of the Agabeg Occult Church, where the woman pastor who presided had violet hair (to match her name) and green-painted eyelids (to emphasize their mystical insight); of the Great White Brotherhood, whose yellow-robed followers celebrate the full moon of May with a special ritual; of the Ancient Mystical Order of Melchizedek; of the Temple of the Jewelled Cross; of Sanford, "food scientist, psychologist, and health lecturer"; of the Baha'i World Faith Center; of the Crusade of the New Civilization; of the Self-Realization Fellowship of America which plans a Golden Lotus Yoga Dream Hermitage near Encinitas; and the lectures of Dr. Horton Held, who believes that California is an unusually healthy place to live since "so many flowers find it possible to grow in this vicinity. The flowers, cultivated or wild, give out certain chemicals which beneficially affect the human body." Los Angeles is the home of the Maz-daz-lan cult of Otoman Bar-Azusht Ra'nish (real name Otto Ranisch), whose followers chant:

> I am all in One individually and one in All collectively;
> I am present individually and omnipresent collectively;
> I am knowing individually and omniscient collectively;
> I am potent individually and omnipotent collectively.
> I am Maz-daz-lan and recognize the Eternal Designs of
>   Humata, Hutata, Hu-varashta
> A-shem Vo-hu, A-shem Vo-hu, A-shem Vo-hu.

It is the home of the Philosophical Research Society, Incorporated, of Manly Palmer Hall, "America's Greatest Philosopher"; the center of Zoroastrianism in America; and the headquarters of the American Association for the Advancement of Atheism. In a single office building in the heart of Los Angeles, Thomas Sugrue found the following listed as tenants: "Spiritual Mystic Astrologer; Spiritual Psychic Science Church, number 450, Service Daily, Message circles, Trumpets Thursday; Circle of Truth Church; Spiritual Psychic Science Church; First Church of Divine Love and Wisdom; Reverend Eva Coram, Giving Her Wonderful Cosmic Readings, Divine Healing Daily; Spiritual Science Church of the Master, Special Rose Light Circle, Nothing Impossible." Southern California, wrote Michael Williams, is a "vertiginous confusion of modern idolatry and sorcery and superstition," which is finding philosophical justification as a "new paganism, made up of Theosophists, Rosicrucians, Christian Mysticism, Hermeticism, and New Thought." It will be noted that most of the movements described in this chapter represent cultic phenomena, that is, they are not sects which have split off from some established faith; they are new cults.

6. CITY OF HERETICS

This was a city of heretics. A themeless city with every theme. Chicago, St. Louis and Denver had each been different; each had its own sordidness and strength and fury. Each was lusty and titanic in its own way, joyful and somber in its own way, and each was indubitably American. But not this Los Angeles. It had an air of not belonging to America, though all its motley ways were American. It was a city of refugees from America; it was purely itself in a banishment partly dreamed and partly real. It rested on a crust of earth at the edge of a sea that ended a world.

—FROM *A Place in the Sun* BY
FRANK FENTON (emphasis mine)

Migration is the basic explanation for the growth of cults in Southern California. "History is replete," writes Dr. William W. Sweet, "with instances of corruption of religion among migrating people." In the process of moving westward, the customs, practices, and religious habits of the people have undergone important changes. Old ties have been loosened; old allegiances weakened. The leaders of the orthodox faith have repeatedly complained, with the exception of those of the Catholic Church, that established church practices and procedures have undergone various mutations in Southern California. For example, entombment in mausoleums and the practice of cremation are much more common here than elsewhere in the nation. Bishop Stevens of the Episcopal Church has said "that people in Southern California jump from one ism to another. It doesn't make much difference if one changes the labels on these empty bottles, and Southern California is full of empty bottles." A church survey made in Los Angeles points up the real problem. "For the most part," it states, "the newly developing religious teachers are sincerely trying to serve their followers, and prove to be strong influences because *traditional habits do not reach the people in this community*. Even the older-type churches have been adopting measures unsanctioned in other parts of the country for a more effective hold upon their people."

In a lesser measure, the cultic aberrations of Southern California are an accidental by-product of its geographical location. Dr. Lee R. Steiner, in her study of quacks and fakirs, has pointed out that, when difficulty besets the quack, "he usually flees to Los Angeles," not so much because it is a haven, as because it is the first metropolitan center west of Chicago. Cult movements have moved westward in America and Los Angeles is the last stop. The cultism of Los Angeles appeared highly exceptional, when it first became pronounced in the early 'twenties, because most other American cities had forgotten that they, too, had passed through a similar phase years ago. For example, San Francisco was the home and center of west-coast cults and fakery from 1860 to 1890. The geography of Los Angeles is important in another respect; it faces the East. "Every migrant," writes Dr. Horace Kallen, "is a cultural carrier." That Los Angeles faces the East accounts for the fact, pointed out some years ago by Dr. Herbert W. Schneider, that every existing religion in the world is represented by branches in Los Angeles. Some idea of the heterogeneous religious scene may be illustrated by the fact that, of 1,833 houses of worship in Los Angeles, 147 are Roman Catholic and 836 are orthodox Protestant; but what are the remaining 850 churches?

Despite the number of churches, many of which cannot be classified under familiar labels, Los Angeles does not show a high average church attendance. "When a city like Los Angeles," complained the Rev. S. H. Bailes in 1933, "with more than 1,000,000 population, can report only 100,000 persons in its churches on an average Sunday morning, it is time for the nation to come back to God." California ranks seventeenth among the states in the number of churches; while Los Angeles ranks ninth, among the cities, in number of churches, and, in 1936, had 427,348 church members. So far as the orthodox faiths are concerned, it is rather interesting to note that the Roman Catholic faith is the largest single denomination in every county in Southern California and that it has shown an increase of 134.8% in membership since 1906. Throughout Los Angeles, as Aldous Huxley observed, one can see "primitive Methodist churches built, surprisingly enough, in the style of Cartuja at Granada, Catholic churches like Canterbury Cathedral, synagogues disguised as Hagia Sophia, and Christian Science churches with pillars and pediments, like banks." Paradoxical in all things, Southern California is a land of exaggerated religiosity and also of careless skepticism, where old faiths die and new cults are born.

While the folk-belief that new religious movements always arise in desert areas is certainly naive, nevertheless there is something about Los Angeles—its proximity to the desert, its geographical position (facing east and west), its history of rapid social change through migration—that leads me to believe that some new religious movement is brewing here. Admittedly the evidence is circumstantial, but I would point to some curiously interesting details recently unearthed by Dr. William York Tindall (see *The Asian Legacy and American Life*, 1945, pp. 175–193.)

When William Butler Yeats and his wife visited California, Mrs. Yeats, a medium, had a series of occult experiences in Los Angeles. For several successive nights, her husband took notes on the daemonic or occult communications which she received. These notes constitute the strange stuff from which his extraordinary volume, *A Vision* (1925), was woven. While visiting in Los Angeles, D. H. Lawrence frequently consulted Lewis Spence, a Rosicrucian, and an authority on the Atlantis legend. Much of the mysticism of his novel, *The Plumed Serpent*, is based on materials acquired from Spence. According to Dr. Tindall, the account of the *chakras*, which appeared in Lawrence's *Psychoanalysis and the Unconscious*, is based upon a book entitled *The Apocalypse Unsealed* (1910), written by James M. Pryse of Los Angeles. In 1937, Aldous Huxley accompanied his friend Gerald Heard to America. After "investigating telepathy in Carolina and Quakerism in Pennsylvania," in search of collaboration for their burgeoning metaphysical beliefs, they settled in Los Angeles. In *After Many a Summer Dies the Swan* (1939), Huxley gives an account of Heard's (the Mr. Propter of the novel) attempt to found a new cult in Southern California. At first a skeptic, Huxley has, within the last two years, become a convert to Indian mysticism. Nowadays he regularly attends the meetings of the Vedanta Society in Hollywood and frequently consults Swami Prabhavananda of the Ramakrishna Mission, editor of *Vedanta and the West*. Still another migrant to be converted in Los Angeles is the brilliant young English writer, Christopher Isherwood. "Soon after his arrival in Los Angeles," writes Dr. Tindall, "Isherwood fell under the power of Heard's Swami, renounced literature, the movies, and the world, and proceeded to meditate in the convenient desert whence he emerges occasionally to assist the Swami in public devotions."

There is, about all this, as Dr. Tindall notes, "the strange recurrence of Los Angeles. To that city Heard, Huxley, and James M. Pryse, *contriving to go East and West at once*, retired to meditate, and it was there that Mrs. Yeats received the daemons. The attraction of this place for spiritual men and even for spirits is plain. But I am not sure that I know what it means" (italics mine). Nor do I know what it means. (See also: *The Mystery of the Buried Crosses* by Hamlin Garland, (1937); and *The Doomsday Men* (1938) by J. B. Priestley.) Emma Harding, in her history of spiritualism, said that cults thrived on the Pacific coast because of the wonderful transparency of the atmosphere, the heavy charges of mineral magnetism from the gold mines which set up favorable vibrations, and the notably strong passions of the forty-niners which had created "unusual magnetic emanations"!

[1946]

EVELYN WAUGH

The Loved One

CHAPTER 3

DENNIS WAS A YOUNG MAN of sensibility rather than of sentiment. He had lived his twenty-eight years at arm's length from violence, but he came of a generation which enjoys a vicarious intimacy with death. Never, it so happened, had he seen a human corpse until that morning when, returning tired from night duty, he found his host strung to the rafters. The spectacle had been rude and momentarily unnerving; perhaps it had left a scar somewhere out of sight in his subconscious mind. But his reason accepted the event as part of the established order. Others in gentler ages had had their lives changed by such a revelation; to Dennis it was the kind of thing to be expected in the world he knew and, as he drove to Whispering Glades, his conscious mind was pleasantly exhilarated and full of curiosity.

Times without number since he first came to Hollywood he had heard the name of that great necropolis on the lips of others; he had read it in the local newssheets when some more than usually illustrious body was given more than usually splendid honours or some new acquisition was made to its collected masterpieces of contemporary art. Of recent weeks his interest had been livelier and more technical for it was in humble emulation of its great neighbour that the Happier Hunting Ground was planned. The language he daily spoke in his new trade was a *patois* derived from that high pure source. More than once Mr. Schultz had exultantly exclaimed after one of his performances: "It was worthy of Whispering Glades." As a missionary priest making his first pilgrimage to the Vatican, as a paramount chief of equatorial Africa mounting the Eiffel Tower, Dennis Barlow, poet and pets' mortician, drove through the Golden Gates.

They were vast, the largest in the world, and freshly regilt. A notice proclaimed the inferior dimensions of their Old World rivals. Beyond them lay a semi-circle of golden yew, a wide gravel roadway and an island of mown turf on which stood a singular and massive wall of marble sculptured in the form of an open book. Here, in letters a foot high, was incised:

The Dream

Behold I dreamed a dream and I saw a New Earth sacred to HAPPINESS. There amid all that Nature and Art could offer to elevate the Soul of Man I saw the Happy Resting Place of Countless Loved Ones. And I saw the Waiting Ones who still stood at the brink of that narrow stream that now separated them from those who had gone before. Young and old, they were happy too. Happy in Beauty, Happy in the certain knowledge that their Loved Ones were very near, in Beauty and Happiness such as the earth cannot give.

I heard a voice say: "Do this."

And behold I awoke and in the Light and Promise of my DREAM I made WHISPERING GLADES.

ENTER STRANGER and BE HAPPY.

And below, in vast cursive facsimile, the signature:

WILBUR KENWORTHY, THE DREAMER.

A modest wooden signboard beside it read: *Prices on enquiry at Administrative Building. Drive straight on.*

Dennis drove on through green parkland and presently came in sight of what in England he would have taken for the country seat of an Edwardian financier. It was black and white, timbered and gabled, with twisting brick chimneys and wrought iron wind-vanes. He left his car among a dozen others and proceeded on foot through a box walk, past a sunken herb garden, a sundial, a bird-bath and fountain, a rustic seat and a pigeon-cote. Music rose softly all round him, the subdued notes of the "Hindu Love-song" relayed from an organ through countless amplifiers concealed about the garden.

When as a newcomer to the Megalopolitan Studios he first toured the lots, it had taxed his imagination to realize that those solid-seeming streets and squares of every period and climate were in fact plaster façades whose backs revealed the structure of bill-boardings. Here the illusion was quite otherwise. Only with an effort could Dennis believe that the building before him was three-dimensional and permanent; but here, as everywhere in Whispering Glades, failing credulity was fortified by the painted word.

This perfect replica of an English Manor, a notice said, *like all the buildings of Whispering Glades, is constructed throughout of Grade A steel and concrete with foundations extending into solid rock. It is certified proof against fire, earthquake and—Their name liveth for evermore who record it in Whispering Glades.*

At the blank patch a signwriter was even then at work and Dennis, pausing to study it, discerned the ghost of the words "high explosive" freshly obliterated and the outlines of "nuclear fission" about to be filled in as substitute.

Followed by music he stepped as it were from garden to garden for the approach to the offices lay through a florist's shop. Here one young lady was spraying scent over a stall of lilac while a second was talking on the telephone: ". . . Oh, Mrs. Bogolov, I'm really sorry but it's just one of the things that Whispering Glades does not do. The Dreamer does not approve of wreaths or crosses. We just arrange the flowers in their own natural beauty. It's one of the Dreamer's own ideas. I'm sure Mr. Bogolov would prefer it himself. Won't you just leave it to us, Mrs. Bogolov? You tell us what you want to spend and we will do the rest. I'm sure you will be more than satisfied. Thank you, Mrs. Bogolov, it's a pleasure . . ."

Dennis passed through and opening the door marked *Enquiries* found himself in a raftered banqueting hall. The "Hindu Love-song" was here also, gently discoursed from the dark oak panelling. A young lady rose from a group of her fellows to welcome him, one of that new race of exquisite, amiable, efficient young ladies whom he had met everywhere in the United States. She wore a white smock and over her sharply supported left breast was embroidered the words, *Mortuary Hostess.*

"Can I help you in any way?"

"I came to arrange about a funeral."

"Is it for yourself?"

"Certainly not. Do I look so moribund?"

"Pardon me?"

"Do I look as if I were about to die?"

"Why, no. Only many of our friends like to make Before Need Arrangements. Will you come this way ?"

She led him from the hall into a soft passage. The décor here was Georgian. The "Hindu Love-song" came to its end and was succeeded by the voice of a nightingale. In a little chintzy parlour he and his hostess sat down to make their arrangements.

"I must first record the Essential Data."

He told her his name and Sir Francis's.

"Now, Mr. Barlow, what had you in mind? Embalmment of course, and after that incineration or not, according to taste. Our crematory is on scientific principles, the heat is so intense that all inessentials are volatilized. Some people did not like the thought that ashes of the casket and clothing were mixed with the Loved One's. Normal disposal is by inhumement, entombment, inurnment or immurement, but many people just lately prefer insarcophagusment. That is *very* individual. The casket is placed inside a sealed sarcophagus, marble or bronze, and rests permanently above ground in a niche in the mausoleum, with or without a personal stained-glass window above. That, of course, is for those with whom price is not a primary consideration."

"We want my friend buried."

"This is not your first visit to Whispering Glades?"

"Yes."

"Then let me explain the Dream. The Park is zoned. Each zone has its own name and appropriate Work of Art. Zones of course vary in price and within the zones the prices vary according to their proximity to the Work of Art. We have single sites as low as fifty dollars. That is in Pilgrims' Rest, a zone we are just developing behind the Crematory fuel dump. The most costly are those on Lake Isle. They range about a thousand dollars. Then there is Lovers' Nest, zoned about a very, very beautiful marble replica of Rodin's famous statue, the Kiss. We have double plots there at seven hundred and fifty dollars the pair. Was your Loved One married?"

"No."

"What was his business?"

"He was a writer."

"Ah, then Poets' Corner would be the place for him. We have many of our foremost literary names there, either in person or as Before Need reservations. You are no doubt acquainted with the works of Amelia Bergson?"

"I know of them."

"We sold Miss Bergson a Before Need reservation only yesterday, under the statue of the prominent Greek poet Homer. I could put your friend right next to her. But perhaps you would like to see the zone before deciding?"

"I want to see everything."

"There certainly is plenty to see. I'll have one of our guides take you round just as soon as we have all the Essential Data, Mr. Barlow. Was your Loved One of any special religion?"

"An Agnostic."

"We have two non-sectarian churches in the Park and a number of non-sectarian pastors. Jews and Catholics seem to prefer to make their own arrangements."

"I believe Sir Ambrose Abercrombie is planning a special service."

"Oh, was your Loved One in films, Mr. Barlow? In that case he ought to be in Shadowland."

"I think he would prefer to be with Homer and Miss Bergson."

"Then the University Church would be most convenient. We like to save the Waiting Ones a long procession. I presume the Loved One was Caucasian?"

"No, why did you think that? He was purely English."

"English are purely Caucasian, Mr. Barlow. This is a restricted park. The Dreamer has made that rule for the sake of the Waiting Ones. In their time of trial they prefer to be with their own people."

"I think I understand. Well, let me assure you Sir Francis was quite white."

As he said this there came vividly into Dennis's mind that image which lurked there, seldom out of sight for long; the sack or body suspended and the face above it with eyes red and horribly starting from their sockets, the cheeks mottled in indigo like the marbled end-papers of a ledger and the tongue swollen and protruding like an end of black sausage.

"Let us now decide on the casket."

They went to the show-rooms where stood coffins of every shape and material; the nightingale still sang in the cornice.

"The two-piece lid is most popular for gentlemen Loved Ones. Only the upper part is then exposed to view."

"Exposed to view?"

"Yes, when the Waiting Ones come to take leave."

"But, I say, I don't think that will quite do. I've seen him. He's terribly disfigured, you know."

"If there are any special little difficulties in the case you must mention them to our cosmeticians. You will be seeing one of them before you leave. They have never failed yet."

Dennis made no hasty choice. He studied all that was for sale; even the simplest of these coffins, he humbly recognized, outshone the most gorgeous product of the Happier Hunting Ground and when he approached the two thousand dollar level—and these were not the costliest—he felt himself in the Egypt of the Pharaohs. At length he decided on a massive chest of walnut with bronze enrichments and an interior of quilted satin. Its lid, as recommended, was in two parts.

"You are sure that they will be able to make him presentable?"

"We had a Loved One last month who was found drowned. He had been in the sea a month and they only identified him by his wrist-watch. They fixed that stiff," said the hostess disconcertingly lapsing from the high diction she had hitherto employed, "so he looked like it was his wedding day. The boys up there surely know their job. Why if he'd sat on an atom bomb, they'd make him presentable."

"That's very comforting."

"I'll say it is." And then slipping on her professional manner again as though it were a pair of glasses, she resumed. "How will the Loved One be attired? We have our own tailoring section. Sometimes after a very long illness there are not suitable clothes available and sometimes the Waiting Ones think it a waste of a good suit. You see we can fit a Loved One out very reasonably as a casket-suit does not have to be designed for hard wear and in cases where only the upper part is exposed for leave-taking there is no need for more than jacket and vest. Something dark is best to set off the flowers."

Dennis was entirely fascinated. At length he said: "Sir Francis was not much of a dandy. I doubt of his having anything quite suitable for casket wear. But in Europe, I think, we usually employ a shroud."

"Oh, we have shrouds too. I'll show you some."

The hostess led him to a set of sliding shelves like a sacristy chest where vestments are stored, and drawing one out revealed a garment such as Dennis had never seen before. Observing his interest she held it up for his closer inspection. It was in appearance like a suit of clothes, buttoned in front but open down the back; the sleeves hung loose, open at the seam; half an inch of linen appeared at the cuff and the V of the waistcoat was similarly filled; a knotted bow-tie emerged from the opening of a collar which also lay as though slit from behind. It was the apotheosis of the "dickey."

"A speciality of our own," she said, "though it is now widely imitated. The idea came from the quick-change artists of vaudeville. It enables one to dress the Loved One without disturbing the pose."

"Most remarkable. I believe that is just the article we require."

"With or without trousers?"

"What precisely is the advantage of trousers?"

"For Slumber-Room wear. It depends whether you wish the leave-taking to be on the chaise-longue or in the casket."

"Perhaps I had better see the Slumber Room before deciding."

"You're welcome."

She led him out to the hall and up a staircase. The nightingale had now given place to the organ and strains of Handel followed them to the Slumber Floor. Here she asked a colleague, "Which room have we free?"

"Only Daffodil."

"This way, Mr. Barlow."

They passed many closed doors of pickled oak until at length she opened one and stood aside for him to enter. He found a little room, brightly furnished and papered. It might have been part of a luxurious modern country club in all its features save one. Bowls of flowers stood disposed about a chintz sofa and on the sofa lay what seemed to be the wax effigy of an elderly woman dressed as though for an evening party. Her white gloved hands held a bouquet and on her nose glittered a pair of rimless pince-nez.

"Oh," said his guide, "how foolish of me. We've come into Primrose by mistake. This," she added superfluously, "is occupied."

"Yes."

"The leave-taking is not till the afternoon but we had better go before one of the cosmeticians finds us. They like to make a few final adjustments before Waiting Ones are admitted. Still it gives you an idea of the chaise-longue arrangement. We usually recommend the casket half-exposure for gentlemen because the legs never look so well."

She led him out.

"Will there be many for the leave-taking?"

"Yes, I rather think so, a great many."

"Then you had better have a suite with an anteroom. The Orchid Room is the best. Shall I make a reservation for that?"

"Yes, do."

"And the half-exposure in the casket, not the chaise-longue?"

"Not the chaise-longue."

She led him back towards the reception-room.

"It may seem a little strange to you, Mr. Barlow, coming on a Loved One unexpectedly in that way."

"I confess it did a little."

"You will find it quite different on the day. The leave-taking is a very, very great source of consolation. Often the Waiting Ones last saw their Loved Ones on a bed of pain surrounded by all the gruesome concomitants of the sick room or the hospital. Here they see them as they knew them in buoyant life, transfigured with peace and happiness. At the funeral they have time only for a last look as they file past. Here in the Slumber Room they can stand as long as they like photographing a last beautiful memory on the mind."

She spoke, he observed, partly by the book, in the words of the Dreamer, partly in her own brisk language. They were back in the reception-room now and she spoke briskly. "Well, I guess I've got all I want out of you, Mr. Barlow, except your signature to the order and a deposit."

Dennis had come prepared for this. It was part of the Happier Hunting Ground procedure. He paid her five hundred dollars and took her receipt.

"Now one of our cosmeticians is waiting to see you and get *her* Essential Data, but before we part, may I interest you in our Before Need Provision Arrangements?"

"Everything about Whispering Glades interests me profoundly, but that aspect, perhaps, less than others."

"The benefits of the plan are twofold"—she was speaking by the book now with a vengeance—"financial and psychological. You, Mr. Barlow, are now approaching your optimum earning phase. You are no doubt making provision of many kinds for your future—investments, insurance policies and so forth. You plan to spend your declining days in security but have you considered what burdens you may not be piling up for those you leave behind? Last month, Mr. Barlow, a husband and wife were here consulting us about Before Need Provision. They were prominent citizens in the prime of life with two daughters just budding into womanhood. They heard all particulars, they were impressed and said they would return in a few days to complete arrangements. Only next day those two passed on, Mr. Barlow, in an automobile accident, and instead of them there came two distraught orphans to ask what arrangements their parents had made. We were obliged to inform them that *no* arrangements had been made. In the hour of their greatest need those children were left comfortless. How different it would have been had we been able to say to them: 'Welcome to all the Happiness of Whispering Glades.' "

"Yes, but you know I haven't any children. Besides I am a foreigner. I have no intention of dying here."

"Mr. Barlow, you are afraid of death."

"No, I assure you."

"It is a natural instinct, Mr. Barlow, to shrink from the unknown. But if you discuss it openly and frankly you remove morbid reflexions. That is one of the things the psycho-analysts have taught us. Bring your dark fears into the light of the common day of the common man, Mr. Barlow. Realize that death is not a private tragedy of your own but the general lot of man. As Hamlet so beautifully writes: 'Know that death is common; all that live must die.' Perhaps you think it morbid and even dangerous to give thought to this subject, Mr. Barlow, the contrary has been proved by scientific investigation. Many people let their vital energy lag prematurely and their earning capacity diminish simply through fear of death. By removing that fear they actually increase their expectation of life. Choose now, at leisure and in health, the form of final preparation you require, pay for it while you are best able to do so, shed all anxiety. Pass the buck, Mr. Barlow; Whispering Glades can take it."

"I will give the matter every consideration."

"I'll leave our brochure with you. And now I must hand you over to the cosmetician."

She left the room and Dennis at once forgot everything about her. He had seen her before everywhere. American mothers, Dennis reflected, presumably knew their daughters apart, as the Chinese were said subtly to distinguish one from another of their seemingly uniform race, but to the European eye the Mortuary Hostess was one with all her sisters of the airliners and the reception-desks, one with Miss Poski at the Happier Hunting Ground. She was the standard product. A man could leave such a girl in a delicatessen shop in New York, fly three thousand miles and find her again in the cigar stall at San Francisco, just as he would find his favourite comic strip in the local paper; and she would croon the same words to him in moments of endearment and express the same views and preferences in moments of social discourse. She was convenient; but Dennis came of an earlier civilization with sharper needs. He sought the intangible, the veiled face in the fog, the silhouette at the lighted doorway, the secret graces of a body which hid itself under formal velvet. He did not covet the spoils of this rich continent, the sprawling limbs of the swimming-pool, the wide-open painted eyes and mouths under the arc-lamps. But the girl who now entered was unique. Not indefinably; the appropriate distinguishing epithet leapt to Dennis's mind the moment he saw her: sole Eve in a bustling hygienic Eden, this girl was a decadent.

She wore the white livery of her calling; she entered the room, sat at the table and poised her fountain pen with the same professional assurance as her predecessor's, but she was what Dennis had vainly sought during a lonely year of exile.

Her hair was dark and straight, her brows wide, her skin transparent and untarnished by sun. Her lips were artificially tinctured, no doubt, but not coated like her sisters' and clogged in all their delicate pores with crimson grease; they seemed to promise instead an unmeasured range of sensual converse. Her full-face was oval, her profile pure and classical and light. Her eyes greenish and remote, with a rich glint of lunacy.

Dennis held his breath. When the girl spoke it was briskly and prosaically.

"What did your Loved One pass on from?" she asked.

"He hanged himself."

"Was the face much disfigured?"

"Hideously."

"That is quite usual. Mr. Joyboy will probably take him in hand personally. It is a question of touch, you see, massaging the blood from the congested areas. Mr. Joyboy has very wonderful hands."

"And what do you do?"

"Hair, skin and nails and I brief the embalmers for expression and pose. Have you brought any photographs of your Loved One? They are the greatest help in re-creating personality. Was he a very cheerful old gentleman?"

"No, rather the reverse."

"Shall I put him down as serene and philosophical or judicial and determined?"

"I think the former."

"It is the hardest of all expressions to fix, but Mr. Joyboy makes it his speciality—that and the joyful smile for children. Did the Loved One wear his own hair? And the normal complexion? We usually classify them as rural, athletic and scholarly—that is to say red, brown or white. Scholarly? And spectacles? A monocle. They are always a difficulty because Mr. Joyboy likes to incline the head slightly to give a more natural pose. Pince-nez and monocles are difficult to keep in place once the flesh has firmed. Also of course the monocle looks less natural when the eye is closed. Did you particularly wish to feature it?"

"No, let us eliminate the monocle."

"Just as you wish, Mr. Barlow. Of course, Mr. Joyboy *can* fix it."

"No. I think your point about the eye being closed is decisive."

The Loved One | 221

"Very well. Did the Loved One pass over with a rope?"

"Braces. What you call suspenders."

"That should be quite easy to deal with. Sometimes there is a permanent line left. We had a Loved One last month who passed over with electric cord. Even Mr. Joyboy could do nothing with that. We had to wind a scarf right up to the chin. But suspenders should come out quite satisfactorily."

"You have a great regard for Mr. Joyboy, I notice."

"He is a true artist, Mr. Barlow. I can say no more."

"You enjoy your work?"

"I regard it as a very, very great privilege, Mr. Barlow."

"Have you been at it long?"

Normally, Dennis had found, the people of the United States were slow to resent curiosity about their commercial careers. This cosmetician, however, seemed to draw another thickness of veil between herself and her interlocutor.

"Eighteen months," she said briefly. "And now I have almost come to the end of my questions. Is there any individual trait you would like portrayed? Sometimes for instance the Waiting Ones like to see a pipe in the Loved One's mouth. Or anything special in his hands? In the case of children we usually give them a toy to hold. Is there anything specially characteristic of your Loved One? Many like a musical instrument. One lady made her leave-taking holding a telephone."

"No, I don't think that would be suitable."

"Just flowers? One further point—dentures. Was he wearing them when he passed on?"

"I really don't know."

"Will you try to find out? Often they disappear at the police mortuary and it causes great extra work for Mr. Joyboy. Loved Ones who pass over by their own hand *usually* wear their dentures."

"I'll look round his room and if I don't see them I'll mention it to the police."

"Thank you very much, Mr. Barlow. Well, that completes my Essential Data. It has been a pleasure to make your acquaintance."

"When shall I see you again?"

"The day after tomorrow. You had better come a little before the leave-taking to see that everything is as you wish."

"Who shall I ask for?"

"Just say the cosmetician of the Orchid Room."

"No name?"

"No name is necessary."

She left him and the forgotten hostess returned.

"Mr. Barlow, I have the Zone Guide ready to take you to the site."

Dennis awoke from a deep abstraction. "Oh, I'll take the site on trust," he said. "To tell you the truth I think I've seen enough for one day."

[1948]

NORMAN MAILER

The Deer Park

CHAPTER TWENTY

T WO DAYS LATER, a half hour before he was to see Lulu, Herman Teppis was waiting for Teddy Pope. From time to time it was Teppis' habit, as Lulu had told me, to have a big chat, or so he called it, with some of his stars. The institution, known to the public through a run of magazine articles written by publicity men, had been advertised as the secret of good family relations at Supreme Pictures. Teppis was always giving little talks at his home, his country club, or the studio commissary, but the big chat took place in his office, the doors closed.

Teppis' office was painted in one of those subsidiaries of a cream color— rose-cream, chartreuse-cream, or beige-cream—used for all the executive suites at Supreme Pictures. It was an enormous room with an enormous picture window, and the main piece of furniture was the desk, a big old Italian antique which had come down from the Middle Ages, and was said to have been brought from the Vatican. Yet, like an old house which is made over so completely that only the shell remains, the inside of Teppis' desk was given to a noiseless tape recorder, a private file, a refrigerator, and a small revolving bar. The rest of the room had some deep leather chairs, a coffee-colored carpet, and three pictures: a famous painting of a mother and child was set in a heavy gold frame, and two hand-worked silver cadres showed photos of Teppis' wife and of his mother, the last hand-colored so that her silver hair was bright as a corona.

The afternoon Teddy Pope came to see Mr. Teppis, he was greeted warmly. Teppis shook his hand and clapped him on the back. "Teddy, it's a pleasure you could manage to get here," he said in his hoarse thin voice, and pressed a button under his desk to start the tape recorder.

"Always happy when you want to talk to me, Mr. T.," Teddy said.

Teppis coughed. "You want a cigar?"

"No, sir, I don't smoke them."

"It's a vice, cigars. My only vice, I say." He cleared his throat with a short harsh sound as though he were ordering an animal to come up. "Now, I know what's going on in your mind," he said genially. "You want to know why I want to see you."

"Well, Mr. T., I was wondering."

"It's simple. I'll give you the answer in a phrase. The answer is I would like to spend the kind of time I ought to with all you young people, all you young stars I've seen growing up right on this studio lot. That's a lack in my life, but it don't mean my personal interest is at long distance. I think about you an awful lot, Teddy."

"Hope you think nice things, Mr. T.," Teddy said.

"Now, what are you nervous for? Have I ever hurt you?" Teddy shook his head. "Of course now, I got a real affection for you, you know that. I'm an old man now."

"You don't look old, H.T."

"Don't contradict me, it's true. Sometimes I think of all the years I been sitting in this room, the stars that came, the stars that fell. You know I think of all the stars I made, and then all these up-and-coming starlets. They're going to be heard from in a couple of years, but they'll never push you out, you can depend on that, Teddy, you can say H.T. said to me, 'You can depend on that almost as a promise, because what I want to say is that I feel the very real affection which all of my stars and starlets feel for me, I can tell when we have these chats, they think I got a large warm heart, I can never remember a single one leaving this office without their saying, 'God bless you, H.T.' I'm a warm individual. It's why I've been a success in the industry. What do you need to be successful here?"

"Heart," said Teddy.

"That's right, a big red heart. The American public has a big heart and you got to meet it, you got to go halfway up to it. I'll give you an example. I'm the father of a grown woman, you know my daughter Lottie, I love her, and I hear from her every single day. At ten o'clock in the morning the call comes through and my secretary, she clears the switchboard for me. If I can't be punctual to my daughter, how can I expect her to be punctual to me? You see, Teddy," he said, reaching forward to pat Pope's knee, "it don't matter the love I got for my daughter, there's a lot left over for my other family, the big family right here at Supreme Pictures."

"The family feels the same way about you, H.T.," Teddy said.

"I hope so, sincerely I hope so. It would break my heart if all the young people here didn't reciprocate. You don't know how much I think about all of you, about your problems, your heartaches, and your successes. I follow your careers. You know, Teddy, you'd be surprised how much I know about the personal lives of all of you. I even follow to see how religious you are, because I believe in religion, Teddy. I've changed my religion and a man don't change his religion like he takes a drink of water. I can tell you I've found great consolation in my new faith, there's a great man in New York, a great religious man, I'm proud to call him one of my dearest friends, and he made things so you and me can go through the same church door."

"I guess I haven't been going to church enough lately," Teddy said.

"I hate to hear that. I'd give you a lecture if there wasn't something else I want to talk about."

Teppis held up his arms. "Look, what am I showing you? Two hands. Two hands make a body. You see, I feel as if I come from two faiths, the one I was born with, and the one I changed to and elected. I think I've inherited the wealth of the tradition from two great faiths. Am I confusing you?"

"No, sir."

"You take my first faith. One of the most heart-warming customs of the people I was born in, it was the concern the parents of the family took in all the doings of their children, the engagements, the weddings, the births of young people. I could tell you stories that make you cry. You know the poorest house, dirt-poor people, they would take the same interest in arranging the marriage of their children as for a royal marriage. Now, this is a democratic country, we can thank God for that, we don't approve of royal marriages, I don't approve of it myself, I would never dream of doing such a thing, but there's a lot to be said on both sides. I was talking to the Bey Omi Kin Bek on this very subject, and you know what he said to me, he said, 'H.T., we don't arrange marriages the way the American public tends to think, we just encourage them, and then it's up to the kids.' That's a first-rate article, genuine royalty. I'll say to any man I'm proud to have the Bey for a friend."

"I think a lot of people like to look down on royalty," Teddy said.

"Sure. You know why they do it? Envy." Teppis took out his handkerchief and spit into it. "People are envious of the people at the top."

"My idea," said Teddy, "is that royalty is like everybody else. Only they express themselves more."

"You're wrong," Teppis interrupted. "Royalty pays a terrible price. Let me tell you a story. What is it about public men that makes them different? It's that they're in the eye of the public. They got to lead a life as clean as a dog's teeth, privately, not only public. You know what scandal is to a public figure? It's a bomb ten times bigger than the atom. They got to do certain things, it breaks their heart to do them, and why? The public responsibility demands it. That's true for royalty and it's true for movie stars, and fellows like me, people like you and me, that's who it applies for. Those are the laws, try and break them. We're talking like equals now, aren't we, Teddy?"

"Face to face," Teddy said.

"You look at that picture I have," said Teppis pointing to the painting. "I would hate to tell you how much I had to pay for it, but the moment I looked at that French picture with that beautiful mother and her beautiful child, I said to myself, 'H.T., it don't matter if you got to work ten years to pay for it, you got to buy that picture.' You know why I said that to myself? Because that picture is life, it's by a great painter. I look at it, and I think, 'Motherhood, that's what you're looking at.' When I think of you, Teddy, and I know what goes on in your heart, I think that you think about settling down with a beautiful bride and children that come out to greet you when you come home from work. I never had anything like that, Teddy, cause when I was your age, I worked long hours, very long hours, hours that would break your heart to tell you about them, and when I'm alone, I sometimes think to myself, and I say then, 'You know, H.T., you missed the fruits of life.' I would hate for a fellow like you, Teddy, to have to say the same thing. And you don't have to. You know with all that's due respect to my wife, may she rest in peace, she had to work very hard herself, only for those early years, but she never complained once, not a peep." Tears filled Teppis' eyes, and he wiped them away with a clean handkerchief he kept in his breast pocket, the aroma of his toilet water passing across the room. "Take any girl you would marry," Teppis went on, "you wouldn't have such problems, you could give her all the financial security, you know why, she'd make you settle down. I'd even sit down with you and your business agent and we'd have a talk how to straighten you out financially so you wouldn't have to borrow from us ahead of your salary." Teppis frowned at him. "It's a shame, Teddy. People will think we don't pay you nothing the way you got to borrow money."

"I'd like to talk to you about that, Mr. T.," Teddy said quickly.

"We'll talk about that, we'll go all into it, but now's not the time. You just remember, Teddy, that you're an idol of the American public, and an idol never needs to worry about money so long as he's clean with his public."

Teppis poured himself a glass of water, and drank it slowly as if he would measure the taste. "I know a young fellow like you with the world at his feet," he went on, "there's a lot of times he don't want to get married. 'Why should I get married?' he says to himself, 'What's in it for me?' Teddy, I'll tell you, there's a lot in it for you. Just think. The whole world is in a strait jacket so it says, 'You, over there, you get in a strait jacket, too.' Know why? The world hates a bachelor, he's not popular. People try to drag him down. The stories you hear, ninety-nine per cent of the time unfounded, but I'd be ashamed, I couldn't look you in the eye to tell you the kind of stories I have to listen to. It's enough to revolt your stomach. I hear a story like that, I let them have it. 'Don't tell me that kind of filth about Teddy,' I say, 'I don't want to hear it. If the boy don't want to get married, it got nothing to do with all those dirty rotten stories you tell me, period.' That's how definite I am. People know me, they say, 'H.T. is on record as being against slander.' "

Abruptly, Teppis pounded his desk. "A rumor about a fellow like you, it spreads like hot cakes. We got letters from your fan clubs all over the place. Kokoshkosh, towns like that. Small-town America. Two-Bits, Kansas. You see what I mean? What do you want? You know what those letters say, they say that the members of the Teddy Pope fan club are brokenhearted cause they heard the most terrible stories about Teddy. Their loyalty is shaken. Listen, Teddy, I go to your defense, you know why? It isn't because of business reasons, or because I know you for a long time, or even because I like you, although I do. It's because I know deep down that you're going to prove I'm right, and I wouldn't go to bat for a person even if they meant a million dollars to me if I didn't think they would prove that H.T. is right in the long run. That's confidence. Should I put that confidence in you?" Teppis held up a finger. "Don't answer, you don't even have to answer, I know I can put confidence in you." He got up and walked to the window.

"You know something, I've had my confidence rewarded already. I took a look in the papers. That picture of you and Lulu where you're holding hands in Desert D'Or. It's one of the most beautiful, impressive, and touching things I've ever seen. Young love, that's what it said. It made me wish that same famous painter on my wall was still alive so I could hire him to paint the photograph of the young love of you and Lulu."

"Mr. Teppis," Teddy said, "that was a publicity picture."

"Publicity! Listen, do you know how many of the most successful marriages in this industry started with just publicity? I'll tell you. The answer is ninety-nine per cent of the most successful marriages began just that way. It's like a dowry in the old country. I know you, Teddy, you're a clean-cut boy. I've seen a lot of photographs. I don't believe that you and Lulu can look at each other like two love-doves and be fakers. Don't try to tell me Lulu isn't crazy about you. That girl is wearing her heart on her sleeve. Teddy, I'll tell you, Lulu is one of the finest girls I know. She's a real fine American-type girl of real American stock. Such a woman is a gift of God. When I look at my mother's picture on this very desk, you know what I get? Inspiration. I carry her picture next to my heart. You should be able to do the same."

Teddy was perspiring. He leaned forward to say something, and said no more than, "Mr. Teppis—you have to allow me the right to say . . ."

"Stop!" said Teppis, "I don't want to hear your ideas. You're a stubborn boy. Why are you so stubborn when you know what's in your heart? You want to agree with me. But you're confused. You need a man like myself to set you straight."

In a quiet voice, Teddy said, "Mr. Teppis, you know very well I'm a homosexual."

"I didn't hear it, I didn't hear it," Teppis screamed.

"That's the way I am," Teddy muttered. "There's nothing to be done about it. What is, is."

"Philosophy?" Teppis shouted. "You listen to me. If a man sits in . . . *shit*, he don't know enough to get out of it?"

"Mr. Teppis, don't you have a big enough heart to understand my feelings?"

"You're the most ungrateful boy I ever knew. You keep me up nights. What do you think, sex it's the whole world? I forget what you said, do you understand? I wouldn't want it on my conscience. You watch. I'll drive you right out of the movie business."

"Let me try to say . . ."

"Lulu, that's what you got to say. I know what goes on. You're a coward. You got a chip against society. You should love society with all it's done for you. I love society. I respect it. Teddy, you're a sick boy, but you and me can lick this thing together." Teppis held up a fist. "I don't want to persecute you, but I never heard of anything so perverted in my whole life."

The buzzer sounded. "All right, all right," Teppis said into the interoffice phone, "you tell the party in question to wait. I'll be with that individual in a minute."

"Mr. Teppis," Teddy said, "I'm sorry. Maybe I'd like to have children, but I've never once had relations with a woman."

Teppis clicked the switch back to its "off" position, and stared for many seconds at Teddy Pope. "Teddy, we've talked a lot," he said. "What I want is that you promise me you won't make up your mind ahead of time that you personally aren't able to boff a beautiful sexy girl like Lulu. Do I have to be there to help you? I'm telling you, you can. That's all I ask of you, Teddy, don't make up your mind. Sleep on it. Is that a bargain?"

Pope shrugged wearily.

"That's the boy. That's Teddy Pope talking." Teppis walked him to the door. "Now, Teddy, nobody is forcing you into anything. If you said yes this very minute, I would still say, 'Teddy, sleep on it.' Now, could anybody claim I was trying to push you into a single thing?"

"Who would dare?"

"You're right. I don't force people. Never. I talk things over with them. Someday, Teddy, you're going to say, 'God bless you, H.T.' "

Once Teddy was out the door, Teppis flipped the buzzer again. "All right, send Lulu in," he said. He waited by the door to greet her and held Lulu at arm's length while he looked at her. "I wish I could tell you the kind of pleasure it is to have you lightening up this office," he said to her. "Sweetie, you take a load off all my worries, and on that desk are sitting one thousand worries." Now, he held her hands. "I love a girl like you who brings sunshine into this room."

Probably Lulu had managed to look no more than seventeen. "I love you, too, Mr. T.," she said in her husky little voice.

"I know you do. Every one of my stars, they tell me that. But with you, I know it's sincere." He guided her to the chair in which Teddy had been sitting, and from a drawer in the Italian desk, he took out a bottle of whisky and dropped some ice cubes in a glass.

"Oh, Mr. T., I'm not drinking these days," said Lulu.

"Nonsense. I know you. Sweetie, you got no respect for me. You think you can twist me around your little finger," he said cordially. "Well, I got news for you. There's no man in the world you can't twist around your finger. But I understand you, sweetie, I'm crazy about you. I don't want you thinking you got to take a drink behind my back."

"I think you're the only man who understands me, H.T.," Lulu said.

"You're wrong. Nobody can understand you. Know why? You're a great woman. You're not only a great actress but there's greatness in you as a person—fire, spirit, charm—those are the sort of things you have. I wouldn't want this to get around, but I don't care if you take a drink. You've earned the right to do anything you want."

"Except when I disagree with you, H.T.," Lulu said.

"I love you. What a tongue. You got impetuosity. I say to myself, 'H.T., what is there about Lulu that's smash box office?' and I don't even have to ask myself the answer. It's in a word. Life," Teppis said, pointing a finger at her, "That's what Lulu's got."

He poured himself a small drink and sipped it politely. "You're wondering why I asked you up here?" he said after a pause. "I'll tell you. I've been thinking about you. Know my personal opinion of Lulu Meyers? She's the greatest actress in this country, and this country's got the greatest actors in the whole world."

"You're the greatest actor in the world, Mr. T.," Lulu said.

"I take it as a compliment. But you're wrong, Lulu, I can't act. I'm too sincere. I feel things too deeply which I can't express. There're nights when I stay awake worrying about you. You know what eats my heart out? It's that I'm not the American public. If I was the American public, I'd make you Number One on the Bimmler Ratings. You know what you are now?"

"Seventeen, isn't it, Mr. T.?"

"Seventeen. Can you believe it? There are sixteen actors in this country the American public buys ahead of you. I don't understand it. If I was the public I'd buy Lulu Meyers all the way."

"Why can't there be ten million people like you, H.T.?" Lulu said. She had finished her drink, and after a little pause, walked up to the desk and poured herself another.

"Lulu, do you know your Bimmler last year? It was twelve. This year you should have gone up, not down. Up to ten, to eight. Three, Number One, that's the way it should have gone."

"Mr. Teppis, maybe I'm a has-been."

Teppis held up his hand. "Lulu, for a remark like that, I ought to take you over my knee and spank you."

"Oh, Mr. T., what a construction I could put on that."

"Ha, ha. Ha, ha. I'm crazy about you, Lulu, listen to me. The trouble is you're weak, publicity-wise."

"I've got the best press agent in the country," she said quickly.

"You think you can buy publicity? Good publicity is a gift of God. The time is past, Lulu, when any sort of girl, you'll see I'm speaking frankly, the kind of girl who's so-called friends with this man and friends with that man until she's notorious. The public wants what's respectable today. You know why? Life ain't respectable any more. Think they want to be reminded of that? Let me show you psychology. Ten years ago, a woman she was faithful to her husband, she wanted excitement, she wanted to dream she was having a big affair with a star—Lulu, I wouldn't talk so frankly to any other person on earth. Today, you know what, that same woman she has boyfriends all over the place, with the man who fixes the television set, people like that. You think she wants to see somebody just like herself on the screen, somebody just as nuts as she is? She don't. She's ashamed of herself. She wants to see a woman she can respect, a married woman, a royal couple, the Number One married lovers of America. That's true psychology."

Lulu shifted in her seat. "H.T., you should have been a marriage broker."

"You tell me that all the time—I'll tell you something. If you could be married to the right kind of boy, let me give you an example, to a star let's say with a Seven Bimmler, a Nine Bimmler, you know what? You think you'd come out with a Bimmler the average between the two of you, you wouldn't you'd end up with the two highest Bimmlers in the country. Know why? Two plus two don't make four. It makes five, and five makes ten. That's compound interest. You think about it. The right kind of marriage is better than compound interest. Lulu Meyers and anybody, Joe McGoe, I don't care what the man's name is just so he has a high Bimmler, and then you have the Number One royal couple of America, and America is the world, that's where you'd be."

Teppis blew a kiss at Lulu. "You're my darling, do you know that? You're my A-1 darling."

"I hope so, H.T."

"You take this young fellow of yours, what's his name, this Shamus Sugar-boy fellow."

"You mean Sergius."

"I've looked into him. He's a nice boy. I like him. I'd hire him. Not for acting, you understand, but some sort of work, moving sets around, driving a truck, he's the kind of boy who'd be good for that, sincere, well-meaning maybe, but I think about him with you, and you know what I decide? Lulu, that boy is not for you. He's insignificant. He would drag you down. I don't care how many planes he says he shot, he's a bum, that's the sort of person he is."

"Oh, you don't have to disparage Sergius, Mr. T.," said Lulu, "he's very sweet."

"Sweet boys, a dime a dozen. He's a kid. You're a woman. That's the difference. I think we understand each other. What I want to say is something I got in mind that's going to stun you. Want to know who I think you should marry?"

"I can never know what you think, Mr. Teppis."

"Guess. Go ahead, guess."

"Tony Tanner," Lulu said.

"Tony Tanner? Lulu, I'm ashamed of you. I looked up his Bimmler myself. One hundred and eighty-nine, that's what a nobody he is. It's a disgrace for a woman not to value herself. I got somebody better to think about. I don't want you to say a word, I want you to sleep on it. Teddy Pope, what do you say?"

Lulu came to her feet. She made a small demonstration of opening and closing her mouth. "I'm shocked, Mr. T.," she said at last.

"Sit down. I'll tell you something. Maybe you don't know it. I got no desire to hide it from you. Teddy Pope is a homosexual. It makes you wonder, don't it? Could H.T. be the kind of man who gets down on his hands and knees to beg a beautiful girl like you to marry a faggola?"

"You could never be that kind of man," Lulu said. "You're too respectable and upright."

"Let's not get off the sidetrack. I want you to answer me one question as honest as you can. Do you admit, paying no attention for the moment to your personal life, that to be married to Teddy Pope, wouldn't that be the biggest benefit you could bestow on yourself, publicity-wise? The Number One couple of America. Say I'm right."

"I can't say you're right, Mr. Teppis." Lulu rattled the ice cubes in her glass, and in a voice which mimicked him, she added, "I think you're being selfish."

"Nobody else in the whole world could say that to me."

"I ought to cry," Lulu said. "I've told everybody you're like a father."

"Don't hurt my feelings, Lulu."

"H.T., I feel as if things can never be the same between us."

"To talk like that," Teppis exclaimed. "It's disgraceful. After all I've done for you."

Lulu began to weep. "I don't like Teddy," she said in a little voice.

"Like him! You stop crying. I know you, Lulu, and I'll tell you something. Teddy Pope is the only man you could ever be in love with. You think I'm crazy. You're wrong. Just cause he's a homo, you think it's an insult to you. But I'm an old man, I know people. You and Teddy can hit it off. He's been hurt, he's got a delicate heart, there's a lot for an actress to learn from him about the subtleties of human nature. Lulu, you're the woman who could straighten him out, and then he'd worship the ground you walk on."

Lulu put a handkerchief to her eyes. "I hate you, H.T.," she sobbed.

"You hate me! You love me, that's why you hate to listen to me. But I'll let you know something. You're a coward. A girl with your looks, your appeal, should rise to a challenge. You're the most attractive girl I ever saw in my life. It don't mean nothing if you get a young healthy nobody excited about the kind of woman you are. That's beneath you. It's like a Hercules award for doing ping-pong. That's the sort of ridiculous thing it is. But think of the respect people would have if you could make a man out of Teddy Pope."

"And what if I couldn't?" Lulu said.

"You're defeated before you start. I'm disappointed."

"Mr. Teppis, I'll quote you. 'Look around before you take a step. There could have been dogs in the grass.' That's what you said, H.T., I have witnesses."

"You make me miserable. I thought you were a gambler like me."

Tears ran down her cheeks. "H.T., I want to get married," she said in a tremulous voice. "I want to love just one man and have a beautiful mature relationship and have beautiful children and be a credit to the industry."

"That's the ticket, Lulu."

"But if I marry Teddy, it won't work, and I'll become promiscuous. You'll see. Will you be sorry when I'm like that?"

"Lulu, you could never be promiscuous. You're too fine. Suppose at the very worst, there should be a fellow or two that you would like and admire and diddle around with, while still being married to Teddy. I don't advise it, but it happens all the time, and you know what? The world don't stop moving."

"H.T., that's an immoral proposal. I'm ashamed of you."

"You're ashamed of me?" Teppis whispered. "You said the wrong thing right then. I sit up nights trying to figure out how to save your career, and this is the thanks you give me. You're wild, that's what you are. Know what a star is? She's like delicious perishable fruit. You got to take her a long distance to market, and when she's there, you got to sell her. If you don't, she rots. She's rotten. Lulu, I'm speaking like a man to a woman. There are a lot of high executives in this studio who are fed up with you. Have you got any idea of the number of times I got to argue in your behalf? 'Lulu needs discipline,' they tell me, 'Lulu's too hard to handle. She gives us more heartaches than she's worth.' Believe me, Lulu, as God is looking into this room, you've made enemies, hundreds of enemies on this very studio lot. If you don't start to co-operate, they'll get into the process of tearing your flesh and picking your bones." His voice had started to rise. "That's exactly the sort of situation it is," he now said quietly. "I don't want to depress you, but Lulu, your Bimmler has got to show improvement this coming year. Otherwise, there's only one way for you." He pointed to the floor. "The way is down. You'll go down and down. You'll get older, you won't look so good, you won't get work so easy, you won't have a studio behind you. Know what a studio means? It's like a battleship. Look at Eitel. You'll become so ashamed you'll change your name. And that's how you'll end up, a dance-hall cutey, that's the sort of girl. I could cut my throat I'm so aggravated."

"I'm amazed you should stoop to intimidate me," Lulu answered.

"You don't fool me," Teppis said, "you're scared stiff. Because you know what I think of people who let me down." He reached forward and squeezed her shoulder. "Lulu, be my witness, don't even answer me right away, this is the only favor I ever asked you. Would you turn H.T. down? Consider carefully. Weigh your words."

Lulu burst into tears again. "Oh, Mr. Teppis, I love you," she cried.

"Then do something for me."

"I'll do anything for you."

"Would you marry Teddy Pope?"

"I'd even marry Teddy Pope. I want to marry Teddy after the way you explained it, Mr. Teppis."

"I don't want to talk you into it."

"I'd marry Teddy in a minute now," Lulu sobbed, "but I can't."

"Of course you can," Teppis said. "Why not?"

"Cause I married Tony Tanner this morning."

". . . . ."

"Mr. Teppis, please don't be angry."

"You're lying."

"I'm not lying. We were secretly married."

"God, how could YOU do this to me?" Teppis bellowed.

"It isn't that terrible, Mr. Teppis," said Lulu from her handkerchief.

"You broke your promise. You're torturing me. You told me you'd tell me if you wanted to get married."

"That was to Sergius."

"I could spit. It's not worth it being alive."

"Do you want a glass of water, Mr. Teppis?"

"*No.*" He smashed his fist into his palm. "I'll annul the marriage."

"You couldn't. Tony would fight it."

"Of course he'd fight it. He's got his lawyer already." Teppis stared down at her. "Would you fight it, too?"

"Mr. T., a wife's duty is to her husband you always say."

"I could rip my tongue out. Lulu, you got married to spite me."

"H.T., I'll prove you're wrong by spending the rest of my life making it up to you."

"I'm sick."

"Forgive me, H.T."

"I'm going to persecute you."

"H.T., punish me, but don't hurt Tony."

"Don't hurt Tony! You disgust me. Lulu, you ain't capable of thinking of nobody but yourself. You could drop dead, I wouldn't even look at your grave." His arms raised, he started to advance on her.

Lulu prepared to flee the room. "Come back here," Teppis said. "I don't want you to leave like this."

"I worship you, H.T."

"You've shortened my life."

"H.T., I don't care what you do. I'll always say, 'God bless you.' "

He pointed to the door, his mouth quivering.

"H.T., please listen to me."

"Get out of here. You're a common whore."

When she was gone, Teppis began to shake all over his body. He stood in the center of the room, shaking visibly. "It's a wonder I don't pop a blood vessel," he said aloud. The sound of his voice must have calmed him a little, for he went to the interoffice phone, pressed the buzzer, and said hoarsely, "You send Collie up here right away."

A few minutes later Munshin was in the office. "When are the wedding bells?" he asked as he came in the door.

"Collie, you're a dummy," Teppis bawled at him. "You're an A-1 stupid moron."

"H.T.! What's up?"

"Lulu got married to Tony Tanner this morning."

"Oh, Jesus," said Collie.

"That Teddy Pope. A degraded homosexual. I had him twisted into a pretzel."

"I'll bet you did, H.T."

"You shut up. This whole thing was your idea. I wash my hands of it."

"You're right, H.T."

"Don't you even know what's happening in front of you? A fact accompli is what Lulu gives me. I could cut her up."

"It's what that twot deserves."

"I'm nauseous. A dime-a-dozen comedian, a coarse person like Tony Tanner. I hate coarse people. Isn't there any class left in the world?"

"You're the class, H.T.," said Collie.

"Shut up." Teppis wandered around the room like an animal with a hole in its flank, and collapsed in a chair. "I made you, Collie," he stated, "and I can break you. I hate to think of what you were when I first knew you, a two-bit agent, a nobody, a miserable nothing."

"It wasn't as bad as that, I hope."

"Don't contradict me. I let you marry my only daughter, I made you my executive assistant, I let you produce your own pictures. I know you, Collie, I know your tricks, you'll cut my throat someday. But you won't because I'll break you first. Do you hear me? What's your ideas?"

Collie stood calmly, almost placidly. "H.T., I'll be frank," he said, "it's my fault about Tony, I admit it."

"You better admit it. I don't know what's the matter with you lately. You can't do nothing right these days. That Air Force boy. I'm sick every time I think of that movie we can't make all because you're such a miserable failure."

"H.T., I've learned everything from you," Collie said, "and I'm not worried. I know you can turn this into something tremendous. I even re-member you saying that that's what failures were for, to give ideas." Collie extended his arms. "H.T., in my book, and I copy your book, you can do more with Tony than you ever could with Teddy. A lot of work, yes, but one thing I learned from you, H.T., Teddy is through. You'll pick up the paper someday and he'll be in the can for scrounging around a character on the vice squad."

"You got a disgusting imagination," Teppis said hoarsely.

"I'm a realist. So are you, H.T. I know there's not another studio in this town that could make a nickel handling Tony. But you can."

"My digestion is upset," Teppis said.

"I glimpse the kind of campaign you see for Tony. Tell me if I'm right." He paused. "No it's a bad idea. It won't work. It would be too hard to bring off."

"You talk and I'll tell you," Teppis said.

"Well, now this is off the top of my head, of course, but I was wondering if you were thinking of making Lulu keep this marriage quiet until we're done shooting her film. Then, we can make the announcement. Maybe even work out a big wedding. The potential it gives us for building up Tony is tremendous. Tony Tanner," Munshin announced, "the kid who stole Lulu Meyers right from under a big lover-type like Teddy Pope. People will say, 'You've done it again, H.T.' and they'll be right."

Teppis failed to respond. "Don't give me compliments," he said, "I'm too upset. Do you know how my stomach feels?"

Munshin lit a cigarette and smoked in silence for some seconds. "The doctor told me you ought to lower your nervous tension," he said.

"You're my son-in-law, and you're a pimp," Teppis burst out. Then he reached for the button under his desk and clicked it to the "off" position. "Did you hear what Charley Eitel said to me once? He said, 'Mr. Teppis, we all got our peculiarities.' I don't like the sound of it. Carlyle, there's word getting around."

"H.T., believe me. It isn't what you do or what you don't do, people will still talk about you."

"There's nothing to talk about."

"That's right."

"I haven't slept with a woman in ten years."

"It's the truth, H.T."

Teppis looked at the ceiling. "What kind of girl do you have in mind?"

"A sweet kid, H.T."

"I suppose you put her on the payroll."

"To tell the truth, I did. A friend of mine introduced me to her in Desert D'Or. Chief, it's better this way, believe me. The kid'll keep her mouth shut because who knows, she might have a career here. She's a cute little stock girl."

"That's what you always say, Collie."

"I had a talk with her. She'll button her lip tight as a virgin's bun."

"You're a foul-mouthed individual," Teppis told him.

"She's really safe."

"If it weren't for Lottie, I'd fire you."

"A genius like you needs relaxation," Collie said. "It's wrong, H.T., to miss the fruits of life."

Teppis tapped one hand against the other. "All right, I want you to send her up."

"I'll have her here in five minutes."

"You get the hell out, Collie. You think a man can break the laws of society? Those laws are there for a purpose. Every time you send up a girl, I don't even want to see her again. I refuse to sleep with her."

"Nobody can work the way you do, H.T.," said Collie going out the door.

After a short interval, a girl in her early twenties with newly dyed honey-colored hair came in unannounced through a separate door to Teppis' office. She was wearing a gray tailored suit and very high heels, and her hair was caught in a snood. Her mouth was painted in the form of broad bowed lips to hide the thin mouth beneath the lipstick.

"Sit down, doll, sit down right here," said Teppis pointing to a place on the couch beside him.

"Oh, thank you, Mr. Teppis," said the girl.

"You can call me Herman."

"Oh I couldn't."

"I like you, you're a nice-looking girl, you got class. Just tell me your first name because I don't remember last names."

"It's Bobby, Mr. Teppis."

He put a fatherly hand on her. "You work here, Collie tells me."

"I'm an actress, Mr. Teppis. I'm a good actress."

"Sweetie, there's so many good actresses, it's a shame."

"Gee, I'm really good, Mr. Teppis," Bobby said.

"Then you'll get a chance. In this studio there's opportunity for real talent-types. Talent is in its infancy. There's a future for it."

"I'm glad you think so, Mr. Teppis."

"You married? You got a husband and kids?"

"I'm divorced. It didn't work out. But I have two little girls."

"That's nice," Teppis said. "You got to plan for their future. I want you to try to send them to college."

"Mr. Teppis, they're still babies."

"You should always plan. I've given to charity all my life." Teppis nodded. "I hope you got a career here, sweetie. You been here how long?"

"Just a couple of weeks."

"An actress got to have patience. That's my motto. I like you. You got problems. You're a human girl."

"Thank you, sir."

"Sweetie, move over, sit on my lap."

Bobby sat on his lap. Neither spoke for a minute.

"You listen to me," Teppis said in his hoarse thin voice, "what did Collie say to you?"

"He said I should do what you wanted, Mr. Teppis."

"You're not a blabbermouth?"

"No, Mr. Teppis."

"You're a good girl. You know, there's nobody you can trust. Everybody tells everybody about everything. I can't trust you. You'll tell somebody. There's no trust left in the world."

"Mr. Teppis, you can trust me."

"I'm the wrong man to cross."

"Oh, I wouldn't cross a swell man like you. Am I too heavy on your lap, Mr. Teppis?"

"You're just right, sweetie." Teppis' breathing became more pronounced. "What did you say," he asked, "when Collie said you should do what I wanted?"

"I said I would, Mr. Teppis."

"That's a smart girl."

Tentatively, she reached out a hand to finger his hair, and at that moment Herman Teppis opened his legs and let Bobby fall to the floor. At the expression of surprise on her face, he began to laugh. "Don't you worry, sweetie," he said, and down he looked at that frightened female mouth, facsimile of all those smiling lips he had seen so ready to serve at the thumb of power, and with a cough, he started to talk. "That's a good girlie," he said in a mild little voice, "you're an angel darling, and I like you, you're my darling darling, oh that's the ticket," said Teppis.

Not two minutes later, he showed Bobby genially to the door. "I'll call you when to see me again, sweetheart," he said.

Alone in his office, he lit a cigar, and pressed the buzzer. "What time is the conference on *Song Of The Heart*?" he asked.

"In half an hour, sir."

"Tell Nevins I want to see his rushes before then. I'll be right down."

"Yessir."

Teppis ground out the cigar. "There's a monster in the human heart," he said aloud to the empty room. And to himself he whispered, like a bitter old woman, close to tears, "They deserve it, they deserve every last thing that they get." [1955]

BEN MASSELINK

All the World's a TV

Q UIET DOWN, everyone, please!" the assistant director shouted. "It's a picture." He turned to a man as thick as a tree. "Hold traffic." The big man spoke into a walkie talkie that was almost invisible in his beefy hand. "Hold traffic, Eddie."

Out of sight, traffic was held by Eddie on Woodley Avenue between Burbank Boulevard and Victory in the San Fernando Valley.

"Rolling," the A.D. said.

The sound man sat at a little cart that was like a peanut vendor's cart with two bicycle wheels, but this cart held a silver console with blinking red and green lights instead of hot peanuts. "Forty-eight, Take One," the sound man said. A beeper beeped "beep beep."

And the clapboard man clapped his clapper in front of the lens of the big Arriflex on a chromium dolly. "Marking."

"Action," the director said quietly.

The tiny pocket bikes coughed and sputtered down the runway. They were so small they looked like the bikes parrots ride. A man and a girl perched on them, legs angled out awkwardly, like parents showing their children how to ride tricycles. The two-wheeled bikes banged and smoked down the narrow runway used for model airplanes, in and out of orange pilings, and around and back again. The riders wore big shiny moon crash helmets with smoked visors and were dressed in elegant golden jumpsuits.

The actors strolled up, dressed identically to the two stunt people who were doubling them on the bikes.

"Cut," Chuck Bail, the director, said.

The bikes rolled to a stop 20 yards before the camera. The stunt people left the bikes there and lowered their heads to duck out from under the big helmets. The crew, dressed in down ski jackets and fleece-lined jackets and jeans, talked and laughed with Debbie Evans and Bobby Foxworth, the stunt people, who on film would be the jewel thieves Bernard and Camille, characters played by actors George Chakiris and Judith Baldwin in this episode of "CHiPS."

Wearing jeans and Bally loafers, Chuck Bail positioned the actors on the tiny bikes. Chuck is a movie director who directed the wild and funny *Gum Ball Rally* and was stunt gaffer for the movie *The Stunt Man* and also played that part in the movie, so Chuck was one of the few in Hollywood who did merge fiction with fact. He had played himself. A boss stunt man playing a boss stunt man.

The makeup man, black-taped mirror sticking out a back pocket of his jeans, brushed Camille-Judith's long blonde hair. When she put on her helmet he winced. She laughed.

Again it was "Quiet, please!" and "Hold traffic" and "Rolling" as now the actors as the characters took over where the stunt people left off. They rode the bikes the twenty yards to camera, but the camera moved back smooth and heavy and fast on aluminum tracks to pan the actors and to now include Sweets, a character played by Robert Hegyes, leaning roguishly against a Rolls-Royce.

"Let's do it again," Chuck said. "And George, this time hold back coming in."

They shot it again. And again. It seemed that each time something different was wrong. A bike wobbled too much. A strand of hair was out of place. Camille-Judith's bike wouldn't start. Bernard-George's bike wouldn't stop.

Finally Chuck was satisfied. This scene would fit in sequence as part of the training for the caper in the story. And Bobby Foxworth would become Bernard would become George Chakiris and Debbie Evans would become Camille who was Judith Baldwin. The old Zen saying, "The way to do is to be," is modified in Hollywood to read, "The way to do is to be somebody else."

Three days later this "CHiPS" crew shot in downtown Burbank. Both interior and exterior of a new Holiday Inn at San Fernando Road and the Mall were used. Debbie and Bobby, after Camille and Bernard had snitched the jewels, raced up and down the carpeted corridors of the Holiday Inn on the pocket bikes to finally escape by soaring through space to an adjoining parking building. The chase was picked up then on the corner of Angeleno and the Mall across from the Holiday Inn.

"All right, hold down the noise," the assistant director yelled. "Rolling," he said. And the sound man spoke and beeps beeped and the clapboard man clapped his clapper, clap!

Erik Estrada as Ponch rolled up on his bike and stopped at an "accident" at the intersection. A prop man hiding under one of the cars and out of the camera's eye lighted a wafer of wheat paste and white smoke poured out from under the car. Ponch legged off his bike like a cowboy off his horse and, wearing a khaki uniform as tight as a leotard, sauntered up to the driver of the big green sedan.

A wino, a real wino, and out of the shot, slid into the real liquor store on the corner. Now reality and fantasy began to fuse.

A big, easygoing man, Chuck Bail said, "Cut," and went over to talk to Erik Estrada the way a coach will talk to a player before sending him out onto the field.

The wino was confused. And it was confusing. This was the wino's liquor store. Every morning at this time he came to this liquor store for his half pint of muscatel in a paper sack and now it looked like there had been a fender bender on the corner, but there were too many cops and too many people for just a fender bender. It was more like a carnival had come to town and set up here along Angeleno and the Mall. Big generator trucks and trailers. RVs. A catering truck. All kinds of lights on standards and reflectors and sound booms. On the green grass of the Mall was a real girls rock band (including real rock musician Laura Branigan) perched on top and around a pink 1956 Caddy convertible. Special effects and grips stood around drinking coffee out of Styrofoam cups.

The wino was dressed in blue and yellow jogging shoes three sizes too large for him, an old Dodgers ball cap, floppy jeans, and gray sweatshirt. Elegantly he stuffed a filter cigarette into an Aqua filter and leaned back against the glass wall of the liquor store, his bottle in the sack in his hand, waiting, prolonging the magic in the sack, watching the magic before his eyes. What was it? Was it real or was it the magic of his dreams? There were the two cops on bikes all cleaned up and tight, but then there were other cops—some on bikes in khaki and some in blue and walking around. This was no ordinary fender bender. Now the wino laughed when the others laughed. When he saw an electrician take a swallow out of his can of soda, he brought his sack to his mouth and drank.

"Hold traffic," the A.D. commanded. "All right. Ready to go. Quiet please. Picture."

And again Ponch rolled up and casually got off his bike and walked up to the smoking sedan.

"Cut and print it!"

A small girl darted out of the crowd with her school notebook for Estrada to autograph and he did and he flashed his famous smile at the little girl and the wino caught some of the dazzle and he laughed and danced about and offered his sack to others. It was family, everyone here was family. The wino was on the stairway to the stars.

Early one morning a writer stood on the Venice pier and looked down at the action on the sand. A camera was set up and the lights and reflectors and people milled about behind the camera, the grips and gaffers, the cameramen. In front of the camera a girl wearing an orange sweat suit chased a small boy around a pier piling.

The writer smiled. "I can't believe my feelings now. Six months ago I stood right here and watched the girl in the orange sweat suit chase her brother in my head and then I went back home to the typewriter and typed the words girl and boy and orange and chased, and now . . ." he waved at the scene. "There it is. The vision became words became real people." He laughed. "If it weren't for me there wouldn't be anyone here."

"Quiet down, please," the assistant yelled.

"Action," the director said. [1983]

IV

Voices
of Dissent

CAREY MC WILLIAMS

Factories
in the Field

*F*ACTORIES IN THE FIELD is subtitled "The Story of Migratory Farm Labor
in California." The subtitle defined my intention: to piece together the
dramatic and fascinating story of migratory farm labor. What prompted me,
a busy young lawyer, to undertake such a task? The answer is quite simple.
A series of dramatic large-scale farm labor strikes captured my interest. The
headlines were so insistent, the social drama so intense, that I felt compelled
to find out what was going on.

The troubles started in the spring of 1930 in Imperial Valley, California's
great truck garden, with a series of spontaneous strikes by Mexican and
Filipino field workers. Hundreds of arrests were made, and eight of the
strike leaders were convicted under the Criminal Syndicalism Act (its first
use against farm labor) and sentenced to San Quentin Prison. Then in 1931
and 1932 a rash of strikes broke out in the San Joaquin Valley, some of which
were suppressed with violence and brutality. The next year workers at The
Tagus Ranch near Fresno walked out in August. A large corporate enterprise,
Tagus was noted for its tough antiunion tactics. When the strike succeeded,
to nearly everyone's surprise, all hell broke loose. Strikes were reported
throughout the state: at Oxnard, Tulare, Fresno, San Jose, Merced, Chico,
Lodi, San Diego, Gridley, and Sacramento. Most of these strikes were
spontaneous. Only a handful of left-wing organizers were involved, and their
role was not significant; workers would not have struck on this scale in the
absence of deep grievances of long standing. The climax came on October
4, 1933, when eighteen thousand cotton pickers went on strike at a string
of cotton "farm factories" that stretched down the San Joaquin Valley for a
distance of 114 miles. The next year another rash of strikes occurred. Co-
inciding with the San Francisco general strike and Upton Sinclair's EPIC
campaign, the 1934 strikes stimulated the formation of a militant anti-labor
organization, the Associated Farmers, which promptly launched a statewide
campaign to prevent the organization of farm workers. A series of mass arrests
was staged, culminating in still another Criminal Syndicalism Act prosecu-
tion, this time in Sacramento, in which eight organizers were convicted after

one of the longest trials in the state's history (the convictions were later reversed on appeal). These 1933–34 strikes were the most extensive in the farm labor history of California and the United States; in scale, number, and value of crops affected, they were quite without precedent. The 1933 strikes alone involved more than fifty thousand workers.

It took little imagination to sense the importance of this extraordinary social upheaval. So as time permitted I began to make forays into various strike areas to see and report on what was happening. In the summer of 1935, I made a tour of areas from Bakersfield to Salinas in the company of my friend Herbert Klein, checking up on the results of the 1933–34 strikes, interviewing workers, labor contractors, growers, and officials, taking a look at living and working conditions, and talking to organizers. Armed guards ordered us off the Tagus Ranch. Near Salinas we inspected a large camp or stockade which had been built, we were told, to protect strikebreakers but seemed much better designed to serve as a concentration camp for striking farm workers in case of mass arrests. I returned to Los Angeles from this trip determined to tell the story of migratory farm labor in California and promptly set to work.

The following year there were still more strikes, including a major strike in the citrus industry in Southern California which lasted for some weeks and was finally suppressed in a crude and brutal fashion. What impressed me most about the strike was not so much the violence, which was commonplace, but the way residents of the beautifully laid out "citrus belt towns," with their ivy-covered Protestant churches, permitted local police to issue shoot-to-kill orders and deputize college football stars to round up Mexican-American strikers and hold them in improvised stockades. But, as I found out, the owners of the groves had little to do with labor relations; that vulgar and often unpleasant activity was handled by the large cooperative fruit exchanges which represented the collective power of the industry. In fact, this was the general pattern of farm labor relations in California. On a regional or crop-by-crop basis, growers would meet in advance of each labor operation and fix a "minimum" rate which invariably proved to be the maximum they would pay, all without benefit of any kind of collective bargaining.

Migratory farm labor was an old if largely unreported California story by the mid-1930s, when it suddenly and dramatically became invested with a new national interest. So-called "Okies" and "Arkies" had been trekking to California since the early 1920s, when cotton first began to be grown in the San Joaquin Valley. As the acreage increased, so did the influx. Then drought sent thousands of refugees moving westward; in 1935 alone some 87,302 Dust Bowl migrants entered the state. Actually the influx was never quite as menacing as it was made out to be. In all, perhaps 350,000 to 400,000 entered California between 1935 and 1938. What alarmed the growers—

and local residents—was the fact that most of these migrants stayed on after the crops were harvested, living in labor camps, improvised "shacktowns" and "Little Oklahomas" on the outskirts of established towns. Most of them lacked the means or any incentive to return to the Great Plains areas from which they had fled. With little federal aid available, local communities became concerned about budgets for schools, hospitals, health services, and, of course, relief payments.

The large growers were particularly disturbed by the fact that Dust Bowl migrants could not be hustled out of the state once the crops were harvested. They were citizens: whites of Anglo-Saxon Protestant backgrounds, former yeomen farmers who had come west seeking a new life for themselves and their families as a majority of Californians had done before them. Although stereotyped as an undesirable minority—lazy, shiftless, ignorant, improvident, with too many children and notoriously loose sexual standards—they stayed on, and others kept coming. So ludicrous expedients were invoked to stem the tide. In May, 1933, a law was passed making it a criminal offense for anyone knowingly to transport an indigent person into the state. In a famous case, the Reverend Fred Edwards was convicted under this statute of having brought his brother to the promised land (the United States Supreme Court eventually held the act unconstitutional). Also, a special border patrol was established in 1935–36 in an unsuccessful but widely publicized attempt to turn back indigent migrants at the Arizona border. Largely ignored in all this headlined excitement was the fact that farm production was increasing while labor costs remained at a low level.

Intrigued by the new turn events had taken and obsessed by a sense of urgency—the times had begun to take on apocalyptic overtones—I somehow managed to finish *Factories in the Field*, working nights, weekends, and holidays. Published in July, 1939, shortly after *The Grapes of Wrath*, it promptly became a best seller. The timing was, of course, excellent. But an unanticipated development catapulted the book into the thick of the controversy then raging in California about farm labor and Dust Bowl migrants. In January, the newly elected Governor Olson had named me to head the Division of Immigration and Housing. A unique agency, set up in 1913 by Governor Hiram Johnson at the time of the Wheatland hop pickers' riot, it had authority to inquire into the welfare of alien immigrants, inspect farm labor camps, and concern itself with some forms of rural housing. Simon J. Lubin, John Collier, and Carleton Parker had worked with the agency in its early years—it was really Lubin's idea—and some remarkable results had been achieved. But under successive conservative Republican administrations it had become moribund. Neither Governor Olson nor his aides had a nominee in mind until someone reminded the Governor that I had written a book about farm labor. I was not an applicant, nor had I known that my name would be proposed. But I had worked in the Governor's campaign and I found his argument unanswerable: if I wanted to do something about farm labor, here was my chance. For all practical purposes, the appointment marked the end of my career as a lawyer.

In that first exciting year, 1939, the division began to come alive. A branch office was opened in Fresno, in addition to those in San Francisco, Sacramento, and Los Angeles. New labor camp inspectors were added to the staff. The number of camp inspections tripled—there were then some 4,500 labor camps in the state, with a peak-season camp population of 160,000 or more—and growers were compelled to spend more than a million dollars in improvements. Most of these camps, often with as many as sixty or more cabins, were located off the beaten paths, invisible to nearby townspeople and to motorists on the main highways. So we organized and took them on guided tours so that they could see for themselves, often for the first time, what the camps were like. Repeated radio appeals were made by way of securing tips on where labor camps were hidden; often they would be set up in abandoned barns or old warehouses. I addressed groups from one end of the state to the other on the need to improve living and working conditions for migratory farm labor. Special reports were issued on labor camps and shacktown settlements. With the Governor's approval, I convened, in Fresno on May 26–27, a large meeting of local, state, and federal officials concerned with various aspects of migratory farm labor, attracting statewide attention. Naturally this burst of activity did not endear me to the large growers and the Associated Farmers. But it was two specific actions that made me, as they put it, "Agricultural Pest No. 1, worse than pear blight or boll weevil."

In May, 1939, I got Governor Olson to let me hold a public hearing in Madera for the purpose of recommending a fair wage rate for chopping cotton (i.e., weeding and thinning). The state could not enforce such a rate, but it could refuse to cut able-bodied adults from relief rolls if they declined to work for less. *These were the first hearings of the kind ever held in California.* When I recommended twenty-seven and a half cents an hour— the going rate was twenty cents—the growers screamed like banshees. And that fall when it came time to pick cotton, I talked the Governor into letting me set up a commission which included growers, academic experts, labor spokesmen, and public citizens to recommend a fair rate of payment. Held in Fresno's City Auditorium September 28, 29, and 30, the hearings drew an estimated attendance of 3,500 and received wide press coverage. That year a man and wife picking cotton for sixty-six days, the average season's length, at the going rate of eighty cents a hundred pounds, would make $140.57. At $1.25, the rate recommended by the minority of which I was one, they would have made $229.41. The majority came up with a lesser rate, but the growers promptly rejected it, and a major strike ensued.

Thus, when *Factories in the Field* appeared on the heels of *The Grapes of Wrath*, the growers were convinced a conspiracy had been hatched to defame large-scale corporate agriculture. A kind of mass hysteria developed, with a concerted public-relations campaign being directed against both authors and their books at luncheons, public meetings, on the radio, and in the press. Answering books appeared with such titles as *Grapes of Gladness* and *Plums of Plenty*. But the more violently the books were denounced, the better they sold. Almost overnight the migrant issue became a national news story. "After mid-1939," writes Walter J. Stein, "Americans could no longer hear the word 'migrant' without thinking of the Joads." The release of John Ford's fine screen version of the Steinbeck novel in January, 1940, gave the issue still greater national exposure. But the conspiracy charge was a fantasy. The fact is I never met John Steinbeck. Both of us were active in the Simon J. Lubin Society, we exchanged a few letters, and I served as chairman of the Steinbeck Committee to Aid Agricultural Workers until succeeded by Helen Gahagan Douglas. (The committee once staged a memorable Christmas party attended by five thousand children of migrant farm workers in a huge circus tent at Shafter, California.) But our paths never crossed.

In the fall of 1938, some of us began a campaign to induce the La Follette Committee to investigate violations of civil liberties in California farm labor disputes, but Senator La Follette remained lukewarm to the idea until *The Grapes of Wrath* and *Factories in the Field* "provided the necessary thrust." Once the committee arrived, I spent a great deal of time with the staff, briefing them, lining up witnesses, and cooperating in other ways. When public hearings opened in San Francisco on December 6, 1939, Governor Olson was the first witness. I remember meeting with him early that morning at the Fairmont Hotel, while he was having breakfast in his nightshirt, to go over the statement I had prepared for him. Later, on December 21, I testified and presented a sixty-page report on farm labor conditions. Unfortunately, the committee's final report and recommendations were not issued until October 19, 1942, and by then we were at war. But the widely publicized hearings and twenty-seven volumes of published transcripts—over four hundred witnesses were questioned—had enormous impact. In effect the hearings put the Associated Farmers out of business.

As a result of all the excitement in 1939, a stream of reporters visited California, and the radio networks were alive with debates, discussions, and interviews. *Factories in the Field* remained on the best-seller lists for months and I was invited to discuss the issues at many public meetings. I debated Phil Bancroft, son of the famous California historian, vice-president of the Associated Farmers, and Republican senatorial nominee in 1938 and 1944, on a *Town Meeting of the Air* program from New York, before the Commonwealth Club in San Francisco, and at the Friday Morning Club in Los

Angeles. Arthur Eggleston, then labor editor of the San Francisco *Chronicle*, summed up the effects of the tumult and the shouting by saying that it had finally become respectable in California to discuss, openly and publicly, any aspect of the farm labor problem. The logjam of taboo, ignorance and misinformation had finally been broken, and "a mighty river of words flooded out over the land" and, he added, "is still flowing."

Before Governor Olson left office, I had so succeeded in arousing the ire of the growers that I became the target of the only bill of attainder ever passed by the California legislature. In February, 1941, Assemblyman Earl Desmond of Sacramento introduced a bill (AB 2162) which proposed to abolish the Division of Immigration and Housing. The sponsors made no secret of the fact that their purpose was to drive me from office. The bill was opposed by an impressive array of unions, church groups, civic and professional organizations, and a significant section of the press. But the war in Europe had crowded the Okies off the front pages, and Olson's enemies had moved in to strike at him by striking at me. The measure passed the Assembly by a vote of forty-eight to seventeen and the Senate by twenty-three to nine, but was pocket-vetoed by the Governor because, so he said, it was primarily aimed at me and he had received no complaints that I was inefficient or incompetent.

Looking back on those years, I find it difficult to believe that so much excitement, action, controversy, and conflict could have been squeezed into such a brief span. But even before the outbreak of war in Europe, I sensed we had come to a big bend in the stream; that nothing would ever be quite the same again. As the preparedness program got under way, the despised Dust Bowl migrants moved into the rapidly expanding shipyards and defense industries, with immense benefit to the state and the nation. And not only that: a new migration of far greater significance had been set in motion.

For every Okie who made the trek from 1935 to 1940 [writes Walter Stein], two Okies came during the wartime boom. For every migrant California gained from 1930 to 1940, she gained three the following decade. Many of the migrants of the war years were as penniless as were the Okies who had displaced the Mexicans in California's fields during the depression years. The new Okies did not frighten Californians, however, for they rapidly found work. In any case, the state had found a new bogey in the Japanese.

It was, as Stein notes, a great pity that "the events of 1940 marked a tragic lost opportunity in America's confrontation with rural poverty." The stage had been set, the issues defined, and an enormous national audience was eagerly attentive; then the war curtain descended. But it was not all wasted effort; those exciting years at the end of the 1930s had "brought the harvest gypsy to national attention for the first time in the nation's history."

It was the misfortune of the Olson administration to come to power too late; by 1939 the New Deal was dead. But if his legislative achievements were disappointing, Olson should be credited with several notable acts of political decency. His first official act had been to present a pardon to Tom Mooney in an impressive ceremony in the State Assembly Chamber on January 7, 1939, which I witnessed. (Mooney and Warren Billings, labor organizers, had been convicted of the bombing of the Preparedness Day parade in San Francisco in 1916. Their case became an international *cause célèbre* during the twenty years they spent in prison for a crime which it is today almost universally conceded they did not commit.) The Governor also supported and approved my efforts to secure the release of Henry Cowell, the distinguished musician-composer, from San Quentin Prison. Cowell's parents had sought my aid shortly after I joined the administration. It took months of patient negotiation—the Hearst press had a vested interest in his conviction—and the aid of John Gee Clark, director of the Department of Penology, and State Senator Robert W. Kenny, both friends of mine, to bring about Cowell's release on parole. He had foolishly pleaded guilty to a morals charge which should never have been filed. Incredible as it sounds today, he had served three and a half years of a fifteen-year sentence before we were able to secure his release. Nothing in my term of service gave me greater pleasure or more lasting satisfaction. In a letter dated July 7, 1940, Cowell wrote to say that his release was "due in much part to your most appreciated efforts on my behalf"; years later I received his personal thanks in New York.   [1978]

JOHN STEINBECK

Their Blood Is Strong

CHAPTER I
The People, Who They Are

At the season of the year when California's great crops are coming into harvest, the heavy grapes, the prunes, the apples and lettuce and the rapidly maturing cotton, our highways swarm with the migrant workers, that shifting group of nomadic, poverty stricken harvesters driven by hunger and the threat of hunger from crop to crop, from harvest to harvest, up and down the state and into Oregon to some extent, and into Washington a little. But it is California which has and needs the majority of these workers. There are at least 150,000 homeless migrants wandering up and down the state, and that is an army large enough to make it important to every person in the state.

To the casual traveler on the great highways the movements of the migrants are mysterious if they are seen at all, for suddenly the roads will be filled with open rattletrap cars loaded with children and with dirty bedding, with fire-blackened cooking utensils. The boxcars and gondolas on the railroad lines will be filled with men. And then, just as suddenly, they will have disappeared from the main routes. On side roads and near rivers where there is little travel the squalid, filthy squatters' camp will have been set up, and the orchards will be filled with pickers and cutters and driers.

Needed and Hated

The unique nature of California agriculture requires that these migrants exist, and requires that they move about. Peaches and grapes, hops and cotton cannot be harvested by a resident population of laborers. For example, a large peach orchard which requires the work of twenty men the year round will need as many as 2000 for the brief time of picking and packing. And if the migration of the 2000 should not occur, if it should be delayed even a week, the crop will rot and be lost.

Thus, in California we find a curious attitude toward a group that makes our agriculture successful. The migrants are needed, and they are hated. Arriving in a district they find the dislike always meted out by the resident to the foreigner, the outlander. This hatred of the stranger occurs in the whole range of human history, from the most primitive village form to our own highly organized industrial farming. The migrants are hated for the following reasons, that they are ignorant and dirty people, that they are carriers of disease, that they increase the necessity for police and the tax bill for schooling in a community, and that if they are allowed to organize they can, simply by refusing to work, wipe out the season's crops. They are never received into a community nor into the life of a community. Wanderers in fact, they are never allowed to feel at home in the communities that demand their services.

Just Who Are They?

Let us see what kind of people they are, where they come from, and the routes of their wanderings. In the past they have been of several races, encouraged to come and often imported as cheap labor; Chinese in the early period, then Filipinos, Japanese and Mexicans. These were foreigners, and as such they were ostracized and segregated and herded about.

If they attempted to organize they were deported or arrested, and having no advocates they were never able to get a hearing for their problems. But in recent years the foreign migrants have begun to organize, and at this danger signal they have been deported in great numbers, for there was a new reservoir from which a great quantity of cheap labor could be obtained.

The drouth in the middle west has driven the agricultural populations of Oklahoma, Nebraska and parts of Kansas and Texas westward. Their lands are destroyed and they can never go back to them.

Thousands of them are crossing the borders in ancient rattling automobiles, destitute and hungry and homeless, ready to accept any pay so that they may eat and feed their children. And this is a new thing in migrant labor, for the foreign workers were usually imported without their children and everything that remains of their old life with them.

Beaten, Bewildered

They arrive in California usually having used up every resource to get here, even to the selling of the poor blankets and utensils and tools on the way to buy gasoline. They arrive bewildered and beaten and usually in a state of semi-starvation, with only one necessity to face immediately, and that is to find work at any wage in order that the family may eat.

And there is only one field in California that can receive them. Ineligible for relief, they must become migratory field workers.

Because the old kind of laborers, Mexicans and Filipinos, are being deported and repatriated very rapidly, while on the other hand the river and dust bowl refugees increases all the time, it is this new kind of migrant that we must largely consider.

The earlier foreign migrants have invariably been drawn from a peon class. This is not the case with the new migrants.

They are small farmers who have lost their farms, or farm hands who lived with the family in the old American way. They are men who have worked hard on their own farms and have felt the pride of possessing and living in close touch with the land.

They are resourceful and intelligent Americans who have gone through the hell of the drouth, have seen their lands wither and die and the top soil blow away; and this, to a man who has owned his land, is a curious and terrible pain.

And then they have made the crossing and have seen often the death of their children on the way. Their cars have broken down and been repaired with the ingenuity of the land man.

Their Blood Is Strong

Often they patched the worn-out tires every few miles. They have weathered the thing, and they can weather much more for their blood is strong.

They are descendents of men who crossed into the middle west, who won their lands by fighting, who cultivated the prairies and stayed with them until they went back to desert.

And because of their tradition and their training, they are not migrants by nature. They are gypsies by force of circumstance.

In their heads, as they move wearily from harvest to harvest, there is one urge and one overwhelming need, to acquire a little land again, and to settle on it and stop their wandering. One has only to go into the squatters' camps where the families live on the ground and have no homes, no beds and no equipment; and one has only to look at the strong purposeful faces, often filled with pain and more often, when they see the corporation-held idle lands, filled with anger, to know that this new race is here to stay and that heed must be taken of it.

It should be understood that with this new race the old methods of repression, of starvation wages, of jailing, beating, and intimidation are not going to work; these are American people. Consequently we must meet them with understanding and attempt to work out the problem to their benefit as well as ours.

It is difficult to believe what one large speculative farmer has said, that the success of California agriculture requires that we create and maintain a peon class. For if this is true, then California must depart from the semblance of democratic government that remains here.

Good Old Names

The names of the new migrants indicate that they are of English, German and Scandinavian descent. There are Munns, Holbrooks, Hansens, Schmidts.

And they are strangely anachronistic in one way: Having been brought up in the prairies where industrialization never penetrated, they have jumped with no transition from the old agrarian, self-containing farm where nearly everything used was raised or manufactured, to a system of agriculture so industrialized that the man who plants a crop does not often see, let alone harvest, the fruit of his planting, where the migrant has no contact with the growing cycle.

And there is another difference between their own life and the new. They have come from the little farm districts where democracy was not only possible but inevitable, where popular government, whether practiced in the Grange, in church organization or in local government, was the responsibility of every man. And they have come into the country where, because of the movement necessary to make a living, they are not allowed any vote whatever, but are rather considered a properly under-privileged class.

Where the Fruit—,

Let us see the fields that require the impact of their labor and the districts to which they must travel. As one little boy in a squatters' camp said, "When they need us they call us migrants, and when we've picked their crop, we're bums and we got to get out."

There are the vegetable crops of the Imperial Valley, the lettuce, cauliflower, tomatoes, cabbage to be picked and packed, to be hoed and irrigated. There are several crops a year to be harvested, but there is not time distribution sufficient to give the migrants permanent work.

The orange orchards deliver two crops a year, but the picking season is short. Farther north, in Kern County and up the San Joaquin Valley, the migrants are needed for grapes, cotton, pears, melons, beans, and peaches.

In the outer valley, near Salinas, Watsonville and Santa Clara there are lettuce, cauliflowers, artichokes, apples, prunes, apricots. North of San Francisco the produce is of grapes, deciduous fruits and hops. The Sacramento Valley needs masses of migrants for its asparagus, its walnuts, peaches, prunes, etc. These great valleys with their intensive farming make their seasonal demands on migrant labor.

A short time, then, before the actual picking begins, there is the scurrying on the highways, the families in open cars hurrying to the ready crops and hurrying to be first at work. For it has been the habit of the growers associations of the state to provide by importation, twice as much labor as was necessary, so that wages might remain low.

Trailed by Starvation

Hence the hurry, for if the migrant is a little late the places will be filled and he will have taken his trip for nothing. And there are many things that may happen even if he is in time. The crop may be late, or there may occur one of those situations like that at Nipomo last year when twelve hundred workers arrived to pick the pea crop only to find it spoiled by rain.

All resources having been used to get to the field, the migrants could not move on; they stayed and starved until government aid tardily was found for them.

And so they move, frantically, with starvation close behind them. And in this pamphlet we shall try to see how they live and what kind of people they are, what their living standard is, what is done for them and to them, and what their problems and needs are. For while California has been successful in its use of migrant labor, it is gradually building a human structure which will certainly change the state, and may, if handled with the inhumanity and stupidity that have characterized the past, destroy the present system of agricultural economics.

CHAPTER II
Squatters' Camps

The squatters' camps are located all over California. Let us see what a typical one is like. It is located on the banks of a river, near an irrigation ditch or on a side road where a spring of water is available. From a distance it looks like a city dump, and well it may, for the city dumps are the sources for the material of which it is built. You can see a litter of dirty rags and scrap iron, of houses built of weeds, of flattened cans or of paper. It is only on close approach that it can be seen that these are homes.

Here is a house built by a family who have tried to maintain a neatness. The house is about ten feet by ten feet, and it is built completely of corrugated paper. The roof is peaked, the walls are tacked to a wooden frame. The dirt floor is swept clean, and along the irrigation ditch or in the muddy river the wife of the family scrubs clothes without soap and tries to rinse out the mud in muddy water. The spirit of this family is not quite broken, for the children, three of them, still have clothes, and the family possesses three old quilts and a soggy, lumpy mattress. But the money so needed for food cannot be used for soap nor for clothes.

Then Come the Rains

With the first rain the carefully built house will slop down into a brown, pulpy mush; in a few months the clothes will fray off the children's bodies, while the lack of nourishing food will subject the whole family to pneumonia when the first cold comes.

Five years ago this family had fifty acres of land and a thousand dollars in the bank. The wife belonged to a sewing circle and the man was a member of the Grange. They raised chickens, pigs, pigeons and vegetables and fruit for their own use; and their land produced the tall corn of the middle west. Now they have nothing.

If the husband hits every harvest without delay and works the maximum time, he may make $400 this year. But if anything happens, if his old car breaks down, if he is late and misses a harvest or two, he will have to feed his whole family on as little as $150.

But there is still pride in this family. Wherever they stop they try to put the children in school. It may be that the children will be in a school for as much as a month before they are moved to another locality.

Starvation Terror

Here, in the faces of the husband and his wife, you begin to see an expression you will notice on every face; not worry, but absolute terror of the starvation that crowds in against the borders of the camp. This man has tried to make a toilet by digging a hole in the ground near his paper house and surrounding it with an old piece of burlap. But he will only do things like that this year.

He is a newcomer and his spirit and his decency and his sense of his own dignity have not been quite wiped out. Next year he will be like his next door neighbor.

This is a family of six; a man, his wife and four children. They live in a tent the color of the ground. Rot has set in on the canvas so that the flaps and the sides hang in tatters and are held together with bits of rusty baling wire. There is one bed in the family and that is a big tick lying on the ground inside the tent.

They have one quilt and a piece of canvas for bedding. The sleeping arrangement is clever. Mother and father lie down together and two children lie between them. Then, heading the other way, the other two children lie, the littler ones. If the mother and father sleep with their legs spread wide, there is room for the legs of the children.

Filth, Flies, Flu

There is more filth here. The tent is full of flies clinging to the apple box that is the dinner table, buzzing about the foul clothes of the children, particularly the baby, who has not been bathed nor cleaned for several days.

This family has been on the road longer than the builder of the paper house. There is no toilet here, but there is a clump of willows nearby where human faeces lie exposed to the flies—the same flies that are in the tent.

Two weeks ago there was another child, a four year old boy. For a few weeks they had noticed that he was kind of lackadaisical, that his eyes had been feverish.

They had given him the best place in the bed, between father and mother. But one night he went into convulsions and died, and the next morning the coroner's wagon took him away. It was one step down.

They knew pretty well that it was a diet of fresh fruit, beans and little else that caused his death. He had had no milk for months. With this death there came a change of mind in this family. The father and mother now feel that paralyzed dullness with which the mind protects itself against too much sorrow and too much pain.

And this father will not be able to make a maximum of four hundred dollars a year anymore because he is no longer alert; he isn't quick at piece-work, and he is not able to fight clear of the dullness that has settled on him. His spirit is losing caste rapidly.

The dullness shows in the faces of this family, and in addition there is a sullenness that makes them taciturn. Sometimes they still start the older children off to school, but the ragged little things will not go; they hide themselves in ditches or wander off by themselves until it is time to go back to the tent, because they are scorned in the school.

The better-dressed children shout and jeer, the teachers are quite often impatient with these additions to their duties, and the parents of the "nice" children do not want to have disease carriers in the schools.

The father of this family once had a little grocery store and his family lived in back of it so that even the children could wait on the counter. When the drouth set in there was no trade for the store anymore.

This is the middle class of the squatters' camp. In a few months this family will slip down to the lower class.

Dignity is all gone, and spirit has turned to sullen anger before it dies.

The next door neighbor family, of man, wife and three children of from three to nine years of age, have built a house by driving willow branches into the ground and wattling weeds, tin, old paper and strips of carpet against them.

A few branches are placed over the top to keep out the noonday sun. It would not turn water at all. There is no bed.

A Little Child—!

Somewhere the family has found a big piece of old carpet. It is on the ground. To go to bed the members of the family lie on the ground and fold the carpet up over them.

The three year old child has a gunny sack tied about his middle for clothing. He has the swollen belly caused by malnutrition.

He sits on the ground in the sun in front of the house, and the little black fruit flies buzz in circles and land on his closed eyes and crawl up his nose until he weakly brushes them away.

They try to get at the mucus in the eye-corners. This child seems to have the reactions of a baby much younger. The first year he had a little milk, but he has had none since.

He will die in a very short time. The older children may survive. Four nights ago the mother had a baby in the tent, on the dirty carpet. It was born dead, which was just as well because she could not have fed it at the breast; her own diet will not produce milk.

After it was born and she had seen that it was dead, the mother rolled over and lay still for two days. She is up today, tottering around. The last baby, born less than a year ago, lived a week. This woman's eyes have the glazed, far-away look of a sleep walker's eyes.

She does not wash clothes anymore. The drive that makes for cleanliness has been drained out of her and she hasn't the energy. The husband was a share-cropper once, but he couldn't make it go. Now he has lost even the desire to talk.

No Will, No Strength

He will not look directly at you, for that requires will, and will needs strength. He is a bad field worker for the same reason. It takes him a long time to make up his mind, so he is always late in moving and late in arriving in the fields. His top wage, when he can find work now, which isn't often, is a dollar a day.

The children do not even go to the willow clump anymore. They squat where they are and kick a little dirt. The father is vaguely aware that there is a culture of hook-worm in the mud along the river bank. He knows the children will get it on their bare feet.

But he hasn't the will nor the energy to resist. Too many things have happened to him. This is the lower class of the camp.

This is what the man in the tent will be in six months; what the man in the paper house with its peaked roof will be in a year, after his house has washed down and his children have sickened or died, after the loss of dignity and spirit have cut him down to a kind of sub-humanity.

Helpful strangers are not well-received in this camp. The local sheriff makes a raid now and then for a wanted man, and if there is labor trouble the vigilantes may burn the poor houses. Social workers have taken case histories.

They are filed and open for inspection. These families have been questioned over and over about their origins, number of children living and dead.

The information is taken down and filed. That is that. It has been done so often, and so little has come of it.

And there is another way for them to get attention. Let an epidemic break out, say typhoid or scarlet fever, and the county doctor will come to the camp and hurry the infected cases to the pest house. But malnutrition is not infectious, nor is dysentery, which is almost the rule among the children.

The country hospital has no room for measles, mumps, whooping cough; and yet these are often deadly to hunger-weakened children. And although we hear much about the free clinics for the poor, these people do not know how to get the aid and they do not get it. Also, since most of their dealings with authority are painful to them, they prefer not to take the chance.

This is the squatters' camp. Some are a little better, some much worse.

I have described three typical families. In some of the camps there are as many as three hundred families like these. Some are so far from water that it must be bought at five cents a bucket.

And if these men steal, if there is developing among them a suspicion and hatred of well-dressed, satisfied people, the reason is not to be sought in their origin nor in any tendency to weakness in their character.

CHAPTER V
Relief, Medicine, Income, Diet

Migrant families in California find that unemployment relief, which is available to settled unemployed, has little to offer them. In the first place there has grown up a regular technique for getting relief; one who knows the ropes can find aid from the various state and Federal disbursement agencies, while a man ignorant of the methods will be turned away.

The migrant is always partially unemployed. The nature of his occupation makes his work seasonal. At the same time the nature of his work makes him ineligible for relief. The basis for receiving most of the relief is residence.

But it is impossible for the migrant to accomplish the residence. He must move about the country. He could not stop long enough to establish residence or he would starve to death. He finds, then, on application, that he cannot be put on the relief rolls. And being ignorant, he gives up at that point.

For the same reason he finds that he cannot receive any of the local benefits reserved for residents of a county. The county hospital was built not for the transient, but for residents of the county.

One Family's Case

It will be interesting to trace the history of one family in relation to medicine, work relief and direct relief. The family consisted of five persons, a man of 50, his wife of 45, two boys, 15 and 12, and a girl of six. They came from Oklahoma, where the father operated a little ranch of fifty acres of prairie.

When the ranch dried up and blew away the family put its moveable possessions in an old Dodge truck and came to California. They arrived in time for the orange picking in Southern California and put in a good average season.

The older boy and the father together made $60. At that time the automobile broke out some teeth of the differential and the repairs, together with three second-hand tires, took $22. The family moved into Kern County to chop grapes and camped in the squatters' camp on the edge of Bakersfield.

At this time the father sprained his ankle and the little girl developed measles. Doctors' bills amounted to $10 of the remaining store, and food and transportation took most of the rest.

The 15-year old boy was now the only earner in the family. The 12-year old boy picked up a brass gear in a yard and took it to sell.

He was arrested and taken before the juvenile court, but was released to his father's custody. The father walked into Bakersfield from the squatters' camp on a sprained ankle because the gasoline was gone from the automobile and he didn't dare invest any of the remaining money in more gasoline.

Can't Get Relief

This walk caused complications in the sprain which laid him up again. The little girl had recovered from measles by this time, but her eyes had not been protected and she had lost part of her eyesight.

The father now applied for relief and found that he was ineligible because he had not established the necessary residence. All resources were gone. A little food was given to the family by neighbors in the squatters' camp.

A neighbor who had a goat brought in a cup of milk every day for the little girl.

At this time the 15-year old boy came home from the fields with a pain in his side. He was feverish and in great pain.

The mother put hot cloths on his stomach while a neighbor took the crippled father to the county hospital to apply for aid. The hospital was full, all its time taken by bona fide local residents. The trouble described as a pain in the stomach by the father was not taken seriously.

The father was given a big dose of salts to take home to the boy. That night the pain grew so great that the boy became unconscious. The father telephoned the hospital and found that there was no one on duty who could attend to his case. The boy died of a burst appendix the next day.

There was no money. The county buried him free. The father sold the Dodge for $30 and bought a $2 wreath for the funeral. With the remaining money he laid in a store of cheap, filling food—beans, oatmeal, lard. He tried to go back to work in the fields. Some of the neighbors gave him rides to work and charged him a small amount for transportation.

He was on the weak ankle too soon and could not make over 75¢ a day at piece-work, chopping. Again he applied for relief and was refused because he was not a resident and because he was employed. The little girl, because of insufficient food and weakness from measles, relapsed into influenza.

The father did not try the county hospital again. He went to a private doctor who refused to come to the squatters' camp unless he were paid in advance. The father took two days' pay and gave it to the doctor, who came to the family shelter, took the girl's temperature, gave the mother seven pills, told the mother to keep the child warm and went away. The father lost his job because he was too slow.

He applied again for help and was given one week's supply of groceries.

Their Blood Is Strong | 261

Many Like This

This can go on indefinitely. The case histories like it can be found in their thousands. It may be argued that there were ways for this man to get aid, but how did he know where to get it? There was no way for him to find out.

California communities have used the old, old methods of dealing with such problems. The first method is to disbelieve it and vigorously to deny that there is a problem. The second is to deny local responsibility since the people are not permanent residents. And the third and silliest of all is to run the trouble over the county borders into another county. The floater method of swapping what the counties consider undesirables from hand to hand is like a game of medicine ball.

A fine example of this insular stupidity concerns the hookworm situation in Stanislaus County. The mud along water courses where there are squatters living is infected. Several business men of Modesto and Ceres offered as a solution that the squatters be cleared out. There was no thought of isolating the victims and stopping the hookworm.

The affected people were, according to these men, to be run out of the county to spread the disease in other fields. It is this refusal of the counties to consider anything but the immediate economy and profit of the locality that is the cause of a great deal of the unsolvable quality of the migrants' problem. The counties seem terrified that they may be required to give some aid to the labor they require for their harvests.

$400 Is Maximum Income

According to several Government and state surveys and studies of large numbers of migrants, the maximum a worker can make is $400 a year, while the average is around $300, and the large minimum is $150 a year. This amount must feed, clothe, and transport whole families.

Sometimes whole families are able to work in the fields, thus making an additional wage. In other observed cases a whole family, weakened by sickness and malnutrition, has worked in the fields, making less than the wage of one healthy man. It does not take long at the migrants' work to reduce the health of any family. Food is scarce always, and luxuries of any kind are unknown.

Typical Diets

Observed diets run something like this when the family is making money:

Family of eight—Boiled cabbage, baked sweet potatoes, creamed carrots, beans, fried dough, jelly, tea.
Family of seven—Beans, baking-powder biscuits, jam, coffee.

Family of six—Canned salmon, cornbread, raw onions.

Family of five—Biscuits, fried potatoes, dandelion greens, pears.

These are dinners.—It is to be noticed that even in these flush times there is no milk, no butter. The major part of the diet is starch. In slack times the diet becomes all starch, this being the cheapest way to fill up. Dinners during lay-offs are as follows:

Family of eight—(there were six children)—Dandelion greens and boiled potatoes.

Family of seven—Beans, fried dough.

Family of six—Fried cornmeal.

Family of five—Oatmeal mush.

It will be seen that even in flush times the possibility of remaining healthy is very slight. The complete absence of milk for the children is responsible for many of the diseases of malnutrition. Even pellagra is far from unknown.

The preparation of food is the most primitive. Cooking equipment usually consists of a hole dug in the ground or a kerosene can with a smoke vent and open front.

If the adults have been working ten hours in the fields or in the packing sheds they do not want to cook. They will buy canned goods as long as they have money, and when they are low in funds they will subsist on half-cooked starches.

Childbirth Problem

The problem of childbirth among the migrants is among the most terrible. There is no prenatal care of the mothers whatever, and no possibility of such care. They must work in the fields until they are physically unable or, if they do not work, the care of the other children and of the camp will not allow the prospective mothers any rest.

In actual birth the presence of a doctor is a rare exception. Sometimes in the squatters' camps a neighbor woman will help at the birth. There will be no sanitary precautions nor hygienic arrangements. The child will be born on newspapers in the dirty bed. In case of a bad presentation requiring surgery or forceps, the mother is practically condemned to death. Once born, the eyes of the baby are not treated, the endless medical attention lavished on middle-class babies is completely absent.

The mother, usually suffering from malnutrition, is not able to produce breast milk. Sometimes the baby is nourished on canned milk until it can eat fried dough and cornmeal. This being the case, the infant mortality is very great.

One Mother's Story

The following is an example: Wife of family with three children. She is 38; her face is lined and thin and there is a hard glaze on her eyes. The three children who survive were born prior to 1929, when the family rented a farm in Utah. In 1930 this woman bore a child which lived four months and died of "colic".

In 1931 her child was born dead because "a han' truck fulla boxes run inta me two days before the baby come." In 1932 there was a miscarriage. "I couldn't carry the baby 'cause I was sick." She is ashamed of this. In 1933 her baby lived a week. "Jus' died. I don't know what of." In 1934 she had no pregnancy. She is also a little ashamed of this. In 1935 her baby lived a long time, nine months.

"Seemed for a long time like he was gonna live. Big strong fella it seemed like." She is pregnant again now. "If we could get milk for um I guess it'd be better." This is an extreme case, but by no means an unusual one.

[1936]

EPILOGUE
Spring, 1938

The spring is rich and green in California this year. In the fields the wild grass is ten inches high, and in the orchards and vineyards the grass is deep and nearly ready to be plowed under to enrich the soil. Already the flowers are starting to bloom. Very shortly one of the oil companies will be broadcasting the locations of the wild-flower masses. It is a beautiful spring.

There has been no war in California, no plague, no bombing of open towns and roads, no shelling of cities. It is a beautiful year. And thousands of families are starving in California. In the county seats the coroners are filling in "malnutrition" in the spaces left for "causes of death." For some reason, a coroner shrinks from writing "starvation" when a thin child is dead in a tent.

For it's in the tents you see along the roads and in the shacks built from dump heap materials that the hunger is, and it isn't malnutrition. It is starvation. Malnutrition means you go without certain food essentials and take a long time to die, but starvation means no food at all. The green grass spreading right into the tent doorways and the orange trees are loaded. In the cotton fields, a few whisps of the old crop cling to the black stems. But the people who picked the cotton, and cut the peaches and apricots, who crawled all day in the rows of lettuce and beans are hungry. The men who harvested the crops of California, the women and girls who stood all day and half the night in the cannerys, are starving.

It was so two years ago in Nipomo, it is so now, it will continue to be so until the rich produce of California can be grown and harvested on some other basis than that of stupidity and greed.

What is to be done about it? The Federal Government is trying to feed and give direct relief, but it is difficult to do quickly for there are forms to fill out, questions to ask, for fear some one who isn't actually starving may get something. The state relief organizations are trying to send those who haven't been in the state for a year back to the states they came from. The Associated Farmers, which presumes to speak for the farms of California and which is made up of such earth stained toilers as chain banks, public utilities, railroad companies and those huge corporations called land companies, this financial organization in the face of the crisis is conducting Americanism meetings and bawling about reds and foreign agitators. It has been invariably true in the past that when such a close knit financial group as the Associated Farmers becomes excited about our ancient liberties and foreign agitators, someone is about to lose something. A wage cut has invariably followed such a campaign of pure Americanism. And of course any resentment of such a wage cut is set down as the work of foreign agitators. Anyway that is the Associated Farmers contribution to the hunger of the men and women who harvest their crops. The small farmers, who do not belong to the Associated Farmers and cannot make use of the slop chest are helpless to do anything about it. The little store keepers at cross roads and in small towns have carried the accounts of the working people until they are near to bankruptcy.

And there are one thousand families in Tulare county, and two thousand families in Kings county, fifteen hundred families in Kern county and so on. The families average three persons, by the way. With the exception of a little pea picking, there isn't going to be any work for nearly three months.

There is sickness in the tents, pneumonia and measles, tuberculosis. Measles in a tent, with no way to protect the eyes means a child with weakened eyes for life. And there are the various diseases attributable to hunger, rickets and the beginnings of pellagra. The nurses in the counties, and there aren't one tenth enough of them, are working their heads off, doing a magnificent job and they can only begin to do the work. The corps includes nurses assigned by the Federal and State Public Health services, school nurses and county health nurses and a few nurses furnished by the Council of Women for Home Missions, a national church organization. I've seen them, red eyed, weary from far too many hours, and seeming to make no impression in the illness about them.

It may be of interest to reiterate the reasons why these people are in the state and the reason they must go hungry. They are here because we need them. Before the white American migrants were here, it was the custom in California to import great numbers of Mexicans, Filipinos, Japanese, to keep them segregated, to herd them about like animals, and, if there were any complaints, to deport or to imprison the leaders. This system of labor was a dream of heaven to such employers as those who now fear foreign agitators so much.

But then the dust and the tractors began displacing the sharecroppers of Oklahoma, Texas, Kansas and Arkansas. Families who had lived for many years on the little "croppers lands" were dispossessed because the land was in the hands of the banks and the finance companies and because these owners found that one man with a tractor could do the work of ten share-croppers families. Faced with the question of starving or moving, these dispossessed families came west. To a certain extent they were actuated by advertisements and hand bills distributed by labor contractors from California. It is to the advantage of the corporate farmer to have too much labor, for then wages can be cut. Then people who are hungry will fight each other for a job rather than the employer for a living wage.

It is possible to make money for food and gasoline for at least nine months of the year if you are quick on the get away, if your wife and your children work in the fields. But then the dead three months strikes, and what can you do then? The migrant cannot save anything. It takes everything he can make to feed his family and buy gasoline to go to the next job. If you don't believe this, go out in the cotton fields next year. Work all day and see if you have made thirty-five cents. A good picker makes more, of course, but you can't.

The method for concentrating labor for one of the great crops, is this. Handbills are distributed, advertisements are printed. You've seen them. Cotton pickers wanted in Bakersfield or Fresno or Imperial Valley. Then all the available migrants rush to the scene. They arrive with no money and little food. The reserve has been spent getting there. If wages happen to drop a little, they must take them anyway. The moment the crop is picked, the locals begin to try to get rid of the people who have harvested their crops. They want to run them out, move them on. The county hospitals are closed to them. They are not eligible to relief. You must be eligible to eat. That particular locality is through with them until another crop comes in.

It will be remembered that two years ago some so-called agitators were tarred and feathered. The population of migrants left the locality just as the hops were ripe. Then the howling of the locals was terrible to hear. They even tried to get the army and the C.C.C. ordered to pick their crops.

About the fifteenth of January the dead time sets in. There is no work. First the gasoline gives out. And without gasoline a man cannot go to a job even if he could get one. Then the food goes. And then in the rains, with insufficient food, the children develop colds because the ground in the tents is wet. I talked to a man last week who lost two children in ten days with pneumonia. His face was hard and fierce and he didn't talk much. I talked to a girl with a baby and offered her a cigarette. She took two puffs and vomited in the street. She was ashamed. She shouldn't have tried to smoke, she said for she hadn't eaten for two days. I heard a man whimpering that the baby was sucking but nothing came out of the breast. I heard a man explain very shyly that this little girl couldn't go to school because she was too weak to walk to school and besides the school lunches of the other children made her unhappy. I heard a man tell in a monotone how he couldn't get a doctor while his oldest boy died of pneumonia but that a doctor came right away after it was dead. It is easy to get a doctor to look at a corpse, not so easy to get one for a live person. It is easy to get a body buried. A truck comes right out and takes it away. The state is much more interested in how you die than in how you live. The man who was telling about it had just found that out. He didn't want to believe it.

Next year the hunger will come again and the year after that and so on until we come out of this coma and realize that our agriculture for all its great produce is a failure. If you buy a farm horse and only feed him when you work him, the horse will die. No one complains at the necessity of feeding the horse when he is not working. But we complain about feeding the men and women who work our lands. Is it possible that this state is so stupid, so vicious and so greedy that it cannot feed and clothe the men and women who help to make it the richest area in the world? Must the hunger become anger and the anger fury before anything will be done?

GERALD HASLAM

The Okies:
Forty Years Later

TODAY they are state legislators and used-car salesmen, waitresses and college professors; they are convicts, guards, country music impresarios, construction workers and contractors, farm laborers and winos; they are, in a word, Californians. But those Okies who struggled into this not-always-golden state during the 1930s have not forgotten the days when an official in Madera said of them: "The squatter is usually . . . nothing more or less than an idler and a parasite on the body politic of the people surrounding them. They are a burden on the taxpayer and the growers. . . ."

"Them thangs hurt," recalls Lemuel Bundy, "but they helped too. I know they made me sore and I just determined we'd make 'er." Make 'er the Okies have, yet scars from those painful, sometimes desperate days occasionally hover near the surface of the original migrants, as well as their progeny. In central California most any old boy can still get his features altered right quick if he calls someone "Okie" in the wrong tone, for the word remains a popular expression of derision in some contexts: siphon hoses used to steal gas are called Okie credit cards; the worst calves in a herd are called Okies. Use of the term has been traced back to 1905, and Ben Reddick of the *Los Angeles Times* is usually credited (or blamed) for having popularized it during the 1930s. Today some Oklahomans both misunderstand and resent the term as meaning "depression drifters."

The actual migrants were of course a heterogeneous collection; mostly, though not all, white. While Oklahoma was the focus of attention, they drifted west from across the Great Plains and rural South: the Dakotas, Nebraska, Kansas, Missouri, Oklahoma, Mississippi, Texas, New Mexico and Arkansas. In the old days, "Texie" and "Arkie" were also common terms, but as time passed, nearly all migrants came to be called Okies once they had reached California. In the 1960s, Dewey Bartlett, then Governor of Oklahoma, tried to improve the word's connotation, but with little luck. However, contemporary achievements, along with the younger generation's growing understanding of what their elders survived, have effected the improvement.

A stubborn, deep pride has grown. Paul Westmoreland, known throughout central California as "Okie Paul," sums it up: "To me, Okies are anyone who went through that period like we did, whether they're from Oklahoma or Illinois or Texas. Okies are anyone who picked that cotton for 50¢ a hundred pounds, or picked potatoes for 15¢ an hour."

If the people were heterogeneous, so were the forces that led them to migrate. Although the Dust Bowl was but a small portion of the area from which they came, it is understandable that the massive dust storms should be popularly identified as the migration's cause, for they were both highly visible and dramatic. The major causes of the migration, all interrelated, as traced by Walter Stein in *California and the Dust Bowl Migration*, were rural poverty; tenant farming practices; mechanization of farming; drought; New Deal crop curtailment policies; soil depletion and depression.

A general rural poverty intensified the other pressures. Recalls Mrs. Frances Walker, who lives now in Keyes, Calif.: "In Oklahoma one year I carried (walked) my 2-year-old daughter a mile and a half to pick cotton, with our lunch and my cotton-pick sack. I bought my oldest kids clothes, and I averaged 85¢ a day. It bought their clothes and a couple of blankets for our beds." Midwest and Southwestern farm people were charged high railroad rates that made shipping their produce to markets barely profitable; further, recurrent droughts created an unstable economic pattern that often made them victims of high bank interest rates. Naturally, the large numbers of folk dependent upon farmers for their livelihood—tenants, laborers, tradespeople, shopkeepers—were profoundly affected by the same problems; they, in fact, formed the bulk of the migrants.

When they finally moved, folks tended to drift west along parallel lines— migrants from the northern plains moved to the Pacific Northwest; California's great length gathered people from the middle and southern plains. In all more than 500,000 people trekked west; some 350,000 settled in California. In addition to its vast corporate agricultural industry, California's reputation as the promised land attracted Okies.

Later research has invalidated the once popular idea that Okies came to California because of the state's "overly liberal" welfare program. Except in 1938, a year of disastrous floods coupled with crop curtailments, Okies strongly resisted welfare. Only in February, a month when there was little or no work in the fields, would welfare rolls shoot up. In fact, self-help became even more the rule during hard times; it was John Steinbeck's Ma Joad who said it most clearly: " 'I'm learnin' one thing good,' she said, 'learnin' it all atime, ever' day. If you're in trouble or hurt or need—go to poor people. They're the only ones that'll help—the only ones' " (*The Grapes of Wrath*, published thirty-five years ago this April). Recalls Flossie Haggard, mother of country singer, Merle:

I remember we broke down in the middle of the desert. We were out of water, and just when I thought we weren't going to make it, I saw this boy coming down the highway on a bicycle. He was going all the way from Kentucky to Fresno. He shared a quart of water with us and helped fix the car. Everybody'd been treating us like trash, and I told this boy, "I'm glad to see there's still some decent folks left in this world." He rode the rest of the way with us, and I still write to him. [Paul Hemphill, the *Atlantic Monthly* September, 1971.]

Historians have also dismissed the widely held belief that handbills put out by California growers lured most Okies to the state. Like the welfare notion, there is a kernel of truth in the handbill theory. Some California growers did circulate them, as did unscrupulous labor contractors, but more evidence points at Arizona growers seeking Okies. The following advertisement appeared in *The Daily Oklahoman* on October 13, 1937:

Cotton Pickers. Several thousand still wanted to arrive here before November 15th; growers paying 85¢ short staple . . . houses or tents free; ideal climate. . . . Farm Labor Service, 28 West Jefferson, Phoenix, Ariz.

Growers hired Okies to chop and pick Arizona cotton, which matured earlier than California's, then encouraged them to move on. A *New York Times* reporter called it "the neatest get rich quick scheme of the century," for Arizonans got their share of the Okies' work, but few of the headaches the influx brought.

And there were headaches. Within rural California, the migrants' desire to settle as quickly as possible went against the state's traditional migratory labor pattern and raised many hackles in the small towns favored by the Okies. An article in the January 13, 1937, *Mid-Week Pictorial* noted that the migrants' ambition was "to get settled down . . . where they can pick cotton and send children to school." So strong was the nesting instinct that it was not uncommon for an Okie family to establish residence even while the father, and often the mother too, continued following crops until a stable job could be found. The family came first—especially the children—and Okies recognized early that education offered the best hope of escape from poverty, though many came to misunderstand and hate the changes it wrought in their children.

It was in education and its related social sphere that Okies most threatened locals. The agricultural areas in which most migrants settled were poorly equipped to assimilate large numbers of newcomers, and some rural counties received whopping numbers indeed; Kern, for example, took in 52,554, or 63.6 per cent of the population between 1935 and 1940. In that same agonizing period, especially from 1938 on, groups such as the California Citizens Association, the Associated Farmers and the California State Chamber of Commerce helped stir anti-migrant sentiments, hinting that the migrants, among other things, were sexual degenerates (and hinting at the same time that they were unusually effective, sexually).

During the 1940s and 1950s, the children of many of the same Californians who most feared and hated Okies found themselves attracted to the children of the migrants. After all, they had been raised on stories of Okie licentiousness, so why not find out for themselves? Many a frowned-upon marriage resulted. There was still another unforeseen complication, one that remains rarely discussed: Okies were white people doing traditionally non-white work; their ambivalent racial position allowed them to date nonwhites, especially Mexicans, and that contributed in no small measure to a realignment of social relationships.

Okies today are still split on racial matters. Most oldtimers remain relatively unchanged in their orientation, though their rhetoric is more fierce than their actions, for the harshness of survival taught them the folly of inflexibility. Among their kids more diversity is evident: some participate in groups like Kern County's erstwhile White Citizens' Council, once reputed to be America's largest outside the Deep South; others have learned from mutual misery that only understanding and respect can help America: an Okie college professor initiated one of the state's most efficient minority recruitment programs and most highly respected ethnic studies curriculums, while Merle Haggard, the powerful Okie bard, has reflected in songs like *Irma Jackson* and *White Man Singin' the Blues* an enlightened and compassionate vision. Most Okies, however, like most other Californians, do nothing one way or another.

Politically and economically, the coming of the Okies was deeply resented. During their poverty years, the migrants did indeed find themselves forced to use county health, education and relief facilities, while adding little to tax income. In those same hard years, they tended to be either Midwestern Populists or Southern Democrats, and California was a Republican state. In 1938, when Culbert Olson defeated incumbent Gov. Frank Merriam, conservatives howled. They found the Okies easy scapegoats for their defeat. More recently Haggard's *Okie from Muskogee* has rattled liberal and radical cages, and resulted in overgeneralized claims about reactionary Okie politics. Yet here, too, generalizations are difficult.

Although Merle Haggard's name is perhaps more closely identified with "Okie music" nationally, the resourceful Buck Owens, a superb entertainer himself, dominates "Music City West" (Bakersfield, that is). And Bakersfield is the heart of Kern County, where Route 66 directed migrants into the lush San Joaquin Valley; it is also the heart of traditional country music, closer to the nonorchestrated past than Nashville itself. Along with Owens, Haggard and Dallas Frazier, such stars as Tommy Collins, Freddie Hart, Lefty Frizzell, Bonnie Owens, Billy Mize, Bill Woods, Buddy Alan, Susan Raye and the late Don Rich are identified with what is proudly called the capital of the Okie sound.

Country music is important on another level, for Okie culture tended to be oral/aural, with singing bards and tellers of tales its indigenous literary people. Where then does Oklahoma's Woody Guthrie stand? His fame grew among intellectual sympathizers, not migrant Okies; surveys conducted in the San Joaquin Valley in the past two years indicate that Woody is far better known in Berkeley's salons than in Bakersfield's saloons. Still, like John Steinbeck, Guthrie remains a masterful interpreter of a time and place that suited his special talents.

Social protest and union activities were two other areas of Okie activity that greatly concerned conservative Californians during the bad old days. Few of the Okies who struggled west joined the attempts to organize California farm laborers during the late 1930s. The United Cannery, Agricultural, Packing, and Allied Workers of America (UCAPAWA), a CIO union, had little appeal for Okie supporters because, by 1938–39, most migrants were in desperate straits, often near starvation, sunk to a level where bare survival, especially for their children, obviated any theoretical economic concerns. The CIO was then often called a Red union, and one migrant summed up his feelings when he said: "We got enough troubles without going Communist." Walter Stein has documented that "Okies played a larger role as strikebreakers than as strikers."

It really isn't surprising—though it may be disappointing—that Okies, given their ambivalent racial attitudes and past experiences with agricultural unions, have not tended to support Cesar Chavez's struggle to organize farm laborers, or that they often parrot allegations about UFWOC's Red taint that sound remarkably like the attacks once launched against UCAPAWA. Most of the arguments used against UFWOC were honed during the 1930s. Ironically, many Okies today are union people who consider Chavez's organization a maverick group.

Contemporary Okie political views, to the extent to which they can be generalized, are not unlike their views of organized labor: among older Okies there is little change from the Southern one-party view and the Midwestern Populism they brought with them. Their children are, by and large, Californians, though momma and daddy's background still makes itself felt. In the view of many Okies, the Democratic Party has moved too far to the Left, so that the American Independent Party's Populism is increasingly attractive now that Republican traditionalism has shown its warts. Withal, their thrust is conservative in most matters, reactionary in some, liberal in spots. Party labels, as generally in California politics, seem less important than specific, sometimes parochial, issues.

Within California's rapidly changing, trendy society, Okies have exerted a tempering, though spicy influence like the country cooking they favor, still retaining strong family ties, clannishness, traditional sex roles, sometimes absurd rites of passage, church affiliations, and a belief in America's promise (for they are proof that, however raggedly, it can be fulfilled). The work ethic has never faltered; "We've always known how to work," observes Okie Paul. "Gawd Almighty did we work. Had to or starve."

Then there is the agrarian myth: despite life in stucco suburbs and in growing cities like Fresno and Bakersfield, not to mention the sprawl of greater Los Angeles, many urban Okies retain rural values, perpetuating the cherished American illusion that we are a nation of yeoman farmers. "When you're urbanized you have to live by the rules," points out Karl Cozad, a Yuba County official whose parents were migrants. "They [Okies] want a little bigger piece of ground." Perhaps in tacit recognition of the enduring strengths of such values, contemporary Okies try to retain at least symbolic contact with the "soil and soul," as Buck Owens has observed.

And many Okies have lived to see the externals of their traditions become part of California's current vogue; an Okie college professor, raised on the music of Bob Wills, Bill Woods and Cousin Herb Henson, tells of having been visited by a student garbed in fashionably faded overalls who, observing the prof's record collection, exclaimed "Wow! Are *you* into country?"

Most Okies remain into country, but as time passes they and their children are even more into California's crazy-quilt culture. If they have become enamored of trail bikes and color television sets and campers, their early poverty explains why. They are a tough, able, complex people who have given strong flavor to California's life. While they seem to have remained relatively static in racial and political matters, no group has struggled farther up the socioeconomic ladder. Perfection is not an Okie characteristic, but a blues-like ability to accept adversity with grace and grit is. And they have not forgotten how to laugh at themselves.

In an often forgotten masterpiece of proletarian writing, *Their Blood Is Strong*, Steinbeck described life in a California ditch bank settlement:

The three year old child has a gunny sack tied about his middle for clothing. He has the swollen belly caused by malnutrition.

He sits on the ground in the sun in front of the house, and the little black fruit flies buzz in circles and land on his closed eyes and crawl up his nose until he weakly brushes them away. . . .

He will die in a very short time. . . .

Surviving such hardships has given Okies a strong sense of their own endurance. Writes Frances Walker:

The Okies were invincible, they won. They are here, they own land, homes, and are comfortable. Their children are here and their grandchildren. I'm part of it.

"Usta be," a college student recently admitted after studying the migrants' experiences, "you'd like hafta put slivers under my fingernails to make me tell that my folks're Okies. But now, well, I understand." Many people—

Okies and non-Okies—have come to understand that the migration was an American epic. Time has softened much of its pain, and added perspective. One of Merle Haggard's songs best summarizes the migrants' current attitude: *I Take a Lot of Pride in What I Am.*   [1975]

CESAR CHAVEZ

The Organizer's Tale

IT REALLY STARTED for me sixteen years ago in San Jose, California, when I was working on an apricot farm. We figured he was just another social worker doing a study of farm conditions, and I kept refusing to meet with him. But he was persistent. Finally, I got together some of the rough element in San Jose. We were going to have a little reception for him to teach the *gringo* a little bit of how we felt. There were about thirty of us in the house, young guys mostly. I was supposed to give them a signal—change my cigarette from my right hand to my left, and then we were going to give him a lot of hell. But he started talking and the more he talked, the more wide-eyed I became and the less inclined I was to give the signal. A couple of guys who were pretty drunk at the time still wanted to give the *gringo* the business, but we got rid of them. This fellow was making a lot of sense, and I wanted to hear what he had to say.

His name was Fred Ross, and he was an organizer for the Community Service Organizations (CSO) which was working with Mexican-Americans in the cities. I became immediately really involved. Before long I was heading a voter registration drive. All the time I was observing the things Fred did, secretly, because I wanted to learn how to organize, to see how it was done. I was impressed with his patience and understanding of people. I thought this was a tool, one of the greatest things he had.

It was pretty rough for me at first. I was changing and had to take a lot of ridicule from the kids my age, the rough characters I worked with in the fields. They would say, "Hey, big shot. Now that you're a *politico*, why are you working here for 65 cents an hour?" I might add that our neighborhood had the highest percentage of San Quentin graduates. It was a game among the *pachucos* in the sense that we defended ourselves from outsiders, although inside the neighborhood there was not a lot of fighting.

After six months of working every night in San Jose, Fred assigned me to take over the CSO chapter in Decoto. It was a tough spot to fill. I would suggest something, and people would say, "No, let's wait till Fred gets back," or "Fred wouldn't do it that way." This is pretty much a pattern with people, I discovered, whether I was put in Fred's position, or later, when someone else was put in my position. After the Decoto assignment I was sent to start a new chapter in Oakland. Before I left, Fred came to a place in San Jose called the Hole-in-the-Wall and we talked for half an hour over coffee. He was in a rush to leave, but I wanted to keep him talking; I was that scared of my assignment.

There were hard times in Oakland. First of all, it was a big city and I'd get lost every time I went anywhere. Then I arranged a series of house meetings. I would get to the meeting early and drive back and forth past the house, too nervous to go in and face the people. Finally I would force myself to go inside and sit in a corner. I was quite thin then, and young, and most of the people were middle-aged. Someone would say, "Where's the organizer?" And I would pipe up, "Here I am." Then they would say in Spanish—these were very poor people and we hardly spoke anything but Spanish—"Ha! This *kid?*" Most of them said they were interested, but the hardest part was to get them to start pushing themselves, on their own initiative.

The idea was to set up a meeting and then get each attending person to call his own house meeting, inviting new people—a sort of chain letter effect. After a house meeting I would lie awake going over the whole thing, playing the tape back, trying to see why people laughed at one point, or why they were for one thing and against another. I was also learning to read and write, those late evenings. I had left school in the 7th grade after attending sixty-seven different schools, and my reading wasn't the best.

At our first organizing meeting we had 368 people: I'll never forget it because it was very important to me. You eat your heart out; the meeting is called for 7 o'clock and you start to worry about 4. You wait. Will they show up? Then the first one arrives. By 7 there are only twenty people, you have everything in order, you have to look calm. But little by little they filter in and at a certain point you know it will be a success.

After four months in Oakland, I was transferred. The chapter was beginning to move on its own, so Fred assigned me to organize the San Joaquin Valley. Over the months I developed what I used to call schemes or tricks— now I call them techniques—of making initial contacts. The main thing in convincing someone is to spend time with him. It doesn't matter if he can read, write or even speak well. What is important is that he is a man and second, that he has shown some initial interest. One good way to develop leadership is to take a man with you in your car. And it works a lot better if you're doing the driving; that way you are in charge. You drive, he sits there, and you talk. These little things were very important to me; I was caught in a big game by then, figuring out what makes people work. I found that if you work hard enough you can usually shake people into working too, those who are concerned. You work harder and they work harder still, up to a point and then they pass you. Then, of course, they're on their own.

I also learned to keep away from the established groups and so-called leaders, and to guard against philosophizing. Working with low-income people is very different from working with the professionals, who like to sit around talking about how to play politics. When you're trying to recruit a farmworker, you have to paint a little picture, and then you have to color the picture in. We found out that the harder a guy is to convince, the better leader or member he becomes. When you exert yourself to convince him, you have his confidence and he has good motivation. A lot of people who say OK right away wind up hanging around the office, taking up the workers' time.

During the McCarthy era in one Valley town, I was subjected to a lot of redbaiting. We had been recruiting people for citizenship classes at the high school when we got into a quarrel with the naturalization examiner. He was rejecting people on the grounds that they were just parroting what they learned in citizenship class. One day we had a meeting about it in Fresno, and I took along some of the leaders of our local chapter. Some redbaiting official gave us a hard time, and the people got scared and took his side. They did it because it seemed easy at the moment, even though they knew that sticking with me was the right thing to do. It was disgusting. When we left the building they walked by themselves ahead of me as if I had some kind of communicable disease. I had been working with these people for three months and I was very sad to see that. It taught me a great lesson.

That night I learned that the chapter officers were holding a meeting to review my letters and printed materials to see if I really was a Communist. So I drove out there and walked right in on their meeting. I said, "I hear you've been discussing me, and I thought it would be nice if I was here to defend myself. Not that it matters that much to you or even to me, because as far as I'm concerned you are a bunch of cowards." At that they began to apologize. "Let's forget it," they said. "You're a nice guy." But I didn't want apologies. I wanted a full discussion. I told them I didn't give a damn, but that they had to learn to distinguish fact from what appeared to be a fact because of fear. I kept them there till two in the morning. Some of the women cried. I don't know if they investigated me any further, but I stayed on another few months and things worked out.

This was not an isolated case. Often when we'd leave people to themselves they would get frightened and draw back into their shells where they had been all the years. And I learned quickly that there is no real appreciation. Whatever you do, and no matter what reasons you may give to others, you do it because you want to see it done, or maybe because you want power. And there shouldn't be any appreciation, understandably. I know good organizers who were destroyed, washed out, because they expected people to appreciate what they'd done. Anyone who comes in with the idea that farmworkers are free of sin and that the growers are all bastards, either has never dealt with the situation or is an idealist of the first order. Things don't work that way.

For more than ten years I worked for the CSO. As the organization grew, we found ourselves meeting in fancier and fancier motels and holding expensive conventions. Doctors, lawyers and politicians began joining. They would get elected to some office in the organization and then, for all practical purposes, leave. Intent on using the CSO for their own prestige purposes, these "leaders," many of them, lacked the urgency we had to have. When I became general director I began to press for a program to organize farmworkers into a union, an idea most of the leadership opposed. So I started a revolt within the CSO. I refused to sit at the head table at meetings, refused to wear a suit and tie, and finally I even refused to shave and cut my hair. It used to embarrass some of the professionals. At every meeting I got up and gave my standard speech: we shouldn't meet in fancy motels, we were getting away from the people, farmworkers had to be organized. But nothing happened. In March of '62 I resigned and came to Delano to begin organizing the Valley on my own.

By hand I drew a map of all the towns between Arvin and Stockton—eighty-six of them, including farming camps—and decided to hit them all to get a small nucleus of people working in each. For six months I traveled around, planting an idea. We had a simple questionnaire, a little card with space for name, address and how much the worker thought he ought to be paid. My wife, Helen, mimeographed them, and we took our kids for two or three day jaunts to these towns, distributing the cards door-to-door and to camps and groceries.

Some 80,000 cards were sent back from eight Valley counties. I got a lot of contacts that way, but I was shocked at the wages the people were asking. The growers were paying $1 and $1.15, and maybe 95 per cent of the people thought they should be getting only $1.25. Sometimes people scribbled messages on the cards: "I hope to God we win" or "Do you think we can win?" or "I'd like to know more." So I separated the cards with the pencilled notes, got in my car and went to those people.

We didn't have any money at all in those days, none for gas and hardly any for food. So I went to people and started asking for food. It turned out to be about the best thing I could have done, although at first it's hard on your pride.

Some of our best members came in that way. If people give you their food, they'll give you their hearts. Several months and many meetings later we had a working organization, and this time the leaders were the people.

None of the farmworkers had collective bargaining contracts, and I thought it would take ten years before we got that first contract. I wanted desperately to get some color into the movement, to give people something they could identify with, like a flag. I was reading some books about how various leaders discovered what colors contrasted and stood out the best. The Egyptians had found that a red field with a white circle and a black emblem in the center crashed into your eyes like nothing else. I wanted to use the Aztec eagle in the center, as on the Mexican flag. So I told my cousin Manuel, "Draw an Aztec eagle." Manuel had a little trouble with it, so we modified the eagle to make it easier for people to draw.

The first big meeting of what we decided to call the National Farm Workers Association was held in September, 1962, at Fresno, with 287 people. We had our huge red flag on the wall, with paper tacked over it. When the time came, Manuel pulled a cord ripping the paper off the flag and all of a sudden it hit the people. Some of them wondered if it was a Communist flag, and I said it probably looked more like a neo-Nazi emblem than anything else. But they wanted an explanation, so Manuel got up and said, "When that damn eagle flies—that's when the farmworkers problems are going to be solved."

One of the first things I decided was that outside money wasn't going to organize people, at least not in the beginning. I even turned down a grant from a private group—$50,000 to go directly to organize farmworkers—for just this reason. Even when there are no strings attached, you are still compromised because you feel you have to produce immediate results. This is bad, because it takes a long time to build a movement, and your organization suffers if you get too far ahead of the people it belongs to. We set the dues at $42 a year per family, really a meaningful dues, but the 212 we got to pay, only 12 remained by June of '63. We were discouraged at that, but not enough to make us quit.

Money was always a problem. Once we were facing a $180 gas bill on a credit card I'd got a long time ago and was about to lose. And we *had* to keep that credit card. One day my wife and I were picking cotton, pulling bolls, to make a little money to live on. Helen said to me, "Do you put all this in the bag, or just the cotton?" I thought she was kidding and told her to throw the whole boll in so that she had nothing but a sack of bolls at the weighing. The man said, "Whose sack is this?" I said, well, my wife's, and he told us we were fired. "Look at all that crap you brought in," he said. Helen and I started laughing. We were going anyway. We took the $4 we had earned and spent it at a grocery store where they were giving away a

$100 prize. Each time you shopped they'd give you one of the letters of M-O-N-E-Y or a flag: you had to have M-O-N-E-Y plus the flag to win. Helen had already collected the letters and just needed the flag. Anyway, they gave her the ticket. She screamed, "A flag? I don't believe it," ran in and got the $100. She said, "Now we're going to eat steak." But I said no, we're going to pay the gas bill. I don't know if she cried, but I think she did.

It was rough in those early years. Helen was having babies and I was not there when she was at the hospital. But if you haven't got your wife behind you, you can't do many things. There's got to be peace at home. So I did, I think, a fairly good job of organizing her. When we were kids, she lived in Delano and I came to town as a migrant. Once on a date we had a bad experience about segregation at a movie theater, and I put up a fight. We were together then, and still are. I think I'm more of a pacifist than she is. Her father, Fabela, was a colonel with Pancho Villa in the Mexican Revolution. Sometimes she gets angry and tells me, "These scabs—you should deal with them sternly," and I kid her, "It must be too much of that Fabela blood in you."

The movement really caught on in '64. By August we had a thousand members. We'd had a beautiful ninety-day drive in Corcoran, where they had the Battle of the Corcoran Farm Camp thirty years ago, and by November we had assets of $25,000 in our credit union, which helped to stabilize the membership. I had gone without pay the whole of 1963. The next year the members voted me a $40 a week salary, after Helen had to quit working in the fields to manage the credit union.

Our first strike was in May of '65, a small one but it prepared us for the big one. A farmworker from McFarland named Epifanio Camacho came to see me. He said he was sick and tired of how people working the roses were being treated, and he was willing to "go the limit." I assigned Manuel and Gilbert Padilla to hold meetings at Camacho's house. The people wanted union recognition, but the real issue, as in most cases when you begin, was wages. They were promised $9 a thousand, but they were actually getting $6.50 and $7 for grafting roses. Most of them signed cards giving us the right to bargain for them. We chose the biggest company, with about eighty-five employees, not counting the irrigators and supervisors, and we held a series of meetings to prepare the strike and call the vote. There would be no picket line; everyone pledged on their honor not to break the strike.

Early on the first morning of the strike, we sent out ten cars to check the people's homes. We found lights in five or six homes and knocked on the doors. The men were getting up and we'd say, "Where are you going?" They would dodge, "Oh, uh . . . I was just getting up, you know." We'd say, "Well, you're not going to work, are you?" And they'd say no. Dolores Huerta, who was driving the green panel truck, saw a light in one house where four rose-workers lived. They told her they were going to work, even after she reminded them of their pledge. So she moved the truck so it blocked their driveway, turned off the key, put it in her purse and sat there alone.

That morning the company foreman was madder than hell and refused to talk to us. None of the grafters had shown up for work. At 10:30 we started to go to the company office, but it occurred to us that maybe a woman would have a better chance. So Dolores knocked on the office door, saying, "I'm Dolores Huerta from the National Farm Workers Association." "Get out!" the man said. "You Communist. Get out!" I guess they were expecting us, because as Dolores stood arguing with him the cops came and told her to leave. She left.

For two days the fields were idle. On Wednesday they recruited a group of Filipinos from out of town who knew nothing of the strike, maybe thirty-five of them. They drove through escorted by three sheriff's patrol cars, one in front, one in the middle and one at the rear with a dog. We didn't have a picket line, but we parked across the street and just watched them go through, not saying a word. All but seven stopped working after half an hour, and the rest had quit by mid-afternoon.

The company made an offer the evening of the fourth day, a package deal that amounted to a 120 per cent wage increase, but no contract. We wanted to hold out for a contract and more benefits, but a majority of the rose-workers wanted to accept the offer and go back. We are a democratic union so we had to support what they wanted to do. They had a meeting and voted to settle. Then we had a problem with a few militants who wanted to hold out. We had to convince them to go back to work; as a united front, because otherwise they would be canned. So we worked—Tony Orendain and I, Dolores and Gilbert, Jim Drake and all the organizers—knocking on doors till two in the morning, telling people, "You have to go back or you'll lose your job." And they did. They worked.

Our second strike, and our last before the big one at Delano, was in the grapes at Martin's Ranch last summer. The people were getting a raw deal there, being pushed around pretty badly. Gilbert went out to the field, climbed on top of a car and took a strike vote. They voted unanimously to go out. Right away they started bringing in strikebreakers, so we launched a tough attack on the labor contractors, distributed leaflets portraying them as really low characters. We attacked one—Luis Campos—so badly that he just gave up the job, and he took twenty-seven of his men out with him. All he asked was that we distribute another leaflet reinstating him in the community. And we did. What was unusual was that the grower would talk to us. The grower kept saying, "I can't pay. I just haven't got the money."

I guess he must have found the money somewhere, because we were asking $1.40 and we got it.

We had just finished the Martin strike when the Agricultural Workers Organizing Committee (AFL–CIO) started a strike against the grape-growers, DiGiorgio, Schenley liquors, and small growers, asking $1.40 an hour and 25 cents a box. There was a lot of pressure from our members for us to join the strike, but we had some misgivings. We didn't feel ready for a big strike like this one, one that was sure to last a long time. Having no money—just $87 in the strike fund—meant we'd have to depend on God knows who.

Eight days after the strike started—it takes time to get 1,200 people together from all over the Valley—we held a meeting in Delano and voted to go out. I asked the membership to release us from the pledge not to accept outside money, because we'd need it now, a lot of it. The help came. It started because of the close, and I would say even beautiful relationship that we've had with the Migrant Ministry for some years. They were the first to come to our rescue, financially and in every other way, and they spread the word to other benefactors.

We had planned, before, to start a labor school in November. It never happened, but we have the best labor school we could ever have, in the strike. The strike is only a temporary condition, however. We have over 3,000 members spread out over a wide area, and we have to service them when they have problems. We get letters from New Mexico, Colorado, Texas, California, from farmworkers saying, "We're getting together and we need an organizer." It kills you when you haven't got the personnel and resources. You feel badly about not sending an organizer because you look back and remember all the difficulty you had in getting two or three people together, and here *they're* together. Of course, we're training organizers, many of them younger than I was when I started in CSO. They can work twenty hours a day, sleep four and be ready to hit it again; when you get to be thirty-nine it's a different story.

The people who took part in the strike and the march have something more than their material interest going for them. If it were only material, they wouldn't have stayed on the strike long enough to win. It is difficult to explain. But it flows out in the ordinary things they say. For instance, some of the younger guys are saying, "Where do you think's going to be the next strike?" I say, "Well, we have to win in Delano." They say, "We'll win, but where do we go next?" I say, "Maybe most of us will be working in the fields." They say, "No, I don't want to go and work in the fields. I want to organize. There are a lot of people that need our help." So I say, "You're going to be pretty poor then, because when you strike you don't have much money." They say they don't care about that.

And others are saying, "I have friends who are working in Texas. If we could only help them." It is bigger, certainly, than just a strike. And if this spirit grows within the farm labor movement, one day we can use the force that we have to help correct a lot of things that are wrong in this society. But that is for the future. Before you can run, you have to learn to walk.

There are vivid memories from my childhood—what we had to go through because of low wages and the conditions, basically because there was no union. I suppose if I wanted to be fair I could say that I'm trying to settle a personal score. I could dramatize it by saying that I want to bring social justice to farmworkers. But the truth is that I went through a lot of hell, and a lot of people did. If we can even the score a little for the workers then we are doing something. Besides, I don't know any other work I like to do better than this. I really don't, you know.   [1966]

SHELDON S. WOLIN AND JOHN H. SCHAAR

Berkeley and the University Revolution

. . . . For some years the Navy has been coming to campus to recruit future sailors. In early 1965, when the Navy set up a recruiting table, students picketed it. They also submitted a formal complaint to the administration, asking why governmental agencies should enjoy privileges on campus not accorded to other non-student organizations. The administration took no action.

On November 28, 1966, the Navy again set up a recruiting table in the lobby of the Student Union building. The executive vice-chancellor claims that elected student officers consented to the placing of the table, but the chief student officers have flatly contradicted this assertion, saying that in fact they had advised against it.

For two days the Navy quietly performed its duty, but the Students for a Democratic Society (SDS) were working too. They were planning an action which would simultaneously oppose the war in Vietnam and show the inequity in the administration's application of the rules governing the use of campus facilities by off-campus organizations. Their method was to set up a table for the dissemination of material opposed to the war and the draft. This table would be placed beside the Navy table, and it would be manned by a non-student. At the same time, students would form a picket around the Navy table.

On Wednesday morning, November 30, a non-student (a lady member of an anti-draft organization) asked the dean of students for permission to set up her table. Her request was refused. Nonetheless, she returned to the Student Union building and set up a table alongside the Navy's with a sign offering "Alternatives to Military Service." Shortly after noon, the SDS pickets arrived and formed their line.

Soon after the pickets came the police, and also the reporters and cameramen. The scene quickly attracted a fair-sized crowd, some sympathetic to the demonstration, some opposed, and some just curious.

At this point, a campus policeman told the anti-draft lady that she would have to leave. After a brief argument she agreed, and the police started to carry her table through the crowd. Many bystanders loudly protested the removal of the table, and several tried to grab it, making the police jerk it from their hands. Just then, a former football player shoved through the crowd, apparently in an attempt to clear a path for the police. Several students shouted at the football player to stop pushing people around. The football player turned, and, according to several witnesses, struck a student in the mouth. When the person who was struck lunged at his attacker, he was restrained and led away by policemen. The crowd grew resentful and apprehensive. In order to reduce confusion and the possibility of more violence and arrests, several students urged the crowd to sit down. Within moments, some seventy-five or one hundred people sat down around the Navy table, jamming the lobby of the Student Union. They began discussions about the arrest and about the Navy's special privileges.

Around 1 P.M. some notables began to arrive, including the president of the student body, the vice-chancellor for student affairs, and Mario Savio, Berkeley's most famous non-student (Savio was denied re-admission to Berkeley for passing out leaflets on campus while not a student).

The vice-chancellor told the demonstrators that he was willing to talk with the students, but not under coercion, and that unless the crowd dispersed he would declare the assembly unlawful. Campus policemen closed all entrances to the lower lobby of the Student Union building, permitting people to leave but not to enter. Three officers also barricaded the stairway leading to the main floor, preventing the persons in the main lobby from joining those in the lower lobby. The three officers were slowly being pushed down the stairs when the barricade broke and students poured into the lower lobby.

Order was soon restored, and the discussions continued. The demonstrators agreed to disperse if the anti-draft table were permitted to remain, if no charges were pressed against the student who had been led away by the police, and if no disciplinary actions were taken against the demonstrators. The vice-chancellor agreed to let the table remain if the student manned it, but he said that he could not promise amnesty for the demonstrators, and that the case of the arrested student was out of his hands. Further discussion produced no agreement. The vice-chancellor declared the assembly unlawful and left. The demonstrators stayed.

While all this was going on downstairs, a crowd of several thousands had formed outside the building and in its main lobby. A degree of organization and leadership emerged among the demonstrators. The talk turned to "student power," the sins of the administration, and the failures of the faculty. "Happy Birthday" was sung for Mario's year-old son, and when the Navy left about 4 P.M., the demonstrators gave them a hearty "Anchors Aweigh."

Shortly before 6 P.M., some twenty or thirty off-campus police entered the locked building. The demonstrators inside had no way of knowing the policemen's intention: did they intend to arrest only a few, or were they going to carry everyone away, in a reenactment of 1964? The police, holding warrants signed by the executive vice-chancellor, arrested six persons, all non-students, on charges of trespassing and creating a public nuisance. Chaos threatened when the police attempted to drag the first person from the crowd of seated protestors. Some persons shrieked in alarm. Others shouted abusively at the officers, and pulled at their arms and legs, getting hit and kicked in return. The other arrests were accomplished without incident. None of the six resisted. Among those arrested were Savio and Jerry Rubin, local leader of the VDC.

Administration spokesmen have offered a very different account of these events. The executive vice-chancellor was reported in the student newspaper as saying that the six were arrested because they played "the key role" in the sit-in. In an official statement to the faculty and staff, he said that "the demonstration today was initiated and led by non-students in direct defiance of University regulations." On the other hand, three faculty eye-witnesses, in a signed document, have reported that "none of the six seemed involved as initiators," that one of the six did not speak throughout the demonstration, and that "two others participated minimally if at all." When confronted with these statements, one of the chancellor's assistants said that the administration had put up with "eighteen months of activists' blackmail" before moving against the students. The chancellor himself, addressing the Academic Senate, stated that the whole thing began when "non-students attempted in violation of our rules to set up a table. . . ." He referred to other recent "provocations," and concluded that "we are dealing, then, not with a single incident but with a chronic situation."

These administration statements overlooked certain critical distinctions among the groups of people involved in the early stages of disturbance: (1) the non-student who set up the anti-war table but was not arrested; (2) the students who, after seeing one of their number struck, sat in; and (3) the six arrested non-students, who, by no account, initiated or organized the demonstration. It appears that the administration, acting on its "outside agitator" theory, was out to get these people, even if that meant calling police onto the campus and committing a possible injustice against individuals.

As the police van moved away, another violent encounter took place. Hundreds of students jammed the street around the van. They were swept aside by a phalanx of policemen. Many persons were shoved and clubbed, some severely. Three students were arrested for interfering with the police.

The Student Union building was now unlocked, and the demonstrators outside were able to join those inside. They began a marathon mass meeting. By 10 P.M. the crowd had grown to around three thousand, jammed into a large ballroom. Many speakers stressed the futility of trying to negotiate reasonably with the administration over questions of political activity. The executive vice-chancellor appeared for about a half hour to answer questions. The hostile audience clearly considered his statements to be evasive or even false, and he was loudly hooted. Savio, who had returned after posting bail, was the last speaker of the evening. He recounted the unsuccessful efforts of individuals to gain due process during the last two years, and described a student strike as the "least disruptive way of pressuring the Administration." At 1 A.M. the students voted, nearly unanimously, to strike. The campus community was offered coffee and rebellion for breakfast.

The next day (December 2, two years to the day after the mass sit-in and arrests of 1964) a rally of about eight thousand confirmed the decision and accepted the demands of the strike: that police must never be called on campus to "solve" political problems; no disciplinary action against participants; off-campus individuals and non-commercial groups should have privileges on campus equal to those enjoyed by governmental agencies; disciplinary hearings must in the future be open and conducted according to the canons of due process; discussions must begin toward the creation of effective student representation on rule-making bodies. The Teaching Assistants' union, the student government, and (later) the student newspaper all supported the strike. Chancellor Heyns, who had been away, returned to an embattled campus.

Throughout the rest of the week the strike and mass rallies continued. Groups of faculty met frequently to discuss the issues and prepare for the forthcoming meeting of the Academic Senate. The chancellor declared himself opposed to the strike and refused to meet with representatives of the strikers.

The strike itself was well organized, but there are no reliable estimates concerning its effectiveness. Although there are a marvelous range and variety of political groups on the Berkeley campus, there was little factionalism or doctrinal infighting apparent in the conduct of the strike. For some time now most campus political groups have united in a loose confederal structure, called the Council of Campus Organizations, for the purpose of doing battle with the administration over issues concerning the legitimacy of the rules governing political activity. Hence, the many organizations participating in the strike had a pre-established system of discussion and communication. Perhaps the two most powerful new forces on the campus political scene are the Teaching Assistants' union and the Free University of Berkeley. The former has a membership of about four hundred graduate teaching assistants, and is affiliated with the AFT. The union voted to strike, supported it to the end, and supplied many of its leaders. The Free University is a "counter-institution" offering courses in everything from psychedelics and modern painting to Marxism and the theory and practice of imperialism. Some 250 persons are in some sense enrolled in the Free University, and some of the strike's leaders are closely associated with it. The strikers quickly elected an executive committee and a negotiating committee, proving once again that Berkeley students have a trained capacity for political organization and action. They can produce a manifesto and arrange a demonstration at a moment's notice. Many of the students have become impressive political speakers and tacticians. While the campus administration intones the language of community, it is the students who have been actually building community among themselves. Although there are student leaders, there is no permanent clique which can manipulate the students. The movement waxes and wanes, leaders come and go, as the situation changes. When the right conditions appear, thousands of students with a shared orientation can be mobilized within hours. If the administration tries to destroy this community by chopping off its head, it may find itself battling a Hydra.

The [Academic] Senate meeting of December 5 opened with an address by the chancellor. He reaffirmed his opposition to the strike, rejected amnesty for rule violators, called the rules "fair and equitable," argued that present hearing procedures met "the highest standards of judicial fairness," and asked for confidence from the faculty. The Senate debated and approved by a vote of 795 to 28, with 143 abstentions, a compromise, omnibus resolution. On the one hand, the Senate called for an end to the strike and affirmed "confidence in the Chancellor's leadership." On the other hand, it urged amnesty for students who had violated rules during the course of the strike. The Senate declared that tactics of "mass coercion" and the use of external police, except in extreme emergency, were both inappropriate to a university. The resolution also asked that new avenues be explored for increasing student participation in rule-making and enforcement, and called for a faculty-student commission "to consider new modes of governance and self-regulation in the University."

Unlike December, 1964, no one was enthusiastic about the result. Many faculty members wanted a more outspoken condemnation of the decision to bring the police on campus. A smaller number was disappointed that the Senate had not even discussed the matter of the arrest of the six non-students. A near majority, sick of the turmoil and persuaded that it had been caused by a few trouble-makers, narrowly failed to pass a "hard" resolution supporting the chancellor without reservation. No one spoke in defense of the students. Only a few dared to challenge the official theory that a small band of subversives had caused the trouble. None dared to say openly what many had declared privately, that the administration's decision to call in the police was more than a mistake, it was a crime. The fragile compromise in the resolutions caused the faculty liberals to abstain from vigorous debate for fear that the resolutions would be mutilated by amendments. Consequently, the speeches were made by faculty conservatives and many were harsh. One compared the Berkeley demonstrators to the Nazi students who had driven the non-Nazi professors from Germany. Another member finished his long speech by declaring in exasperation that he didn't want to hear any more arguments, only a vote of confidence in defense of order and authority.

It is doubtful that the chancellor was pleased by resolutions which coupled police action with the student strike and condemned them both; nor could the faculty declaration for amnesty be viewed by him as other than a rebuff. The students interpreted the resolution as final evidence of faculty unreliability. "The faculty cannot solve our problems," declared a student manifesto. "They did not choose to implement the December 8 Resolution, and [they have] demonstrated their inability to deal . . . with the educational ills of the University." Thus the faculty managed to disappoint itself, the administration, and the students.

The next day the Board of Regents met in emergency session. Regent Edwin Pauley, who had declared that "if people on the payroll can't understand their conditions of employment they shouldn't be there, and I'm for getting rid of them," introduced a resolution calling for retroactive punishment of striking Teaching Assistants and faculty. It was defeated and a substitute was passed that supported the chancellor, refrained from punishing the students, and condemned the "interference" of "outsiders." "The Regents support all necessary action to preserve order on all campuses of the University." Separating the student strikers from their supporters among the Teaching Assistants and faculty, the Regents produced the only unequivocal action of the week, a resolution that radically redefined the nature of academic freedom and tenure. Henceforth, "University personnel . . . who participate in any strike or otherwise fail to meet their assigned duties, in an effort to disrupt University administration, teaching, or research, will thereby be subject to termination of their employment . . . denial of reemployment, or the imposition of other appropriate sanctions." Obviously, the Regents had sown the seeds of future controversy.

Meanwhile the politicians of the state were angrily demanding that the striking faculty and Teaching Assistants be dismissed. The governor-elect warned the students "to obey the prescribed rules or get out. . . . The people of California . . . have a right to lay down rules and a code of conduct for those who accept that gift [of public education]." The president *pro tem* of the Senate advised Reagan that all that the university needed was "a new president and some regents with more guts than liberalism." The Speaker of the Assembly, and sometime Chubb Fellow of Yale, who had gotten his investigating committee from the 1964 crisis, made his usual statesmanlike suggestion: instead of appointing a new commission, the Governor should appoint the former CIA head to the Board of Regents. As of this writing, a bill has been introduced into the state legislature which would drastically reduce the powers of the Regents and place the university under closer legislative control.

The strike dragged to a close that evening and a haggard faculty and student body prepared for finals. In their last mass meeting, the students found a measure of joy and humor—graces sadly lacking this time. Half the joy was relief: they had been naughty, but hadn't gotten spanked too hard, at least not yet. There also emerged at the rally a spontaneous coalition between the hippies and the political activists. While the Teaching Assistants, like good trade unionists, sang "Solidarity Forever" in one room, the hippy–activist coalition sang "The Yellow Submarine" in another, and promised that next term they would "blow the Administration's mind." Instead of resorting to such "square" tactics as strikes and sit-ins, they might clog the machine, mock its logic, and drive its operators out of their minds by such tactics as flooding the deans with thousands of petitions, misplacing their identity cards, returning books to the wrong libraries, flocking to the student medical clinic for all manner of psychosomatic complaints, and wearing masks to class. It is impossible to anticipate how the chancellor will respond to that escalation.

II

It is doubtful whether the strike settled anything. Surely it added to the legacy of bitterness and anxiety. Perhaps it provided the jolt needed to start the university on the work of self-examination which it has so far shirked. More likely, Berkeley will enter an era of strong solutions—an obsession with total control, possibly a purge of dissident elements. That way may bring peace, but it will be the peace of intellectual and moral torpor.

The only hope for the university lies in replacing the narrow and fatal premises which have produced the present impasse with others more appropriate to the general social situation in which the university now stands. The social situation is one that can be called revolutionary in the sense that while the forces of change gather momentum, the society cannot find the appropriate response either in thought or act.

The troubles which beset American society are unprecedented and paradoxical. Stated broadly, our condition is one of widespread affluence, growing social expectations, scientific and technological dynamism, extensive welfare programs, and a high degree of formal democracy. In spite of all this, there is pervasive contempt for the very system which has given its members more comfort and leisure than any society in history. There is in this progressive, tolerant, and literate society a frightening lack of intellectual loyalty and spontaneous affection for the system. Above all, there lurks the fear that behind the greatest concentration of economic, scientific, and military power in history there is a moral weakness so thoroughgoing that when the society faces a substantive problem, such as racial discrimination, its cities are thrown into turmoil, or when it becomes embroiled in a foreign policy misadventure, its political creativity is limited to throwing increasing military might against a small country in a cause whose hopelessness rises in direct ratio to the violence employed.

Historically, revolutions have been occasions for attempting something new in the political world: a new vision of society, a new concept of authority, a new ideal of freedom or justice. We are accustomed to think of revolutions as arising out of poverty and injustice, exacerbated by the governing class's refusal to "modernize"—France of 1789, Russia of 1917, China of 1945. But the revolution brewing in America, this richest and most advanced of societies, is different. It is nourished by a sense of failure rather than hope. Our physical success is accompanied by spiritual despair. America is proving that modern man can create powerful and rich societies in which the rate of change is so intense that men cannot endure it, let alone master it. The paradox of our revolutionary condition, then, is the existence of despair, disaffection, and contempt within a society that is prosperous, progressive, and democratic.

Berkeley is the perfect example of the kind of university which a democratic and progressive society might be expected to produce. Its faculty is distinguished, its students highly selected, and its facilities superb. Like the society around it, the university is dynamic and growing, and it can claim excellence in science and professional training. Despite these achievements, it is a university whose administrators find ungovernable, whose educational leaders find unreformable, and whose students find unliveable. For two years its life has been marked by an enervating anxiety and hostility which cannot be dismissed as "a failure in communication." The melancholy truth is that there is no widely shared understanding about the meaning and purpose of the institution. Lacking the unifying force which flows spontaneously from common understandings, the system is held together by a bureaucratic organization whose weakness is exposed whenever it is directly challenged.

This is partly the result of Berkeley's legacy as a public university, a legacy which contrasts with the traditional idea informing the ancient public universities of Europe, as well as the private universities and colleges of this country.

The striking difference between the traditional university and the modern public university is best seen in the small place assigned to administration in the former. The older university could flourish with a "housekeeper" administration because of one basic presupposition: that a genuine and autonomous community of scholars existed to be served. The modern public university, however, was born in a state of dependence on the outside society, and in most instances, the administration was created first. It never had the chance to become a community. Its survival depended upon public support and administrative power, not on the moral and intellectual fellowship of its members.

The public university adheres to a conception of knowledge which differs greatly from that of its ancestors. The knowledge it produces must be useful to the social and economic interests of an expanding society. At Berkeley, there are installations, institutes, and laboratories in which trained experts develop knowledge in such fields as naval medicine, sanitary engineering, space science, marine food products, nuclear weapons, mining, and range management. The demand for all these services is strong and growing. But it goes without saying that there is no irresistible demand that the university preserve the knowledge and experience of the past or encourage reflection on the intangibles of the good life. The old idea of the university as a community of conservants has been pushed aside by the Baconian vision of knowledge as power. But practicality has not by itself created the ideal of knowledge which now threatens all universities, public or private. The notorious concern of most faculties with publication and research is directly related to the requirement that a scholar be "original." He must turn up novelties of fact or theory, and his novelties must pay off, either because they are practical or because they "generate" further research. Knowledge is no longer associated with wisdom, or with the fruits of contemplation or rediscovery. It is not guided by reflection, but fired by the hope of a "breakthrough." This conception of knowledge brings a new pace to academic life: the researcher is forever racing to the frontiers where the future beckons. He must continuously invent new concepts, models, and techniques. The greatest sin lies not in being trivial, but in appearing old-fashioned.

At Berkeley these concerns amount to an obsession. It is virtually official doctrine that the ruthless pursuit of productivity is the key to Berkeley's rapid rise to a position where it is no longer just "another state university," but can compare with such renowned institutions as Harvard.

The assumption that a university is a place where knowledge is "pursued" and "cumulated" seems harmless enough until its effects are considered. This approach entails destruction of and contempt for the old, and for the fuddyduddies who profess it. The perfect illustration of the new spirit is the popularity of Whitehead's battle cry among social scientists: "A science which hesitates to forget its founders is lost." Forgetting and destroying are necessary preconditions for productivity; he travels faster who travels lightest; he travels lightest who sheds civility, tradition, and care for the common culture of the intellect.

The new conception of knowledge produces human casualties as well. In departments throughout Berkeley there are endless macabre discussions, amounting to ritual murder, about the older professors left stranded alongside the main stream of research. Young men are ready, but the old men are protected by tenure. The curiosity is that the superannuated professor is probably in his thirties.

The competitive ethos of the modern research-oriented university has created "dysfunctional" or "deviant" human types, to use the current idiom. These are, lamentably, the very types which were "functional" in the traditional university. Foremost among them is the teacher. The teacher who is threatened is not the one who loves to be surrounded by admiring undergraduates and who makes a cult of non-writing, but rather the one who naively believes that teaching and research can be creatively combined. But, as an academic member of the Berkeley administration responsible for promoting educational reform has said, "A professor's bread is buttered by his relationships within his field, and they are established by research. You don't get an international reputation for giving a great course at Berkeley." Nor need the academic face a Kierkegaardian choice between teaching and research. Numerous agencies are eager to pay for the professor's "released time" from the classroom so that he can pursue his research free from the distractions of teaching. In some fields, it is tacitly agreed that the professors who carry normal teaching loads are those whose research is not so valuable as to justify their giving full time to it.

If the teacher is "dysfunctional," the student is worse. To the jet-age frontiersman he is a distraction and an anomaly, except when he is an apprentice researcher. Most graduate students present few problems, for they have been "socialized" and can even instruct their seniors in the art of grantsmanship. Those undergraduates and graduates who are left outside the system and who feel hurt and betrayed have formulated their own counter-idea of knowledge. Against the professionalism of the insiders, they proclaim the primacy of passion, subjectivity, and openness. Knowledge which is not obviously related to their immediate personal needs and situations is irrelevant. To be relevant, knowledge must speak *now* to *their* needs. The ancient values of detachment and disinterested inquiry are seen as evasions of responsibility; or, worse, as typifying the vice of "objectivism" which transforms thought and feeling into alienated objects and serves as an ideological figleaf for a corrupt establishment.

It would be a foolish man who, given the complex problems confronting the modern university, would claim to have a new constitution in his pocket. Nevertheless, certain things are clear. If something of the traditional idea of the university is to be salvaged, there must be revitalization of a common culture and a lessening of the centrifugal tendencies of specialization. It must be recognized that the pursuit of knowledge can take forms incompatible with the unique cultural and educational character of the university. This is not to say that the university should turn away from new modes of knowledge and inquiry and lovingly cultivate all that is precious and old. A creative tension between tradition and innovation should be the guiding principle.

It has become clear that the University of California is no longer viable in its present form. The whole vast state-wide complex, with its centralized bureaucratic apparatus of control, should be decentralized toward something like a "Commonwealth of Campuses" model, but it is unlikely that this will happen. Two years ago, a committee appointed by the Regents proposed that the state-wide system be devolved into a looser alliance of largely autonomous campuses. After creating a brief sensation, the report was conveniently forgotten. The best hope for the future lies in devising ways to reintegrate faculty and students around smaller structures which are allowed genuine powers of decision-making and broad opportunities for educational experiments. If smaller communities are to be established, there must be serious openminded discussion of the possibilities of student participation in a far broader range of university matters than hitherto.

At this moment, the Academic Senate is considering a concrete proposal to establish a student–faculty commission to explore ways of improving "the

292 | *Voices of Dissent*

participation of students in the formulation of educational policies, including measures for the improvement of teaching." The proposal lays special emphasis on the need to develop "patterns of student–faculty cooperation" at the departmental level.

These proposals move in the direction recently suggested by President Kerr. In a newspaper interview of a month ago, he described Berkeley's steps toward educational reform as "somewhat too conservative." He also said that "the University of California had the most restrictive policies [regarding political activity] of any university I've ever known about, outside a dictatorship." He also declared "that this is a generation that wants to participate" and "there ought to be 100, or 1,000 opportunities" for it to do so.

In contrast, too many faculty members have resisted trying to understand the contemporary student and have indulged themselves, instead, in grotesque analogies between Berkeley and Latin American-style universities or Nazi youth movements. These spectral analogies, like the outside agitator theory, are appeals to fear and rest upon the belief that men can be frightened into order.

Today's student finds himself in a world of complexity and change, of exciting possibilities and ominous threats, of uncertain landmarks for personal conduct and all too certain prescriptions for success in the straight world. He sees a world whose promise is constantly violated by destruction, discrimination, and cruelty. In an older and simpler age he would have entered the university with greater confidence and stability, for many institutions would have helped prepare him for adulthood. But family, church, neighborhood, and school have now declined in effectiveness and where they once contributed to his confidence, they now reinforce his uncertainty. Consequently, the student is led to demand more from his university experience than ever before. Such students embarrass the university for the same reason that Kierkegaard embarrassed Christendom: by the purity of their demands. They want the university to be a place where education and knowledge are pursued out of love for the pursuit itself. They are in revolt against all that is remote and impersonal in human relations. They want an educational community whose members will look at each other, not one in which relationships are defined by rules and treated as simple problems of order and compliance. Because they take the democratic ideal seriously, they want a voice in the decisions which shape their lives. It is these students who provide hope.

Opportunities for creative change still exist at Berkeley, but the problems are profound, reflecting as they do the sickness of our society and the disaffection of a whole generation. This time the campus must face the future with a fuller appreciation of the radical nature of the reforms needed.

[1967]

Berkeley and the University Revolution | 293

THOMAS PYNCHON

A Journey
into the Mind of Watts

THE NIGHT of May 7, after a chase that began in Watts and ended some fifty blocks farther north, two Los Angeles policemen, Caucasians, succeeded in halting a car driven by Leonard Deadwyler, a Negro. With him were his pregnant wife and a friend. The younger cop (who'd once had a complaint brought against him for rousting some Negro kids around in a more than usually abusive way) went over and stuck his head and gun in the car window to talk to Deadwyler. A moment later there was a shot; the young Negro fell sideways in the seat, and died. The last thing he said, according to the other cop, was, "She's going to have a baby."

The coroner's inquest went on for the better part of two weeks, the cop claiming the car had lurched suddenly, causing his service revolver to go off by accident; Deadwyler's widow claiming it was cold-blooded murder and that the car had never moved. The verdict, to no one's surprise, cleared the cop of all criminal responsibility. It had been an accident. The D.A. announced immediately that he thought so, too, and that as far as he was concerned the case was closed.

But as far as Watts is concerned, it's still very much open. Preachers in the community are urging calm—or, as others are putting it: "Make any big trouble, baby, The Man just going to come back in and shoot you, like last time." Snipers are sniping but so far not hitting much of anything. Occasional fire bombs are being lobbed at cars with white faces inside, or into empty sports models that look as if they might be white property. There have been a few fires of mysterious origin. A Negro Teen Post—part of the L.A. poverty war's keep-them-out-of-the-streets effort—has had all its windows busted, the young lady in charge expressing the wish next morning that she could talk with the malefactors, involve them, see if they couldn't work out the problem together. In the back of everybody's head, of course, is the same question: Will there be a repeat of last August's riot?

An even more interesting question is: why is everybody worrying about another riot—haven't things in Watts improved any since the last one? A lot of white folks are wondering. Unhappily, the answer is no. The neighborhood may be seething with social workers, data collectors, VISTA volunteers, and other assorted members of the humanitarian establishment, all of whose intentions are the purest in the world. But somehow nothing much has changed. There are still the poor, the defeated, the criminal, the desperate, all hanging in there with what must seem a terrible vitality.

The killing of Leonard Deadwyler has once again brought it all into sharp focus; brought back longstanding pain, reminded everybody of how very often the cop does approach you with his revolver ready, so that nothing he does with it can then be really accidental; of how, especially at night, everything can suddenly reduce to a matter of reflexes: your life trembling in the crook of a cop's finger because it is dark, and Watts, and the history of this place and these times makes it impossible for the cop to come on any different, or for you to hate him any less. Both of you are caught in something neither of you wants, and yet night after night, with casualties or without, these traditional scenes continue to be played out all over the south-central part of this city.

Whatever else may be wrong in a political way—like the inadequacy of Great Depression techniques applied to a scene that has long outgrown them; like an old-fashioned grafter's glee among the city fathers over the vast amounts of poverty-war bread that Uncle is now making available to them—lying much closer to the heart of L.A.'s racial sickness is the co-existence of two very different cultures: one white and one black.

While the white culture is concerned with various forms of systematized folly—the economy of the area in fact depending upon it—the black culture is stuck pretty much with basic realities like disease, like failure, violence and death, which the whites have mostly chosen—and can afford—to ignore. The two cultures do not understand each other, though white values are displayed without let-up on black people's TV screens, and though the panoramic sense of black impoverishment is hard to miss from atop the Harbor Freeway, which so many whites must drive at least twice every working day. Somehow it occurs to very few of them to leave at the Imperial Highway exit for a change, go east instead of west only a few blocks, and take a look at Watts. A quick look. The simplest kind of beginning. But Watts is country which lies, psychologically, uncounted miles further than most whites seem at present willing to travel.

On the surface, anyway, the Deadwyler affair hasn't made it look any different, though underneath the mood in Watts is about what you might expect. Feelings range from a reflexive, angry, driving need to hit back somehow, to an anxious worry that the slaying is just one more bad grievance, one more bill that will fall due some warm evening this summer. Yet in the daytime's brilliance and heat, it is hard to believe there is any mystery to Watts. Everything seems so out in the open, all of it real, no plastic faces, no transistors, no hidden Muzak, or Disneyfied landscaping, or smiling little chicks to show you around. Not in Raceriotland. Only a few historic landmarks, like the police substation, one command post for the white forces last August, pigeons now thick and cooing up on its red-tiled roof. Or, on down the street, vacant lots, still looking charred around the edges, winking with emptied Tokay, port and sherry pints, some of the bottles peeking out of paper bags, others busted.

A kid could come along in his bare feet and step on this glass—not that you'd ever know. These kids are so tough you can pull slivers of it out of them and never get a whimper. It's part of their landscape, both the real and the emotional one: busted glass, busted crockery, nails, tin cans, all kinds of scrap and waste. Traditionally Watts. An Italian immigrant named Simon Rodia spent thirty years gathering some of it up and converting a little piece of the neighborhood along 107th Street into the famous Watts Towers, perhaps his own dream of how things should have been: a fantasy of fountains, boats, tall openwork spires, encrusted with a dazzling mosaic of Watts debris. Next to the Towers, along the old Pacific Electric tracks, kids are busy every day busting more bottles on the steel rails. But Simon Rodia is dead and now the junk just accumulates.

A few blocks away, other kids are out playing on the hot blacktop of the school playground. Brothers and sisters too young yet for school have it better—wherever they are they have yards, trees, hoses, hiding places. Not the crowded, shadeless tenement living of any Harlem; just the same one- or two-story urban sprawl as all over the rest of L.A., giving you some piece of grass at least to expand into when you don't especially feel like being inside.

In the business part of town there is a different idea of refuge. Pool halls and bars, warm and dark inside, are crowded; many domino, dice, and whist games in progress. Outside, men stand around a beer cooler listening to a ball game on the radio; others lean or hunker against the sides of buildings—low, faded stucco boxes that remind you, oddly, of certain streets in Mexico. Women go by, to and from what shopping there is. It is easy to see how crowds, after all, can form quickly in these streets, around the least seed of a disturbance or accident. For the moment, it all only waits in the sun.

Overhead, big jets now and then come vacuum-cleanering in to land; the wind is westerly, and Watts lies under the approaches to L.A. International. The jets hang what seems only a couple of hundred feet up in the air; through the smog they show up more white than silver, highlighted by the sun, hardly solid; only the ghosts, or possibilities, of airplanes.

From here, much of the white culture that surrounds Watts—and, in a curious way, besieges it—looks like those jets: a little unreal, a little less than substantial. For Los Angeles, more than any other city, belongs to the mass media. What is known around the nation as the L.A. Scene exists chiefly as images on a screen or TV tube, as four-color magazine photos, as old radio jokes, as new songs that survive only a matter of weeks. It is basically a white Scene, and illusion is everywhere in it, from the giant aerospace firms that flourish or retrench at the whims of Robert McNamara, to the "action" everybody mills along the Strip on weekends looking for, unaware that they, and their search which will end, usually, unfulfilled, are the only action in town.

Watts lies impacted in the heart of this white fantasy. It is, by contrast, a pocket of bitter reality. The only illusion Watts ever allowed itself was to believe for a long time in the white version of what a Negro was supposed to be. But with the Muslim and civil-rights movements that went, too.

Since the August rioting, there has been little building here, little buying. Lots whose buildings were burned on them are still waiting vacant and littered with garbage, occupied only by a parked car or two, or kids fooling around after school, or winos sharing a pint in the early morning. The other day, on one of them, there were ground-breaking festivities, attended by a county supervisor, pretty high-school girls decked in ribbons, a white store owner and his wife, who in the true Watts spirit busted a bottle of champagne over a rock—all because the man had decided to stay and rebuild his $200,000 market, the first such major rebuilding since the riot.

Watts people themselves talk about another kind of aura, vaguely evil; complain that Negroes living in better neighborhoods like to come in under the freeway as to a red-light district, looking for some girl, some game, maybe some connection. Narcotics is said to be a rare bust in Watts these days, although the narco people cruise the area earnestly, on the lookout for dope fiends, dope rings, dope peddlers. But the poverty of Watts makes it more likely that if you have pot or a little something else to spare you will want to turn a friend on, not sell it. Tomorrow, or when he can, your friend will return the favor.

At the Deadwyler inquest, much was made of the dead man's high blood alcohol content, as if his being drunk made it somehow all right for the police to shoot him. But alcohol is a natural part of the Watts style; as natural as LSD is around Hollywood. The white kid digs hallucination simply because he is conditioned to believe so much in escape, escape as an integral part of life, because the white L.A. Scene makes accessible to him so many different forms of it. But a Watts kid, brought up in a pocket of reality, looks perhaps not so much for escape as just for some calm, some relaxation. And beer or wine is good enough for that. Especially good at the end of a bad day.

Like after you have driven, say, down to Torrance or Long Beach or wherever it is they're hiring because they don't seem to be in Watts, not even in the miles of heavy industry that sprawl along Alameda Street, that gray and murderous arterial which lies at the eastern boundary of Watts looking like the edge of the world.

So you groove instead down the Freeway, maybe wondering when some cop is going to stop you because the old piece of a car you're driving, that you bought for $20 or $30 you picked up somehow, makes a lot of noise or burns some oil. Catching you mobile widens The Man's horizons; gives him more things he can get you on. Like "excessive smoking" is a great favorite with him.

If you do get to where you were going without encountering a cop, you may spend your day looking at the white faces of personnel men, their uniform glaze of suspicion, their automatic smiles, and listening to polite putdowns. "I decided once to ask," a kid says, "one time they told me I didn't meet their requirements. So I said: 'Well, what are you looking for? I mean, how can I train, what things do I have to learn so I *can* meet your requirements?' Know what he said? 'We are not obligated to tell you what our requirements are.' "

He isn't. That right there is the hell and headache: he doesn't have to do anything he doesn't want to do because he is The Man. Or he was. A lot of kids these days are more apt to be calling him the *little* man—meaning not so much any member of the power structure as just your average white L.A. taxpayer, registered voter, property owner; employed, stable, mortgaged, and the rest.

The little man bugs these kids more than The Man ever bugged their parents. It is the little man who is standing on their feet and in their way; he's all over the place, and there is not much they can do to change him or the way he feels about them. A Watts kid knows more of what goes on inside white heads than possibly whites do themselves; knows how often the little man has looked at him and thought, "Bad credit risk"—or "Poor learner," or "Sexual threat," or "Welfare chiseler"—without knowing a thing about him personally.

The natural, normal thing to want to do is hit the little man. But what, after all, has he done? Mild, respectable, possibly smiling, he has called you no names, shown you no weapons. Only told you perhaps that the job was filled, the house rented.

With a cop it may get more dangerous, but at least it's honest. You understand each other. Both of you silently admitting that all the cop really has going for him is his gun. "There was a time," they'll tell you, "you'd say, 'Take off the badge, baby, and let's settle it.' I mean he wouldn't, but you'd say it. But since last August, man, the way I feel, hell with the badge— just take off that gun."

The cop does not take off that gun; the hassle stays verbal. But this means that, besides protecting and serving the little man, the cop also functions as his effigy.

If he does get emotional and say something like "boy" or "nigger," you then have the option of cooling it or else—again this is more frequent since last August—calling him the name he expects to be called, though it is understood you are not commenting in any literal way on what goes on between him and his mother. It is a ritual exchange, like the dirty dozens.

Usually—as in the Deadwyler incident—it's the younger cop of the pair who's more troublesome. Most Watts kids are hip to what's going on in this rookie's head—the things he feels he has to prove—as much as to the elements of the ritual. Before the cop can say, "Let's see your I.D.," you learn to take it out politely and say, "You want to see my I.D.?" Naturally it will bug the cop more the further ahead of him you can stay. It is flirting with disaster, but it's the cop who has the gun, so you do what you can.

You must anticipate always how the talk is going to go. It's something you pick up quite young, same as you learn the different species of cop: the Black and White (named for the color scheme of their automobiles), who are L.A. city police and in general the least flexible; the L.A. county sheriff's department, who style themselves more of an elite, try to maintain a certain distance from the public, and are less apt to harass you unless you seem worthy; the Compton city cops, who travel only one to a car and come on very tough, like leaning four of you at a time up against the wall and shaking you all down; the juvies, who ride in unmarked Plymouths and are cruising all over the place soon as the sun goes down, pulling up alongside you with pleasantries like, "Which one's buying the wine tonight?", or, "Who are you guys planning to rob this time?" They are kidding, of course, trying to be pals. But Watts kids, like most, do not like being put in with winos, or dangerous drivers, or thieves, or in any bag considered criminal or evil. Whatever the cop's motives, it *looks* like mean and deliberate ignorance.

In the daytime, and especially with any kind of crowd, the cop's surface style has changed some since last August. "Time was," you'll hear, "man used to go right in, very mean, pick maybe one kid out of the crowd he figured was the troublemaker, try to bust him down in front of everyone. But now the people start yelling back, how they don't want no more of that, all of a sudden The Man gets very meek."

Still, however much a cop may seem to be following the order of the day read to him every morning about being courteous to everybody, his behavior with a crowd will really depend as it always has on how many of his own he can muster, and how fast. For his mayor, Sam Yorty, is a great believer in the virtues of Overwhelming Force as a solution to racial difficulties. This approach has not gained much favor in Watts. In fact, the mayor of Los Angeles appears to many Negroes to be the very incarnation of the little man: looking out for no one but himself, speaking always out of expediency, and never, never to be trusted.

The Economic and Youth Opportunities Agency (E.Y.O.A.) is a joint city-county "umbrella agency" (the state used to be represented, but has dropped out) for many projects scattered around the poorer parts of L.A., and seems to be Sam Yorty's native element, if not indeed the flower of his consciousness. Bizarre, confused, ever in flux, strangely ineffective, E.Y.O.A. hardly sees a day go by without somebody resigning, or being fired, or making an accusation, or answering one—all of it confirming the Watts Negroes' already sad estimate of the little man. The Negro attitude toward E.Y.O.A. is one of clear mistrust, though degrees of suspicion vary, from the housewife wanting only to be left in peace and quiet, who hopes that maybe The Man is lying less than usual this time, to the young, active disciple of Malcolm X who dismisses it all with a contemptuous shrug.

"But why?" asked one white lady volunteer. "There are so many agencies now that you *can* go to, that *can* help you, if you'll only file your complaint."

"They don't help you." This particular kid had been put down trying to get a job with one of the larger defense contractors.

"Maybe not before. But it's different now."

"Now," the kid sighed, "*now*. See, people been hearing that '*now*' for a long time, and I'm just tired of The Man telling you, '*Now*, it's OK, *now* we mean what we say.' "

In Watts, apparently, where no one can afford the luxury of illusion, there is little reason to believe that now will be any different, and better than last time.

It is perhaps a measure of the people's indifference that only 2 per cent of the poor in Los Angeles turned out to elect representatives to the E.Y.O.A. "poverty board." For a hopeless minority on the board (7 out of 23), nobody saw much point in voting.

Meantime, the outposts of the establishment drowse in the bright summery smog; secretaries chat the afternoons plaintively away about machines that will not accept the cards they have punched for them; white volunteers sit filing, doodling, talking on the phones, doing any kind of busy work, wondering where the "clients" are; inspirational mottoes like SMILE decorate the beaverboard office walls along with flow charts to illustrate the proper disposition of "cases," and with clippings from the slick magazines about "What Is Emotional Maturity?"

Items like smiling and Emotional Maturity are in fact very big with the well-adjusted, middle-class professionals, Negro and white, who man the mimeographs and computers of the poverty war here. Sadly, they seem to be smiling themselves out of any meaningful communication with their poor. Besides a nineteenth-century faith that tried and true approaches—sound counseling, good intentions, perhaps even compassion—will set Watts straight, they are also burdened with the personal attitudes they bring to work with them. Their reflexes—especially about conformity, about failure, about violence—are predictable.

"We had a hell of a time with this one girl," a Youth Training and Employment Project counselor recalls. "You should have seen those hairdos of hers—piled all the way up to here. And the screwy outfits she'd come in with, you just wouldn't believe. We had to take her aside and explain to her that employers just don't go for that sort of thing. That she'd be up against a lot of very smooth-looking chicks, heels and stockings, conservative hair and clothes. We finally got her to come around."

The same goes for boys who like to wear Malcolm hats or Afro haircuts. The idea the counselors push evidently is to look as much as possible like a white applicant. Which is to say, like a Negro job counselor or social worker. This has not been received with much enthusiasm among the kids it is designed to help out, and is one reason business is so slow around the various projects.

There is a similar difficulty among the warriors about failure. They are in a socio-economic bag, along with the vast majority of white Angelenos, who seem more terrified of failure than of death. It is difficult to see where any of them have experienced significant defeat, or loss. If they have, it seems to have been long rationalized away as something else.

You are likely to hear from them wisdom on the order of: "Life has a way of surprising us, simply as a function of time. Even if all you do is stand on the street corner and wait." Watts is full of street corners where people stand, as they have been, some of them, for twenty or thirty years, without Surprise One ever having come along. Yet the poverty warriors must believe in this form of semimiracle, because their world and their scene cannot accept the possibility that there may be, after all, no surprise. But it is something Watts has always known.

As for violence, in a pocket of reality such as Watts, violence is never far from you: because you are a man, because you have been put down, because for every action there is an equal and opposite reaction. Somehow, sometime. Yet to these innocent, optimistic child-bureaucrats, violence is an evil and an illness, possibly because it threatens property and status they cannot help cherishing.

They remember last August's riot as an outburst, a seizure. Yet what, from the realistic viewpoint of Watts, was so abnormal? "Man's got his foot on your neck," said one guy who was there, "sooner or later you going to stop *asking* him to take it off." The violence it took to get that foot to ease up even the little it did was no surprise. Many had predicted it. Once it got going, its basic objective—to beat the Black and White police—seemed a reasonable one, and was gained the minute The Man had to send troops in. Everybody seems to have known it. There is hardly a person in Watts now who finds it painful to talk about, or who regrets that it happened—unless he lost somebody.

But in the white culture outside, in that creepy world full of pre-cardiac Mustang drivers who scream insults at one another only when the windows are up; of large corporations where Niceguymanship is the standing order regardless of whose executive back one may be endeavoring to stab; of an enormous priest caste of shrinks who counsel moderation and compromise as the answer to all forms of hassle; among so much well-behaved unreality, it is next to impossible to understand how Watts may truly feel about violence. In terms of strict reality, violence may be a means to getting money, for example, no more dishonest than collecting exorbitant carrying charges from a customer on relief, as white merchants here still do. Far from a sickness, violence may be an attempt to communicate, or to be who you really are.

"Sure I did two stretches," a kid says, "both times for fighting, but I didn't deserve either one. First time, the cat was bigger than I was; next time, it was two against one, and I was the one." But he was busted all the same, perhaps because Whitey, who knows how to get everything he wants, no longer has fisticuffs available as a technique, and sees no reason why everybody shouldn't go the Niceguy route. If you are thinking maybe there is a virility hangup in here too, that putting a Negro into a correctional institution for fighting is also some kind of neutering operation, well, you might have something there, who knows?

It is, after all, in white L.A.'s interest to cool Watts any way it can—to put the area under a siege of persuasion; to coax the Negro poor into taking on certain white values. Give them a little property, and they will be less tolerant of arson; get them to go in hock for a car or color TV, and they'll be more likely to hold down a steady job. Some see it for what it is—this come-on, this false welcome, this attempt to transmogrify the reality of Watts into the unreality of Los Angeles. Some don't.

Watts is tough; it has been able to resist the unreal. If there is any drift away from reality, it is by way of mythmaking. As this summer warms up, last August's riot is being remembered less as chaos and more as art. Some talk now of a balletic quality to it, a coordinated and graceful drawing of cops away from the center of the action, a scattering of The Man's power, either with real incidents or false alarms.

Others remember it in terms of music; through much of the rioting seemed to run, they say, a remarkable empathy, or whatever it is that jazz musicians feel on certain nights; everybody knowing what to do and when to do it without needing a word or a signal: "You could go up to anybody, the cats could be in the middle of burning down a store or something, but they'd tell you, explain very calm, just what they were doing, what they were going to do next. And that's what they'd do; man, nobody had to give orders."

Restructuring of the riot goes on in other ways. All Easter week this year, in the spirit of the season, there was a "Renaissance of the Arts," a kind of festival in memory of Simon Rodia, held at Markham Junior High, in the heart of Watts.

Along with theatrical and symphonic events, the festival also featured a roomful of sculptures fashioned entirely from found objects—found, symbolically enough, and in the Simon Rodia tradition, among the wreckage the rioting had left. Exploiting textures of charred wood, twisted metal, fused glass, many of the works were fine, honest rebirths.

In one corner was this old, busted, hollow TV set with a rabbit-ears antenna on top; inside, where its picture tube should have been, gazing out with scorched wiring threaded like electronic ivy among its crevices and sockets, was a human skull. The name of the piece was "The Late, Late, Late Show."   [1966]

OSCAR ZETA ACOSTA

The Revolt
of the Cockroach People

CHAPTER EIGHT

THE WEEK after McIntyre got the ax, I first encountered death as a world of art.

It is early one morning when the family of Robert Fernandez arrives. The sign outside the basement office only announces *La Voz*, but these strangers come in asking for me. Via the grapevine, they have heard of a lawyer who might help them. Nobody else is around. It is just them and me:

"We gotta have someone to help us, Mr. Brown. The deputies killed my brother."

A hefty woman with solid arms and thick mascara burnt into her skin is talking. She says her name is Lupe. She is the spokesman, the eldest child in a family of nine. The woman beside her is the mother, Juana, an old nurse. Juana is still in shock, sitting quietly, staring at Gilbert's paintings hung on the wall. John, Lupe's husband, sits on her other side. His arms are crossed, bright tattoos over corded muscle. He wears a white T shirt and a blue beanie, the traditional garb of the *vato loco*, the Chicano street freak who lives on a steady diet of pills, dope and wine. He does not move behind his thick mustache. He too sits quietly, as a proper brother-in-law, a *cuñado* who does not interfere in family business unless asked.

"Why do you say they killed your brother?" I ask.

"*¡Porque son marranos!*" Juana cries out and then falls back into silence. Aztec designs in black and red meet her glazed eyes.

I ask for the whole story. . . .

Robert was seventeen when the weight of his hundred and eighty pounds snapped the bones and nerves of his fat brown neck. He, too, lived in Tooner Flats, a neighborhood of shacks and clotheslines and dirty back yards. At every other corner, street lights hang high on telephone poles and cast dim yellow glows. Skinny dogs and wormy cats sniff garbage cans in the alleys. Tooner Flats is the area of gangs who spend their last dime on short dogs of T-Bird wine, where the average kid has eight years of school. Everybody there gets some kind of welfare.

You learn about life from the toughest guy in the neighborhood. You smoke your first joint in an alley at the age of ten; you take your first hit of *carga* before you get laid; and you learn how to make your mark on the wall before you learn how to write. Your friends know you to be a *vato loco*, a crazy guy, and they call you "*ese*," or "*vato*," or "man." And when you prove you can take it, that you don't cop to nothing even if it means getting your ass whipped by some other gang or the cops, then you are allowed to put your mark, your initial, your sign, your badge, your *placa* on your turf with the name or initial of your gang: White Fence, Quatro Flats, Barrio Nuevo, The Jokers, The Bachelors, or what have you. You write it big and fancy, scroll-like, *cholo* print. Graffiti on all the stores, all the garages, everywhere that you control or claim. It's like the pissing of a dog on a post. And underneath your *placa*, you always put C/S, "*Con Safos*," that is: *Up yours if you don't like it, ese!*

There is no school for a *vato loco*. There is no job in sight. His only hope is for a quick score. Reds and Ripple mixed with a bennie, a white and a toke. And when your head is tight, you go down to the hangout and wait for the next score.

On the day he died, Robert had popped reds with wine and then conked out for a few hours. When he awoke he was ready for more. But first he went down to Cronie's on Whittier Boulevard, the Chicano Sunset Strip. Every other door is a bar, a pawn shop or a liquor store. Hustlers roam freely across asphalt decorated with vomit and dogshit. If you score in East

Los Angeles you score on The Boulevard. Broads, booze and dope. Cops on every corner make no difference. The fuzz, *la placa, la chota, los marranos, la jura* or just the plain old pig. The eternal enemies of the people. The East LA Sheriff's Substation is only three blocks away on Third Street, right alongside the Pomono Freeway. From the blockhouse, deputies come out in teams of two, "To Serve And Protect!" Always with thirty-six-inch clubs, with walkie-talkies in hand; always with gray helmets, shotguns in the car and .357 Magnums in their holsters.

The *vato loco* has been fighting with the pig since the Anglos stole his land in the last century. He will continue to fight until he is exterminated.

Robert had *his* last fight in January of 1970. He met his sister, Lupe, at Cronie's. She was eating a hamburger. He was dry, he told her. Would she please go to the store across the street and get him a six-pack on credit? No, she'd pay for it. Tomorrow is his birthday so she will help him celebrate it early. Lupe left Robert with friends. They were drinking cokes and listening to the jukebox. Robert liked *mayate* music, the blues. They put in their dimes and sip on cokes, hoping some broad, a *ruka*, would come buy them a hamburger or share a joint with them.

I know Cronie's well. I live two blocks away with the three cousins. I know if you sit on the benches under the canopy long enough, *someone* comes along with *something* for the evening's action. This time the cops brought it.

By the time Lupe returned with a six-pack, two deputies were talking with Robert and his friends. It all began, he told her when she walked up, just because he shouted "Chicano Power!" and raised his fist.

"The cop told me to stay out of it, Mr. Brown. I told him Robert is my brother. But they told me to get away or else they'd arrest me for interfering, you know."

Juana says, "Tell him about the dirty greaser."

"Oh, yes. . . . We know this pig. He's a Chicano. Twice he's arrested Robert," Lupe says.

"Yes, Mr. Brown!" Juana could not restrain herself. "That same man once beat up my boy. He came in one day, about a year ago, and he just pushed into the room where Robert was sleeping. He dragged him out and they held him for three days. . . . They thought he had stolen a car. . . . But the judge threw the case out of court. That pig hated my boy."

Robert had been in jail many times. He'd spent some time at the Youth Authority Camp. But he'd been off smack over a year now. He still dropped a few reds now and then. And yes, he drank wine. But he was clean now. The cops took him in from Cronie's, they said, to check him out. They wanted to see if the marks on his arms were fresh. But anyone could tell they were old.

The Revolt of the Cockroach People | 305

Lupe appeals to John:

"That's the truth, Brown," the brother-in-law says. "Robert had cleaned up. He even got a job. He was going to start working next week."

"And we were going to have a birthday party for him that Friday," Juana says.

The deputies took Robert and told Lupe not to bother arranging bail. They told her he'd be released within a couple of hours. They thought he might just be drunk, but mainly they wanted to check out his arms. They said for her not to worry.

An hour after he was arrested, Robert called his mother. The cops had changed their minds, he said. They had booked him for Plain Drunk, a misdemeanor. The bail was set at five hundred dollars.

"He told me to call up Maldonado, his bail bondsman. Robert always used him. I could get him out just like that. All I had to do was make a phone call and then go down and sign, you know? The office is just down the street. I didn't even have to put up the house or anything. Mr. Maldonado always just got him out on my word!" the mother cries.

Juana had called the bail bondsman before she received the second call. This time it was a cop. He simply wanted to tell her that Robert was dead. He'd just hung himself. And would she come down and identify the body.

"He was so cold, Mr. Brown. He didn't say he was sorry or anything like that. He just said for me to wait there and he'd send a deputy to pick me up," she says bitterly.

"I went with her," John says. "When we got there I told the man right away that they'd made some mistake. I told him Robert had just called.

"Then they brought in a picture. And I said, 'gracias a Dios,' I knew him. It wasn't Robert, it was somebody named Sanchez. But that lieutenant said there was no mistake. He said the picture just didn't come out too good. . . . But Juana told him, 'Well I should know, he's my son.' And I told him Robert wouldn't do a thing like that. He'd never kill himself. He was católico, Señor Café. He even used to be an altar boy one time. And he was going to get married, too. He was going to announce it at his party. I talked to Pattie and she told me. She said they were going to get married as soon as he got his first paycheck."

"Pattie is pregnant," Lupe says. "You might as well know, Mr. Brown."

"So what happened after that?" I ask.

"We had the funeral and they buried him last week," Juana says.

Lupe says, "We just got the certificate last night. It says he killed himself. Suicide, it says."

"That's a goddamn lie," John says. "Excuse me. . . . But it is."

"How do you think he was killed?"

"I *know*," Lupe says. "At the funeral . . . you tell him, John."

"Yeah, I was there. I saw it."

Doris, another sister, had discovered it. At the funeral, while the others sat and cried, Doris had gone up to get her last look at the body. She bent over the casket to kiss him. Tears from her own eyes landed on the boy's face. She reached over to wipe the wetness from his cheek when she noticed purple spots on the nose. She wiped away the tears and the undertaker's white powder came off his face. It was purple underneath. She called John over and he verified it. They began to look more closely and noticed bruises on the knuckles.

"We told the doctor at the Coroner's Office," John finishes. "But he said not to worry about it. It was natural, he said."

"Anything else?"

"Just what Mr. de Silva told me," the mother says.

"Who's that?"

"Andy de Silva. . . . Don't you know him?"

"You mean . . . *the* Andy de Silva? The man who makes commercials? Chile Charlie?"

"Yeah, that's Mr. de Silva."

I know of him. He is a small-time politico in East LA. A bit actor in grade B movies who owns a bar on The Boulevard. And he considers himself something of a spokesman for the Chicano. He served on Mayor Yorty's Chicano Community Board as a rubber-stamp nigger for the establishment. He and his cronies, the small businessmen and a few hack judges, could always be counted upon to endorse whatever program the Anglo laid out for the Cockroaches. He had been quoted in all the papers during our uprising against the Church. He had agreed with the Cardinal that we were all outside agitators who should be driven out on a rail.

"What did Andy say to you?" I ask.

"Well, I don't even know him. I used to go to his meetings for the old people. Anyway, he called me the next day after Robert died. He said, 'I heard about your boy and I want to help.' That's how he started out. I was so happy to get someone to help I told him to do whatever he could. He said he was very angry and he would investigate the case. He said he would have a talk with the lieutenant and even with the captain if necessary."

"What happened?"

"He called me back the next day. He said he had checked it all out and that the captain had showed him everything, the files and even the cell. He said not to make any trouble. That Robert had hung himself."

"Did he say how he knew about it?"

"Yeah. I asked him that, too," John says.

"He said his nephew was the guy in the cell with Robert."

"His nephew?"

"Yeah, Mickey de Silva . . . He's just a kid like Robert. He was in there for something. . . . Anyway, Andy said his nephew told him that Robert killed himself."

"But we don't believe it," Lupe says fiercely.

"Can you help us, Señor Brown?"

I pick up the phone and dial the office of Thomas Noguchi, the Coroner for the City and County of Los Angeles.

"This is Buffalo Z. Brown. I represent the family of Robert Fernandez," I tell Noguchi. "And we want to talk with you about the autopsy. . . . Your doctor listed it as suicide. However, we are convinced that the boy was murdered. We have information unavailable to the pathologist conducting the autopsy. I plan to be in your office this afternoon. I'm going to bring as many people as I can and hold a press conference right outside your door."

"Mr. Brown. Please, calm yourself. I can't interfere with the findings of my staff."

"I'll be there around one."

I hang up and tell the family to go home, call all their friends and relatives and have them meet me in the basement of the Hall of Justice. They thank me and leave. I then call the press and announce the demonstration and press conference for that afternoon. I know my man. And since Noguchi can read the newspapers, my man knows me. The afternoon will be pure ham.

Noguchi has been in the news quite a bit. He was charged with misconduct in office by members of his own staff. They accused him of erratic behavior and incompetence. They said he took pills, that he was strung out, and hinted that perhaps he was a bit nuts. After the assassination of Robert Kennedy he allegedly said he was glad Kennedy was killed in his jurisdiction. He was a publicity hound, they contended. He was removed from his position of County Coroner. He hired a smart lawyer and challenged it. The Civil Service hearings were televised. The white liberals and his own Japanese friends came to his defense. He was completely exonerated. At least he got his job back.

A month prior to the death of Fernandez, both the new City Chief of Police, Edward Davis and the Sheriff of LA County, Peter Pittches, announced they would no longer request Coroner's Inquests. The publicity served no useful purpose, the lawmen stated. Since the only time the Coroner held an inquest was when a law enforcement officer was involved in the death of a minority person, they contended that the inquest merely served to inflame the community. Noguchi made no comment at the time of this statement, although his two main clients were emasculating his office.

When we arrive at the Hall of Justice, the press is waiting. The corridor is lined with Fernandez' friends and relatives. The television cameras turn on their hot lights as I walk in with my red, white and green briefcase, the immediate family at my side.

"Are you making any accusations, Mr. Brown?" a CBS man asks.

"Not now, gentlemen. I plan to have a conference with Dr. Noguchi first. Then I'll speak to you."

I hurried into the Coroner's Office. The people shout "Viva Brown!" as I close the door. The blonde secretary tells me Noguchi is waiting for me. She opens the door to his office and ushers me in.

"Ah, Mr. Brown, I am so happy to make your acquaintance."

He is a skinny Jap with bug eyes. He wears a yellow sport coat and a red tie and sits at a huge mahogany desk with a green dragon paperweight. The office has black leather couches and soft chairs, a thick shag rug and inscrutable art work. It seems a nice quiet place. He points me to a fine chair.

"Now, Mr. Brown, I'd like you to read this." He hands me a typed sheet of white paper.

I smile and read the paper:

The Coroner's Office announced today that it will hold a second autopsy and an inquest into the death of Robert Fernandez at the request of the family through their attorney, Mr. Buffalo Z. Brown. It will be the first time in the history of the office that an inquest is being held at the request of the family.

Thomas T. Noguchi
County Coroner

I looked into the beady eyes of Mr. Moto. He is everything his men say. "I've been wanting to meet you, sir," I say.

"And I've heard about you, Mr. Brown. You get a lot of coverage in your work."

"I guess the press is interested in my cases."

"Would you be agreeable to holding a joint press conference?"

"Sir, I would be honored. . . . But one thing . . . If we have another autopsy, the body will have to be, uh. . . ." I am coy.

"Exhumed . . . We will take care of that, don't you worry."

"And who will perform the autopsy?"

"I assume the family will want their own pathologist."

I look down at his spit-shined loafers. I shake my head and sigh. "I just don't know. . . . The family is extremely poor."

"I understand, sir. I offer my staff, sir."

"Dr. Noguchi . . . would it be too much to ask you, *personally*, to examine the boy's body? I know you are very busy. . . ." It is my trump card.

"I would be honored. But to avoid any . . . problems, why don't I call up the Board of Pathologists for the county. I will request a panel. Yes, a panel of seven expert pathologists. It will be as careful and as detailed an autopsy as we had for Senator Kennedy. And it won't cost the family anything . . . I have that power."

I stand up and, walking over to him, I shake his hand.

"Dr. Noguchi, I'll be glad to let you do all the talking to the press."

"Oh no, Mr. Brown, it is *your* press conference."

He calls his secretary and tells her to bring in the boys. When they arrive with their pads and cameras, he greets them all by their first names. He is better than Cecil B. DeMille. His secretary has passed out copies of his statement. He tells them all where to sit and knows how many lumps of sugar they want in their coffee. Then he introduces me to them and stands by while I speak.

"Gentlemen, I'll make it short. . . . We have reason to believe that Robert Fernandez died at the hands of another. The autopsy was inconclusive and we have since found some new evidence that was not available to Dr. Noguchi's staff. . . . The Doctor has graciously consented to exhume the body and hold a full inquest before a jury. On behalf of the family and those of us in East LA who are interested in justice, I would like to thank Dr. Noguchi."

After the press leaves, I reassure the family and all the arrangements are nailed down.

The following Tuesday, I again enter the Hall of Justice. Above me are Sirhan Sirhan, the mysterious Arab who shot Kennedy, and Charles Manson, the acid fascist. Both await their doom. I am told to go straight down the corridor, turn right and the first door to my left is where I'll find Dr. Noguchi and his seven expert pathologists. The light is dim, the hard floors waxed. Another government building with gray walls, the smell of alcohol in night air.

I open a swinging yellow door and immediately find myself inside a large dark room full of hospital carts. Naked bodies are stretched out on them. Bodies of red and purple meat; bodies of men with white skin gone yellow; bodies of black men with blood over torn faces. This one has an arm missing. The stub is tied off with plastic string. The red-headed woman with full breasts? Someone has ripped the right ear from her head. The genitals of that spade are packed with towels. Look at it! Listen! The blood is still gurgling. There, an old wino, his legs crushed, mangled, gone to mere meat. And there, young boys die too. And there, a once-beautiful chick, look at her. How many boys tried to get between those legs, now dangling pools of red-black blood?

Don't turn away from it, goddamnit! Don't be afraid of bare-ass naked death. Hold your head up, open your eyes, don't be embarrassed, boy! I walk forward, I hold my breath. My head is buzzing, my neck is taut, my hands are wet and I cannot look away from the dead cunts, the frizzled balls, the lumps of tit, the fat asses of white meat.

I have turned the wrong way. Backtracking, I find the room with Dr. Noguchi and the experts.

The doctors wear white smocks. They smoke pipes. Relaxed men at their trade. They smile and shake my hand. In front of us, the casket is on a cart with small wheels. On a clean table we have scales and bottles of clear liquid. There are razor-sharp tools, tweezers, clips, scissors, hacksaws, needles and plenty of yellow gloves. The white fluorescent light shines down upon us. It reminds me of the title of my first book: *My Cart for My Casket.*

"Shall we begin, gentlemen?" Dr. Noguchi asks the experts.

The orderly, a giant sporting an immense mustache, takes a card and a plastic seal from the casket. He booms it out to a gray-haired fag with sweet eyes who sits in a corner and records on a shorthand machine.

"We shall now open the casket, Coroner's Number 19444889, Robert Fernandez, deceased."

We all gather close to get the first look.

The body is intact, dressed in fine linen. Clearly, Robert was a bull of a man. He had big arms and legs and a thick neck now gone purple. Two experts lift the body and roll it on the operating table. It holds a rosary in the hands. The orderly removes the rosary, the black suit, the white shirt, the underwear and brown shoes. The chest has been sewn together. Now the orderly unstitches it. Snip, snip, snip. Holding open the rib cage, he carefully pulls out plastic packages from inside the chest cavity. I hold my breath.

"Intestines." The meat is weighed out.

"Heart . . . Liver . . ."

A Chinese expert is making notations of everything. So is the fruity stenographer.

There is no blood, no gory scene. All is cold and dry. Sand and sawdust spill to the table.

"Is this your first autopsy?" a doctor with a Sherlock Holmes pipe asks me. I nod.

"You're doing pretty good."

"He'll get used to it," another one says brightly.

When the organs are all weighed out, Dr. Noguchi says, "Now, gentlemen, where do you want to begin?"

Sherlock Holmes asks, "Are we looking for anything special?"

"Treat this as an ordinary autopsy, Dr. Rubenstein. Just the routine," says Noguchi.

"Circumstances of death?"

"Well, uh . . . Mr. Brown?"

"He was found with something around his neck."

"Photographs at the scene?"

"No, sir," a tall man from the Sheriff's Department says.

"Self-strangulation? . . . or . . ." Rubenstein lets it hang.

"That's the *issue*," I say. "The body was found in a jail cell. The Sheriff claims it was suicide. . . . We, however, believe otherwise."

"I see."

"We have reason to believe that the boy was murdered," I say.

"Nonsense," the man from the Sheriff's Department says.

"Now, gentlemen, please. . . ." Noguchi oils in.

Dr. Rubenstein is obviously the big cheese. He comes up to me and says, "You think there was a struggle before death?"

"It's very possible."

He ponders this and then announces: "Gentlemen, we will have to dissect wherever hematoma appears."

"What's that?" I ask.

"Bruises."

I look at the body closely. I noticed purple spots on the face, the arms, the hands, the chest, the neck and the legs. Everywhere. I point to the face. "Could *that* be a bruise?"

"There's no way to tell without microscopic observation," Rubenstein answers.

"You can't tell from the *color*?"

"No. . . . The body is going through decomposition and discoloration . . . purple spots . . . is normal. You find it on all dead bodies."

"Are you saying we have to cut out all those spots?"

"That's the only way to satisfy your . . . yes."

"Well, Mr. Brown?" says Noguchi. "Where do you want us to begin?"

I look around at the men in the room. Seven experts, Dr. Noguchi and a Chinese doctor from his staff, the orderly and the man from the Sheriff's . . . they want *me*, a Chicano lawyer, to tell them where to begin. They want *me* to direct them. It is too fantastic to take seriously.

"How about this? Can you look there?" I point to the left cheek.

Without a word, the Chinese doctor picks up a scalpel and slices off an inch of meat. . . . He picks it up with the tweezers and plunks it into a jar of clear liquid.

"And now, Mr. Brown?" says Noguchi.

I cannot believe what is happening. I lean over the body and look at the ears. Can they get a notch from the left one?

Slit-slit-slice blut! . . . into a jar.

"Uh, Dr. Rubenstein? . . . Are you *sure* there's no other way?"

He nods slowly. "Usually, we only try a couple of places . . . It depends on the family." He hesitates, then says, "Is the case that important?"

"Would you please take a sample from the knuckles . . . here?"

No trouble at all, my man. Siss-sizz-sem . . . blut, into another jar.

The orderly is precisely labeling each jar. Dr. Noguchi is walking around like a Hollywood mogul. He is smiling. Everything is going without a hitch. He touches my shoulder.

"Just tell us what you want, Mr. Brown. . . . We're at your service."

"Would you please try the legs? . . . Those big splotches on the left."

"How about the chin?"

"Here, on the left side of the face."

"What's this on the neck?"

"Try this little spot here."

"We're this far into it. . . . Get a piece from the stomach there."

Cut here. Slice there. Here. There. Cut, cut, cut! Slice, slice, slice! And into a jar. Soon we have a whole row of jars with little pieces of meat.

Hrumph! Yes, men? Now we'll open up the head. See where it's stitched? They opened it at the first autopsy. See the sand fall out from the brain area? Yes, keeps the body together for a funeral. No blood in here, boy. Just sand. We don't want a mess. See that little package? That, my lad, is the brain. I mean, it was the brain. Well, actually, it *still* is the brain . . . it just isn't working right now.

Yes, yes! Now we pull back the head. Scalp-um this lad here. Whoops, the hair, the full head of hair, now it lays back, folded back like a Halloween mask so we can look *into* the head . . . inside, where the stuffings for the . . . Jesus H. Christ, look at those little purple blotches. . . . You can tell a lot from that, but you got to cut it out . . . Then cut the fucking thing out, you motherfucker! This ain't Robert no more. It's just a . . . no, not a body . . . body is a whole . . . this is a joke . . . Cut that piece there, doctor. *Please!*

Uh oh! Now we get really serious. If he died of strangulation . . . We'll have to pull out the . . . uh, neck bone.

Go right ahead, *sir!* Pull out that goddamn gizzard.

Uh, we have to . . . take the face off first.

Well, Jesus Christ, go ahead!

Slit. One slice. Slit. Up goes the chin. Lift it right up over the face . . . the face? The face goes up over the head. The head? The head is the face. Huh? *There is no face!*

What do you mean?

The face is hanging down the back of the head. The face is a mask. The mouth is where the brain . . . The nose is at the back of the neck. The hair is the ears. The brown nose is hanging where the neck. . . . Get your goddamn hand out of there.

My hand?

That is the doctor's hand. It is inside the fucking face.

I mean the head.

His hand is inside. It is pulling at something. What did he find in there? What *is* it?

He's trying to pull out the . . . if we put it under a microscope, we'll be able to make some strong findings. It's up to you. . . .

Slice, slice, slice . . . No dice.

"Give me the saw, please."

Saw, saw, saw, saw, saw . . . No luck.

"Give me the chisel and hammer, please."

The goddamn face is gone; the head is wide open; no mouth, nose, eyes. They are hanging down the back of the neck. God! With hammer and chisel in hand, the Chinese doctor goes to town. Chomp, chomp, chomp . . . Hack, hack, chuck, chuck, chud, chomp!

Ah! Got it!

Out it comes. Long, gizzard-looking. Twelve inches of red muscle and nerve dripping sawdust. Yes, we'll dissect this old buzzard, too.

How about those ribs? You want some bar-b-que ribs, mister?

Sure, *ese*. Cut those fucking ribs up. Chomp 'em up right now!

"How about the arms? Is there any question of needle marks?"

Yes, they'll claim he was geezing. Cut that arm there. Put it under your machine and tell me later what I want to hear. Tell me they were *old* tracks, you sonofabitch . . . And try the other one.

Why not? The body is no more.

Should we try the dick?

What for? What can you find in a peter?

Maybe he was raped, for Christ's sake. Or maybe he raped someone. How should I know? I just work here.

I see the tattoo on his right arm . . . God Almighty! A red heart with blue arrows of love and the word "Mother." And I see the little black cross between the thumb and the trigger finger. A regular *vato loco*. A real *pachuco, ese*.

And when it is done, there is no more Robert. Oh, sure, they put the head back in place. They sew it up as best they can. But there is no part of the body that I have not ordered chopped. I, who am so good and deserving of love. Yes, me, the big *chingón*! I, Mr. Buffalo Z. Brown. Me, I ordered those white men to cut up the brown body of that Chicano boy, just another expendable Cockroach.

Forgive me, Robert, for the sake of the living brown. Forgive me and forgive me and forgive me. I am no worse off than you. For the rest of my born days, I will suffer the knowledge of your death and your second death and your ashes to my ashes, your dust to my dust . . . Goodbye, *ese*. Viva la Raza! [1973]

RANDY SHILTS

The Mayor of Castro Street

A WARM BREEZE rustled through the Black Cat bar in San Francisco's North Beach neighborhood on a soft October night in 1951. Hazel, the piano player, had just announced last call, and Jose, one of the waiters, in his usual sequined gown and red high heels, stepped forward to deliver his nightly oration.

"Remember, there's nothing wrong with being gay. The crime is getting caught," he shouted. It was a criminal act in those days to serve liquor to homosexuals and the proprietors of the Black Cat had been caught doing it more than once. "Let's all stand up and form a circle," Jose said. The crowd slowly went into a formation. "For one moment, I want you to stand and be proud of who you are."

With an evangelist's fervor, Jose led the chorus:

> God save us nelly queens,
> God save us nelly queens,
> God save us queens.

Moments later, the sergeant at the old Hall of Justice across the street motioned to the prisoners of the gay tier. "There's your leader," he laughed, pointing out the window to Jose.

Jose had moved his sing-along to the Black Cat's front door, where they could look up to their friends who had been unfortunate enough to be caught in that week's sweep of gays. The small figures on the sidewalk stood singing up to those behind bars: "God save us queens."

Decades later, grown men would break into tears when they remembered those nights in the 1950s, singing to their friends in jail.

Generations before people like Harvey Milk came west to build a political movement that would one day capture the nation's attention, a homosexual underground thrived in San Francisco. The early settlers dubbed the cosmopolitan city "Baghdad by the Bay," but ministers throughout the West quickly gave the town another nickname, "Sodom by the Sea."

Necessity, if nothing else, forced a see-no-evil attitude toward homosexuality. Between 1848 and 1858, San Francisco leaped from being a backwater hamlet of 1,000 residents to being a major metropolis of 50,000—and virtually all the gold-seeking newcomers were men. The late twentieth-century homophile vogue of denoting sexual inclinations by colored handkerchiefs dates back to those forty-niner days when raucous miners used hankies to separate male and female roles for their all-male square dances.

In the 1930s, gays had to run the gauntlet with "Lily Law," as police were called by homosexuals then. Police knew that one Market Street theater was a popular pit stop for wandering gay men, so authorities routinely assigned seats there to the most comely police cadets. Once a gay man sidled into the next seat, the cadet would wriggle his legs suggestively. After the preliminaries of fellatio, the plainclothesman would suggest that the pair meet outside for more fun. In the lobby of the theater, vice squaders would be waiting to arrest the guilty party.

World War II marked the first conflict in which the armed services tried to systematically identify and then exclude homosexuals. In the process of examining the nearly 36 million men eligible for service, thousands were found to be homosexual and classified as such by the draft boards. Purge after purge of gays in various branches condemned them to the "blue discharge," named for the blue paper on which homosexual discharges were written. The discharge was stamped with a large *H* and guaranteed the bearer the status of persona non grata, especially during the patriotic war years. The action created an entire class of social outcasts who were public homosexuals. Most of the men discharged from the Pacific theater were processed out in San Francisco, and that's where they stayed.

It was in these turbulent postwar years that the modern gay bar started. Unlike the clandestine gay speakeasies and private parties of the past, these were public institutions, the first places where homosexuals could publicly assemble. The patrons had less to lose than their predecessors—many had already been publicly identified as gays by the military. Once plucked from the isolation of generations past, it was only a matter of time before this new San Francisco minority would begin its slow and irresistible movement toward civil rights.

The Invasion: There Goes the Neighborhood

Cleve Jones was just one of the thousands who knew he was different long before the guys at Scottsdale High School in Phoenix realized he was.

Once they did, Jones had to learn how to bend over at just the right moment to avoid the full force of the punch that ground him into the locker room's tiled walls. When simple brutality grew tedious, Jones's classmates took to dunking his head in the toilet. In another generation, Jones might have resigned himself to be another hapless miscreant doomed to liaisons in the Phoenix Greyhound depot.

But Jones had read articles about how homosexuals were influencing elections in San Francisco in the 1970s, coalescing into gay neighborhoods and even holding parades. From the age of fifteen on, he decided he had only one goal—to move to San Francisco and march in a Gay Freedom Day parade. Jones hitchhiked to San Francisco in 1973, just weeks after his eighteenth birthday. That first night he ended up wandering the streets of the seedy Tenderloin District and was lucky enough to meet up with Joey, a seventeen-year-old hustler from Mexico who introduced him to other gay hippies in the Haight Ashbury. Every night, Jones, Joey, and the rest of the gang rendezvoused at Bob's Burgers in the heavily gay area of Polk Street. Those hustlers who had had a generous trick that day treated the less fortunate to cheeseburgers and fries.

Soon Jones and his young friends started drifting over the hill to the rundown street where there were bars full of young gay and hippie men like themselves. Those were exhilarating times to be gay on Castro Street. The materialism of the early homosexual gentry was passé. These new gays were not going to devote their lives to acquiring tasteful end tables and spotlighted impressionist paintings. Orange crates and Jimi Hendrix posters did just fine. No expensive colognes, just patchouli oil. The carefully tailored suits of the gay upper crust or the flamboyant silk scarves and sheer shirts of the glitterati were nowhere to be seen. Instead came a new homosexual fashion born out of the J.C. Funky secondhand clothing store, which sold army fatigues and used blue jeans for $2 a pair, flannel shirts for $1.50, and hooded sweatshirts for $1.75. The new gay fashion matched a new gay attitude. The clothing spoke of strength and working-class machismo, not the gentle bourgeois effeteness of generations past. Most of the gays made a living as bicycle messenger boys or part-time housecleaners, but the main focus of their lives centered on the streets.

When Jones was hanging out on a street corner one day, he stumbled into a camera store, where he met a long-hair merchant who had a fondness for helping the young gay refugees who were pouring into the neighborhood. Maybe the aging hippie foresaw that the lively young men might be useful in campaigns; maybe he just liked lively young men. It didn't matter then, because in 1973, Harvey Milk was just a small camera shop owner and Cleve Jones was just another eighteen-year-old drifter far more interested in manning the dance floors than the barricades. But things were changing on

Castro Street, and it was all because boys like Cleve Jones got beat up and called sissy in high school and because a man named Harvey Milk was sensing how an unusual blending of lifestyle and politics might rewrite the script by which gays had acted out their lives for so long.

The son of two Scottish immigrants, Allan Baird was born just seven blocks from the central Castro shopping strip in 1932. That's the farthest from Castro Street he had ever lived. During World War II he had hawked newspapers on the corner of Castro and Eighteenth streets, his wife, Helen, had lived in the same house on Collingwood Street for 40 years—even after she was married. The gentle slopes surrounding the street seemed to cut the neighborhood off from the rest of San Francisco, lending the cozy, working-class area all the trappings of an insular small town.

The city maps had always referred to the area as Eureka Valley, but to most of the people who lived there it was just Most Holy Redeemer parish. The Catholic Church dominated every facet of neighborhood life, from the schooling of children to the family picnics and weekly bingo games. Wives stayed at home to take care of their large broods; families stayed in the area generation after generation. But now all that was changing.

First came the whispers. Maybe it was Mrs. O'Malley talking to Mrs. O'Shea over the cod at the open-air fish market. Or it could have been Mrs. Maloney fretting to Mrs. Asmussen, who was a good friend even though she was a Lutheran. The word went out: a former police officer, not a good Castro boy, but—the housewife flicked her wrist, raised her eyebrows, and paused meaningfully—a *funny* one, bought the Gem bar, right here in Most Holy Redeemer parish.

Baird had never seen anything like the panic that followed the establishment of the first gay bar on Castro Street in the late 1960s. The stolid Irish families sold their Victorians at dirt-cheap prices, fearing greater loss if they waited. They had seen what the hippies had done to the Haight Ashbury neighborhood—now the gays were doing it to their neighborhood.

Allan Baird figured he had better learn how to get along with the invaders—that's what the old-timers called them. He heard that Harvey Milk was the man to talk to if you wanted to work with the gays. Milk and his lover, Scott Smith, had come to the Castro from New York in 1972 and set up a small camera shop in the neighborhood just two blocks from Baird's house. Castro Camera had become a gathering spot for all kinds of waifs, drifters, and new settlers in the gay community even before Milk ever decided to make his eleventh-hour run for supervisor in 1973.

The other guys at the Teamsters might think I'm crazy, Baird thought as he headed toward Castro Camera, but it's worth a try.

"I'm Allan Baird, a representative of the Teamsters and director of the Coors beer boycott in California," he began formally upon walking into the store.

"I know who you are," Milk said, smiling.

Baird realized he didn't need to be formal. "I know you're the spokesperson for the gay community here, and I think I can use your help."

The beer truck drivers' local was striking the six major beer distributors, which refused to sign the proposed union contract. So far Baird had enlisted a group representing more than 400 Arab grocers and the federation of Chinese grocers who would boycott scab drivers. If gay bars chipped in, they could win it.

"I'll do what I can," said Milk, pausing to add one condition. "You've got to promise me one thing. You've got to help bring gays into the Teamsters' union. We buy a lot of the beer that your union delivers. It's only fair that we get a share of the jobs."

Baird liked Milk's straightforwardness. After years of union politics, the beefy teamster thought he could spot a bullshitter. Harvey Milk was no bullshitter. Baird grew more impressed when he later learned that Milk was in the middle of his first campaign for a seat on the county board of supervisors. Any other politician would have asked for an endorsement, Baird thought. Milk just asked for jobs.

The project gave Milk a chance to test out his theories about achieving gay power through economic clout. He enlisted his gay friend, Bob Ross, publisher of the *Bay Area Reporter*, to help connect him to bar owners and started buttonholing support for the boycott. Baird was amazed at Milk's ability to get attention for the effort.

The boycott worked. Gays provided the coup de grace to the already strained distributors. Five of the six beer firms signed the pact. Only Coors refused to settle. Harvey used the refusal as a basis to launch a more highly publicized boycott of Coors beer in Bay Area gay bars. And Baird kept his end of the bargain. Gays started driving for Falstaff, Lucky Lager, Budweiser, and soon all the distributors, except, of course, Coors.

"Some people call me the unofficial mayor of Castro Street," Milk would always say. Harvey Milk first tried the title out during his unsuccessful run for supervisor. Once he threw himself into the Coors beer boycott and a host of other local issues, he always brought the title up to any reporter who happened by Castro Camera to see what was going on. Nobody was ever sure who the "some people" who thought up the nickname were, but the appellation made good copy, so nobody groused.

When Milk was in his shop, Castro Camera became less a business establishment than a vest-pocket city hall from which he held court. An old overstuffed maroon couch was stretched in front of the store's large bay window, next to the old barber chair where the Kid, Milk and Smith's dog, sat much of the day, lapping at the hand of any customer who had a penchant for mutts. Milk could often be found on his frumpy couch when new Castro residents came to inquire where to look for apartments or jobs, or what to do with a lover who had an alcohol problem. Local merchants discovered that Milk was the man to see if police took too long to answer a suspected burglary or if the sewer overflowed. He always knew whom to call at City Hall or the reporter to buzz with the proper story of moral indignation if nothing was done. Every night Milk took the addresses from every check cashed at the store that day and put them on his political mailing list.

Milk loved circuses and holidays, especially Christmas, and the store's picture window sprang to life every December with ornate holiday displays. On Christmas Eve, the window would be packed with unopened presents under a fully decorated tree; the next morning, bows, cards, ribbons, torn wrapping paper, and empty boxes would be scattered haphazardly about the window, to be joined by bottles of Alka-Seltzer and Anacin a week later, on New Year's Day.

More than one young boyish-looking patron would be surprised when they came to pick up their photos and Milk would giggle, "I see you have a new boyfriend." Smith had worked out a system of marking the envelopes of incoming film from men who were particularly noteworthy, while Milk thumbed through the daily delivery of processed photos to check for names of men he had always wanted to see in less formal surroundings. Neither Milk nor Smith put much faith in fidelity. Promiscuity was practically an article of faith among the new gays of Castro Street, stemming both from the free love hippie days and the adoption of aggressive male images. As Milk explained it, the homosexual's intensified sexuality was one of the benefits of not being able to hold hands or express affection publicly. "What happens," he said, "is you get inside that room and the door closes. The intensity of the relationship increases to make up for all the times you had to hide it."

The old Irish businesses fought hard against the rapid shift in the Castro area. To counter the resistance of the established businessmen, Milk assembled the younger gay merchants in the back room of a pizza parlor and resurrected the Castro Village Association (CVA), a short-lived merchants group that had been organized by hippies a few years before. Milk was dutifully elected president of the CVA if for no other reason than that nobody else wanted the job.

As president of the CVA, Milk took to promoting his theories about achieving gay power through economic clout. He decided his organization needed the respectability of having established institutions as members. The street's two banks were ideal prospects—one was a branch of the gigantic Bank of America, the other a branch of the Irish, locally owned Hibernia Bank. Executives at both branches rejected Milk's suggestion that they join. Most of the CVA members avoided Bank of America because of its bad-guy image as the world's largest bank, so Hibernia held most of the area's gay money. Milk carefully wrote a straightforward letter to the Hibernia branch: "We strongly urge you to send the $20 to join our group." Instead of signing the letter with the CVA members' names, Milk had each business affix its bank deposit stamp to the bottom of the request.

Rarely have the words "for deposit only" produced such quick results. Hibernia's $20 dues came in the return mail. Milk took his newly revised list of CVA members to the Bank of America branch manager, mentioning he would hate to have it get around that the bank was anti-gay. The branch signed on.

By the end of 1974 politicians began coming to CVA meetings. Membership swelled. The political possibilities titillated Milk, who rarely looked further than the next election. He pushed his friends into being voter registrars. Customers in Castro Camera were rarely greeted with a pitch to buy film; instead, the first question was, "Are you registered to vote?" Milk considered his most important accomplishment of 1974 to be the registration of 2,350 new voters for the governor's race. Surrendering the right to vote was, to Milk, surrendering the chance to make a difference in the world.

Early in 1975 Milk confided to Allan Baird that he was going to run for supervisor again. The problems with the police had peaked several months before, on Labor Day weekend, when the cops rounded up a group of gays Milk later dubbed the "Castro 14" and hauled them off to jail for "obstructing a sidewalk." The increasing violence between police and Castro citizens and the unresponsiveness of City Hall to the needs of the neighborhood were major problems that needed to be solved, Milk told Baird.

His first race for supervisor in 1973 had been a last-minute affair in which his style—ponytail, mustache, and hippie clothes—was noted more than his ideas. Still, he was able to tally 17,000 votes, a solid showing for a man who had moved to San Francisco from New York only a year earlier. Two weeks after his campaign Milk cut off his ponytail and swore two oaths to himself: he would never smoke dope and would never go into a San Francisco bathhouse again. "I decided this was all too important to have it get wrecked because of smoking a joint or being caught in a raid at some bathhouse," he told a reporter.

The Campaigns: Vote Union, Vote Gay

Harvey Milk, at last, was a serious candidate. He was taking on six incumbent supervisors who were all seeking reelection. His strongest tactical allies came from unions. Baird introduced him to labor leaders who were impressed by his no-nonsense, straightforward manner.

"I know the guy's a fruit, but he shoots straight with us. Let's support him," said cigar-chomping union boss George Evankovich. He was not a man to take alliances lightly, so Stan Smith, the new secretary-treasurer of the San Francisco Building & Construction Trades Council, had to take his advice seriously. "That guy has charisma," Evankovich told his labor buddies as he saw Milk campaigning. "A lot of our guys think gays are little leprechauns tiptoeing to florist shops, but Harvey can sit on a steel beam and talk to some ironworker who is a mean son of a bitch and probably beats his wife, but he'll talk to Harvey like they've known each other for years."

The announcement that the giant building and construction trades council joined the laborers' union and beer truck drivers' local in endorsing Harvey Milk had the hard hat hiring halls buzzing. Milk relished the symbolism of gaining the endorsements from the city's three most macho unions—teamsters, firemen, and hard hats. Milk loved seeing the shock on his gay volunteers' faces when groups of tough firemen and teamsters trooped into the shop to fold flyers and stamp envelopes.

The antipathy gay moderates had felt toward Harvey Milk as the Johnny-come-lately of the 1973 election turned into open hostility in 1975, when it looked like he actually had a shot at capturing a supervisorial seat. Members of the staid Alice B. Toklas Memorial Democratic Club thought that Milk had taken a politically suicidal route of bucking the anti-labor tide by chumming up with rednecks like teamsters and hard hats. Once again, the Toklas club and most of the gay leadership shunned Milk's candidacy, backing liberal incumbents.

The gay moderates' extolling of liberal friends' virtues made Milk's blood boil, and he compared the Toklas club to the homosexual groupies who had once idolized Judy Garland. For all their liberal friends, gays still had not received a single city commission appointment or gotten a comprehensive civil rights law. "To hear those who are already working for a particular candidate praise that person, one would think that the gay community has already achieved gay rights," Milk said. "But we haven't. There is no reason why any gay should go to any candidate. Let them come to us. The time of being political groupies has ended. The time to become strong has begun."

But if gay moderates needed to prove the power of liberal friends, they had to point no further than the California legislative session in which the legislators of San Francisco's Democratic machine—mindful of the 1975 mayoral race—produced results of national significance. Assemblyman Willie Brown had pushed for years to strike down the 1872 statute that prescribed felony penalties for "crimes against nature," but any attempt was always voted down by the legislature. Now state senator George Moscone, the majority leader and leading San Francisco mayoral candidate, shepherded the measure through committees, jawboned reluctant moderate Democrats from rural California, and pulled in every outstanding IOU in the Capitol. The bill passed the assembly and the senate, though in the case of the latter only by a tie-breaking vote. The demise of the antisodomy statutes had far-reaching implications for gays' legal status around the country. California had long been a leader in criminal justice law; the fact that the nation's largest state legalized all sex between consenting adults gave the libertarian posture new credibility. The biggest political plum, however, fell in the lap of George Moscone, who clinched virtually all the major gay support, earning a constituency that would remain in his camp for the rest of his life.

On election night in 1975, Milk's diverse throng of supporters gathered at the Island restaurant to drink their non-Coors beer and wait for the results. They cheered as Senator Moscone surged into an early lead in the mayor's race. Moscone ultimately won, though by one of the slimmest margins in San Francisco history, in this the most liberal city in the country. Dianne Feinstein's humiliating defeat—third behind the mercurial conservative supervisor John Barbagelata—showed that the city's new political spectrum had little room for moderates, as it had become polarized between the more extreme left and right.

Milk made an initial strong showing and ended up finishing the race in seventh place, one slot away from victory. He lost the seat only because of his poor returns on the conservative west side of town. He carried the Castro and the Haight districts by landslide proportions and swept aside all contenders in the young, hip "Brown Rice Belt" neighborhoods. The better-heeled liberals of Pacific Heights also backed the maverick in high numbers. The finish startled many political observers, since few believed a gay candidate could really be a serious contender.

Harvey Milk was appointed the nation's first openly gay city commissioner in the early weeks of Mayor Moscone's term. But the post was marked by one of the shortest tenures ever served by a city commissioner. Milk infuriated Moscone and the liberal establishment by deciding to run against their hand-picked candidate for the Castro neighborhood's state assembly race and was booted off his commission.

The assembly race proved both boon and bane to Milk. He tirelessly campaigned, significantly broadened his base of support, and ended up polling an impressive number of votes, nearly winning the election. But nearly wasn't enough. The assembly loss was his third defeat in as many years, and dark, bitter days followed. Harvey's father had died toward the end of the campaign. Milk had long been estranged from his older brother, and his mother had died years before, so his father's death severed the last family tie. Milk's five-year relationship with Scott Smith, who had been the perfect political wife, managing both Milk's business and campaigns, also ended.

Milk's spirits soared in November, however, when San Francisco voters ended citywide, at-large elections of supervisors and enacted district elections, carving up the city into eleven supervisorial districts. One district was centered on Castro Street. At last, the ward politician got his ward and announced his candidacy for the 1977 supervisorial race from the new District Five. His announcement speech would become the standard pitch for the rest of his campaign:

I'll never forget what it was like coming out. . . . I'll never forget the looks on the faces of those who have lost hope, whether it be young gays, or seniors, or blacks looking for that almost impossible to find job, or Latinos trying to explain their problems and aspirations in a tongue that's foreign to them.

No, it's not my election I want, it's yours. It will mean that a green light is lit that says to all who feel lost and disenfranchised that you can now go forward. It means hope, and we—no—you and you and you and, yes, you, you've got to give them hope.

By the time Rick Stokes announced he was one of the seventeen candidates in the board of supervisors race from District Five, story of his electric shock treatment to cure his homosexuality had been neatly packaged into a nationally televised documentary and sealed as part of the San Francisco gay community's heritage, along with comparable stories of bar raids, suicide attempts, and dishonorable discharges.

To most, the confrontation between the two gay candidates fell into easily definable components, as starkly contrasted as black and white. Stokes was the gentleman politician, a moderate Democrat who had built a substantial reputation as a gay rights lawyer, working for the gay cause in some of the highest legal circles in the state, a reasonable, coolheaded, and respectable homosexual. Harvey Milk, by contrast, was the *enragé*, given to shoot-from-the-hip hyperbole, the maverick, forging a populist political niche, representing the scruffy studs on Castro Street, the shirtless ones. Respectable? Hardly. A reputable professional? No. Milk conceded that his business was little more than a front for his political activities.

Born to an impoverished, Oklahoma family of cotton pickers, Stokes spent his first years living in a dirt-floored shack. His parents pursued an upwardly mobile dream and moved to a ranch outside Shawnee, Oklahoma. It was on the ranch, about the time he turned six, that Stokes knew he was different. He spent most of his time playing with the kids on the ranch down the road, especially his best friend. By the time the two boys were teenagers, they had started a passionate affair that lasted ten years, even after his friend got married. Stokes was depressed and jealous when his friend got married, and he confided to his parents the story of his homosexual relationship. So when Stokes was seventeen, his parents knew all about his homosexuality. That was 1951, the year Harvey Milk joined the navy. While Milk was leading a discreet but active gay life in the navy, Stokes struggled to live up to the sexual norm, marrying and having a daughter. While Milk contentedly lived his double life in New York City in the waning years of the 1950s, Stokes was undergoing shock therapy and psychiatric treatment for his "sickness."

The same year Milk was passing out Barry Goldwater leaflets in Manhattan subways, Stokes had found a political cause, too—in Sacramento, where he had fled from his family and founded the area's first gay organization. While Milk was arguing vociferously that America should bullishly win the Viet Nam War, Stokes was organizing gay rights protests in San Francisco.

By 1977, of course, their roles had reversed. Harvey Milk had been through his transition from conservative Republican to hippie dropout and had begun to live an openly gay life in the early 1970s. He was the candidate who talked most convincingly of the terrors perpetrated by a heterosexual society, even though Rick Stokes surely was the candidate who had more intimately experienced them. Milk was the candidate who talked of the importance of coming out to parents and friends, even though Stokes had done it years before the concept had even dawned on Milk. And all the compounded contradictions meant nothing in that election because politics reduces complexities to facile catch phrases and flossy symbols. To most, the choice between Harvey Milk and Rick Stokes did not represent a conflict between two complex men, but between two ways of life, two styles.

On a personal level, the conflict had been building since the first day Harvey Milk was rebuffed by a man named Jim Foster, who considered himself Mr. Gay San Francisco after his gay rights speech at the 1972 Democratic convention and resented Milk moving in on his territory, and since the first time Milk talked publicly of the Alice Toklas club's "Uncle Toms." But broader historical forces were fueling the juggernaut of Milk's campaign. For proof, Milk needed only to step outside his ex officio city hall and look down Castro Street. By the thousands, these men had flocked to the golden gates of the Castro. It had become the nation's chief liberated zone, as if the neighborhood's massive Castro Theatre marquee had announced, GIVE ME YOUR WEAK, YOUR HUDDLED, YOUR OPPRESSED, AND YOUR HORNY LOOKING FOR A LITTLE ACTION.

Machismo was no longer fashionable on Castro Street, it was ubiquitous. The hair was kept closely cropped a la Korean War era. Those who dared grow more than a few inches kept it tightly combed back, Rick Nelson fashion. The dress was decidedly butch, as if God had dropped these men naked and commanded them to wear only straight-leg Levi's, plaid Pendleton shirts, and leather coats over hooded sweatshirts. Everywhere, drugstore cowboys eyed laundromat loggers winking at barfly jocks. No more used jeans, but brand-new straight-leg models, pulled tight at the ass and stretched suggestively around the crotch. The fashion models were derived from the most virile male images of the society—cowboys, construction workers, and military men. Cowboy hats and western boots became common. Engineer boots, keys dangling from the belt, and a shiny hard hat lent the contractor's look. Fatigues, army jackets, and leather bomber jackets also became de rigueur.

The mating rituals were carefully honed as hundreds of young men cruised the strip. Eye contact first, maybe a slight nod, and, if all went well, the right strut over to the intended with an appropriately cool grunt of greeting. Getting that far was three-quarters of the battle, and a few sentences more were all that was necessary to complete arrangements for a tryst. But if the nod came off as prissy, or if the first stare was too longing, if the salutation's tone was not aloof or masculine enough, then you could blow the whole thing—*that* easy. Before long, the posturing became a caricature of the heterosexual ideal, as if this new generation of gays were out to deliver one big "f—— you" to society: tell us we're femmy queers who need wrist splints and lisp lessons and we'll end up looking like a bunch of cowboys, loggers, and MPs. Whaddaya think of that?

Most estimates put the gay population of San Francisco in 1976 at around 130,000—more than one in five citizens. Milk privately estimated that at least 25,000 had settled in the Castro. One of his friends called them the "Jeep People," since they were refugees who came not in tiny boats but in their macho four-wheel-drive Jeeps. The uniformity in dress and style had the Castro denizens jokingly branding each other "Castroids."

Milk's Castro Village Association had grown to include 90 merchants as the neighborhood's business district sprawled from the two-block Castro Street strip to include virtually all the adjacent side streets. Milk estimated that businesses on the Castro strip alone grossed $30 million in 1976, up 30 percent from the year before. The mere rumor that beer magnate Joseph Coors had donated to Anita Bryant's antigay campaign in Dade County,

Florida, resurrected the old Coors boycott, and every gay bar in the city dropped the popular beer. That helped to end Coors's long-held status as California's top-selling beer. Florida orange juice, which Anita Bryant endorsed on television, also became a prime no-no, and every gay bar prominently displayed signs explaining that all OJ came strictly from California groves.

Milk the candidate, however, had plans for the entire city—not just the Castro area. He wanted to reorient the tax structure to bring light industry back to the deserted factories and warehouses near downtown. The city could also use the structures for day-care centers, where senior citizens, who frittered away their last years in lonely Tenderloin apartments, could tend the children of low-income mothers trying to work their way off welfare. The vision fit perfectly with the essentially capitalistic core of Milk's own version of urban Jeffersonian democracy, focused on small business and industries working around decentralized neighborhoods that, like the Castro, could return the small-town flavor to big-city life.

The central element of Milk's campaign appearances was always the last paragraphs of his hope speech. "It was funny," Frank Robinson, his speechwriter and close friend, later reflected. "Harvey had so much hope for the generic you and so much personal fatalism about his own life."

Milk always had a penchant for young waifs with substance abuse problems, so Jack Lira's appearance on the scene surprised few who had known Milk in the early days. Most of Milk's San Francisco associates, however, had known only Scott Smith, who had for years served as the quintessential political wife before he and Milk broke up. According to most accounts, Milk had discovered 25-year-old Jack Lira one night on Castro Street, as he stared absently into the window of Castro Camera. His compact body made the young Latino irresistible to Milk, and the pair made time for sexual trysts whenever they could be fit into Milk's hectic campaign schedule.

Milk quickly nicknamed Lira "Taco Bell"; Milk's friends called him "the mistake." While campaign volunteers worked late into the night leafletting and stuffing envelopes, Lira spent afternoons watching soap operas and evenings drinking with a set of queeny buddies who also gained the disdain of Milk's friends. When they confronted Milk about his questionable choice of lovers, he would sketchily out-line Lira's troubled past. The youngest child of a poor Mexican American family, Lira had little education and no useful skills. Milk insisted he was just trying to help out a troubled kid.

Milk campaigned on manically, even as all the pieces fell his way. He canvassed every precinct twice. The shocker came in the campaign's closing days, when the *San Francisco Chronicle* endorsed him for supervisor from District Five. The endorsement editorial noted Milk's business experience as part of his qualifications, sending his friends into hysterics. For all the things Milk had been charged with over the years, no one had ever accused him of being a good businessman.

On election day Milk dashed madly from precinct to precinct. His nightmare was that he would again lose by the razor-thin margin that had marked his assembly defeat. He relentlessly pushed on his well-organized corps of get-out-the-vote workers to knock on every door. The fears, at last, proved unfounded.

At Castro Camera that night the crowd cheered at the sight of Harvey Milk, the upset winner who had polled the highest tally of any nonincumbent supervisorial candidate in the city, making him the first openly gay elected official of any big city in the United States. Milk had beaten Rick Stokes by a better than two-to-one margin, garnering 30 percent of the vote against sixteen other candidates.

The elections of Harvey Bernard Milk, the Jewish, gay neighborhood politico, and Daniel James White, the Irish cop turned politician, to the board of supervisors were the natural peg to the election follow-ups. The media like quick, easy juxtapositions that can be translated into the brief 90 seconds generally allotted to each television news story. On one level, both men typified the ultimate goal of district elections—to reflect the diverse citizenry of the city. Dan White reflected his working-class, traditional, native San Francisco district, just as Harvey Milk reflected his hip, heavily gay, non-native district. The contrast was too tantalizing for the television producers to pass up. In the weeks following the election, White and Milk made a number of joint appearances on local talk shows. Each warmly praised the other. White even publicly assured Milk that his brochure's comments about "social deviates" referred to junkies, not gays. Milk began privately telling friends that he might be able to work with the conservative White.

"But Harvey, that guy's a pig," one of his friends told him after he had seen a White and Milk TV show.

"As the years pass, the guy can be educated," Milk insisted to his friend, adding huffily, "*Everyone* can be reached. Everyone can be educated and helped. You think some people are hopeless—not me."

It was well past midnight a week after the election when Milk sat down to tape the three messages he simply entitled "In Case." There was a chilling anatomical specificity to it all when Milk's recorded voice was later heard saying, "May the bullets that enter my brain smash through every closet door in the nation." In his tape Milk named those who were acceptable as successors, people who had become friends and allies in past campaigns: Frank Robinson; Bob Ross; Anne Kronenberg, his lesbian friend who managed his successful campaign; and Harry Britt, president of the San Francisco Gay Democratic Club, a group Milk had founded in 1976.

Harry Britt leaned over the pool table, peering at the intransigent six ball that stood between him and the guy across the table, a stud in cowboy boots, plaid shirt, and button-fly Levi's with the bottom button provocatively unhitched. That guy's hot, Britt thought. No doubt about it. Not that Britt tricked around a lot. But there he was at Toad Hall almost every day for the two years between 1975 and 1977, even on Christmas Eve.

Britt had spent all his life being good. He grew up in Port Arthur, Texas, and had been president of the regional Methodist Youth Fellowship (MYF). He liked the MYF because it was the one environment in which men did not expect him to live up to the macho ideal that so intimidated him. Britt was on the debating squad, served in student government, and won the only National Merit scholarship in his part of East Texas the first year they were given out. He went off to Duke University because it looked like all the colleges he had seen in the movies. He was president of his fraternity. He sped through college in a little more than three years, but he couldn't decide on a major. His life didn't seem to fit together.

Then came Fran, the daughter of a Methodist minister. He married Fran—that's what he knew he was supposed to do. He even became a Methodist minister, holding parishes in East Texas, then Chicago. He compounded his acts of goodness by living near Martin Luther King, working in the civil rights movement, and pleading for integration of his Central Park United Methodist Church on Huron Street. He had worked so hard to justify his existence; he had known all that time that he was vile in the eyes of God, always lusting after the handsome young guy across the aisle. By the time he was a 28-year-old preacher in Chicago, he had bloated out to 270 pounds and was smoking four packs of Old Gold Straights a day.

Britt left his wife and moved to San Francisco in 1972—he had become interested in the growth of the human potential movement in California. His life had never had direction; maybe a guru could provide it. He watched Jim Foster address the Democratic convention on TV in 1972. That marked the first time Harry Britt ever saw a human being stand up and say he was gay. Britt knew he was gay, too, but still he wrestled hard against the truth for another two years. In 1974 he answered an ad in the *Berkeley Barb*. "I'm coming out and scared," Bob's classified read. Britt answered the ad, and the pair cautiously sidled into their first gay bars. Britt needed only a few months before he shifted into the intense gay life of the Castro. Finally, he did something he never thought he would do in his life—he made love to a man.

For Harry Britt, being gay in the Castro in 1975 meant buying a sun lamp, losing 100 pounds, joining a gym to pump up his sagging pectorals, and changing from glasses to contact lenses. His Texas twang and lean Castro look made him a hit at the pool tables. Since he had taken a night auditor's job at the Hilton Hotel, he had all day to shoot pool at Toad Hall, walk through the Twin Peaks bar for a draft, and then saunter past the stores, window-shopping both the wares and the salesmen. Just seeing such a panoply of available partners was enough to set a guy's head spinning. Though he didn't come to the Castro for the politics, Britt did his political number, too, walking precincts for Harvey Milk's campaigns.

Harvey's Show: Getting Down to Business

"What do you think of my new theater?" Milk would ask his friends as he guided them up the grand marble staircase of City Hall. Milk left little doubt that his term would be marked more by his unique brand of political theater than by the substantive tasks of the board. He managed to turn his ceremonial swearing-in into a major media event when he and Jack Lira led a procession of 150 supporters from Castro Camera down the fifteen blocks to the wide front steps of City Hall.

The formal inauguration in the elaborately carved, oak-paneled board chambers was marred only when Milk turned to introduce Lira. Dan White had introduced his wife and paid tribute to his grandmother, an Irish immigrant. Milk relished the juxtaposition of introducing his male lover, but Lira had slipped out of the room even before the meeting started, afraid of the cameras and bright lights being trained on him. "It's well known that I'm a gay person. I have a loved one, but he was too nervous to stay here, and he left," said Milk. He had waited so many years for the day of his inauguration, when he could stand as a homosexual to introduce the man he loved, and the moment had fled him.

Lira remained Milk's biggest personal problem throughout his first months in office. Lira had a love-hate relationship with Milk's politics. On one hand he enjoyed the chance to be Milk's First Lady and sometimes pushed for invitations to dinners and social events. But he was ill prepared for the skills such a role demanded, and he would often become drunk and stomp out of the events he attended.

The new supervisor from District Five turned out to be more than the gay legislator, and he used his first months on the board to build his populist image, inveighing against the interests he considered the bane of a healthy San Francisco—downtown corporations and real estate developers. He pushed for a commuter tax so the 300,000-plus corporate employees who went downtown each day from suburbia would pay their share for the city services they used. When the Jarvis-Gann tax revolt started drying up local revenue sources, he joined Moscone in a push for higher business taxes, legislation that business-oriented board president Dianne Feinstein managed to kill.

As the early months in office wore on, Milk gained greater confidence and poise. He reined his once galloping pace of speech to a reasonable canter. The formerly frenzied waving of arms gave way to a calmer, more confident gesture of one arm, index finger extended, which photographed better. He did his homework meticulously. When a friend went to rouse him for a 2 A.M. emergency one morning, he found Milk wide awake in his pajamas, reading the complicated city charter.

Early in his term as supervisor, Milk squared off with Dan White. White's biggest setback, and the one that permanently soured his relationship with Milk, came over a proposed psychiatric treatment center to be housed in an empty convent in his district. Even before White was sworn in, he was eagerly lobbying against the center, echoing neighbors' fears that the center would put "arsonists, rapists, and other criminals" at their doorstep. Before learning much about the issue Milk indicated he would probably vote with White, but as the gay legislator learned more about the center he pondered switching his vote. "They've got to be next to somebody's house," Milk finally decided, and tilted the majority for the center. After the vote, Supervisor Quentin Kopp reportedly heard White mutter, "I see a leopard never changes his spots."

The loss infuriated White, who had made the center a major campaign issue in his district. White's immediate anger fell on Milk's pet project, the gay rights bill. At a committee meeting before Milk's vote on the psychiatric center, White supported the bill, talking at length about his experiences as a paratrooper in Viet Nam. "I found a lot of the things that I had read about that, had been attributed to certain people—blacks, Chinese, gays, whites—just didn't hold up under fire, literally under fire," he said. "I learned right there that the sooner we leave discrimination in any form behind, the better off we'll all be." When the gay rights law came for a vote before the entire board—a week after Milk voted against White on the psychiatric center—White had significantly changed his views.

White was not alone in his fears. Supervisor Feinstein, whose interest in the gay leather scene bordered on obsession, openly wondered if the bill would make landlords rent to S&M cultists. In the end she overcame her trepidations about leather-men tenants and voted for the bill. By 1978 the political stakes were too high for any serious politician with ambitions for higher office to raise gay dander.

Milk still maintained that White could be "educated," as Milk liked to put it. He sometimes contrasted White with Feinstein—the "Wicked Witch of the West," Milk called her—whom he thought politicked from a sense of noblesse oblige. He considered Feinstein intelligent enough to take a more progressive place in city politics, while White's conservatism stemmed from ignorance. Milk worked to curry favor with White. He attended the young supervisor's baby shower. He tried softening White with humor. During one exchange on gays, Milk told White, "Don't knock it unless you've tried it." Dan White was not amused.

"I can't believe it," sputtered an aide to another supervisor as he tossed the morning *Chronicle* across a table in the City Hall lunchroom. "Every time you pick up the paper, there's Harvey doing something new. How in the hell does that guy do it?" Milk had long since learned that the city's newspapers considered gays good copy, and he manipulated every situation he could into a press advantage. Thinly veiled queer joking has always been considered good copy in San Francisco newspapers, and Harvey was always quick to oblige. One gossip writer listed him as the "number-one most ineligible bachelor of San Francisco," while columnist Herb Caen added that Dianne and Harvey were fighting it out to see who got to be City Hall's official Avon lady.

The media coup of the year and the issue that best symbolized Milk's theories on how government should work centered on the subject of dog feces. Survey after survey showed that sidewalk dog droppings were San Franciscans' biggest complaint about city life. Milk, therefore, sponsored a bill requiring dog owners to clean up after their pets, waxing philosophically that "it's symbolic of all the problems of irresponsibility we face in big, depersonalized, alienating urban societies. Whoever can solve the dog shit problem can be elected mayor of San Francisco, even president of the United States." Years later some would claim Milk was a socialist or some other kind of ideologue, but in reality his political philosophy was never much more complicated than the issue of dog shit. Government should solve people's basic problems.

Bienvenido, Castro, Willkommen, Castro. Bienvenue, Castro. In seven languages, the large canvas banner festooned over the intersection of Eighteenth and Castro spoke to the new role the Castro neighborhood now fulfilled in the homosexual collective consciousness. The corner had been dubbed the crossroads of the gay world, and by the summer of 1978 the neighborhood had become an international gay tourist mecca. A new gay chauvinism ran rampant, complete with a lexicon of pejoratives. Heterosexuals became known as "breeders"—"Today's breeders, tomorrow's cows," went one slogan—and the game of spotting heterosexuals on Castro Street replaced the old heterophile game of picking out queers.

The neighborhood represented less a trend than a bona fide sociological phenomenon. An entire Castro lifestyle evolved, fixed squarely on machismo. A gym membership became a prerequisite to the neighborhood's social life. No longer was the area a social experiment in the throes of creation —the lifestyle had solidified. Gays no longer came to the Castro to create a new lifestyle. They came to fit into the existing Castro Street mold. The summer of 1978 seemed the Castro gays' equivalent of the Haight Ashbury hippies' summer of love eleven years earlier. Like the summer of love, the hot sunny days of 1978 marked the end of an epoch as well as the beginning.

The continuing influx of gays from across the country strained housing stock, and once distinct neighborhoods adjacent to the Castro soon became Castroized. The gay immigrants bought heavily—often at extravagant prices— into neighboring black and Latino areas whose low-income minorities could not compete economically. By the end of 1978 gay neighborhoods dominated roughly 20 percent of the city's residential expanses.

No single strip in San Francisco felt the pinch of the inflated real estate values like the two-block core of the Castro District. With characteristic delicacy, Milk posted the old and new rent figures for his shop and apartment above—$350 and $1,200 for his shop alone—on his store window, alongside the name of the offending realtor, and moved to a small cubbyhole on Market Street right off Castro. Milk's friends looked at the move as symbolic of the end of an era on Castro Street and sneered when the space was soon taken up by a bourgeois boutique that sold such utilitarian items as $350 crystal vases.

Virtually all of Milk's aides and friends saw the move from his Castro Street apartment as an opportunity to unload Jack Lira. But Milk had prepared a dozen reasons to keep him. Lira was improving; he might take a job next week; he might go back to school; he seemed to be getting better the last few days; and, of course, the old standby, "He needs me."

It would be another year before Milk's good friend Anne Kronenberg understood Harvey's ill-fated attraction to Lira and other men with dependent and often suicidal personalities. She was studying alcoholism and ran across research about "coalcoholism": the caretaker of the alcoholic is the coalcoholic, a person who, like Milk, is often a nondrinker. The coalcoholics are the people who drive the drunk home from the bar, pay the rent, and offer hope to otherwise dismal lives. By doing this, the coalcoholic fulfills an addiction as dangerous as alcohol—the need to be needed. Milk had all the classic symptoms of the coalcoholic, Kronenberg thought to herself.

One August night, after a long day at City Hall, Milk walked to his new apartment. He fumbled for his keys as he arrived at his flat. The first thing he saw as he opened the door mystified him. A trail of voter registration forms led from the front door, down the hall, into the living room. Milk quizzically followed the trail from the living room to the dining room to the back porch. A huge black velvet curtain was draped from a curtain beam. Lira had pinned a note to it: "You've always loved the circus, Harvey. What do you think of my last act?"

Milk pulled back the curtain and saw Lira's body, cold and discolored, hanging from the beam. A long suicide message scrawled in both Spanish and English rambled about the antigay tide he saw sweeping the country. Other notes ranted vindictively against Milk. "You're a lousy lover, Harvey." Over the next few days Milk found many notes tucked into odd drawers, out-of-the-way nooks, in the seams of his underwear, and between the pages of books and magazines that Lira knew Milk would pick up some day.

Both the police and press treated the death gingerly. Though the suicide made page one the next day, it quickly faded. An avalanche of sympathy notes poured into Milk's office.

In the following months Milk immersed himself in the No on Proposition 6 campaign to defeat the Briggs amendment. Anita Bryant's 1977 landslide victory to repeal a gay rights law in Dade County, Florida, marked the beginning, not the end, of a nationwide backlash against the gay civil rights movement. In California, state senator John Briggs had put his anti-gay initiative to ban homosexuals from teaching in public schools on the ballot for November. Milk formed his own group to fight Prop 6, with Cleve Jones, who had become one of Milk's protegés, as its director. The grass roots politicking at his headquarters created a cadre of activists—many of them brought in by Harry Britt—well trained in Milk's meet-the-people methods. For once, gay factionalism disappeared as the various No on 6 groups united in a common cause.

On election night, all the pollsters who predicted the passage of Prop 6 were proved wrong. The vote wasn't even close. In San Francisco the proposition was losing by a 75-percent-to-25-percent margin; the proposition didn't even pass in District Eight, Dan White's district. It looked like the measure would lose by more than a million votes statewide.

The Final Act: Countdown in City Hall

Three days after the Prop 6 victory, Milk and his new boyfriend, Doug Franks, were sitting in Castro Camera, closing up the shop for the day. Milk took a phone call and within moments was jumping up and down shouting, "That's too terrific to believe. Dan White's resigned. Now I've got my sixth vote—the sixth vote. Now I'll really be able to get things moving on the board."

As Dianne Feinstein had said on inauguration day, "The name of the game is six votes." Milk and the other liberals had lost so many battles to the six-to-five conservative majority that year that White's resignation—

caused, White said, by the financial hardship of the supervisors' puny salaries—seemed a godsend, the final move that would give liberals complete control over City Hall.

Never had Milk's star seemed brighter. His role as chief gay spokesperson during the Prop 6 campaign had thrust him to the forefront of the national gay movement. He also was looking forward to his reelection campaign the next fall, when, for the first time in his political career, he would be a shoo-in. He confided to Allan Baird that he was far less concerned with the problems of winning District Five than with winning the race by such a huge margin that he could replace Feinstein as the board president. He also told Baird that he intended to run for mayor in 1983. He had enlisted the popular assemblyman Willie Brown to be his honorary campaign chairman and lined up most of his major 1977 supervisorial opponents—including Rick Stokes—to serve as Brown's cochairs.

White acted like a new man after he resigned from the board, thought White's colleague, Supervisor John Molinari. The pressures that had forced White's impromptu resignation had, by now, become front-page news: the supervisors' $9,600 annual salary wasn't enough for White to support his wife and four-month-old son. The fried potato stand he operated at the new Pier 39 complex needed his attention or it would fold. White's resolution to quit politics seemed the right thing to do. He was more cheerful and relaxed than he had ever been. That's why the city's political establishment was surprised when, ten days after his sudden resignation, White said he wanted his seat back. (White had been pressured by police and real estate interests not to resign, as they feared they would lose their six-to-five majority.)

The news that George Moscone was actually going to reappoint the former police officer shocked Milk, who quickly set up an appointment with the mayor. Milk reminded Moscone that White had been the swing vote in many of the six-to-five defeats that the mayor's proposals had suffered on the board. Beyond that, White was the only city politician who had stepped forth as an active antigay spokesperson. You are up for reelection next year, Milk goaded Moscone, and reappointing the city's major antigay politico is no way to lock up the gay vote.

The fight over White's reappointment was little more than a political sideshow. Most of the politicking was done behind closed doors. Feinstein, who had taken White under her wing when he was elected supervisor, was the only board member to publicly back Dan White.

Mayor Moscone set Monday, November 27, as the day he would announce whether he would reappoint Dan White or put someone else on the board. With Peoples Temple and Moscone's involvement with Jim Jones (he was a close ally) in the news, the mayor knew that the gay constituency was important. Newspaper stories, meanwhile, started carrying comments from "an unnamed supervisor" vociferously opposing White's reappointment. That this supervisor was Harvey Milk soon became one of the city's worst-kept political secrets.

On Saturday, November 25, a newspaper reported that there were at least 780 dead, maybe more, in Jonestown. The same paper reported that Dan White intended he would be in the board chambers to take his seat whether Moscone appointed him or not. "I'm worried about Dan White," Moscone reportedly confided to his wife. "He's taking this hard. He's acting sort of flaky."

Mary Ann White returned from a trip to Nebraska at about seven o'clock on November 26. She expected Dan to ask her if she had had a good time or a nice flight back, but he said nothing when she walked into the house. He just walked through the hall, plopped himself on the bed, and started watching television. His attitude didn't particularly surprise Mary Ann. The pair had stopped having sex weeks before. White spent the nights in a sleeping bag on the living room couch.

Mary Ann heard the phone ring in the other room, though she couldn't make out what Dan was saying.

"I'm Barbara Taylor from KCBS. I have received information from a source in the mayor's office that you are not getting that job," the caller told White. "I am interested in doing an interview to find out your reaction to that."

"I don't know anything about it," White said and hung up the phone.

White stayed up all night, eating cupcakes, drinking Cokes, and watching the sun work its way over the horizon. He was moping around the house when Mary Ann woke to go to work at the Pier 39 fried potato stand. She dressed the baby and left for the babysitter's at seven-thirty.

White's aide, Denise Apcar, called at nine to tell White that a group of his supporters planned to present Moscone with petitions and letters of support from District Eight voters. Since Mary Ann had the car, White asked if Apcar would come and take him to City Hall. White hung up the phone, showered, shaved, and slipped into his natty three-piece tan suit. He walked downstairs to his basement den and picked up his .38 Smith & Wesson, the Chief's Special model so favored by police officers. He checked the chamber; it was loaded. Stepping into a small closet off the den, he reached to the top shelf and pulled down a box of Remington hollow-point bullets. He methodically pulled each bullet from the styrofoam case in which they were individually packed. He counted out ten, two chambers' full, slipped the gun into his well-worn holster, snapped the holster to his belt, and then carefully tucked the gun under his vest.

Cyr Copertini, George Moscone's appointments secretary, was surprised to see the mayor's black Lincoln limousine parked by the Polk Street entrance of City Hall when she arrived to work at eight-forty. The mayor rarely arrived before her, but then she remembered he had a lot to do that day. He had originally planned a ten o'clock press conference to announce the appointment of a new supervisor, but he asked Cyr to delay the gathering until eleven-thirty. Moscone decided to take care of some phone work before then.

A cadre of Dan White's supporters were waiting in the mayor's office when Cyr arrived. They wanted to present a stack of petitions to the mayor. Cyr offered to take the papers to him, because the mayor told her he did not want to see the delegation. Copertini was not surprised. Moscone was by nature a jovial man who avoided potentially nasty confrontations at all costs. He still had not told Dan White that he would not be reappointed.

Moscone dialed Dianne Feinstein's Pacific Heights home. No, he was not going to reappoint White, he explained, even though the former supervisor insisted he would physically take his seat at that day's board meetings, whether he got it back or not. Moscone returned to writing out by hand his comments for the press conference later that morning. His close ally, Willie Brown, dropped in briefly, and the two made arrangements to do some Christmas shopping that weekend.

A worried Feinstein was sitting in her small City Hall office a half hour after talking to Moscone. As president of the board, the decorum-minded Feinstein felt it was her responsibility to prevent the kind of donnybrook that might arise when two men, both claiming to be the supervisor from District Eight, tried to get into the same chair at that afternoon's board meeting. She decided she would try to dissuade White from forcing his way into the chambers. She told her aides to try to find White and tell him she would like to have a chat before the meeting.

When Denise Apcar picked up White at about ten-fifteen, he told her he wanted to see both Moscone and Milk once he got to City Hall. Apcar noted he was rubbing his hands together and blowing on his fingertips as he talked. "I'm a man. I can take it," he told her. "I just want to talk with them, have them tell me to my face why they won't reappoint me."

Apcar dropped White off at City Hall and left to gas up her car. William Melia, a city engineer with a lab overlooking the supervisors' parking lot, first noticed a nervous young man pacing by his window at about ten-twenty-five. The man walked back and forth, anxiously glancing into the window where Melia was working. The phone rang, and Melia stepped briefly into another room to take the call. As soon as he left the room, he heard the lab window open and the sound of someone jumping to the floor and running out of the lab and into the hall.

"Hey, wait a second," Melia shouted. He knew such an entrance was a sure way to avoid passing through the metal detectors at the public entrances of City Hall.

"I had to get in," White explained. "My aide was supposed to come down and let me in the side door, but she never showed up."

"And you are—"

"I'm Dan White, the city supervisor. Say, I've got to go." With that, White spun on his heel and left.

Mildred Tango, a clerk typist in the mayor's office, saw White hesitating near the main door of the mayor's office as if he didn't want to use that entrance. Inside sat the mayor's police bodyguard. White knew that, since he had once worked the relief shift as the mayor's police bodyguard during the Joseph Alioto administration. White saw Tango unlock a side door to the mayor's office on her rounds to collect the morning mail. She recognized White and let him follow her into the hallway that led to the mayor's suite. White presented himself at Cyr Copertini's desk at about ten-thirty.

"Hello, Cyr. May I see the mayor?"

"He has someone with him, but let me go check."

Moscone grimaced at the news. "Give me a minute to think," the mayor said. "Oh, all right. Tell him I'll see him, but he'll have to wait a minute."

Copertini asked if Moscone wanted someone to sit in on the meeting. Press secretary Mel Wax often served such duty to make sure disgruntled politicos did not later lay claim to specious mayoral promises.

"No, no," Moscone said. "I'll see him alone."

"Why don't you let me bring Mel in," Copertini persisted.

"No, no. I will see him alone."

Copertini told White the mayor would be a few minutes. White seemed nervous.

"Would you like to see a newspaper while you're waiting?" Copertini asked.

He didn't.

"That's all right. There's nothing in it anyway, unless you want to read about Caroline Kennedy having turned 21."

"Twenty-one? Is that right?" White shook his head. "Yeah. That's all so long ago. It's even more amazing when you think that John-John is now eighteen."

Moscone buzzed for White.

"Good girl, Cyr," Dan White said.

Around the same time Dan White walked into George Moscone's office, Harvey Milk was stepping up the marble staircase to his aides' offices. Dick Pabich, a legislative aide, was working on correspondence. Jim Rivaldo, another assistant, was talking to a gay lawyer who, Milk knew, had a fondness for leather during his late-night carousing.

"Well, where are your leathers?" Milk asked.

"Don't worry," Rivaldo joked. "He's got leather underwear on."

White and Moscone hadn't been in the mayor's large ceremonial office for more than five minutes before Copertini heard White's voice raised, shouting at Moscone. The mayor hated scenes and decided to try to mollify the former supervisor by inviting him to a small den off his office, where he kept a wet bar. He lit a cigarette, poured two drinks, and turned to see White brandishing a revolver. White pulled the trigger and fired a bullet into Moscone's arm, near the shoulder, and immediately shot a second slug into the mayor's right pectoral. Moscone sank to the floor as the second bullet tore into his lung. Dan White knelt next to the prostrate body, poised the gun six inches from the right side of Moscone's head, and fired a bullet that ripped through Moscone's earlobe and into his brain. He pulled the trigger again, and another bullet sped from the revolver, through Moscone's ear canal, and into the brain.

White methodically emptied the four spent cartridges and the one live bullet from his Smith & Wesson and crammed them into the right pocket of his tan blazer. He had special bullets for his next task, the hollow-point dumdum bullets that explode on impact, ripping a hole in the victim two to three times the size of the slug itself. White slipped the five bullets into the revolver's chamber, stepped out a side door, and dashed toward the other side of City Hall, where the supervisors' offices were.

The four dull thuds sounded like a car backfiring, Copertini thought, so she looked out her office window but saw nothing. Rudy Nothenberg, Moscone's deputy mayor, had an eleven o'clock appointment with the mayor. He was ready to cancel it when he noted that Moscone's meeting with White was taking longer than expected. He was relieved when he saw White hurriedly leave the office—he would get his chance to talk to the mayor, after all.

Dick Pabich saw White dashing toward the supervisorial offices. What a jerk, Pabich thought, running around here like he's still somebody important.

Peter Nardoza, Feinstein's administrative assistant, saw White rushing into the hallway outside Feinstein's office.

"Dianne would like to talk to you," Nardoza said.

"Well, that will have to wait a couple of moments," White answered sharply. "I have something to do first."

Harvey and one of his assistants, Carl Carlson, were getting ready to go to the bank when White stuck his head into Milk's office.

"Say, Harv, can I see you?"

"Sure."

White took Milk to his old office across the hall. He noticed that his nameplate had already been removed from the door. Once Milk stepped inside, White planted himself between him and the door. He drew his revolver and fired. A sharp streak of pain sped through Milk.

"Oh no," Milk shouted. "N—" He reflexively raised his hand to try to protect himself.

White knew that bullets went through arms, and he fired again, cutting short Milk's cry. The slug tore into Milk's right wrist, ripped into his chest and out again, finally lodging near his left elbow. Another dumdum bullet pounded Milk in the chest. He was falling now, toward the window. As he crumpled to his knees, White took careful aim from across the office. The first three bullets alone would not have killed Milk. White fired a fourth. Milk was still staggering when the fourth bullet sliced into the back of his head and out the other side, spraying blood against the wall. The shots sounded so loud—louder than the shots in Moscone's office—that they startled White. Milk had fallen to the floor. White gripped the revolver's handle and pulled the trigger once more. The bullet left only a dime-size wound on the outside of Milk's skull, but shards from its hollow tip exploded when they struck, tearing and ripping into his brain. Harvey Milk died at approximately ten-fifty-five on the dark gray morning of November 27, 1978, eleven months after he took office, a year and a half short of his fiftieth birthday.

"This is Harvey Milk, speaking on Friday, November 18, 1977. This is to be played only in the event of my death by assassination. I've been thinking about this for some time prior to the election and certainly over the years. I fully realize that a person who stands for what I stand for, an activist, a gay activist, becomes the target or potential target for a person who is insecure, terrified, afraid, or very disturbed with themselves. . . ."

Most of the people in the room had known Milk had made this tape. Now, only three hours after the shootings, they were following Milk's wish that it be played. He knew enough about City Hall politics to understand that sorrow would not keep politicos from immediately maneuvering to grab his seat. He had made the tape to ensure that his post would not fall into the hands of the gay moderates, whom he had so long opposed. He then listed the four people whom he said should be considered as replacements.

"I cannot prevent some people from feeling angry and frustrated and mad," the tape continued, "but I hope they will take that frustration and that madness and instead of demonstrating or anything of that type, I would hope they would take the power and I would hope that 5, 10, 100, 1,000 would rise.

"May the bullets that enter my brain smash through every closet door in the nation. I would like to see every gay doctor come out, every gay lawyer, every gay architect come out, and let the world know."

The crowd started gathering at seven-thirty that evening on the corner of Castro and Market streets, the place that would one day be called Harvey Milk Plaza. Hundreds, then 5,000, and soon 10,000 came with their candles.

The crowd soon stretched the entire distance from City Hall to Castro Street, some 40,000 strong, utterly silent. A carload of punks sped by and shouted "God damn queers"—and nobody bothered to shout anything back as the procession moved toward the grand rotunda. The Civic Center plaza was awash with the still flickering tapers, stretching out around the wide granite stairs of City Hall, while the strong and resonant voice of Joan Baez sang "Swing Low, Sweet Chariot." The march ostensibly memorialized both Moscone and Milk, but few speakers quarreled that the crowd had amassed chiefly to remember the gangly ward politician who had once called himself the mayor of Castro Street.

Like all the shrouded mornings of that week, the Saturday after the assassination promised to be another overcast day, but brilliant sunshine broke through the clouds late in the morning while two dozen of Milk's closest friends gathered at the San Francisco pier where an antique 102-foot schooner, the *Lady Frei*, was berthed. Milk's old lovers, friends, and political cronies arrived. One passed around cigar-size joints while another freely shared whiskey from his hip flask. After a dreary week of death and eulogies, they were ready for a party. A curious shrine greeted the revelers when they went below into the ship's cabin. Neatly arranged on the top of a color television set was a dictionary-size box wrapped in Doonesbury comics and topped by a single long-stemmed crimson rose. Spelled out in rhinestones on the cartoons were the initials R.I.P. Arranged neatly around the package was a box of bubble bath and an array of grape Kool-Aid packs, the drink with which, according to early news reports, The Reverend Jim Jones had mixed cyanide during the Guyana suicide ritual. Jack McKinley, one of Milk's ex-lovers from New York, explained that he had decided to wrap the box in comics since Harvey would never want to be seen publicly in plastic.

The ship glided gently across the Bay, under the Golden Gate Bridge, and into the open sea. Once out to sea, the funny papers were torn off the plastic box while McKinley ripped open the Kool-Aid packs and bubble bath. Under the clear California skies, the ashes, Kool-Aid, and bubble bath fell gently from the schooner, and Harvey was gone, a bubbly patch of lavender on the cold, glittering Pacific Ocean. [1982]

Two days after the assassination, the board of supervisors elected Dianne Feinstein to succeed George Moscone as mayor of San Francisco. Five weeks after Feinstein took office, she named Harry Britt to Harvey Milk's seat.

On May 21, 1979, Dan White was convicted of two counts of voluntary manslaughter. He will be released from prison in January 1984.*

* Editor's note: Dan White was released from prison in 1984.

V

Paving
Paradise

JOHN MCKINNEY

The Boutiquing
of California's Coast

I FIND Richard Henry Dana's memorial overgrown with weeds and overlooked by motorists whizzing by on Highway 1. His little bronze plaque
abuts a cyclone fence separating the gated, guarded, residential community
of Monarch Bay from the highway. If you remember your California history,
you'll recall that one October day in 1835, Richard Henry Dana, a young
sailor on the *Alert*, lowered himself over the two-hundred-foot cliff that now
bears his name to retrieve some cowhides he and his fellows were attempting
to toss down to their ship. Later, Dana described his adventures in an
eloquent passage in *Two Years Before the Mast*, one of the greatest books
ever written about life on the high seas and a California classic.

I wonder why California's earliest and most enduring literary landmark
stands forgotten among broken bottles and burger wrappings. Why has Dana
been marooned so far from his beloved sea and more than two miles north
of his famous Point?

As I stand with Dana's memorial in the shadow of Monarch Bay's walls,
the sun, which I cannot see, drops toward the ocean, which I cannot see,
showering golden light on sandstone cliffs, where I cannot legally walk. I
stare at California Historical Landmark number 169 and review what has
been a simply awful day of walking Orange County's coast, a day so dis-
heartening I'm compelled to rethink my dream of hiking the entire California
coastline.

My day's hike began at Doheny State Beach. Hiking up-coast along
water's edge I soon reach the southern breakwater of Dana Harbor. On the
cliffs overlooking the harbor, the bulldozers are busy, making building pads
out of bluffs. Lantern Bay is the name of the development, consisting of 198
expensive homes, two hotels, and a New England seacoast village shopping
center.

I walk across the acres of hot asphalt comprising the Dana Harbor parking
lot. The sight of the huge plasticky and antiseptic marina takes the wind out
of my sails. A favorite surfing spot of my adolescence has been totally destroyed. Before Dana Cove became Dana Marina, better surfers than I rode

waves as big as twenty-five feet and called the place "Killer Dana." More often though, the waves came in smaller, less radical sets, and we surfers loved Dana Cove, for it had everything a beach should have: white sand, aquamarine water, a lack of truant officers.

The marina builders did not completely overlook Dana, however. Along the concrete promenade I discover a statue of young Richard Henry, bare chested, notebook in hand, his back to the sea. The sculptor has captured him in mid stride, making Dana appear to be struggling to loose himself from his pedestal and flee the marina.

Leaving Dana to his fate I clamber up collapsing sandstone cliffs and past a closed restaurant that is collapsing with the cliffs onto the beach. Atop these cliffs is supposed to be Dana Point. I seem to remember, from childhood, a little wooden observation tower, complete with ten-cent telescopes. The tower has vanished, which may be just as well because if the telescopes were up here today, all they'd view is a wall of residences. Alas, even Dana Point looks smaller with an adult's perspective. Still, it's the largest chunk of rock for miles around and would provide an inspiring coastal panorama if a few houses were pushed off the cliffs.

I find a vacant lot between two expensive homes and squeeze through to the cliff edge. Ah, this is more like it. A superb view! I marvel at the severely deformed light-colored shale and Monterey sandstone beds of the Point, the translucent Capri-like waters swirling below. My mind paints pictures of Dana and his fellows hefting those stiff heavy hides stripped from the backs of tough Mexican cattle, and heaving them over the cliff. I imagine other sailors on the beach, retrieving the plywoodlike hides, balancing them on their heads, and fighting the surf to the waiting longboats, which delivered tall stacks of them to the *Alert* anchored a hundred yards offshore. For an instant history comes alive for me and I smile at how these majestic headlands impressed young Dana. "The only romantic spot in California," he wrote.

A man walking a Doberman interrupts my reverie.

"This is private property," he announces.

"Yes, I know."

"Well . . . you'd better move on."

I briefly contemplate how satisfying it would be to toss his hide over the cliff, but move on peacefully.

Intersecting an eroded surfer trail, I switch back down the bluffs to the far side of Dana Point and back to the sand. A little beach-walking brings me to Salt Creek, or what *used to be* Salt Creek. The creek mouth is now a cement spillway, scrubbed clean of the salt bush that gave it its name; Salt Creek is destined to become a drainage ditch for a new suburb. From Salt Creek Beach to Coast Highway and from Coast Highway a mile inland, the land is being torn and terraced by giant earthmovers. A construction worker tells me scores of half-million-dollar-plus villas and a golf course will line the creek and a luxury hotel will be "terraced" into the coastal bluffs fronting the beach.

I continue hiking up-beach but am soon halted in my tracks by a mass of barbed wire and cement, a residential Maginot Line, defeating my best efforts to continue north. I climb up the bluffs and over a wall, retreating along Monarch Bay's private streets and suffering the hostilities of a guard ("This is private property . . . you're subject to arrest . . . the *public* beach is located . . .") when I emerge at his outpost on Coast Highway.

Fifty yards south of the Monarch Bay Guardhouse is where the powers-that-be have installed Dana's memorial.

Today is the first day on my 1,400-mile coastal hike that I witness such historical outrage.

But not the last.

Today is the first day I observe the desecration-in-progress of a stretch of natural beach.

But not the last.

Today is the first day the works of man prevent my passage up the coast.

But not the last.

During my months of hiking northward along land's end, I find mounting evidence in the form of plans and planning commissions, stucco and steel, indicating our citizenry has not learned or chosen to forget that the California coastline is a natural ecosystem, as vital, as dynamic, as special as a redwood forest or Sierra lake, and continues to treat the coast as a commodity to be auctioned off to the highest bidder. All along the coast, but particularly in Southern California, rivers no longer run to the sea to deposit sand for beaches; estuaries, the tideland's genetic reserves, are drained for development; longshore currents are disrupted by groins and jetties; cliff erosion is thwarted by blankets of cement. The utilitarian function of shoreline, its ability to carry out nature's chores, is being grossly altered. The coast is also losing its utilitarian value to most Californians as the coastal industries of fishing, dairy farming, and agriculture disappear and the last affordable seaside cottages are razed and replaced by high-priced condos.

Like proprietors of a boutique, where the fashionable and the expensive are sold, Californians are selling off their coastline and heritage to the highest bidder. This real estate sale affects both public and private lands and is having profound influences on California culture. A unique coastal history is cheapened when the marketable is substituted for the memorable. Coastal architecture suffers when the frivolous is substituted for the functional. Coastal ecosystems are degraded when the expensive replaces the priceless. In short, economically and ecologically, what we are witnessing in the 1980s is the boutiquing of California's coast.

The boutiquing of a coastal town does not end with the building of a few dozen or even a few hundred expensive homes. Theme parks—collections of shops and homes done in a nostalgic nineteenth-century style—complete the boutiquization process. Three dominant motifs prevail along the California coast: the New England seacoast village, the Victorian, and the Mission.

The New England seacoast look is favored by Ye Olde Shopping Mall developers, though the illusion of authenticity suffers when palm trees are included in the landscaping. Whaler village-style condominiums, complete with plank boardwalks and braided rope handrails, electric gas lights, and fake lighthouses, have proved attractive to consumers. The Cape Cod bungalow is also a popular condo style imported from the East Coast.

Of Queen Anne tract houses, fake cupolas and gables, and other manifestations of ersatz Victorian architecture along the coast, the less said the better. This congested sort of architecture appears ill at ease along the coastline, though perhaps in a million years or so, when the next Ice Age arrives, the steep-pitched Victorian roof will prove invaluable in shedding snow.

Dominating the new architecture along the coast, however, is the Mission-style. Mission Savings and Loan, Mission Auto Body, Mission Inn, Mission Shell, Mission Cemetery. On a hot day, all that whitewashed stucco strains the eye. The characteristic black iron grillwork adds a vaguely sinister flavor, giving even a luxury apartment house the profile of a Mexican penitentiary. It is said that Mission-style architecture is "natural" for California, but when I gaze out at all those red-tile roofs crowning Santa Barbara, I have to disagree. I know of no shade of red in nature like those tiles, save that of boiled crustaceans.

So widespread is the Mission-look that visitors often jump to the conclusion that coastal towns like Carlsbad, Oxnard, and Palos Verdes, given their presiding architectural bias, are mission towns, founded by the Spanish padres. Their Mission motif, however, is afterthought facade; in fact, these towns were born of boosterism, not Catholicism. Local chambers of commerce downplay circumstances of their towns' birthrights, for fear of being considered illegitimate perhaps.

Only a few angry Western historians have suggested Californians regard the mission era with less romance and more realism. They claim the missions were little more than Chumash Indian concentration camps, and portray mission founder Father Junipero Serra as a kind of marketing expert, franchising missions like so many Jack-in-the-Box drive-ins. Despite these revisionist historians, advocacy of the missionary position continues unchallenged. Junipero

Serra will soon be honored by Serra Plaza, currently under construction in San Juan Capistrano. The padre's life will be depicted on large tile murals installed near the Bank of America building and other offices.

Much of what passes for homage to the past is really a hustle of the present. Witness the condominiums being built on the historic San Diego Ferry Landing site on Coronado Island. From 1886 to 1969 the San Diego & Coronado Ferry shuttled a quarter of a billion passengers back and forth from the mainland to Coronado. Generations of visitors flocked to the "Del," that queen of Victorian-era hotels, the Hotel Del Coronado. In 1970 the Coronado Bay Bridge opened, considerably altering Coronado's charm and retiring the ferry. At the old ferry landing site, Watts Industries is building The Landing, a $90 million condominium complex of 196 units on the last major undeveloped piece of private property on San Diego Bay. The public will be accommodated by a pedestrian mall leading to the shoreline and by view corridors permitting glimpses of San Diego Bay. Construction of The Landing was approved by various planning commissions in large measure because the condos will architecturally ape the old Hotel Del Coronado, with pitched-roof design, dormers, and awnings. Of course, the ersatz Del will be constructed of stucco, not wood.

On Catalina Island, not far from Avalon, the $180 million Hamilton Cove development nears completion. Avalon's mayor declares the 330 condos, with prices ranging to $1.2 million, "will bring a nice type of person to the island." A Hilton Hotel is slated to join the condos. In homage to the nearby historic Casino Building and ballroom, the developers have adopted a 1940s Big Band theme to promote their project, chauffeuring prospective buyers to the condos in a 1941 Cadillac limousine.

Countless more examples of boutiquization could be given, but it's sufficient to note that nothing is sacred. No, not even a national park. The National Park Service is considering building extensive tourist facilities on the Channel Islands. A Park Service report contemplates an "early twentieth-century island resort" on Santa Cruz Island and mentions the possibility of inns, airports, and all-terrain shuttle buses, all designed for a "high quality leisurely experience."

Richard Henry Dana's legacy is a marina and bluffs-full of expensive homes. Father Serra's life is inspirational decor for a new Bank of America. Those historical figures lacking ornamental value are overlooked. Homesteaders Pfeiffer, Gamboa, Wheat, and Flores have left their names on coastal slopes, but the importance of their lives has been allowed to fade away. Trailblazers Anza, Portola, and Brewer are forgotten and so are their expeditions up the coast. Uniquely Californian events such as the installation of the world's first water-to-water airplane flight, from Balboa to Catalina, have sunk into oblivion.

Monterey's Cannery Row, formerly the site of a flourishing sardine canning industry, is one of the most intensively boutiqued stretches of coastline. The street immortalized by John Steinbeck has become, depending on your point of view, either a unique array of specialty shops or a tourist trap. The old cannery buildings have been gutted, prettied, and stuffed chock-full of knickknack shops, restaurants, and art galleries. Visitors with a historical interest find few clues to the rise and fall of the sardine. In fact, so extensive is the boutiquization that visitors are unable to reach the waterfront. The Coastal Commission in recent months has had to browbeat Monterey merchants in order to secure coastal access for the public. In a particularly ironic juxtaposition, a bust of Steinbeck mounted on a pedestal faces a row of cutesy shops. Steinbeck's words, taken from his novel, *Cannery Row*, and imprinted on his pedestal read:

"Cannery Row is a stink, a grating sound. . . ."

When history is boutiqued, past genius, past labors, past lives, and even life itself, are nullified, as if obliterating them from the pages of history. The boutiquization of history and historical landmarks trivializes our civilization and what our civilization is entitled to—namely, the accumulation of the best products and visions of preceding generations.

If merely coastal architecture was suffering the pox of boutiquization, one might have a good laugh and carry on, but a more sobering prospect is on the horizon, the boutiquing of the natural world. All along the coastline, whole ecosystems are being replaced with, in the future-world jargon of planners, "pocket beaches," "pocket parks," "SEAS" (Significant Environmental Areas), "scenic turnouts," "vista points," and "view corridors."

The Battle for Bolsa Chica, one of Orange County's most valued and undeveloped coastal properties, epitomizes oceanfront boutiquization. Signal Oil Company, the owner of the oil drilling–degraded Bolsa Chica marshland, envisions a residential development of 5,700 homes and apartments, a shopping center, and a marina with 1,800 boat slips. Conservationists wish to rehabilitate the wetland as habitat for fish and fowl. So far, 150 acres of the once extensive wetland have been restored by the U.S. Department of Fish and Game, but the future of the remaining 1,000 acres is in serious jeopardy. Wildlife biologists argue that encircling a "duck pond" with homes, boat slips, and commercial development is not the same as preserving a sizable, unstressed, ecological reserve.

Ninety percent of Southern California's wetlands have been drained for exclusive residential and marina developments. Habitat for native and migratory waterfowl has disappeared. Commercial and sport fishing has suffered. Still, even the last tideland remnants are threatened. Summa Corporation has offered to preserve a duck pond–sized portion of Ballona Wetlands near Marina Del Rey in exchange for permission to drain much of the rest and build a community to be called Playa Vista, consisting of 8,837 housing units, 2,400 hotel rooms, 4.5 million square feet of commercial space, and a marina.

Coastal bluff ecosystems are also subject to boutiquization. Depending on how you look at More Mesa in Goleta, it's either one of the last untouched natural habitats on Santa Barbara County's south coast or an ideal site for 300 high-priced condominiums. A UCSB research team has determined the mesa, with its wide variety of habitats including a creek, oak woodlands, wetlands, and grassland, to be "environmentally sensitive." The mesa is home to such creatures as frogs, lizards, turtles, and several bird species including the marsh hawk, the white-tailed kite, and the short-eared owl.

"The short-eared owl doesn't pay taxes," scoffs the developer, Bill Simonsen of Simonsen Group. "We're going to use the land for something that will be producing income, taxes, the things that make society work. We're developing an outstanding development."

Though his development would obliterate a natural environment, Simonsen suggests that the public should be content with the 60-acre park he has offered to put in.

What passes for ecology along the coast often consists of identifying a few rare species, such as the California least tern or peregrine falcon, and giving them just enough habitat between housing developments to permit their survival. Often, this results in a temporary increase in the population of an endangered creature and it's proclaimed "saved." However, in terms of the long-term success of a species, it's a serious ecological error to believe an increase in population can substitute for the elimination of habitat.

Time will tell if many endangered plants and animals can survive in the ever-smaller niches allowed them. Surely a time will come when a smaller representative environment can no longer substitute for a larger habitat. As quiet is more than an absence of sound, and peace more than an absence of war, an ecosystem is more than an absence of building. Boutiquing the shoreline tampers with the collective gene pool, nullifies species, decimates habitats, and makes it impossible for many life forms to survive.

As I hike along the coast, I have a recurring fantasy: When the millennium arrives, when navy battleships return to San Diego for conversion into floating universities, their guns, as a last act before being spiked, will be allowed to blow to sand the hideous, continuous, and disfiguring chain of hotels, haciendas, and shopping malls which by then will have completely smothered the coastline.

Other than subversive dreams, what alternative to boutiquization can I offer the Captains of Industry that will absorb the unemployment problem, the housing shortage, etc., so well?

It will be useless for me to point to the billowing brome grass, the cry of the gull, the crescents of white sand.

No, the Master Planners conjure seaside condos facing a concrete promenade.

It will be useless for me to point out that we have no right to destroy what's left of our rural citizenry by taking their land and employing them for our own money-making purposes, negating their identity and merging them into Metropolis.

No, the Joint Chiefs of Shaft insist on extending the benefits of boutiquization to every coastal nook and cranny.

Combating boutiquization is tough because of the difficulty in recognizing the enemy. Often the conflict is oversimplified by the media into ecology versus economy or rich versus poor. Of the first false division, let it be noted that ecology and economy share a common Greek root, *oikos*, meaning "household," and a common ground; the degradation of one leads to the degradation of the other. As for the rich versus poor division, I think there's only so much indignation one can raise at the affluent and their conspicuous consumption of the coastline.

Some boutiquers befouling the coast for private gain, such as the well-organized and well-financed Signal Oil Company or Summa Corporation, are easy to spot. Other boutiquers are ordinary working folk, who've simply cut their ties to the coastline on which they live. And still other boutiquers are all the rest of us—all of us who look but don't see or who look the other way.

Rarely questioned is the Board of Realtors rationale for boutiquization: "Doesn't an owner have the right to do with his land as he pleases? If he wants to bulldoze his coastal bluffs and put up Moorish castle condos, well isn't that his business and isn't this a free country and what right has anyone to stop him?"

Nearly all Californians agree that some regulation of coastal development is necessary. It's acknowledged that to go as you please is not always to arrive at what is pleasant. But those who would regulate boutiquization are faced with a dilemma: We know a man's home is his castle, but we recognize the dangers of building castles on sand.

The answer to boutiquization in this age of deregulation cannot come from lawmakers. The new taste must grow from within the populace; it cannot be decreed from above, as the Coastal Commission has found out. It is beyond the commission's mandate to encourage a new coastal ethic. No Harry Truman–like commissioner has a sign on his desk reading: "The Boutique Stops Here."

Perhaps Californians can take consumer advocate David Horowitz's approach: Become educated consumers and fight back. Sunsets and tidepools are not products to be consumed, of course, but they are vital processes to be appreciated, and the difference between a boutiqued environment and a real one is obvious. The consumer has become a fair judge of home computers, jug wines, and new cars and is keenly interested in their looks and quality. If consumers can rate products, can they not evaluate living processes? Citizens should be encouraged to judge both built and unbuilt environments by what they are, not by what they pretend to be.

The coast's condition reveals California's culture and tradition as directly as does a newspaper, because the coastline, even its most natural parts, are shaped by this culture. The coastline, either boutiqued or wild, is a historical document. Whether future historians report a path of preservation or the track of a bulldozer is up to us. Today's choice is tomorrow's experience. A bulldozer biting into a coastal terrace can perform the equivalent of a thousand years of erosion in one hour. The choice not to boutique involves a conscious exercise of human will.

Those battling the boutiquers must not try to effect a retreat to the real past, wherever that may be, but to plead for an honesty in the treatment of the built and unbuilt environment. Coastal conservation is more than saying, "Look how wonderful the past is, let's keep it that way." There's no modeling the future solely on the past. The coast's future depends to a large extent on citizens adopting a new *visualization*, another way of looking at land and sea, a vision of the coastline not as a sandbox for play but as a living thing placed in our trust. Until a new visualization is generally accepted, the problems of zoning, population density, housing, erosion, and cliff collapse will be extremely difficult to solve and boutiquing will continue unabated. Until a new visualization is accepted, the forces of Cut and Fill and Grade and Pave will continue their assaults against landmark and landscape.

While searching for a style, Californians will have to put up with the current orgy of revivalism along the coast. Nineteenth-century–style condos are nothing but surface fashions of course, the architectural thorazine of a dazed age, but they indicate that the flow of tradition is lost and not yet found. As the hideousness created by these revivals brings a reaction, perhaps we'll realize that tradition is not a wave breaking and retreating, but a wide slow current flowing on from the past to the future. If this current is so feeble and so negligible along the coast, architects are hardly to blame.

Like it or not, we have a generation of Californians valuing things for their boutiqueness (no matter how spurious) instead of for their suitability and harmony with the coastline, uncomfortable at the very mention of the word beauty. Among this generation are coastal commissioners, developers, and other planners of the built and unbuilt environment, the men and women in whose hands the whole coastline is passing. Unless some means can be found of sharing with them, not an unblinking reverence for the good old days, not a superficial knowledge of the way we were, but a live, dynamic sense of history, beauty, and natural proportion, the present path of vulgarization and defilement of California's coast will continue.

It's too late to save Dana Point and San Juan Capistrano. Once a pleasant mixture of the urban and rural, they are fated to become, in the parlance of developers, "destination resorts." But it's not too late for Leucadia, North Malibu, Catalina, Carpinteria, Davenport, Gualala, and Petrolia.

Richard Henry Dana wrote of California, "In the hands of an enterprising people, what a country this might be."

The future is in the hands of our enterprising people.

Under boutiquization, if it comes to dominate the California coast, we shall look westward and receive no inspiration from the earth. Dune and cliff and wave and beach will be only spectacle and the binding force they once exerted on the character of Californians will have to be entrusted to Planning Commissions. May Planning Commissions be equal to the task.

[1984]

STANLEY POSS

Spaced Out West

ALONG WITH other urban blessings, the franchised quick-order food joints such as "Colonel" Sanders, The Big M (McDonald's Hamburgers), Dairy Delite, and their legion of competitors have been taken reasonably enough to signify the end of the American dream of westering, the end of the frontier, the end of the Open Road (which has now been seen to lead to a used car lot). But the peculiarly American felt relationship between space and moral and political simplicities survives in pockets and may even be increasing its appeal. As one might expect, the more isolated areas of the West Coast have become attractive gathering spots for those who believe that if only they can get some land, lotsa land (or even a patch so long as it's sufficiently removed from their neighbors), they will fulfill the Thoreauvian ideal of simplification. No one, I suppose, among these New Agrarians thinks of the West in the old way, that is, as a place where a man's a man, a woman's a woman, and there's none of this modern equivocation. But they do seem to think not only that this land is or can be their land but also that, planted on it, rooted in it, they'll draw sustenance from it that will clarify and make whole their lives. Like Steinbeck's Joads, they're avatars of Antaeus.

Chief among their West Coast bases is Humboldt County, an underpopulated and thickly forested area on California's north coast whose southern boundary is two hundred miles above San Francisco. Named for the German naturalist, who, however, did not include it in his travels, it's about one hundred fifty miles long (it's the next to last county before Oregon) and extends inland between fifty and seventy-five miles. Its 3500 square miles support some 100,000 people, that is, about twenty-nine inhabitants per square mile, as compared with San Francisco County's 15,000 for each of its forty-five miles. Like New Hampshire, it has always seemed to me to mark the line where the real north begins, the mythic north; and passing into it from the infinite extensions of San Francisco and Bay Area urbanization is like passing into, say, scruffy, violent, anarchic Keene from sleek and predictable Amherst.

Humboldt County shares some of its amenities with its Eastern counterpart, others are unique. It has redwoods, unswimmable beaches, rain, headlands, Indians; funny place-names such as Kneeland, Samoa, Manila, Fickle Hill, Trinidad, the Mad River, Petrolia, and Hoopa; a big lumber industry, space, clean air, old houses, incipient urban freeways, a small bay mostly mud flats (the bay was called "Humboldt" before the county), some commercial fishing, the coolest summers south of Juneau, cranes and egrets, a depressed economy, and a powerful attraction for those who define the good life as being spaced way out from urban centers: hippies, hairies, vandwellers, eco-freaks, and the kids generally. Old America overlaid by The Youth, its centers are Eureka and Arcata. Eureka ("You've Found It," the billboards say) is a bare town of 30,000 with more Victorian houses per inhabitant than one might reasonably expect, including that ultimate specimen of Carpenter Gothic, the Carson House. The much smaller Arcata, ten miles north on highway 101 at the top of the bay, has a pretty plaza, hills, shops and small restaurants in the Grand Funk style, cheap movies, a good bookstore, and Humboldt State University, successively Humboldt Normal, Humboldt State Teachers College, Humboldt State College, California State University, Humboldt (Arcata), Hohum (or Bumhole) Tech, and Dumbo (or Limbo) State, an institution with a hilly campus, popular natural-resources programs, anomie, and political influence.

Though a local columnist has it otherwise, nothing much happened in this dim northern land between, say, 1860 and 1960. (At least it's become traditional to say so.) The woods were clearcut, some Indians were killed, Bret Harte wrote journalism for a local paper, it rained. Even today, according to the latest au-thoritative survey, most Angelenos and San Franciscans believe it's in Oregon. Traditionally insulated from the rest of the state, more or less untouched by population explosions and the problems of the cities, it went its oblivious way. All the upheavals of the early '60's, civil rights, farm labor, the war, seem to have touched it lightly or not at all. Its political apathy is still almost as intense on campus as off. Gown recently voted against open personnel files while Town was simply puzzled by a few bedraggled Safeway pickets ("Cesar Chavez? Who's he when he's at home?"). But times change and even Humboldt County changes with them, chiefly because it has become the West Coast headquarters for young New Agrarians fleeing the cities.

Believing that their lives are well served to the degree they manage to avoid urban and suburban milieus, these new friends of the earth are reifying a con-stellation of some of our oldest political and social notions. Pervasive anteced-ents can be found in Brook Farm, Thoreau, the twin concepts of westering and the frontier, the myths of the village and of Eden itself and the opposing myths of metropolis and the jungle of the cities, in *Faust, Candide*, W. B. Yeats, John Synge and his islanders, Ken Kesey, Forster's *Howards End*, you name it. Naturally, the Agrarians recoil from the concept that More Is Better and eschew the dream of success, except on their terms. They favor wild or at least rural areas, handcrafts, small co-ops, Victoriana, camp, unwritten social contracts. As nearly everyone knows by now, their values cluster around a few familiar verities. Progress as it's usually defined operationally is a fraud. ITT and the oil companies run Amerika. War is insane. Social and religious and educational and political institutions exist chiefly to maintain the same snouts in the trough (though as we'll see the Agrarians believe one can affect local political issues). White sugar gives you cancer and kills your sexuality. Processed foods generally are poison. History isn't bunk, it's shit. Everything they tell you is a lie because they hate us youth. On the other hand, as everyone knows who hasn't sold out, movies, rock, sandals, beards, jeans, boots, old clothes generally, vans, pot, open-air sex, and natural foods are good (not that any of these comes as the hottest of news).

One would think them a mobile group by definition, but a fair number stay put long enough to vote. And since they tend to vote in a bloc for the anti-freeway, pro-environmental candidates, they've directly affected recent elec-tions. Although the local (Republican) Congressman who's never been known to offend the lumber interests or any other institution for that matter is still on the job, the trend has been Left in city and county races. The Mayor of Arcata (wife of a sociology don) presides over an enterprising, not to say free-swinging, City Council, a car dealer was threatened with removal for building on environmentally hallowed ground, and in general the moldy figs are no longer unquestionably in the ascendant. As one can imagine, these events have distressed many of the indigenes and their representative *The Times-Standard*, a Eureka daily that's no foe of the obvious. Linked with the Thompson chain, it's distinguished by its adherence to received ideas, its infallibly platitudinous editorials, its love affair with the Chamber of Commerce and the giant Louisiana-Pacific Lumber Company, its disinclination to fault any institution, and its fascination with area sports. Well, this distress peaked in a recent Arcata City Council election when two young anti-freeway candidates were elected over a large field, one of whom, a member of the Sheriff's Department, put his defeat in perspective when he informed his constituents that they'd turned the city over to a bunch of Hitlerites and punks and made it a little Berkeley. The references had no real referents, as far as I can see, except that one of the winners was the director of the local recycling enterprise. Since Hitler could be said to have recycled the paper of Versailles into the armaments of the Ruhr, perhaps it makes sense to regard recyclers generally as cryptofascists (or commies, it makes no matter).

A similar division occurred in a recent county election when the voters confronted the issue of whether to dam the Mad River in remote and privately owned Butler Valley some twenty miles upstream. The Army Corps of Engineers was set to go but the voters turned their backs on progress and rejected the proposal. This was by no means a straight Environment vs. Growth issue since Humboldters might have had to accept a considerable tax liability for the dam. Nor was the vote on Town-Gown lines: the Nays carried precincts far removed from the influence of HSU. Nonetheless, the anti-dam position of the University weekly and its special supplements, and the hard work of some of the kids, together with the youth vote, generally ensured a defeat for the dam proponents, though it's fair to say the defeat might well have occurred in any case.

The local ad man who chaired the pro-dam committee made it sound pretty ominous without the dam and pretty good with. "We must have some growth and progress," he said, "or this area will become the most depressed area imaginable. Butler Valley is our opportunity to effect moderate growth, to build payrolls, to encourage tourism, which incidentally is our greatest area of opportunity for economic development. This is a desirable type of development as people visit our area, spend money and leave, not posing an over-population problem." But even though he stressed the benefits and amenities consequent upon the dam, even though he pointed out that the land would become public and that floods would be eliminated, the voters weren't persuaded. My point in raising the issue is to call attention to the rejection here of the boosterism argument. As I've said, part of that rejection was merely self-interest in the form of fear of more taxes. But another part stemmed from a wholesale opposition to the mode of living implied in the language of the boosters. And given the stagnant economy of the county, that opposition is remarkable (remarkably short-sighted, its enemies would say). It's not very risky to say that it would hardly have existed ten years ago, since change has traditionally been identified with growth in Humboldt, and both have been thought good.

I shouldn't imply that the loosely cohesive group I've attempted to describe is more than loose. Whether they're real back-to-the-landers or just college kids who like to hike, their chief article of faith is suspicion of federations of all sorts. But, like anarchists who can sometimes put aside their detestation of organizations, they can be counted on to vote in favor of Letting It Be. They don't know Thoreau but instinctively they feel as he thinks. They see themselves as the real Americans, as he did, and like him they're social revolutionaries mostly by indirection. They endorse his idea that "A town is saved, not more by the righteous men in it, than by the swamps and woods that so surround it." They stand for Old America, they believe, and their radicalism is nowhere so apparent as in their deliberate preference for the old-fashioned. The irony is that they come here as to a last frontier for the true America of their imagining, and, coming, change it, despite their howdies and overalls and boots and grannies and calico dresses and VW covered wagons. This change was dramatized by the Fourth of July celebrations on Two Street in Old Town Eureka, the mainline street of yesterday whose Victorian crazies are now undergoing renewal. Two Street is about as close to Eureka's small commercial waterfront as you can get, and in the old days was the place for the whores and high-rollers. Subsequently it became Northern California's most famous Skid Row. Now, as I said, an urban renewal program is underway to smarten it up and capitalize on its raffish charms by bringing in the tourists.

The Fourth celebrations on the Street were revived last year and blossomed hugely into this year's gala. All the straights go fishing and kids take over with booths, music, street dancing, beer, love-ins, grubby and nutty clothes, makeup. The event really deserves a long and lovingly circumstantial and richly Proustian account only the bare outlines of which I can sketch here in this brief Social Note from All Over (Humboldt County). It's a saturnalia, a frolic, a rite of spring, a licensed folly, a carnival (though no one is thinking of giving up meat) in which bikers, Agrarians, children, aging hippies, students straight and emeriti, freaks, and some bourgeoisie mingle as the great Carson House at the top of the street broods inscrutably on the odd goings-on. One has fish and chips, shouts Wow at ten-minute intervals, digs the hairy and colorful Children of Paradise, and drinks beer with the Two Street Poet whose pad lies in an alley just off the Street and thus smack in the center of the pulsing heart of the Great City. Author of the observation that "The fly is on the lip of the Vinegar Jug" and a boyo on whom there are absolutely no flies, the Poet is a translator of Spanish and Mayan literature and a mud man ("without strength, runny vision, mind of mud, can't turn his head to look behind") who reads frequently in local pubs and occasionally works packing fish or teaching an extension course. Never daunted, he is said to have reassured his friends on emerging from a vasectomy by observing dispassionately, "Urethra, I've lost it." His pad was the scene of a large-scale tostada operation in behalf of a local free school whose booth was selling them like, well, hotcakes. Then back to the street and the Roman license thereof. One expected, in the memorable words of Faulkner's Jason Compson, to find them at it like a couple of dawgs in the middle of the square or under a wagon in front of the courthouse. And (again quoting the misogynist Jason) damme if they don't dress so's to make every man they pass want to reach out and clap his hand on it.

And yet for all the gaiety of a Two Street Fourth and the ostensible small-town friendliness of Humboldt County, alienation and anomie abound. Fog hangs on for much of the summer while the winters are mild but the rain almost never stops. The social atomization in parts of the University is pervasive and extreme. You tire of seeing the same people and they you, with the result that everyone tends to clam up (appropriately, I suppose, in view of the Hoopa creation myth that ascribes the curious behavior of the whites in the area to an original union between their progenitors, an ancient fisherman, first of his race to settle here, and an especially succulent *saxidomus* for which he conceived a passion). A lot of not knowing and not wanting to know goes on. In fact, a Cloud of Unknowing blankets the place for months at a time. Friends go by default, paranoia thrives. Shaky marriages fail. The ramshackle and Middle Eastern quality about North Coast life that seemed rather winning initially begins to drive you around the bend. (An English teacher said you have to get over the idea that you're in California because really you're in a wet Cairo.) Phone calls don't get through, memos aren't answered, secretaries disappear. One feels a long way from anywhere by February. Two Street can seem the end of the road instead of Fat City to many of its regulars on the fifth consecutive wet gray Thursday morning. The houses and yards have a Puritan austerity; where once their Sartrean bareness and fragility seemed moving and appropriate and symbolized unaccommodated man, the very image of America, as in *The Last Picture Show*, now they're simply dull. Huddled between sea and hill, crouched under the low sky, the houses are oppressed, spiritless, mean, while their typically treeless yards signify the provincial isolation and smugness of the place as one forgets the real reasons for this North Coast trademark, which are partly economic, partly esthetic, and partly a matter of climate ("With all those redwoods and all that fog who needs trees? We want sun"). The continued existence of the dark forests on Fickle Hill and endlessly beyond is merely pointless. You don't really want to make another trip to Ferndale, the pretty Victorian village down the road, and San Francisco's too far. The local arts are zilch except for a few ceramicists, the music third rate. Morris Graves lives nearby but, while not the recluse Salinger is, almost never shows his work. Life in the hills where some hard-core environmentalists *cum* recyclers are rumored to be living—in redwood stumps or on the reservations or the Samoa Peninsula, a subsistence-level collection of beaten little houses, or in the vans students live in—doesn't bear thinking on. The converted Mother's Cookies truck that seemed so funky in October looks now merely raunchy and the old Corvair van with the jaunty orange Popsicle decal has a flat and looks unsafe at no speed at all. You long for splendid redwood and stone and glass multilevel "Sunset" houses of the sort you might reasonably expect to see in an area like this but almost never do. (Two of the most elegant, both by architect owners, lie off the coast south of the old fishing town of Trinidad but are quite invisible from the road.) You want the frankly sybaritic instead of the everlasting wafflestompers and jeans and minicampers and vans. Swish and posh never seemed so desirable; you find yourself spending more time with *The New Yorker* than is healthy. Away with Volkswagens and Datsuns! Begone, universal ferns and colei! Out, cozy little short-order spots with camp decor and carefully negligent charm! Down with all driftwood mobiles! Back where you came from, great rusty bolts, shells, stones, and other sea treasures! Nobody comes to visit, the winds keep drilling the rain into you, you've just seen Jennifer Jones as Mme. Bovary, you feel the redwood curtain descending for good, you're in the ultimate provinces.

Money of course is the root but the money doesn't live here, it's in San Francisco, Portland, Chicago. That's why there is no economic base to support the local arts. You can't have an active sponsorship of the arts in a capitalist order without some form of salon system, it appears; you can't have salons without *grandes dames*; you can't have *grandes dames* without money. With money you'd see fewer of the ephemeral houses and more redwood and glass ones. With money you'd have swish villages like Amherst or Williams or some of those other fantastic Western Massachusetts towns that rival those of Kent and Sussex in their happy harmony of trees and houses, fields and farms. With money you could comb and groom the landscape as it is in southern England. But these raw North Coast towns that we believe and die in have their own powerful appeal as they are, if one has a bit of money, that is. There's no question but that Humboldt County gets in your blood if you're at all susceptible to its charms of forest and shore together with a town life notable for its conspicuously undizzying pace and sense of community. In common with other exurbanites, I love the place immoderately, and also, in common with them, feel more native than the natives, like the Anglo-Irish whose assimilation has come to be total, at least from their point of view. Possibly we need a term for this acculturation such as "San Francisco Eurekans" or "Urban Humboldters" or "Angeleno Arcatans," possibly not. In any case, as I mentioned, I and other newcomers change the place by our presence, no matter how great our sense of instinctive rapport with it. But the change is reciprocal as well, so it's a question of who changes first and most. I hope it wins, that is, changes least, this dim northern land, this remote Western Slope, this afterthought of California, this great empire of trees, this garden of earthly delights, this other Eden, this cloudy gem set on a steel-gray sea, this blessed plot, this realm, this Humboldt. [1977]

RICHARD STAYTON

When You Wish Upon a Star: Notes from a Season in the Fantasy Factory

> *The 70 acres of the Disneyland stage is a miniscule part of the earth's surface. It is separated from the outside world by an earthen berm. There is some question whether Disneyland is reality or fantasy . . . if you tune out the outside world . . . turn on . . . get with it . . . you'll find . . .* —"Your Role in the Disneyland Show"
>
> *I wanted flat land I could shape.* —WALT DISNEY

"I'M SORRY, but you're too tall to be a dwarf."

I am not prepared for rejection, not after the sacrifices already endured: moving from San Francisco to Los Angeles; giving up drugs and sex, since the two were inevitably connected; then entering the cheapest Orange County barber shop I could find and commanding the alcoholic barber to, "Cut it close. I'm seeking employment as a dwarf in Disneyland."

No, I *had* to get inside the Magic Kingdom—because I'd had it. This was the summer of 1974, and I'd just barely survived a decade of drugs, Haight-Ashbury communes, bisexuality, political craziness in ultra-hip San Francisco. I desperately needed to get back, to find sanctuary, to be like I was as a youth, a Boy Scout leader and winner of the coveted God and Country Award. Get back to my Middle American roots, yes, back when I first saw Disney's *Snow White and the Seven Dwarfs*, yes by God I was happy then. . . . Besides, this was Impeachment Summer, and from what better location could one watch the Fall of Nixon than from the ramparts of "The Happiest Place On Earth"? Anyway, I'd just spent two years getting a master's in creative writing from San Francisco State, so a job in Disneyland seemed the logical postgraduate study program.

"How about the Big Bad Wolf?" I am totally sincere. "He's my size."

The Disney employment interviewer smiles kindly and says, "I'm afraid all Character positions have been filled." I like her because she didn't find it at all strange that I'd want a job as a dwarf. I like her even more because she didn't check my application, which is nothing but an outrageous series of distortions, lies, and delusions.

"However, there are a few openings in Foods."

"What's that mean?"

"Selling popcorn," she explains. "Officially, a Fantasyland Utility Man. And should a position open in the Character Division, you could always transfer."

I muse . . . Popcorn Man in Fantasyland . . . What the hell? "I'll take it." We settle a few formalities, such as when my "Orientation" in the University of Disneyland will begin.

"One more thing. Your hair—it's much too long."

"THIS!" I grip all I can of my butchered locks, a bare finger's worth. I start to rave, but check myself and don't blow my cover.

"The Disneyland Look," she lets me know gently, "is a neat and natural look with no extremes."

> *Our product is happiness.*   —WALT DISNEY
>
> *Our look hasn't changed since 1955.*
> —Disneyland University Employee Brochure

The University of Disneyland is an unimposing building just beyond the Kal-Kan Club Pet Motel at the eastern end of the 107.3 acre parking lot—or, as they say here, the "outer lobby." Its symbol is a Mickey Mouse in cap-and-gown, clutching a diploma.

Orientation takes place in a dentist-office type room while Jiminy Crickett's voice is piped in, "When you wish upon a star . . ." We sit in director's chairs emblazoned with the names of Disney stars (Annette Funicello, Fess Parker, Julie Andrews, etc.). We sit around a large conference table and we smile a lot. "Use the Magic Mirror of Your Smile to Reflect the Happiness We Produce" is a key slogan in the "3-Step Formula" for making it here.

Orientation lasts two days. It's handled like a story conference from some Hollywood B picture. We learn we've not been hired, but "cast." We are all to be stars and starlets "Onstage"—at minimum wage. Films are shown illustrating The Disney Philosophy.

Brochures from Wardrobe are handed out. One of mine, "The Disneyland Look for Hosts," has a detailed list of "don'ts," plus photographs of D-land employees depicting "well-groomed acceptable haircuts." Appropriate and inappropriate shoes and jewelry are explained.

A quiz is given, "Become a Disney Information Expert . . ." and we fill in the blanks. Sample question: "(4) Mice are very important to Walt Disney Productions. In addition to Mickey, there are several other mice that are Disney stars. Name eight of them."

A succession of Disney executives, corporate jocks spun from old "Spin and Marty" episodes, take turns lecturing us. Their looks remind me that Ron Ziegler, Nixon's press secretary, worked between semesters at USC as a captain on Adventureland's Jungle River cruise boats.

"When you park your car," we are advised, "leave your prejudices inside, close your door on yourself and pretend the gates of Disneyland are curtains, spreading before a stage, and you're entering a new role."

"STOP role playing!" another commands. "Be yourself!"

"This is critical!" we learn. "On accidents, stand by, keep close if you're a witness. Maybe you can get Disneyland off the hook. Keep your eyes and ears open."

"If you have a contagious disease, please don't come to work—at least not to Tomorrowland or Fantasyland."

"Know the questions, know the answers," we are told, and a list of facts are given, along with a Wallet Fact Card to be kept on our persons at all times: the Matterhorn is 147 feet high; there are 500 trashcans; 9,000 gallons of water in the submarine lagoon; 20,000 different kinds of signs; 40,000 spreads of colors; 10,000 . . .

Finally, a Security Host addresses us:

"Disneyland, contrary to popular opinion, does not operate on pixie dust." He grins to signal this is humor, waits for the obligatory titters. "There are no German Shepherds guarding the wire fences surrounding the Park, but likewise there aren't any pole-vaulters trying to sneak in. . . . Any disturbances, call Security. On misunderstandings, call City Hall. In everything, from damaged camera to physical injury, *don't discuss with guests!* . . . There will always be one of us nearby."

We discover that on Main Street, U.S.A., the Keystone Kop is an official undercover policeman; in Frontierland, it's the Cowboy; on Tom Sawyer Island, the Cavalrymen.

He concludes: "In Disneyland we have removed all contradictions."

I glance at my fellow Seasonal Hosts and Hostesses as they applaud. It seems I'm the only one who didn't know what he meant.

Our Orientation ends at last with a crucial walk around the Park. Since the most frequently asked question will be "Where is the bathroom?," we are led by a Tour Hostess from toilet to toilet. There are 156 bathrooms in the Magic Kingdom.

> In Disneyland (a land in itself), we have our own
> language. —"Your Role in the Disneyland Show"

At the employee watering hole, the Offstage Cafeteria, you find the metamorphoses taking shape for the season.

Losers outside the Magic Kingdom, here these Southern California youths become more than winners: they are myth.

Here Cinderella is not the shy wallflower she was in high school. She's gone beyond even the Prom Queen: she *is* Cinderella. Better yet, someday her Prince *must* come—it's in the script.

That shy, good-looking but awkward boy who never found the courage to invite a girl to the Senior Prom? Here he's issued a Prince costume and— lo and behold!—he's dating Cinderella. . . . All pain of adolescence sheds like a cocoon as Cinderella and her Prince Charming select a center stage table in the Cafeteria. They sit, their costumes sparkling, and they hold hands, but their eyes aren't meeting one another's. . . . Their eyes sneak glances to gauge their magic's power. Are our dreams coming true?

And their fellow Hosts and Hostesses, co-conspirators in enchantment, meet the challenge: "How charming a couple! Just made for each other!"

That oversized teenager who never quite got it together to make the football team? Here he pulls on boots, suspenders, a holster, badge, vest, hat—abracadabra, please and thank you!—larger than life, he's King of the Wild Frontier(land) . . .

This masquerade is subtly programmed by the "Imagineers" running the show. Those casting look for the teenagers in need of the ultimate drug: magic. And then they make sure the roles stick. Snow White must sign a

Contract not to get a tan all summer. Mickey and Minnie must not hold hands or kiss Onstage. Pinocchio is an obvious homosexual closet case, extremely uptight about his sexual identity: but as Pinocchio he need never grow up. Within the ranks, they promote mediocrity because it's easier to control. Those who rise tend to be intimidated by real personality. And talent leaves. No one serious about a career stays because the pay is so low.

Those who remain are true D-land addicts. They don't deal with the "real world" any more than they must. They come to work. They mainline Disney myth. Nothing matters but the high of make believe. Here they can be kind and gentle without fear of rejection. Here children laugh with them, not at them. And kindness is the goal.

When they clock out at the stroke of midnight this enchantment threatens to dissolve. They complain about two days off in a row: better only one day off at a time, thus easier to return in the prescribed mood of happiness. So they spend their Off Days as Guests in the Magic Kingdom. Or they go to Las Vegas, where another insulated environment maintains the spell. They go to the beach, where the sun helps to "Oz out" the brain. They collect toys. They participate in the Disneyland Recreation Club. They have "costume parties" after work. They date each other.

They do anything—absolutely anything—to keep the "real world" away until the next fantasy fix.

> *To be on the safe side, the advice is to be nice to everyone.*
> *You can never tell when it may be a relative of ours on*
> *the family tree at Walt Disney Productions.*
> —"The Maintenance of Magic in the Magic Kingdom"

Night, and I'm stationed by the Matterhorn. The mountain (two acres of metal lathe, covered with cement two or three inches thick, topped with 2,500 gallons of white acrylic resin for sparkling snow) is a soothing presence: taped wind sounds whistle from the speakers in the crags, the waterfalls splash in a computer-balanced rhythm, and the trees are cropped to duplicate those at high, windswept ledges.

Popping popcorn, I grow aware of a strange tap dance: shoes skipping in a circle around my wagon. I discover a blond, grinning young man with that surfer look so common to Southern Cal climes.

"Hi there," he says, shuffling about. "My name's Rob. Yours?"

He tells me he's an employee of D-land, works in Foods over on Main. "Orange Juice." He goes on about how the popcorn smells good on a night like this, and it sure would be good to have some. I suggest he buy some.

He's broke, but suggests I give him a bag, free. I remind him of the sacred Law of the Kingdom: Thou Shalt Not Give Food Away Gratis.

"So? Everybody does it, man, come on, gimme a bag, nobody's gonna know any different."

He abruptly stops his dance, peers close into my eyes, and begs: "Please, man, let me have a bag."

Could he be a popcorn addict?

"Please!"

"Here!" Into his hand I thrust the hard won bag.

Immediately he cools out. "Don't forget, the name's Roy," he peers close at my nametag: ". . . Richard." He pops a single kernel into his mouth, then strolls into the shadows of the Matterhorn.

Perhaps two minutes later my Working Leader and his Assistant march up to my wagon. The Assistant takes over my duties while my Working Leader draws me aside: "Did you give away a bag of popcorn tonight?"

I confess, certain I'll be fired. But I bitch that Roy or Rob or whoever/whatever should be hunted down and caged, perhaps tortured in the Castle's dungeon.

"We've heard about the guy, he's a troublemaker."

"We've got our eyes on him, too," adds the Assistant.

They make me recite the "Ten Specific Taboos Governing All Members of the Disneyland Cast." They finally leave me with: "One Last Chance at Probation."

A Hostess from Foods passes by. I tell her what happened.

"You were set up," she calmly observes. "He was obviously a Customer."

Customers, I discover, are D-land employees from Security Division paid to act as spies. They roam the Kingdom disguised as Guests and simply interact with Hosts and Hostesses. They buy things. They watch your smile. They ask questions like "Where's the bathroom?" You never know who they are or where. But one word from a Customer and it's over and out.

"You were lucky," my Hostess informs me. "He must have liked you or you'd be gone."

> The Golden Duck Award has been traditionally pre-
> sented on a yearly basis to the security guard whose
> performance has merited special attention by his
> peers. —"Disneyland Line," Employee Newspaper

The weirdest Security game haunts Tom Sawyer Island.

The Island is D-land's escape valve. It's designed to capture a real wilderness feel, and the illusion is total. Guests who have nearly OD'd on fantasy desperately sit quiet among the real trees and listen to real water spill into the real river. . . . All made by man, of course. The plantings in D-land are treated with growth-retardant hormones to keep trees and bushes from disrupting the carefully maintained five/eighths scale design. And the Rivers of America are chemically clouded to conceal the cables and wires pulling the Mark Twain Steamboat and Columbia Sailing Ship.

Security patrols the Island disguised as United States Cavalry. They wear boots, bandanas, ribboned hats, suspenders, blue uniforms with yellow stripes. Straight out of a John Ford western, except in their holsters, instead of pistols, are intercoms for radioing the Mainland Headquarters.

A Security Cavalryman tells me they know Tom Sawyer Island so well, "Every bush and tree is numbered." Another boasts, "It's the perfect setup for Dopers." They watch the rafts which bring the newcomers to the Island. They've developed a sixth sense for detecting Dopers.

The Cavalrymen keep an eye on the dangerous users of illegal fantasy substitutes. They know which trails lead to the best spots for getting stoned, and when they see the Dopers wander down certain trails, they wait.

The Dopers, completely suckered by the atmosphere of Mother Nature, find what looks like an isolated cove. They lie back and light up.

The Cavalrymen wait, give them time to get ripped, completely into the time-warp fantasy of Mark Twain's Steamboat paddling by, the mechanical moose munching the plastic lily, the Indian Village across the Rivers of America. . . . Suddenly the Cavalrymen trek down the trail and the hallucination is total.

In the Doper's stoned eyes, the Security Cavalrymen see themselves mirrored transcendent: their power awesome; no longer Orange County losers, but Custer's ghosts returned from those thrilling days of yesteryear to right today's wrongs; and about to scalp these violators of frontier law.

"How's the view?"

Score it a bull's-eye: it will take the Dopers hours to recover from their vision. They're led off to the Backstage Anaheim Police Department jail . . . a *real* jail. . . .

Evening ritual: each dusk the Security Cavalrymen sweep the Island from end to end, emptying it of the children. Once certain they're alone, they sit on the Fort Wilderness stockade walls to watch the sunset and smoke the day's confiscated weed. If it's been a good day's catch, with a little luck they'll hallucinate themselves into true Cavalrymen guarding civilization from the barbarian wilderness. Stoned, they lower the American flag, then walk and talk like John Wayne to the raft for the dreaded trip back to reality.

Our security officers do not act as a law enforcement agency, but as a service enforcement agency, and as a service organization always available to assist with any problems that may arise . . . day or night.

—"Working Our Way"

A few comrade Hosts have some weird angle on my persistent questions about Security. They hint the game I'm hunting can be found if I visit the Security Hut on the roof of the Pirates of the Caribbean.

So one afternoon I climb the ladders to the roof. I follow a narrow plank walkway zigzagging to a three-walled Hut. The planks creak when I stop behind the Security Host seated on a stool, his binoculars trained on the parking lot below. He scans the parked cars and Guests, making sure no theft, boozing, doping, violence, or loitering takes place.

"Go ahead, it's in focus," he says, never lowering his binoculars or giving me a glance.

I discover to his right, aimed in the opposite direction, a telescope on a tiny tripod. I peer through the lens.

In perfect focus I see illuminated one of the bedrooms of the Disneyland Hotel. A maid moves through the room in stark closeup, sheets under arm. She bends to make the bed . . .

After what seems like a safe length of time, I get up to leave. "Well, thanks," I manage to say.

"See anything?" Security asks, never looking at me, his binoculars still pressed to his eyes.

"No."

"Too early. Come tonight during the fireworks. They tend to get it on when Tinker Bell flies."

"Sure, thanks, I'll come then."

A long time ago, in a far away land, lived a sparkling little spirit named Tinker Bell . . . who sometimes, to this day, returns to fly above the magic land of fantasy. And the story is told for children of all ages, that if you wish hard enough, and believe strong enough, Tinker Bell may appear to light—fantasy in the sky!

—Voice from the Sky

And with that cue Tinker Bell flashes from the top of the Matterhorn, down a wire, waving her pixie dust wand, while the night sky bursts with fireworks and "Zip-a-dee-doo-dah" crackles from speakers in the trees.

One evening I decide to follow the wire into the forest behind the Castle and see how Tinker Bell lands. I move up a path winding through undergrowth and trees, until I hear voices ahead. I enter a clearing and discover a low wooden platform. A nurse is seated on it, reading a magazine. Several Maintenance Men stand next to the wire, holding handled cushions for braking Tinker Bell's landing. Security Hosts line the edge of the platform. All look at me in stunned silence. Instantly I know I've made a mistake and turn to go.

"Hold it!"

A Security Host blocks my path. He examines my nametag, then:

"What do you want here?"

I tell him I was just curious to watch Tinker Bell hit the ground.

"*Hit* the ground?" There is a perceptible heightening of tensions. ". . . That's not a good idea, fella."

He tells me Tinker Bell's wire has been cleverly cut nearly in half to make it snap during her flight. The supports on her pulley have been found unscrewed. Other devices have been tried too hideous to mention.

"Why would anyone want to assassinate Tinker Bell?" I ask.

"That's what we'd like to know. Any suggestions?"

I resist the urge to accuse Captain Hook. Security's eyes are busy probing the back of my brain, eager tentacles feeling for signs I'm the saboteur. "I can't imagine anyone wanting to do such a thing," I finally answer.

"Maybe a labor dispute," Security mutters. "Maybe a crazy."

"It's crazy allright." I'm real eager to get the hell out of there. I can think of fifty fast reasons for wanting Tink out of the way.

"We keep her landing pad guarded twenty-four hours," Security says, as if warning me. "We're always watching." He encourages me to stay away from the area. I promise never to come back and hurry down the path.

Soon computers will be checking my record, deep in the bowels of D-land. The Security Host will interview my Supervisor.

Just as I exit the woods behind the Castle, the nightly "Fantasy in the Sky!" fireworks show goes off. Tinker Bell flashes down her wire, whizzes over me, legs dropping down for landing, and disappears into the trees—*plop/plop/plop* comes the sound of cushions braking her descent.

I hide in the shadows among the Castle's Offstage vending machines. I wait. Meanwhile, the Voice in the Sky announces: "And now, Walt Disney salutes America the Beautiful!" To a medley of patriotic tunes the sky explodes in red, white, and blue, sparkling between the leaves like deranged fireflies.

Out of the forest comes Tinker Bell, hidden within a phalanx of Security Personnel. All are bathed in a strobe effect from the fireworks. A cloak is over Tinker Bell's shoulders, she's carrying her wings and wand, her hair is peroxide white, and she has to be in her late sixties. With this kind of protection, I figure only a sniper with a crossbow on the Castle parapets has a chance.

I make a study of Tinker Bell's habits. I learn she is a mother and an ex-circus acrobat. But there have been other Tinks before her. . . . The first was seventy-two when she retired, a former Ringling Brothers aerialist—then she returned for a few more years before ending her night flights forever. The second Tink was only nineteen and a French circus acrobat. For a few years a model of Mary Poppins would roll down a second wire, but "she" kept getting jammed, and would hang over the Castle till the Kingdom closed. Once one of the Tinker Bells got caught above King Arthur's Carousel; a hook-and-ladder fire engine had to come to the rescue. Another Tink always traveled to D-land by bus: "I'm afraid to ride in a car on the freeways. They're not safe."

I decided not to join D-land's underground army of assassins.

> *Our most precious natural resource is the minds of our children.*
> —WALT DISNEY

Thank Disney I'm not a dwarf, for they are the most helpless in the Kingdom of Fantasy, daily victims sacrificed on the altar of Crowd Control.

When they drop that dwarf head-and-shoulders costume over their bodies, the kids of the Character Department surrender to the Disney mythology. The arms that dangle are lifeless wires encased by cloth, ending in rubber hands; while their "real" arms remain trapped inside the rubber head. Thus balance becomes an art. Their only view of the outside world is through a screen "third eye" in their foreheads. Thus all peripheral vision is lost.

The dwarfs move in caravan, "The Together Seven," and not just for effect, but to avoid being mobbed when isolated. They wear taps on their shoes: a cute touch, but actually crucial signals to one another. "How far behind are you, Grumpy?" one dwarf will tap-dance. "Three feet, Dopey, slow down," comes the tapped response. Dopey has a plastic cloak which drags the ground: this sound also becomes a critical source of communication. They follow the narrowest paths: this protects their flanks. They move in circles, in charming dances, but with reason: to keep one another in sight. They prefer to be photographed with their backs to a wall.

Their most dreaded days come when the Kingdom opens its gates to kids' conventions, such as Little Leaguers, Cub Scouts, 4-H Clubs, or Junior

Bowling Leagues. These groups break down into packs, are swayed by obscure passions, descend on the dwarfs without warning.

When ambushed, the dwarfs can do little to defend themselves. They can press close and endure the furious blows. Or they can appease the savagery by tricks: Dopey wiggles his ears; Sneezy lets loose a monumental "Ahhh-chooo!"; Sleepy snores; Happy laughs; and all can arch their painted eyebrows and pucker their rubber noses. But such tricks only humor true blood lusts for a few seconds. Then the dwarfs launch their single weapon: circling, twirling their boneless arms like propellers—the heavy rubber hands batter the children, keep the beasts at bay until Snow White or Prince Charming comes to the rescue. But twirling tactics involve serious risk, for a kid can drop beneath the flailing arms and topple the unbalanced dwarf. Fallen, the dwarf is unable to rise, especially when hordes of Buster Brown shoes stomp his rubber head. Once a dwarf was nearly tossed off the drawbridge and into the moat.

But The Three Little Pigs are less protected, and targets of even more vicious and frequent assaults. Everyone hates a pig, it seems, and their swollen bodies with navy caps and coveralls attract sadists of all ages. Yet the dwarfs will argue that the Pigs are better protected, with a wider and thicker head for a shield, so safety in numbers doesn't count.

Pity the poor kids from the Character Department! On hot, smoggy days, encased within these heavy costumes, how they suffer! And all martyrs to the faith of escape.

> *All ten million guests will be coming to Disneyland to be happy and have a good time and counting on you to make it come true. . . . The challenge is bringing the sparkle back to the eyes of the man with a family of six whose car vapor-locked on the Santa Ana freeway coming to Disneyland on a typical summer day.*
> —"Showmanship . . . Disneyland Style"

Scenes of Battle:

Donald Duck being teased by a boy pulling his tail feathers. . . . Donald times it just right, twirls and *slams* the boy with his beak. The boy crashes, howling, to the pavement. Instantly his Mother is on the noble Duck, and the two topple, locked in a wrestler's death-grip. Security quickly drags Mother and Duck offstage where they can be pried apart away from the tourists' Kodaks.

Goofy is reprimanded repeatedly for accidentally scaring small children.

In his bizarre outfit, with huge clumsy shoes, awkward suspenders, and an unbalanced head, his tendency is to aim at some distant landmark and charge straight ahead. But Goofy must also wave, skip, and act . . . goofy. So it's common to find in his wake crushed children.

One of the Character Reliefs has an accident. As a Relief, this college student must take over for the various Characters in need of Rest and Recuperation. Every hour he dons a new identity: Winnie the Pooh; then Pluto; next the Walrus; the Mad Hatter; the Dormouse; ad nauseam. . . . It's a hot day and the Masses are restless. Suffering acutely from the heat, crowds, and from a schizophrenic identification with his changing roles, he can take no more. As Goofy, he throws up. His vomit fills his huge rubber head. He nearly chokes before making it Offstage to pull off his head.

The Parade Characters fight Offstage for the right to be The Fairy Godmother on the Cinderella pumpkin-coach. . . . There is a large Gay contingent within the Parade Division.

Alice in Wonderland, when riding on her mushroom, actually stands waist-deep in a hole in the top. False legs partially concealed by her skirt dangle side-saddle over the mushroom. One of the Alices, during a Character Parade, starts turning in circles so it looks like her upper torso moves separately from the legs. "Hi, little kiddies!" she waves, turning. "I'm Linda Blair from *The Exorcist!*"

. . . Sometimes, unable to endure more, desperate for comic relief, and in a furious rejection of their imprisoning myth, the Seven Dwarfs descend on Snow White and perform make-believe rape. They bend and strain to lift her skirts with their conical caps. They pretend to push their gigantic heads between her thighs. If Snow White is carrying a basket of apples, she will dump these over the dwarfs. Otherwise, she gently slaps the thrusting heads: "Oh, you cute little devils!"

Such mock attacks are spontaneous and brief, for fear of Security.

> *The total concept has proven to be one of the great wonders of the world. Disneyland has been copied and duplicated (with varying success) throughout the world. It is a model for cities.*
> —"The Maintenance of Magic in the Magic Kingdom"

"Buzzz . . . Buzz! Buzz!"

A Sweeper lurches up to my popcorn wagon, moving like a robot, in a spastic series of twitches and jerks, his broom and bucket clattering. "Buzz!

Buzz! This is Danny of Walt Disney Productions. Unfortunately, this Audio-Anamatronic is about to go 101" (101 is D-land code for out-of-order).

The name is strange: Audio-Anamatronic. Disney considered it his most pioneering creation. It's animation plus electronics plus sound: equals life-life, life-*substitution*. The "Lincoln" in the "Great Moments with Mr. Lincoln" exhibit is the most chilling example. A duplicate model of the original, the "creature" is constructed of steel and plastic. Duraflex composes "his" skin, and actually "sweats" an oily substance, and so uses makeup. It's operated by sixteen air lines to the plastic skull, ten air lines to the hands and wrists, fourteen hydraulic lines to control the body, and two pairs of wires for every line. It stands up, or, more precisely, *lurches* to its feet, then gives a three-minute speech which is a composite of five Lincoln speeches edited and selected by the Board of Directors of Lincoln Savings. This abridged "speech" is made to seem one of Lincoln's intact originals, and it's a Right-wing isolationist theme with overtones of paranoia.

> *I hope we never lose sight of one fact . . . that this was all started by a mouse.* —WALT DISNEY
>
> *Mickey is Walt.* —ROY DISNEY
>
> *Mickey Mouse.*
> —Secret Code for Allied Invasion, Coast of Normandy, D-Day, June 6, 1944

One Mickey Mouse is an actual dwarf who's grown weary of the children constantly mobbing him. Occasionally he loses control and hits the kids with his baton. But they can't fire him, being the first Mick in a long proud line, and Walt's favorite pet during Our Founder's life. Besides, this Mick's made Permanent Full Time.

Another Mick is known to hiss dirty comments to the children while posing for photographs.

Sometimes the various Onstage Mice drift by mistake into the same area. This always creates panic and anarchy. How can there be more than one Mickey Mouse?

Because of the height restrictions, the majority of the Mickey Mice are girls.

Walt Disney had a secret hideaway here, an apartment above the firehouse overlooking Main Street, U.S.A. He loved to spend what free time he had hidden in it, spying on his Guests below. When strolling the Park, crowds always surrounded him, asking him to draw Mickey or for his autograph. This was always a source of embarrassment to him, because he'd never been a great animator; in fact, he never drew Mickey for the screen (Ub Iwerks did the original). So during his strolls through the Park, children got confused when they asked him for a Mickey drawing, then saw the scrawl with a tail. "That's not Mickey!" He took lessons from his animators, but still he couldn't duplicate the mouse.

Even more frustrating to Disney was an inability to duplicate his world famous signature. His animators again tried to teach him to sign his name consistently, but without success. Guests examining his signature would suspect him to be an imposter.

Walt always did the voice of Mickey Mouse, until late in his life when his throat, scarred by his chain-smoking which eventually gave him lung cancer, no longer produced the proper squeaks.

> *At Disneyland, we go out of our way to make a person feel like an individual. . . . Among other things, we never hesitate to offer to take a group picture which includes everybody in a family.*
> —"Your Role in the Disneyland Show."

> *We believe in returning loyalty with loyalty.*
> —DICK NUNIS, President, Walt Disney Productions

"You shouldn't be here!" A Guest is shouting at me because I'm depressed and it shows. "You should not be working here!" he insists. I know, but how does he know?

Little children gaze up at me and ask, "Do you like working here?"

"Sometimes," I answer.

But the fact is, for all its faults and kinkiness, D-land belongs to the children. Sure, it's a con game, but better than most, and a bargain at today's rates. The disguised Right-wing political propaganda oozing from all the products and attractions doesn't faze the children. They belong here. I don't.

One afternoon, working the Fantasyland Ice Cream Train, I notice the Vendor beside me feeling the frozen bananas before he sells them. I keep my eye on him, and soon discover he only does this just before selling a banana to a particularly good-looking woman. Inside the freezer, his hand moves rapidly up, around, down the bananas—and then he passes it to the beauties.

He notices I've noticed.

"I warm it up a little for the hot lookers," he explains. His eyes intensely watch the sexy woman unwrap her frozen banana, nibble its tip. "You think they notice?"

"I think they think it's soft," I say.

This deflates him. He gulps, watches desperately while the sexy woman eats her banana. "No," he finally concludes. "They like it."

Right—I don't belong here.

> *But is Mickey a mouse?* . . . *certainly one would not recognize him in a trap. . . .*
> —"Mickey and Minnie," E.M. FORSTER

"I tell people it's all right to work here," one of the Characters tells me, "but be careful: it becomes a trap for a lot of people." He is talking about a Sweeper who, six years after earning his engineering degree, still sweeps garbage off Main Street, U.S.A.

But this is my final night here, and I finally see why D-land gets such loyalty from its employees. Tonight there are just a few hundred Guests, and so there is a celebratory air throughout the Magic Kingdom. as my relief says to me, "Tonight it's the way it's supposed to be."

At dusk, those Permanent Part-Time employees leaving till the next holiday season give Mickey and Minnie the Superstar treatment: they get their photographs taken with the famous Mice. Mickey and Minnie give autographs, blow kisses and wave goodbye as the departing Hosts and Hostesses clock out for the last time . . . all this happens Offstage.

The last Parade of the long season moves down Main Street, U.S.A. Only a few Guests line the curbs, and so the many Characters skip, dance, play tag—safe to explore fantasy.

I spot what might be called our Average American Family: Father, Mother, Son Senior, Daughter Senior, Son Junior, Daughter Junior, Grandma, Grandpa—in line along a curb. I notice them because they stare at the Characters without any expressions whatsoever.

At the tail end of the Parade skip the Seven Dwarfs. They have miner's lamps attached to their caps for night vision. Their heels click, they swirl and dance, truly light on their feet. A far cry from the peak attendance days when the Masses cornered them.

The oldest Son of our Average American Family runs into the street. He catches the trailing dwarf—Dopey—and with all his strength slugs the dwarf in the back. There is no hate or joy in the blow, no expression at all, just some kind of solemn response to some private need. Then Son Senior races back to the curb and resumes his place in line with our Average American Family. They could not have missed his attack on the dwarf. But no one reprimands him, nor do they give him a glance. They simply continue to watch the passing Parade as if before their TV set. None must know they've been programmed for happiness.

Meanwhile, the dwarf staggers from the blow, misses a step, but manages to maintain his balance. He continues in line with the other dwarfs, none knowing of this assault on their comrade. But the dance is gone from his steps. I imagine the youth inside the costume, bewildered by this unprovoked attack from nowhere, struggling to maintain his/her composure—but free to weep, hidden inside.

> *Once we hire and motivate and orient them, they stay.*
> *Because life at Disneyland and Walt Disney World is*
> *good. We operate on a first-name basis. The environment*
> *is clean and happy. In many ways we're part of a make-*
> *believe world. A fantasyland.*
> —GARY FRAVEL, Ex-Head, University of Disneyland

It is for each other this band of Disney employees perform. Summer done, the Magic Kingdom is once again in the hands of the precious few who feed its fantasy life. The season is over—and the antique, delicate, intricate toy is to be carefully laid back in its winter drawer. The Permanent Full Time Hosts and Hostesses have free reign again. Disney is dead—long live D-land!

And I get the hell out.   [1983]

JEFFREY SHORE

Bouncing
at the Whisky

L OUD MUSIC. That was my first impression of the Whisky-A-Go Go. Scratchy, raunchy, techno, but always very loud. I stood outside the front door in the smoggy Sunset Boulevard air and let the music surround me, grab my shirt tail and pull me inside. This wasn't the first time I thought I'd like to experience the Whisky, but my cornfed background and ever-present skepticism had heretofore kept me away. Finally, however, the end of unemployment checks drove me inside. I needed a job.

I thought I'd try for a bartender's job. I've never been a bartender before, but what could be so tough about it? All writers have been bartenders at some point in their lives, after all. I found the manager, Ray Sexton, slumped over a downstairs bar supervising the unloading of several cases of beer. He eyed me up and down. "Sorry, no bartender jobs." I was disappointed. "What about bussing, or cleaning up?" He shook his head. "We got Mexicans to do that." One more try. "Bouncing? I could be a bouncer." He checked me out again. "Maybe. We always need bouncers. You ever had a litre bottle of burgundy broke over your head?" I was taken aback. "No." He nodded. "Good. You'll work out fine until it happens." He handed me a time card and a flashlight, shook my hand, and disappeared into his office. I was a bouncer.

The Whisky is a barn. A big ugly. barn. There's not a square inch that hasn't been puked on. It's not unusual to find blood smears on the wall and old, wild-eyed drunks asleep under the tables. As a building, the Whisky is tired. If it were alive it would probably kick Elmer and the rest of the crew down Sunset and reopen itself as a church, or something equally tame. Elmer, by the way, is Elmer Valentine, a nice old gentleman, an ex-cop from Chicago who is one of the owners. The other owner is Mario Magliani, also an ex-cop from Chicago, the real Godfather of rock 'n' roll in Los Angeles, who rules from the Roxy Theatre, up the street. He watches over the employees with a benevolent smile, an open kitchen, and an evil eye. Mario don't take no shit.

The employees at the Whisky are many and nearly all weird. I got to know all of them pretty well, my comrades in arms, so to speak, but when I first walked in there, I don't believe I'd ever seen a bunch of crazier looking folk. The waitresses seemed bizarre, nightmarish. One was wearing a basketball jersey and tights, another had green hair, black lipstick, and six-inch heels. Karen, our hostess, wore black leather.

And the bouncers. First there was Dan, who worked the door checking I.D.s. He was big, strong, and ugly—reminded me of the Frederick Forrest character in *Apocalypse Now*: he wasn't wrapped tight enough for West Hollywood. He was also a graduate of the University of Vietnam. Then there was Morgan, another vet. He was a tall Texan who favored ten gallon hats and big-eyed women. He often worked the floor with a toothpick in his mouth until Sexton clapped him on the back one night and damn near choked him. The Vietnam alums were capable of mountainous violence in molehill situations, often with little or no provocation. A third bouncer was Bobby, peace-loving Bobby, a little guy with curly blond hair who carried a crossword puzzle book to work. We were the regulars: Bobby, Morgan, Danny and myself. On punk nights we used seven or eight more, all rent-a-muscle quality, college football players or ex-cons who enjoyed breaking heads for five bucks an hour. They were part of a mercenary group of headhunters who worked concerts all over Los Angeles, and who specialized in accruing assault charges.

I really enjoyed the job for the first couple of weeks. It was mid July, the air was hot, the bands were good, and my first layer of naivete hadn't worn off yet. I worked the top of the stairs and kept the aisles clear. Can't beat that. There were lines of gaffer's tape on the floor that marked where people could stand. I just kept them behind the tape. I smiled a lot, chatted with the customers and kept out of the fights, I was amiable. I'd shine my light on the stairs so the patrons wouldn't trip.

Three months later I'd growl at anyone who got in my way, trip people on the stairs and sucker punch anyone who so much as looked at me in the wrong way.

The honeymoon ended the night I worked my first punk concert. Up until that time I worked outside during the punk bands since I was low man on the seniority pole. It was easy work. I'd sit on a cement stair behind the Whisky and keep people out of the employee parking lot and away from the back doors. Occasionally, someone would toss an egg at me or a bottle-throwing fight would start, but I'd simply hide behind the nearest car and let the Sheriff handle the guilty. At the end of July, however, Sexton hired another man, and I had to move inside. I saw my first punks and their dancing, and work wasn't fun anymore.

The punks were incredible, especially to an ex-frat rat from Ashtabula, Ohio. They just don't grow them like that in the Midwest. The worst looking were the Huntington Beach skinheads. They shaved their heads, wore black leather jackets covered with Nazi paraphernalia, chains, and, strangely enough, crosses. They wore faded, grimy blue jeans and huge stomping boots with steel toes, stirrups, bootstraps, and bandanas loosely tied around their ankles. The chains were padlocked or soldered together. Around their wrists and neck they wore leather bands dotted with sharpened studs. And those dudes were mean! One punk painted his eyebrows and sharpened his teeth. Groups of skinheads would huddle together during the night and pop capsules of amyl nitrate, then start punching each other.

The bouncers, usually Danny and I, would wade in and stop the fight. We had to establish control. That was much later, though. During that first night, I stayed away from them. I was frightened; I was ignorant. I wasn't scared of the people behind all the weird garb, I was afraid of what the weird garb represented. Later I got scared of the people.

There were other punks, the ones that weren't skinheads. They wore raincoats and overcoats and torn T-shirts and buttons, lots of buttons: X buttons, Circle Jerks buttons, Sex Pistols buttons; they loved their buttons. I saw a punk crawl around on his hands and knees for 45 minutes after we closed the Whisky one night, looking for a Dead Kennedys button.

On that first hot July night all hell broke loose. X was playing, the most highly touted and vocal of the punk bands. They walked onstage, mean, sassy, towering and controlling the crowd like hypnotic aliens escaped from a *Twilight Zone* set. The punks roared and the skanking began. Skanking is what their peculiar dance is called. The tight group of punks pushed everyone off the dance floor. This had a domino effect on the crowd and smashed people in the back of the club. When they had enough room they began to skank. It's a cross between a wild Lindy Hop and the Roller Derby. The dancers bent at the waist, jerked their arms over their heads in time to the music, and slammed themselves into one another like human dodge 'ems, electrically wired marionettes with flashing eyes swinging themselves around in a cacophony of light and sound. The slamming became quite violent when some fraternity boys slumming from UCLA joined the fray and fistfights broke out. The Huntington Beach skinheads didn't have much use for the alligator shirt crowd.

Danny, Morgan and I surrounded the dancers, slowly tightening the circle until the hardcores were isolated. The circle wouldn't close, so Danny picked out a wimpy-looking punk on the perimeter, winked at me, then jerked him out, slammed him against the wrought-iron fence that separates the dance floor from the tables and dragged him out the back door. My hand shook, and I couldn't catch my breath. The punks saw that we meant to keep order, and the less brave skanked off the dance floor. The hardcores continued, however, and we slowly tightened the noose, according to the rules.

The rules (unstated) were that when they fought, they were ejected. When a fist was raised in anger, the raisee would be out the back door with a bloody nose. When they jumped onstage, they were ousted. Some of the punk bands, like the Dead Kennedys, didn't mind if they skanked onstage; any other band, they were tossed. The roadies caught them as they climbed onstage and flung them back into the crowd. Some of the larger roadies would get astounding height and distance on their throws, and it wasn't unusual for a punk to fly, terror-stricken, over the crowd and off the dance floor. Sometimes other punks would try and catch their friends, but more often than not they would hit the floor with a sickening thud, and we'd simply drag the carcass out. When they ignored repeated orders to calm down, we ejected them. Anyone skanking with reckless abandon and who had premeditated injury in mind would be collared, flung behind the circle of bouncers and warned. If he smiled and nodded, he was allowed back into the skank. If he gave the finger and swore, he was restrained and led out the door.

Of course, these are only the general rules; each bouncer had a set of his own that he would rigorously enforce. For example, if anyone dared touch Morgan's hat they were open game for a bumpy trip outside. Danny's rule was simpler: Don't touch. If a punk skanked into Danny, he was lifted up by the scruff of his neck, shook until his teeth chattered like loose Chiclets, and dropped back on the floor.

That first night I tried to develop a rapport with the punks, a rapport I worked hard to maintain in the ensuing weeks, by letting them know how far they could go and enforcing it. I kept them separated from the weekend curious, and if the two were fighting, the nonpunk was carried out. After all, the dance floor was the punk's turf, and anyone else who entered the war zone was only asking for trouble. The wrist bands they wore had studs so sharp that they could slash your cheek into ribbons and you wouldn't feel it until you got home. Some of the punks were so dusted (on PCP) that they would have fought a battalion of marines, let alone a clean-cut guy like myself who looks as though he just stepped out of the Sigma Nu Christmas Ball.

I stood at the edge of the madness with both hands in front of me, flashlight poised in my right hand, and pushed the crazies away from me. X dug in onstage, Exene wailed away on verses that Lenin would have loved, and the punks skanked. They slammed into me and ground their boots into my toes and writhed on the floor like dying dogs. I sweated through two T-shirts and my ears hurt for days. I survived the first night by standing behind Danny. He taught me a choke hold and laughed at my ineptitude and unwillingness to inflict pain. I thought about quitting.

I came back the next night. And the next. Through the next month, as a matter of fact, regardless of how frightened I was, I enjoyed going to work. I cautiously learned how to play the tough guy, how to intimidate and buffalo large groups of people, how to handle ex-paratroopers who were just divorced and out looking for a good time, and I learned a bit about myself, too. There was an excitement, a feeling about the place. I was special. I was a bouncer at the world-famous Whisky-A-Go Go, on the Strip! I would clock in at 7:30 p.m. and sit bug-eyed as some strange new wave band would go through its sound check. I was intrigued by the swirling, grasping, Bohemian music world and its participants: the party-loving, insecure musicians; the slick-talking, tough-acting managers; the pathetic groupies; the nomadic roadies.

Two weeks later, in early August, Fear came to the Whisky. Fear is a band, not an emotion. They haven't the musical talents of X nor the hardline political background of the Dead Kennedys or Gun Club. But Fear are in a class of their own. I thought I'd seen everything there was to see in Punkdom, except the spitters, and Fear were spitters. Each song began with a staccato ONE, TWO, THREE, FOUR! and preached death, violence, individual acts of perversion, sex, mayhem, and the like. The punks, their women, and anyone else with a load of saliva crowded the stage and expectorated on the band. Fear loved it! The lead singer grinned apishly as he was covered with hawkers and spit back at the crowd. Between songs he screamed at the punks, "Go back to the valley!" or, "Register for the draft and get killed in Iran!," liberally punctuating the insults with enough profanities to curl an Irishman's ear.

The punks responded with volleys of spit that covered his face, shirt and pants. During the late show, the lead guitar player had to stop playing and wipe the spit off his face with a white towel that he threw into the crowd. At first I laughed. I laughed hard. Then I was disgusted, and I almost threw up. That was the strange thing about the Whisky: it was a vacuum of relativity, a time-warp nightclub where you willingly surrendered your objectivity at the door along with your four bucks and entered a world where the most asinine, stupid, incredible acts seemed normal and acceptable. Later that same evening, I found a young woman on the floor of the ladies' room plunging an ice pick into her palm. Blood was spurting out of her hand and dripping on the floor. She looked at me and said, "I'm into pain."

Shortly afterwards, the Surf Punks rolled into the Whisky for a weekend. The Surf Punks are like the ten-lane freeways—they could only exist in L.A. Their hit song "My Beach" is a testament to the chauvinistic attitudes of a surf-loving 18-year-old. Their followers were mostly young, tan, blond-haired types who drank lots of beer and had good-looking girlfriends. The stage was dressed like a Malibu beach, complete with lifeguards, bikinied big-breasted high school girls and surfboards. Midway through the show, KLOS disc jockey Frazier Smith ran onstage, ripped off one of the girls' bikinis and disappeared backstage.

Unfortunately, these shows were few and far between. I was beginning to look for ways to stay off the floor. I began to spend more time backstage, the holding area of the zoo and the gathering spot of the mirror and razor blade crowd. The hallways outside the dressing rooms were jammed nightly with jabbering cocaine freaks telling outrageous lies about record deals and friendships with Bruce Springsteen and how to get backstage at the Forum. The technicians' room was often camouflaged with a thick, billowing haze of marijuana smoke, and the general atmosphere was one of early Roman hedonism. I once observed the lead singer of a well-known female band sucking up lines of cocaine on the lid of a toilet.

Some nights were just plain boring. After the weekend punk and new wave bands, the rest of the week would be filled with ear-shattering rock and roll dinosaurs, or pop bands so bad the sound men would fall asleep in their booth. The rock and roll nights, however, could display a higher level of primal violence than the weekend nights. Scores of drunks, most covered with tattoos and Kiss T-shirts, would initiate knock-down, drag-out, bar-clearing brawls that would send the waitresses scurrying to the restrooms and cause the quieter, calmer customers to cover their heads and slip out the front door. I would watch the fight and call the sheriff. This was my "discretion is the better part of valor" technique.

I was learning to avoid confrontations. I was becoming the master of non-violent bouncing. Gone were the days when I would jump into the fray and go for the gusto. As time went on, the distance between the customer and myself became very pronounced. I never let anyone too close to me, just in case he was carrying a knife or a razor or was quick with his fists. Why the paranoia? A Charles Atlas type threatened to shoot me unless I let him backstage. I was horrified at the low value of my life. I saw one former member of the Byrds wield a knife upstairs and damn near kill a pouting groupie. I was sucker-punched by an angry giant who later tried to climb the front of an apartment building across from the Whisky. Morgan caught a guy on the dance floor with a gun stuck in his pants. Danny had his arm broken in a fight at the front door. Bill, a part-time bouncer who's since left California, had his mouth busted open by a young girl who hit him with a dog collar she had wrapped around her fist. No, I wasn't paranoid. I was past that.

September was one long month. My friends, even strangers at parties, advised me to quit the Whisky. I couldn't. There was something, repugnant as it was, that held me there. Maybe it was the violence. When I did get involved, it was thrilling despite the dangers, if not sexually exciting or cathartic.

Three incidents precipitated my departure from the Whisky. The first occurred during the Go-Go's show in mid-September. The Go-Go's are an all-girl band who draw a boisterous crowd, punk and non-punk alike. The skanking was at its all-time ferocious high. A shaking, spastic Rude Boy (one who follows the English ska movement) was jerking about on the dance floor like a dying fish. I was about to unleash one of my patented restraining-warning holds when I felt a tug on my shirt. I turned to find a small, purple-haired, white-skinned girl with fear in her eyes beckoning me to follow her.

She took me to the ladies' room, where I found a tall, emaciated young man floating in a puddle of blood. A girl kneeling behind him and propping his head up said that he had broken his neck. I had never seen a man die before, and I wasn't looking to an inaugural event. We turned him over. His neck wasn't broken, but he had a deep gash in his skull. We lifted him up and carried him outside. I called an ambulance. I asked the purple-haired girl how the man had gotten injured, and she calmly remarked that he had been hit with an iron bar in an argument over a single Quaalude.

The second incident was much more well known, indeed, infamous. Black Flag, a notoriously wild and subhuman band, was scheduled. Their last three shows had been stopped by the police, and most insiders were surprised that they were booked. The Whisky did not advertise the show, allowing word of mouth to sell it. Two weeks prior, I had a chat with some of my skinhead friends who told me, point blank, that they meant to "rip the Whisky down" when Black Flag appeared. I told Sexton, who shrugged his shoulders. He didn't book the bands, he only ran the club.

Well, October 8th came off as planned. The club was sardined with hundreds of half-human specimens, all of them loaded for bear. A couple of bouncers prudently called in sick. While the first show raged on, the line for the second show wound down Sunset, up Clark. Some of the kids were drinking beer, others smoking joints. Someone threw a beer bottle into the street, another followed, and another. One struck a car, and the occupant got in a fight with the suspected thrower. More beer bottles hit the street. Fist fights broke out. Punks hanging out on the other side of Clark threw bottles onto Sunset, disrupting traffic. A sheriff's car sped to the scene and was pelted by bottles. Ten minutes later, by all accounts, 22 sheriff's vehicles flooded Sunset, and riot-geared sheriffs and special forces waded into the crowd.

I knew I had reached my limit, the end of my proverbial rope. The whole punk scene seemed a harbinger of new dangers, pseudo-thrills and massive freaked-out antics that I had no desire to be a part of. Unfortunately, I worked one more weekend, long enough to see the Plasmatics. The Plasmatics were a New York-based band making their first trip out west. The drummer and three guitar players wore Mohawk haircuts, one green, one blue, and, on the only black man in the group, one white. The lead guitarist wore heavy boots, tights, and a pink tutu. The singer, Wendy Williams, was dressed in a tight pair of short-shorts and a ripped shirt.

They jammed the Whisky that weekend. People were hanging off the ceiling and the heat was intolerable. The evening began with three short films of the Plasmatics, driving cars and smashing them, blowing them up onstage, and the music was loud enough to peel the wallpaper and wake up even the most stoned patrons. As soon as she stepped onstage, Miss Williams sledgehammered two transistor radios, much to the delight of the audience. I stood at the top of the stairs and watched in amazement. A television set was brought behind Williams and set on a ladder, and, to the accompaniment of dirge-like music, she performed fellatio on the sledge-hammer, avariciously licking the chrome business end; then she whirled and buried the hammer in the screen, knocking the set off the ladder to the stage floor, where she finished it off with dozens of well-aimed strikes. The crowd roared with a bloody edge that reminded me of a bullfight I had once seen.

After an interminable period during which I shoved paper into my ears, Williams hopped back onstage, this time dressed in a bikini bottom and whipped cream that she had smeared over her chest, hiding a pair of massive breasts discreetly covered with two pieces of electrician's tape. She licked the cream off herself as she sang the next song. I stopped working and leaned over the rail and watched. Williams produced a shotgun that she again licked with relish. Then she pointed it over the crowd's head and fired. The explosion inspired panic in waves, slow-motion hysteria as the crowd ducked and fell backward at the same time. I was on one knee before I realized that she must be shooting blanks, an obvious conclusion, but one slow in coming in that bizarre atmosphere.

Williams swung the gun around and shot at her amplifier, which burst into flame and crumpled to the floor. Then she aimed the gun skyward, fired, and five or six chickens—live chickens—fell out of the ceiling to the stage floor, sprinkling the pulsating audience with loose plaster. Tens of punks at the edge of the stage grabbed for the chickens, and one was taken into the crowd. The roadies jumped offstage to recover the fowl, and a fight ensued. Finally, they rescued the chicken and threw it back onstage. It had lost most of its feathers and quickly hid behind one of the amplifiers.

My sensibilities were failing me, escaping into the smoky, acrid shotgun haze that hung over the center of the room like a snow cloud. I felt as though I had stumbled in on a secret tribal rite, complete with feathers, drums, fertility dances and mass religious hysteria. This was theatre of Organized Self-Indulgence, the Me Generation's answer to self-inflicted pain. I was nauseated by the last act and the people's reaction to it.

While the last echoes of the shotgun blasts were still bouncing off the walls, Miss Williams approached her climax. A new guitar was carried onstage by two hooded men, set on an easel. Then Miss Williams was handed a chainsaw, which she coaxed into life. Finally, she turned the frightening machine on the guitar. As she sawed the guitar in half, she wriggled her tongue and pulled on her nipple. I left my post and walked downstairs. The crowd was mesmerized, caught up in a communal nightmare, undulating and whining like hungry animals.

I decided to slip out the back door into the night. Walk away from it while I still understood it. Then a fight erupted on the floor. I saw two bouncers trying to pull a massive, dark-haired man out the back door. I turned away. No more fights. Then Bobby saw me and cried out my name. I stopped for a moment, made my decision, and jumped on the fellow's back. He growled like a trapped lion and shook me off like so much water. The audience ignored us and watched Williams massacre the guitar.

We got him past the bar, but he was tenacious, grabbing T-shirts and waitresses as we hit him and tried to force him out the back. He screamed wildly and hung on to the door frame. A bouncer named Larry hit him in the throat and he let go, while Bobby slammed the door. My hand was still on the frame. The iron door hit me with a crunchingly deciding blow and blood spurted out of a deep purple ravine that crossed my thumb. I slumped to the floor. Larry knelt beside me for a moment, then rushed to stop another fight. Miss Williams finished with the guitar and raced offstage. The crowd yelled for more, and the house lights came up. I propped myself in a corner and held my wrist.

Time slowed to a crawl. I heard voices, but they seemed to be coming from another time zone. My crushed cells sent screams of pain racing over my nerve synapses and jarred my brain into thinking positively for the first time in three months. The job was too much for me, and I knew it. I lurched to my feet and looked around like a strange man in a strange country. Sexton walked by and I handed him my flashlight. He stared at my wrist but said nothing. I walked onto the main floor, through the beer cans and liquor bottles and out the front door. Danny looked at the wrist, then my eyes, and clapped me on the back. Bobby waved his crossword puzzle book. I plowed through a bevy of radical punks and turned up Clark and went away.

And I never looked back. Never.   [1981]

JAMES D. HOUSTON

Byting the Apple

THE SAN FRANCISCO CIVIC CENTER is noted for its pigeons and for its restful, prewar architecture. Pre-First World War. The high rotunda of the city hall has a cathedral-like serenity that can put the mind at ease. The pigeons swarm and swoop in the bright sunlight, in the granite bowl these buildings make. Sitting there watching them, and watching the winos positioned knee to knee in the April shade, as they pass back and forth the poorboy of muscatel, I would never have guessed what was going on some ten or fifteen feet below my bench. If I had not paid my $10 to pass through the door of the Civic Auditorium and then descend by escalator, I would never in my life have envisioned the menagerie of equipment on display in the underground extravaganza room called Brooks Hall.

"The biggest event of its kind in history," the organizer told me later. "Not as big as the NCC next month in Chicago, but the emphasis there has always been mainframe, the big federal and industrial stuff."

"Of its kind" meant equipment that brings computers down to the individual human scale. "Biggest" meant five hundred booths and over thirty-two thousand people—a record that eventually stood for several months. "In history" meant since 1976, when fairs of this type began.

As he said that date, '76 did seem a long way back. History is so compressed—in the accelerated world of electronics technology—that this morning's breakthrough is already old news. The spring of 1981, when the Sixth Annual West Coast Computer Fair took place, seems now as ancient as Rome. But it happened to be my first computer fair. It had for me the shine of the Ringling Brothers Barnum and Bailey Circus that came to San Francisco when I was twelve. And I was not alone. I saw many that day who gazed in wonder. I saw grizzled computer veterans whose eyes were filled with true surprise. Excitement was in the air. A sense of discovery filled Brooks Hall, because in those days the personal computer was still a rather recent idea. Moreover, many of its basic features had been invented or developed right down the Peninsula there, forty miles south, in Silicon Valley, and this was the season when it was being introduced in a big way to the public at large.

The main hall was a blizzard of light, a blur of toaster-size screens humming and busy with numbers and rolling print and here and there little robot people acting out stories for kids. Under the steady *ack-ack* from the printout machines, you could see gorgeous full-color butterflies, a perfectly reproduced dollar bill, a ticking watch, a sinuous mountain of topo lines. Rapid-fire eighth and sixteenth notes followed the honky-tonk tinkle of a computerized player piano doing "The Muskrat Ramble."

After my eyes and ears stopped jumping—actually it was during my second tour around the hall—it dawned on me that every other booth at the fair featured the same piece of equipment. It was The Apple II. No single booth was selling the Apple by itself. But dozens, hundreds sold components that interfaced with Apple—graphics programs, tax accounting programs, music readers, war games. It was impressive. I made a third trip around the hall, to look closer. It went beyond electronics. In those days— back in early 1981—the TRS-80 out of Texas still held the nationwide edge in sales. But Apple was clearly running first in something else. Call it pizzazz. Or mystique. In a juggler you might call it style. In a religious leader it would be charisma.

A cult had formed around the Apple. In Vacaville, California, a retail outlet called itself The Apple Orchard. From Burbank you could order a text-editing program called APPLE P.I.E. (Programma International Editor). From Lake Havasu, Arizona, programs were being sold in packages called Apple Sacks. In Aptos, California, a college biologist was offering a course called The Biology of the Apple. In San Francisco there was a computer club, The Apple Core, with a publication named *The Cider Press*. In Venice there was another club, The Original Apple Corps, and at their booth you could subscribe to *Applesauce*. Meanwhile, everywhere you looked the T-shirts were visible. Large, medium, and small, light tan in color, with no words on the shirt, just a big juicy red apple across the chest, and one bite gone.

Should I have been startled by the sight of a lovely young woman at the computer fair walking around in her clogs and her jeans and her snug-fitting Apple T-shirt, with a big bite chomped out of the apple?

Does that suggest anything?

What about Eve?

Is Eve too traditional? The Garden of Eden?

That is what she brought to mind, there in the basement, with the monitors winking and the printouts chattering. Eve. The Garden. The Tree. The Original Apple. The question is, When Eve sank her teeth in to take that first karmic bite, what was she after? She wasn't after vitamins and minerals, as I understand the story. She was after more knowledge, more information. The eternal human quest. And the more forbidden, or forbidding, the information, the more urgent and attractive that quest becomes.

I looked again at the front page of *Applesauce*, at the exuberant members of The Original Apple Corps, at the battalion of components that interface with Apple II, and I remembered a full-page ad someone had sent me from the *Wall Street Journal*, which begins like this:

What is a personal computer?

Let me answer with the analogy of the bicycle and the condor. A few years ago I read a study—I believe it was in *Scientific American*—about the efficiency of locomotion for various species on earth, including man. The study determined which species was the most efficient, in terms of getting from point A to point B with the least amount of energy exerted. The condor won. Man made a rather unimpressive showing, about one third of the way down the list.

But someone there had the insight to test man riding a bicycle. Man was twice as efficient as the condor! This illustrated man's ability as a tool maker. When man created the bicycle he created a tool that amplified an inherent ability. . . .

Now, there are not many places in the world where you will find this particular gathering of images. A bicycle. A condor. An apple. And a personal computer. Something more than circuitry is going on here, I thought. A sense of poetry. Perhaps even a sense of history. I decided then that when the fair was over I would have to find and talk to whoever could think up a computer with such a name, and such an ad for the *Wall Street Journal*, and such a T-shirt.

A while back someone wrote to the San Jose *Mercury News* complaining about the way the term "Silicon Valley" turns up more and more often as a synonym for Santa Clara Valley. "They are not the same," this citizen cried out. And I agree with him. The valley called Santa Clara has been here in its present shape for many thousands of years—a flat and fertile basin, in times past a submerged and southerly extension of San Francisco Bay, and still bordered by parallel ridges of the Coast Range. Silicon Valley is a very recent event, and it exists much more in the mind than it does in the landscape.

Physically it is a collection of low buildings that have been added, laid into various niches and cleared spaces like a scattering of heat-resistant ceramic tiles, around and among the various towns that now contain it: Palo Alto, Los Altos, Mountain View, Sunnyvale, Cupertino, Santa Clara, San Jose. The four long, low buildings that house Apple Computer—sand-colored, with red roof-tiles in the mission manner—are so new, green plastic nursery tape still flutters around the saplings staked outside. They have to be new. Six years ago the personal computer industry did not exist. At the moment, according to the fellow I am about to meet, it is the fastest-growing industry in the history of American business. "In six years," he will soon be telling me, "from zero to a billion dollars."

His name is Steve Jobs. Together with his partner, Steve Wozniak, he developed the first Apple when he was twenty-one years old. Now he is twenty-six, lean and purposeful as he comes striding toward me through the lobby of one of his buildings. He wears jeans, sandals, a plain checkered shirt. His dark brown hair is collar length, his dark beard trimmed. Behind the rimless glasses his eyes, very shrewd and watchful eyes, show a glint of amusement as he says—and this is his opening line—"I have to walk down and draw some money out of the bank. How's that for an introduction to Silicon Valley?"

He is flying out tonight to Boston, to a gathering of some ten thousand people who use his company's equipment, a gathering called The Apple Fest, where he will be the keynote speaker, and he has run short of cash. So we walk two blocks to the nearest Bank of America, another new, low building that presides over a recently completed shopping plaza. From the way Steve prowls around looking over the tellers' fences I figure that whoever usually handles his accounts is not here. Finally he steps into the long line of customers waiting for service.

I am struck by the humbleness, or perhaps it is the sheer youthfulness, of this move. Here he is, vice chairman of a company that, in recent months, moved $250 million through the securities markets, a company that, according to *Time* magazine, enjoyed "one of the biggest and most successful stock launchings in the history of Wall Street," here is Steve standing in line at the neighborhood bank waiting to get some spending money for his trip to Boston.

This is not, as I quickly discover, an uncharacteristic moment. *Loose* is his middle name. He is loose of limb and loose on formalities. At the corporate headquarters he has no parking slot of his own. In his office, which is the size of a small kitchen, the desk is right-angled into one corner, more like a tinkerer's workbench. On the wall above it, there is one embellishment, a small frame around the red and vibrating word:

THINK

We have come back to his office to talk about the history of Apple—which is really the history of his relationship with Wozniak and with these two coexisting valleys—and when we sit down at the round, breakfast-sized conference table in the center of the room, he slips off his sandals and puts his bare feet up there next to the table's one decoration, a small transparent apple made of solid glass.

"I first met Woz when I was thirteen," he says, "in another friend's garage. He was four years older than me and had just graduated from the same high school I was about to go to. He was the first person I met who knew more than I did about electronics. I started hanging around him after that, soaking up all I could. We became friends and have been friends ever since. I've known him now for thirteen years. That's half my life."

Jobs was still in high school when they teamed up for their first collaboration, which he begins to describe, then hesitates.

"I don't know if I can tell you this."

He turns to look out the window. "What's the statute of limitations, seven years? Woz and I . . ." Another pause. Then he laughs.

"Did you ever hear of a blue box? You know how when you make a long distance phone call, you hear these tones that go"—and he sings the bleeping rise and fall—"doo-doo-doo-doo-doo-doo? Well, you can make a little box that goes doo-doo-doo-doo-doo-doo. And you can basically make free phone calls all over the world. And we made the best one ever. We put a note down in the bottom of each one, it was our little trade mark. It said, 'He's got the whole world in his hands.' You could get on a pay phone and get over White Plains, New York, and take a satellite to London and cable to Tokyo, and another satellite back to Paris, and take a cable back to White Plains, and call the pay phone next door."

I ask Steve if he was taking any electronics courses back in those high school days.

He shakes his head. "There really weren't any. You just got it by osmosis."

"Osmosis?"

"It's in the atmosphere."

Some kids grow up on the ranch and become cowboys. Some kids grow up in Beverly Hills immersed in show business and become studio executives. Steve Jobs grew up five miles from where we're sitting, in what appears to be a suburban neighborhood like thousands across the land, but you talk to him for a while and you see that he and Woz came of age in this new realm called Silicon Valley just as its headlong energy reached full acceleration. Neither of them holds a college degree or any of the other emblems of formal training. Wozniak's father was an electronics engineer at Lockheed, who had his son designing logic circuits by the time he was in the fourth grade. A few years later he was already building his own computers. Jobs in turn learned a lot from Woz, and from belonging to local computer clubs, and from hanging around the neighborhood garages.

He is the first to acknowledge that Apple could only have happened within the unique support system this Valley has to offer. He feels a sense of lineage that goes back at least as far as the 1930s, and he feels immersed in an environment he is eager to talk about. He calls it the culture of entrepreneurial risk.

"You do not get penalized for failure here," he says. "You are expected to try things. If you go out on your own and try something and fail, your career isn't over. You can actually be more valuable to the next person you work for, because of what you have learned in the process. It operates at every level. There was a point, when Woz and I were working on the first Apple, we needed ten thousand dollars' worth of parts. So we went to a parts distributor and asked him to help us out. And he did. He lent us the parts on a twenty-nine-day loan with no credit, because there is a role model for doing things that way. And you need that infrastructure. You need the engineer who is willing to go out on his own, and you need the parts distributor who is not going to say, 'Well, I want you guys to sign over your house.' He has to be able to say, 'Okay, I'll tell you what. You don't have a house, but I'll take a gamble anyway.' So he lent us the parts, and we went off and built the equipment and paid them back in twenty-nine days."

Adventurous risk is all around you, along with the legendary results, the breakthrough devices that keep this atmosphere charged up and ever challenging. Steve's voice rises with urgency and fills the office when he exclaims, "Look what's come out of this valley. Basically, the first integrated circuit. The first micro-processor was invented ten miles from here. The first personal computer. Now, the first genetics companies. Probably five out of the top ten things we're going to look back fifty years from now and say, these are the ten things that impacted the world the most, five of them are going to come from right here in this valley."

The passion in his voice almost has the ring of patriotism, making it that much clearer to me that Steve is talking about his true homeland and native surroundings—this volatile mix of microchips and circuit boards and commerce in the fast lane. He grew up in the midst of it, with a native's grasp of how it all works.

The more he talked, the more I began to wonder where this new valley had actually come from, this little country unto itself where, among other things, a new kind of apple had sprouted. What was it doing here? When I finished high school in Santa Clara Valley back in 1951, the word "silicon" was still something you maybe heard mentioned once in chemistry class and never remembered. By the time Steve finished high school, twenty-one years later, an entirely new type of valley had made its appearance, superimposed upon the original. But why? Why here, in a sunny basin that for a hundred years had been cherished for its apricots, pears, walnuts, peaches, and prunes? The new industry did not require any of the things the old farms and ranches required, unless it be vision, and hustle, and a gambler's nerve. The basic ingredient is a crystalline substance that can be processed in labs anywhere but happens to be processed in large quantities here—in some of these low buildings spread around among the suburbs, often in the shade of surviving walnut trees.

It is strange. It is almost out of character in a state where most of the industry and so much of the fame has been directly tied to the physical endowments. Gold. Oil. Soil. Harbors.

If you add climate to that list, electronics too might be said to have a regional and earthly anchor. Climate explains a lot of what goes on in California, and has helped keep this industry centered here. But climate is not where it begins. When I started asking around, everyone sooner or later mentioned Stanford University and a two-way flow of brain power between New England and the Bay Area. The phrase "critical mass" also came up several times: a gathering of ingredients, which acquires its own magnetic effect. A clustering begins, and breeds more of itself.

The earliest name you hear is that of Lee De Forest, who was living in Palo Alto in 1912 when he invented the triode, key component in the vacuum tube, which made it possible for the first time to modulate or amplify electric current. De Forest, who had studied at Yale, was working for Federal Telegraph, a company founded in 1909 by a Stanford graduate, with some help from David Starr Jordan, Stanford's first president. Today, in one of Palo Alto's tree-lined, vintage neighborhoods, a small plaque near the corner of Channing and Emerson marks "The Birthplace of Electronics."

The next name you hear—and this one lurks right at the center of the critical mass—is that of Frederick Terman. He graduated from Stanford in 1920 with a degree in chemical engineering, went to M.I.T. for a doctorate in electrical engineering, then returned to Stanford, where he eventually became a department head and later provost. Two of his students in the early 1930s were William Hewlett and David Packard. Both received electrical engineering degrees in 1934. Five years later, with Terman's support, they founded Hewlett-Packard in Palo Alto, now one of the world's largest electronics firms, with annual sales over $3 billion.

Hewlett and Packard are the archetypal Silicon Valley pioneers. The way they started—in a garage—has become the classic way. This is where Apple got started. According to Steve Jobs, this is where some of next year's discoveries are already in the works. "There are guys in garages all over," he says. "I could show you thousands." This is why Jim Warren, who organized the West Coast Computer Fair, has special booths available called micro-booths. "They are smaller and priced more economically per foot," he told me, "so that some fellow with an original idea can come in here and try it out on the public. We have people who started out on a shoestring two or three years ago, renting a micro, coming back this year in a full-size booth."

After World War II Terman promoted a number of ideas that put Stanford on course toward its present position in the forefront of innovative technology. He advocated top salaries to draw scientific talent to the campus. He worked to bring in federally funded projects. He encouraged the collaboration with private industry and supported what has come to be known as the Stanford Industrial Park, some six hundred sixty acres from the university's eighty-two-hundred-acre holding, which was an early home for Hewlett-Packard, Varian Associates, and the Shockley Semiconductor Lab—all within easy biking distance of Stanford's research facilities.

In the legend of Silicon Valley the name "William Shockley" is heard over and over again, usually accompanied by a raise of the eyebrows and a dip in the voice. He is another figure at the center of this critical mass, which had truly begun to exert its magnetic powers by the time he arrived in 1955. Shockley later joined the Stanford faculty and embarrassed everyone there by advancing the idea that blacks are genetically of lower intelligence than whites. But that came toward the end of his long career. And I.Q. testing, as some apologists have pointed out, was not really his area. He was a physicist, with degrees from Cal Tech and M.I.T. In 1947, while employed at Bell Labs in New Jersey, he co-invented the junction transistor, which launched the modern age of electronics and won him a Nobel Prize.

In 1955 Shockley left Bell and moved to Palo Alto, a return, in fact, to his boyhood town. Beckmann Instruments had offered him a higher salary and a free hand with his own researches. A number of talented young specialists were soon drawn West to work with Shockley, among them Robert Noyce and Gordon Moore, two men whose careers have been almost perfectly joined to the boom times.

Today Noyce is vice chairman at Intel Corporation in Santa Clara, while Moore is chairman of the board. Noyce is a native of Iowa. In 1956 he had recently completed his doctorate in electrical engineering at M.I.T. Moore grew up twenty-five miles due west of where his office stands today. By the age of twenty-four he held a Ph.D. in chemical engineering from Cal Tech. In 1957 they were among eight men who left Shockley's firm to found Fairchild Semiconductor in nearby Mountain View. Silicon Valley was officially ushered in, it has been said, with the development of the first practical integrated circuit at Fairchild some three years later. Shockley's transistor had miniaturized the process for controlling current flow, reduced it down to a small chip of semiconducting material, usually silicon. The integrated circuit is a multiple transistor, whereby ten or a hundred or a thousand circuits are squeezed into something the size of your little toenail.

Fairchild, in turn, was soon to become the industry's most prolific breeding ground, or launch pad. At least fifty Silicon Valley companies have been started by former employees.

"This is an extremely flexible technology," Gordon Moore told me, remembering his ten years at Fairchild, where he had directed research and development. "You can do a lot of different things with it. And Fairchild wasn't able to pursue all the ideas that were coming around. Engineers would see opportunities and take it in a slightly different direction and maybe set up an important company."

One of these spin-off companies was Intel, formed by Moore and Noyce in 1968. In 1980, *California Business* listed it as the fastest-growing corporation in the state. Among its main products is the micro-processor, developed at Intel in 1971 (while Steve Jobs was a junior at Homestead High School, five miles away: see *osmosis*). A chip that can actually execute instructions, the micro-processor was another giant step forward, or rather a leap downward and inward, since this happens to be an industry where you advance by getting smaller.

These tiny, miraculous and infamous chips—the memory chips that can store information; and the chips that work like minuscule computers—they are no bigger than shirt buttons and they have spawned and spurred this runaway industry with all its components and interfaces. The firms that have clustered in and around the critical mass now number in the hundreds—some say six hundred, some say a thousand, some give up trying to count. The technology proliferates around the world. But for the time being the center remains here, in this valley of the mind that has traded in walnuts for circuit boards and traded the name of a Spanish saint for the name of, according to my dictionary, "a nonmetallic chemical element found always in combination and more abundant in nature than any other element except oxygen."

Until the mid-1970s the main applications had been industrial, federal and military. Bell was computerized, and the IRS, and the Jupiter space capsule. But the common home owner, the trimmer of lawns, or the woman waiting for the stoplight to change, had only heard about computers from a distance, had seen computer-villain movies like *The President's Analyst* and *2001*, and had seen the effects on mail-order offers from the *Reader's Digest*, where a name had been added to what appeared to be a typed letter, beginning *Dear Mr. and Mrs.* with only a faint discrepancy in the shadings of ink to tell you that your pen pal was really a room-size machine somewhere in the Midwest.

When Steve Jobs and Steve Wozniak met up again, after a few years of going their separate ways, when they began to tinker again in the family garage in the summer of 1975, the home computer, the classroom computer, the computer for the small partnership and the backyard businessman, the preassembled, personal, and affordable computer you could unwrap and plug right in was an idea whose time had come. Like one of those radiating lightbulbs above the inventor's head in the old-time cartoons, the idea was hanging in the air above the entrepreneurial garage door, which from the street still looked much like any number of garage doors between San Jose and Daly City.

After high school, Jobs spent a year and a half at Reed College in Oregon. When he ran out of money he came back and worked awhile for Atari, the video game company, in Sunnyvale. They sent him to Europe, and not long afterward he was off by himself on a six-month trek through India. Wozniak in the meantime had been to the University of Colorado and had done a few quarters at Berkeley. He had designed a computing calculator and a low-cost hobby kit. He was working at Hewlett-Packard, designing hand-held calculators, when he and Jobs began thinking their way toward a new kind of machine.

"We had designed—mostly Woz, actually, but a little bit on my part— a little terminal you could hook up to another computer to use cheap. And we thought, well, we don't just want a terminal, we really want a computer."

They spent six months designing the prototype. Now, from a cabinet below his desk he pulls out an uncovered circuit board and casually tosses it onto the table, in the same way I have seen writers showing the galleys of a first novel long out of print, a thin packet of ink-filled pages that represent a year of one's life. It is the size of a small hand-tray, packed tightly with rows of dark blocks. In one corner I see the stamped letters *Apple I*.

"Only two hundred of these were ever made," he says. "That was the first computer we designed together, and we basically designed it because we couldn't afford to buy one."

When they showed their idea to a local retailer, he immediately said, "Great! I'll take fifty!"

In a matter of seconds they had gone from zero to a $25,000 order. All they lacked was a company, and some start-up capital, and some merchandise to sell.

Making what some Californians would consider the ultimate sacrifice, Jobs sold his VW van. When Woz sold his HP-65 calculator, they had a total of $1,300. They borrowed some parts, and while Woz worked overtime perfecting Apple I, Jobs got on the phone to organize the fledgling corporation.

"What was your feeling at that point?" I ask him. "Did you know you were on to something very large?"

"Yeah. But not this large. Woz and I had done a lot of stuff together, the blue boxes, and other ideas. At that point 'large' meant, Boy, if this really flies, maybe we can afford to buy a house, or get the car back."

By the summer of 1976 they were designing Apple II. Simultaneously, as Steve says, "We had to learn about marketing and distribution. And so we did. I wrote the first ad myself. And we got it placed. We wrote a technical article. And we got that placed. We started finding dealers. We called up Intel and asked who their ad agency was, and they said Regis-McKenna, so we called up Regis and went over there and said, 'We want you to do some ads for us but we don't have any money to pay you.' "

Regis-McKenna is a Palo Alto agency that specializes in high-tech Silicon Valley companies. On the day I visited Apple, Rene White, the fellow supervising their account, had spent the morning with a writer from the *Wall Street Journal* briefing him on the mechanics of genesplicing. Five years earlier, when Jobs and Woz came asking for ads on credit, Regis-McKenna said, "Go away."

"They told us 'Go away' four times," Steve says, smiling. "Finally they said, 'Okay, we'll do it,' and we became their largest account."

Call it brass. Call it moxie. Call it self-assertiveness. Or call it, as Steve does, "the entrepreneurial risk culture." Whatever its source, Jobs and Woz were never afraid to ask for what they wanted, or to go right to the best people they could reach to find answers to whatever they needed to know next. In Steve's case, he seems to have discovered it early in life, perhaps by osmosis. "When I was thirteen," he says, "I called Bill Hewlett on the phone and asked him for some parts I needed to build a little piece of electronic equipment I was working on. And he helped me out." With another smile he adds, "I actually got a summer job at H-P too."

From other Silicon Valley firms they hired away some top management people to help orchestrate the company's growth. Healthy sums of venture capital soon followed. In 1977, the year Apple II was introduced, sales hit $2.5 million. In 1978 the gross was over $15 million, and in 1979 it had jumped to $70 million. By the time I talked to Steve that annual figure had increased fivefold, eighteen hundred people were on the company payroll, a quarter of a million Apples had been sold, and there was no end in sight.

It had been a triumph of timing and superb design, together with a brilliantly simple packaging idea. Something about the Apple catches the imagination in a way that the equipment inside—the integrated circuits, the micro-processors—never could. The name, it turns out, was Steve's idea, along with the condor and the bicycle.

"I thought it up," he says. "But Woz and I talked about it for a long time. We wanted a name that wasn't so harsh and didn't have such a heavy connotation. For a lot of people, 'computer' is still a scary word. Apple is sort of warm and takes the edge off it."

"It's earthy," I say, "organic, nonthreatening . . ."

He interrupts me, bristling slightly, and I see that his sense for connotation is carefully tuned. " 'Organic' is probably the wrong word," he says. "We just wanted something simple and friendly."

"What about the bite?" I ask, still thinking of Eve, at her fateful moment. "Who decided to take the bite out of the side?"

"Oh that." He laughs lightly. "A fellow at the agency is the one who designed our logo. He did it sort of for fun. It's a pun. *Byte* is a computer term. Technically, eight bits of information. I guess the main reason, graphically, was he wanted to make sure everyone knows it's an apple."

"What else could it be?"

"A cherry. He wanted to make sure no one would mistake it for a cherry."

Hmmmmm, thinks the writer, deflated. So much for biblical symbols. I have been ready to ask him about my Garden of Eden theory. At the mention of puns and cherries, I decided against it.

Steve is getting restless. He takes his feet off the table and slips them back into his sandals. He has things to do before catching the plane to Boston. A writer from *Fortune* magazine is waiting to talk to him. Then he has to pick up a suit. "All my suits are either in a state of disrepair," he mutters, "or at the cleaners. And they close in an hour."

There is time for a final question, and I am relieved to hear that his reply answers the one I did not ask. In an oblique way he confirms my reading of the logo. Eve bit into the apple and opened whatever secrets had been locked inside The Tree of Knowledge. It is Steve's belief that a bite into Apple II, or Apple III, is a 1980s way to liberate some new resources of the mind.

I ask him if he actually foresees the day—the one we so often hear predicted now—when every home owner will have the console and the personal keyboard.

"They are going to be in every school and office first," he says. "Eventually in every home. We think there is a revolutionary process going on here, which is the integration of personal computers into the society at a very individual level. That is going to take about ten years to happen, and we want to be a driving force behind that."

He leans forward and his voice accelerates, with the same fervor I heard when he summed up this valley's history.

"It's my belief that each time there has been a new source of free energy, civilization has taken a step forward. We are living now off the wake of the petrochemical revolution, based on petrochemical energy, which is still basically free, relative to the energy inside. And look at the impact *that* had! We have very rarely had things that free *intellectual* energy. Language was a big breakthrough. And mathematics. And printing, to some degree. But this thing"—pointing to the twelve-pound, typewriter-sized Apple I sitting on his desk, with video display terminal attached—"it takes about a third of the power of one lightbulb, and it saves me two hours a day. That is basically free intellectual energy. In a very limited way. But it is going to get much more interesting in the next decade. I think the revolution is going to come through free intellectual energy. It is going to dwarf the petrochemical revolution, and I think it is going to happen in my lifetime."

At Brooks Hall the various shapes this revolution might take had been visible everywhere. Signs and portents. It had been half carnival and half window into the near and distant future, and you could not afford to dismiss any of it, since you never know when or where next season's Jobs-and-Wozniak will emerge to make their unannounced debut. It had ranged from the awesome and dazzling to the zany and absurd.

Back in one corner I came across a game called Interface with Fiction. A long-haired fellow was getting up the nerve to add some of his own dialogue to a novel that had been programmed onto a storage disk. The novel was called *Wheeling and Dealing: A Gripping Tale of Skullduggery in High Places*. The story line was incomplete. Spaces had been left for the viewer/ writer to add whatever came to mind.

The fellow at the keyboard was giggling. His two pals were giggling too, wisecracking for the small crowd. When the rolling print stopped, four words appeared at the bottom: PRESS ENTER TO CONTINUE. Then the name *Henry* appeared. Long-hair made his move. He typed in, *Do you like rock and roll?*

His friends cackled loudly as the words popped onto the screen. Instantly the next line emerged from the programmed narrative: *Lorraine does not answer.* PRESS ENTER TO CONTINUE.

Henry reappeared, and long-hair typed, *I want to get better acquainted.*

To which Lorraine replied, *Have you ever been to Seattle?*

Five more programmed lines rolled across the screen, leaving the next line to Henry: *It looks like the sun is going down.*

The computer replied, *Lorraine: The bank is only four blocks away.* PRESS ENTER TO CONTINUE.

Upstairs in the meeting rooms that surround the civic auditorium, other personal computer stories were being told, in the seminars and forums scheduled throughout the three-day weekend. I heard an attorney describe how one can be used in an anti-trust suit. I heard a nurseryman talk about growing flowers out of season. I heard a math teacher talk about how it works in his high-school classroom. He looked about fifty, crewcut, light-gray suit. "We're trying to utilize this thing that has been against us all these years," he said. "The tube. The screen. Kids nowadays, they are questioning more and more, and yet they are believing less and less. Let me give you an example of what I mean.

"I can take a math problem involving a lot of calculations about, say, velocity and speed, and I can work it all out on the blackboard, and half the kids in the class won't believe me. They just do not believe I know the right answer. But if I program that same information into a microcomputer, and they see that same answer come out on the screen, then they believe it. And so they learn it. I am not saying I like that situation. But this is the world we're living in, and we may as well confront it right now."

He paused then, to let that sink in, and I slipped out the door.

It was getting late. In the main hall the booths were shutting down. Sales reps were listening patiently to the last questions from lingering browsers. Over the sound system a firm voice informed us that the auditorium was closed for the day. Anyone who did not hold an exhibitor's pass was now invited to leave.

Stepping into the Civic Center plaza, I was slightly amazed to see that the world was still there and that the sturdy granite buildings had not moved or changed their shapes. It was six o'clock. The sun was out of sight beyond Twin Peaks, but the sky was rich with color, adding russet hues to the stonework and the domed City Hall across the square.

I moved in next to the wall of the Civic to pick up some of the heat the day's sunshine had stored there, and I noticed then the date of construction, which is carved into the cornerstone: "Anno Domini MCMXIV."

It was odd, both startling and comforting, to see those ancient numbers, just upon leaving the scene inside. I wondered if the men who had built this building back in 1914 had any inkling, when they carved the stone, what would be going on here in 1981. They couldn't have, not when they were living in an age that still reached back to Rome and Latin lettering as a way to validate the moment. I started thinking about that, about languages, and the ways they slide and change and overlap and replace one another, and about the things we hold on to. On the outside of the building, "Anno Domini." On the inside, analogs and binary programs, the lingo of the eighties.

It brought to mind a man I had seen in the lobby when I first walked in. Past the door a glossy ASCII word processor had been set up, with a little sign inviting you to try it. The demonstration keyboard was smooth and flat and seamless, its letters and numbers embedded in vinyl or Plexiglas. A dozen people stood gazing at this machine with a kind of blank wonder, looking like a group of Arkansas farmers might have looked on the day the first horseless carriage chugged into town. They too had just walked in off the street, and this was the first thing they encountered. At last a slender fellow in a windbreaker stepped forward, as if fate had chosen him to be the one who risks his hands and fingers. His face empty of emotion, he pecked out *How now brown cow*. The script popped onto the screen, beneath another line, still flickering there from another time zone, earlier that morning perhaps, or yesterday, when someone else had typed, *Now is the time for all good men . . .*

It was just a small moment in the hurtling rush of technological advance. But it struck me as a kind of emblematic touch point—the touching of that man's fingers to the keyboard. Steve Jobs and Steve Wozniak had seized the day, leaped into an opening, and thereby joined the ranks of those who are changing our lives, the ways we organize our time and work, our storage space and our memories. And now, this weekend, in the basement underneath the Civic Center, one of the world's newest industries was making its next incremental leap into the marketplace, giving large numbers of the general public close-in looks at all this scaled-down electronic wizardry. Meanwhile, the man on the street, this fellow in the windbreaker who has just wandered in to see what is happening at the Sixth Annual West Coast Computer Fair, he cannot make the leap all at once, or he chooses to make it tentatively, makes his cautious reach for the vinyl keyboard. Holding a few moments longer to what he knows, he tries to tame the unknown with some last little shred of the tested and familiar, *Now is the time* PRESS ENTER PRESS ENTER *Now is the time for all good men to come to the aid of the quick brown fox jumps over the fence how now* PRESS ENTER *How now brown cow* PRESS ENTER TO CONTINUE. [1982]

BIOGRAPHICAL NOTES

HERBERT GOLD, a major author praised for his humor and sensitivity, has written, among other works, *The Man Who Was Not With It*, *Salt*, *Fathers*, and *Love and Like*. His articles and stories have appeared in *The New Yorker*, *Harper's*, *Esquire*, *New West*, and other journals. Born in Cleveland, Ohio, in 1924, he has lived in San Francisco for many years.

WALLACE STEGNER is a major American writer, and author of many articles, short stories, and novels. Among the awards he has received are the Pulitzer Prize in 1972 for *Angle of Repose* and the National Book Award in 1977 for *The Spectator Bird*. His works include *The City of the Living*, *Sound of Mountain Water*, and *Recapitulation*.

JOHN GREGORY DUNNE, a former New Yorker who resides in California, is the author of a number of works, including *Delano: The Story of the California Grape Strike*, *The Studio*, *Vegas: A Memoir of a Dark Season*, *True Confessions*, and *Dutch Shea, Jr.* He is also author of a number of film scripts, including *Play It as It Lays*, coauthored with his wife, Joan Didion. He has been a contributor to *Commonweal*, *The New York Times*, and *California*.

LEWIS LAPHAM, a native of San Francisco, worked as a reporter on the *San Francisco Examiner*, *The New York Herald Tribune*, *The Saturday Evening Post*, *Life*, and *Harper's*, where he became editor.

JOHN MUIR is obligatory reading for anyone who has love and respect for the planet. Born in Scotland, he immigrated to America in 1849 and made extensive trips across the continent, usually on foot, settling in California in 1868. He is probably America's premier backpacker/journalist, the Thoreau of the West. Like Thoreau he had his troubles with Emerson, whose love for the outdoors was no match for his own. A supreme diarist, Muir was a participant-observer of natural process and splendor, particularly of Yosemite and the Sierras. He is currently the guardian angel of the Sierra Club.

SAMUEL LANGHORNE CLEMENS (Mark Twain) is not well known these days for his California writing, but it was there he lived and worked for a time and developed his monumental talent. He was in the goldfields ostensibly mining for gold, but what he won was material. "The Celebrated Jumping Frog of Calaveras County" is his best-known California tale.

NIGEY LENNON is the author of *Alfred Jarry: The Man with the Axe* and *Mark*

Twain in California. She has written for numerous journals, including *Playboy, The Village Voice,* and the *Los Angeles Times.*

HENRY GEORGE was a popular nineteenth-century political economist and radical luminary whose best-known work, *Progress and Poverty* (1879), advocated the "single tax" theory, which proposed a tax on land ownership as a remedy for social inequity. He edited a weekly, *The Standard,* and twice ran unsuccessfully for mayor of New York City, though he was only narrowly defeated. In 1857 he was settled in California, working as a printer, gold hunter, editor, and author.

LOUISE CLAPP lived among the miners in the California gold rush of 1848, and for several years she recorded her thoughts and observations as the letters of "Dame Shirley." These letters were published intermittently over the years, the most recent edition by Knopf in 1945.

WILL IRWIN is resurrected in this volume for the first time to our knowledge since his book *Old Chinatown* appeared in 1911. He is, however, one of the most interesting observers of California we have encountered, seminal in his comprehension and depiction of San Francisco's Chinatown.

GERALD HASLAM, a native of the San Joaquin Valley, was raised in the small town of Oildale, near Bakersfield. Three collections of his stories—*Okies: Selected Stories, The Wages of Sin,* and *Hawk Flights: Visions of the West*—have been published, as has one novel, *Masks.*

WARREN HINCKLE was editor of *Ramparts* magazine from 1964–69. He and his magazine ignited a political spark in the 1960s in the tradition of Upton Sinclair and I. F. Stone. His books include *If You Have a Lemon, Make Lemonade, The Fish Is Red,* and *The Ten Second Jailbreak.*

LIONEL ROLFE describes himself as a "California journalist." He is the author of *The Menuhins: A Family Odyssey* and *Literary L.A.* He is widely published in California journals, establishment and underground.

FRANK ROBERTSON has written articles for *Rolling Stone, California,* and *San Francisco,* among other publications. Currently a reporter for the *Sebastopol Times* and a contributing editor at *California,* he lives in Guerneville.

KATE COLEMAN is a freelance writer based in Berkeley. She has written for many magazines, including *Ms., New Times, Mother Jones,* and *Ramparts.*

HENRY MILLER, one of America's most brilliant writers, was born in 1891 and lived in Europe in the thirties before settling in Big Sur, California, in 1942. The work for which he is best known, *Tropic of Cancer* (1934), was banned, to the nation's shame, until 1961. It was followed by *Tropic of Capricorn* (France 1939, U.S. 1962) and *Black Spring* (France 1936, U.S. 1963). *The Cosmological Eye* (1939) and *The Wisdom of the Heart* (1941) are collections of stories and essays. Among his many other works are *The Air-Conditioned Nightmare* (1945), *Big Sur and the Oranges of Hieronymus Bosch* (1958), and the trilogy *The Rosy Crucifixion* (1949–60). He spent his last years writing and painting in the Pacific Palisades section of Los Angeles, his reputation secured as one of America's most significant contemporaries.

CYRA MCFADDEN is the author of a satirical novel, *The Serial,* about "a year in the life of Marin County," San Francisco's affluent bedroom community to the north, from which we have drawn two chapters. The novel became a successful film, starring Martin Mull, Tuesday Weld, and Sally Kellerman.

JACK SMITH writes for the *Los Angeles Times*. His column remains one of the newspaper's most popular items.

RICHARD REEVES has written regularly for *The New York Times*, *The New Yorker*, and most of the more literate magazines in America as a keen observer of all things American.

WILLIAM IRWIN THOMPSON, born in 1938, is the author of *At the Edge of History*, *Passages About Earth: An Exploration of the New Planetary Culture*, *Evil and World Order*, *The Time Falling Bodies Take to Light: Mythology, Sexuality and the Origins of Culture*, and other works of distinction.

CAREY MCWILLIAMS was a great warrior for social justice, a man whose writings and tireless efforts won some basic human rights for California farm workers and the homeless and unemployed during and after the Depression. Born in Colorado, he moved to Los Angeles in 1922, where he earned a law degree and served as a labor attorney, wrote a good number of articles, and became an active liberal force in California politics. He moved to New York in 1951 and from 1955–1975 served as editor of *The Nation*. His books include *Brothers Under the Skin*, *Factories in the Fields*, *California: The Great Exception*, *North from Mexico*, *Southern California: An Island on the Land*, and *Ill Fares the Land*.

EVELYN WAUGH, British novelist, satirist, and biographer, is the author of *Brideshead Revisited* and *A Handful of Dust*, among other major novels. He came to Hollywood in 1947 to adapt *Brideshead* for an MGM film, one result of the journey being his graveyard novel, *The Loved One*, a brilliant satire inspired by his morbid fascination with Forest Lawn Cemetery.

NORMAN MAILER began his career as a novelist with *The Naked and the Dead* (1948). His latest novel is *Real Men Don't Dance*. In between he has written, among other works, *Barbary Shore*, *Advertisements for Myself*, *An American Dream*, *On the Steps of the Pentagon*, *Of a Fire on the Moon*, and *The Executioner's Song*. The excerpt we include here is from *The Deer Park* (1955), his Southern California movie-colony satire.

BEN MASSELINK sent his first story to *The New Yorker* in 1935 and says, "I haven't made it yet. . . . I have been published in over thirty magazines from the old *Colliers* and the old *Saturday Evening Post* to *TV Guide*. Little, Brown has published one novel, *The Crackerjack Marines*, and three young adult novels. Methuen published a book of short stories, *Partly Submerged*. I have over sixty writing credits in TV, ranging from Disney to Movie of the Week."

JOHN STEINBECK is one of America's most widely read and beloved writers. His long writing career began in 1929 and culminated in a Nobel Prize in 1962. Among his best-known California novels and story collections are *The Pastures of Heaven*, *Tortilla Flat*, *In Dubious Battle*, *Of Mice and Men*, *The Red Pony*, *The Grapes of Wrath*, *Cannery Row*, and *East of Eden*. A writer of limitless compassion, he brought a readable simplicity to his work, woven through with plots and characters of powerful imagination and realism.

CESAR CHAVEZ is best known for his indefatigable organizing efforts on behalf of the migrant farm worker in America. A man of deep, abiding conscience, he was successful in a broad range of legal and political battles with California agribusiness in helping attain some alleviation of the crushing poverty and exploitation of the migrant workers. His union is the United Farm Workers of America.

SHELDON WOLIN and JOHN SCHAAR were on the political science faculty of the University of California at Berkeley when the university was a center of radical political consciousness and a force for social change. Schaar is the author of *Loyalty in America* and *Escape from Authority*. Wolin authored *Politics and Vision*.

THOMAS PYNCHON is a major American novelist who has managed to keep his private life just that. Born in 1937, he attended Cornell University. His novel *V* won the William Faulkner First Novel Award in 1963. A second novel, *The Crying of Lot 49* (1966), is set in Southern California. *Gravity's Rainbow*, his third, won the National Book Award in 1973.

OSCAR ZETA ACOSTA has written two autobiographical novels, *The Autobiography of a Brown Buffalo*, set in San Francisco, and *The Revolt of the Cockroach People*, set in Los Angeles and dealing with the struggle of Mexican Americans for justice against the Los Angeles white power structure. A lawyer and a friend of journalist Hunter Thompson, Acosta appeared in *Fear and Loathing in Las Vegas* as the freaked-out Dr. Gonzo, a 300-pound Samoan lawyer. Not long after the publication of his second novel in 1973, Acosta dropped out of sight and has not been heard from since.

RANDY SHILTS, a resident of San Francisco, has been with the *San Francisco Chronicle* and has covered city hall and the gay community as a newspaper and television reporter. The selection used here is a magazine abridgement of his book *The Mayor of Castro Street: The Life and Times of Harvey Milk*.

JOHN MCKINNEY, former outdoors editor of *New West* magazine (now *California*), is the author of *California Coastal Trails* and is on the staff of *Islands Magazine*. He was born in Los Angeles in 1952 (during an earthquake) and now lives and writes in Santa Barbara.

STANLEY POSS is a professor of English at California State University at Fresno. He publishes literary and social criticism.

RICHARD STAYTON is on the staff of the *Los Angeles Herald Examiner* and serves as drama critic. He is a member of the Los Angeles Drama Critics Circle. Born in Linton, Indiana, he moved to Los Angeles during the "great gold rush" of 1960, left L.A. in 1967 to attend San Francisco State College, and lived in a Haight-Ashbury commune. He "got crazy" and "got sane." He is married to Hunter Drohojowska, art editor/critic for *L.A. Weekly*.

JEFFREY SHORE worked as a bouncer for the night spot Whisky-A-Go Go before he turned to writing. He has been a contributing editor to *L.A. Weekly* and a television stage manager, art director, sequence coordinator, and associate producer. He was also publisher of a magazine, *Dead*. His play, *Act of Contrition*, won the 1979-ON Art Center Playwriting Contest.

JAMES D. HOUSTON is an astute observer of the California scene and has written about it in such works as *Californians: Dancers on the Brink of the World* and *Continental Drift*.